THE PERSIAN GULF
AT THE MILLENNIUM

THE PERSIAN GULF AT THE MILLENNIUM

ESSAYS IN POLITICS, ECONOMY, SECURITY, AND RELIGION

Edited by

Gary G. Sick and Lawrence G. Potter

St. Martin's Press
New York

THE PERSIAN GULF AT THE MILLENNIUM

ISBN 0-312-17449-7 (cloth)
ISBN 0-312-17567-1 (paperback)

Library of Congress Cataloging-in-Publication Data

The Persian Gulf at the millennium : essays in politics, economy,
    security, and religion / edited by Gary G. Sick, Lawrence G. Potter.
        p. cm.
    Includes bibliographical references and index.
    ISBN 0-312-17449-7
    1. Persian Gulf Region—Politics and government. 2. Persian Gulf
Region—Economic conditions. 3. Persian Gulf Region—Strategic
aspects. 4. Islam—Persian Gulf Region. I. Sick, Gary, 1935- .
II. Potter, Lawrence G.
DS326.P4732 1997
953.6—dc21

                                                        97-13020
                                                        CIP

Map on page vii created by Mehrdad Isady, Professor of History © 1997.

Design by The Tern Book Company, Inc.

First edition: August, 1997
10 9 8 7 6 5 4 3 2

CONTENTS

LIST OF TABLES

Persian Gulf Region

——————	International borders
FARS	Provinces
<u>Manama</u>	Capital city

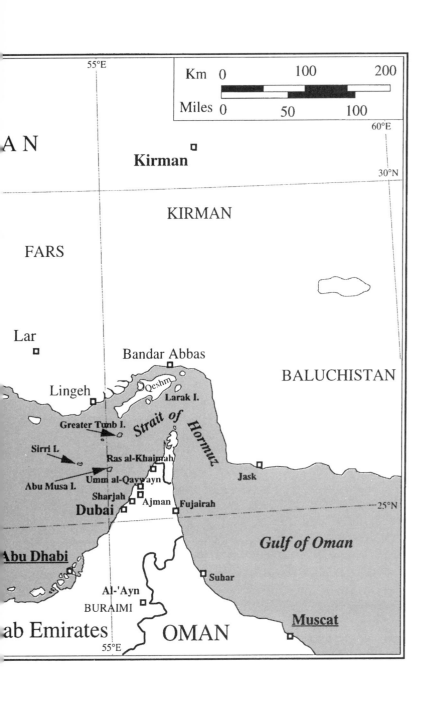

INTRODUCTION

Gary G. Sick and Lawrence G. Potter

The Persian Gulf[1] was the scene—and often the source—of international political and economic turmoil throughout the second half of the twentieth century. Blatant great-power intervention in the domestic affairs of regional states was a familiar feature of Gulf politics from World War II until the British withdrawal in 1971, when it assumed more subtle forms. The regional states repaid the favor beginning with the oil shocks of the 1970s, which triggered international economic dislocations that brought down or crippled governments from Bonn to Tokyo, followed closely by the Iranian revolution and subsequent hostage crisis, which helped unseat an American president and upset a security structure that had been developed over a generation.

Two wars followed at ten-year intervals. Both were initiated by Iraqi president Saddam Hussein for apparently quite similar reasons: oil, rectification of Iraq's boundaries, visions of regional leadership, and an exaggerated sense of grievance. The first war, with Iran (1980-88), was largely ignored by the United Nations and the West for most of its eight years, and saw approximately 370,000 men killed and nearly twice that many maimed and injured.[2] The second, against Kuwait (1990-91), prompted the formation of the largest and most capable international military coalition in a generation. This force ejected Iraqi forces from Kuwait in a lightning campaign and subsequently enmeshed Iraq in an intricate cocoon of international sanctions; but the international community permitted the brutal

Iraqi suppression of indigenous opposition movements (the Kurds in the north and the Shi'i community in the south) and left Iraqi president Saddam Hussein in power.

The Persian Gulf also made its own modest contributions to Western political science. The rise and demise of development theory in academic circles paralleled the fortunes of the shah of Iran, not entirely by coincidence. A substantial literature was generated around the concept of the anomalous "rentier state," which derived its state revenues from royalties paid for the extraction of natural resources. The oil-rich Arab states of the Gulf, with their tiny populations and traditional forms of government, were the archetypes.

By the end of that fateful half-century, the United States had definitively replaced Great Britain as the supreme military and political power in the Gulf. At the same time, the Soviet Union, which had been perceived by the United States as its principal rival and the declared *raison d'etre* of the U.S. regional presence, collapsed. The U.S. policy of containing Soviet influence had succeeded, but at the expense of a strategic rationale, a void only partially filled by Saddam Hussein's Iraq and the revolutionary Islamic regime in Iran.

The Persian Gulf has been the periodic subject of intense media attention since the first oil shocks of the 1970s, but most reporting has focused on the crisis du jour. People today are perhaps better able to locate the Persian Gulf on a world map than their predecessors a generation earlier, but it is not clear that citizens or decisionmakers or all but a handful of scholars have a firm grasp of the political and economic dynamics of this unique region.

THE GULF/2000 PROJECT

The Gulf/2000 project at Columbia University was created in an effort to help close the information gap. The project grew out of a series of discussions with officials of the W. Alton Jones Foundation of Charlottesville, Virginia. There was a shared concern that public information about developments in the Gulf region was so meager and distorted that the United States was at risk of stumbling into a new crisis in that volatile region out of a false sense of security reinforced by inadequate or misleading information.

One concern related to the "cold war" in the Gulf, where historical enmities and political insecurities fueled suspicions and stifled dialogue, reminiscent of the U.S.-Soviet rivalry. Another problem was the absence of a forum for the exchange and analysis of timely and accurate information about events in the region. The community of scholars working on the Gulf was not a community at all. It consisted of a relatively small number of individuals scattered around the globe, who seldom saw each other and who had no mechanism for routinely sharing research data or assessments. This isolation and separation inhibited the development of an intellectual critical mass and, consequently, a discernible and credible voice.

In response to the first, we decided to assemble a group of knowledge-able observers from each of the eight countries of the Gulf: Bahrain, Iran, Iraq, Kuwait, Oman, Qatar, Saudi Arabia and the United Arab Emirates. Drawing on the model of the Pugwash and Dartmouth conferences during the Cold War, which brought together non-official American and Soviet scientists and policy specialists for regular private discussions even when their governments were at odds, this group would meet periodically to discuss issues of mutual concern. With luck, the trust and personal friendships forged in those meetings would facilitate a level of informed discourse that would transcend the acerbity of the public debate and perhaps even feed back quietly to their respective governments.

Second, since this gathering would necessarily be limited to a small and select group of individuals, a global meeting place needed to be created where a wider community of Gulf specialists could meet, share views, and draw from a common body of information and opinion. Such an endeavor, which would have been inconceivable even a few years earlier, was made possible by the growing worldwide access of scholars and other observers to the Internet. An electronic library and forum was created to link Gulf specialists from all parts of the world.[3]

With funding support from the W. Alton Jones Foundation (later joined by the Rockefeller and MacArthur foundations), Executive Director Gary Sick spent six months interviewing officials from several different countries who had extensive experience in the Gulf. He also met with a wide range of scholars inside and outside the region. This preparatory phase yielded two results. First, these individuals identified a series of structural problems and issues that had the potential to affect future developments in the Gulf but that were poorly understood and therefore worthy of more systematic examination. Many of these issues (e.g. rapid demographic change, the relationship of the oil market to political stability and development, the resurgence of political Islam, heavy expenditures on defense, and new geostrategic realities after the end of the Cold War) were not limited to a single country or a subset of countries but applied in some degree to all eight of the Gulf states. Consequently, it seemed feasible to adopt an integrated strategy of examining functional issues in the context of the entire region, rather than the more common approach of a country-by-country analysis.

The second product of these interviews was the development of a list of scholars, officials, lawyers, businessmen, and journalists from each of the Gulf states who might contribute to a study of this nature. One of the objectives of the project from the start was to engage primarily specialists from the region, with only a few non-Gulf experts. Eventually, a list was compiled of twenty to thirty "core" participants from all eight Gulf states. The meetings were to be small, limited to approximately twenty-five people, and the ratio of Gulf citizens to non-Gulf residents was to be about four to one. Those guidelines shaped the planning of three meetings in 1994-95. This volume is one product of that extended dialogue.

Approximately five papers were commissioned for each conference and were made available to the participants well in advance of the meeting. At the beginning, most of the papers were by Western scholars. By the third meeting, a majority of the papers were produced by the regional participants. A full half day was devoted to discussion of each paper, and a rapporteur noted the main points of argument and controversy. Based on the discussion, each paper was revised by the author following the meeting and was then further edited for this volume. The papers are not intended to reflect a consensus of the meetings—there was no attempt to fashion a formal consensus—and any individual participant may disagree with any specific point of analysis. However, the papers were subjected to a searching review by a body of exceptionally knowledgeable specialists, and that input is reflected in the final product.[4]

Much contemporary writing on the Persian Gulf has focused on conflicts, political rivalries, and dramatic internal developments within and among individual states in the region. This volume, while not ignoring those critical historical markers, places its primary emphasis on underlying trends that are no less consequential but that tend to be submerged in the torrent of current events. The authors in this volume focus less on immediate conflicts and rivalries, and place more emphasis on the conditions that helped to produce those conflicts and that will shape the future of the region. For the most part, they also widen their focus to include many or all of the states in the region, rather than the more common approach of looking at individual states.

The reader may be surprised at the relatively limited amount of attention paid to Iraq. This lacuna is not because Iraq was ignored in the discussions of the Gulf/2000 seminars. Quite the contrary. Nor is it due to any doubt on the part of the authors and editors that Iraq will play an important role in regional politics in the twenty-first century. It will. But during the years that this volume was being developed, Iraq was under the idiosyncratic rule of one man and was embedded in a suffocating web of international sanctions. Until the sanctions were removed and some degree of political and economic normality restored to Iraq, the country's fate would be determined largely by the actions and decisions of one man, President Saddam Hussein, who had repeatedly showed himself to be unpredictable and willing to sacrifice the well-being of his country to his quixotic pursuit of territory and power.

LEANING INTO THE FUTURE

The intellectual premise of this project was change. The states of the Persian Gulf region, it was hypothesized, were engaged in the politics of transition from a tumultuous but now familiar past to an uncertain future. Although the future could not be predicted, it would probably grow out of seeds that had already been planted. The object, therefore, was to keep one's analytical feet planted firmly in the past and present, while remaining alert to trends and underlying structures that might provide useful clues about what was yet to come.

Thus, each author was presented with a question or series of questions about some major issue of policy relevance to the regional states. There was no formula, but each author was asked to be critical of the conventional wisdom, to be deliberately provocative, and to attempt to peer beneath the surface of events for structural problems that would potentially challenge existing policies and attitudes. The papers, it was hoped, would then stimulate an informed discussion among the diverse participants around the table, who brought a wide range of national backgrounds and perceptions as well as an exceptional depth of understanding of regional issues and decisionmaking.

There was no intention, either in the papers or in the discussion, to force a consensus of views or to prescribe policy solutions. We did not presume to instruct the eight regional states about how to deal with their problems. There was every intention, however, to identify the important questions and to seek a more profound and nuanced understanding of fundamental issues from a variety of perspectives. Participants were urged to take home with them the cumulative insights and constructive suggestions of the discussion and to introduce them into the discourse of their respective governments and societies.

STRUCTURE OF THE VOLUME

The present volume contains twelve chapters that discuss the politics, economy, security and religious issues of the Gulf states. The lead article by Gary Sick, "The Coming Crisis in the Persian Gulf," draws on a growing body of evidence to suggest that the Gulf countries are experiencing "a crisis in slow motion." The author identifies fundamental structural distortions—budgetary uncertainties, inadequate revenues, the absence of political participation and consequent lack of accountability, the dominance of the public sector and, especially, unemployment—that, if left unattended, could lead to disaster in the future. Oil, he concludes, while the blessing of the twentieth century, could turn out to be the curse of the twenty-first.

The following chapter, on "The New Geo-Politics of the Gulf: Forces for Change and Stability" by Richard K. Herrmann and R. William Ayres, suggests a new framework for understanding the Gulf given the obsolescence of the former paradigm of East-West struggle. The senior author is a leading expert on Soviet foreign policy behavior toward the Middle East, and this fresh analysis draws on both Western and Russian sources. The authors maintain that at present the main determinant of geopolitical dynamics in the Gulf results from the confrontation between the United States, Israel and the GCC states and Iran and Iraq. They argue that in the future, domestic conditions in the Gulf states will be more important in influencing change than extra-regional powers or even regional states.

Professor F. Gregory Gause's chapter, on "The Political Economy of National Security in the GCC States," is a groundbreaking critical examination of domestic conditions in the Gulf monarchies. Gause maintains that the key to regime security is domestic, not external threats, and he highlights the difficult choices Gulf rulers are now facing. Many of these result from the breakdown or change in the rentier state, and include issues such as guns versus butter, the demographic explosion, problems of maintaining the welfare state, and the key issue of balancing economic and political reform. The author, an expert on the politics of the Arabian peninsula states, concludes that the choices made by local rulers in the next few years will determine the character of politics in the GCC states into the next century, and wonders if they will meet the challenge.

How the oil industry will influence politics in the Gulf in the future is discussed by economist Paul J. Stevens, professor of petroleum policy at the University of Dundee, Scotland, in "Oil and the Gulf: Alternative Futures." Stevens constructs a set of scenarios to speculate on how the market for Gulf oil will operate in the future, and explores their political implications. He concludes that the oil states face poor prospects for increased revenues over the next few years, although they have not adjusted their planning for this.

Increased privatization is a frequently mentioned remedy for the ailing economies of the Gulf states, and this prospect is addressed by Karim Pakravan in "The Emerging Private Sector: New Demands on an Old System." The author, a vice-president and senior economist at the First National Bank of Chicago, focuses on the situation in Iran and Saudi Arabia, both of which have a legacy of heavy state involvement in the economy. His discussion of the domination of the Iranian economy by *bonyads*, or private foundations outside of state control, is particularly valuable. He concludes that, while conditions for successful privatization exist in Saudi Arabia, major obstacles persist, and in the case of Iran, so far the process has been severely constrained.

With the exception of Iran and Oman, the Persian Gulf states are creations of the twentieth century, and their boundaries were largely imposed by imperial powers. Resistance to these borders has cropped up repeatedly and has even led to wars, such as those between Iran and Iraq and between Iraq and Kuwait. In "Border Disputes in the Gulf: Past, Present, and Future," geographer Richard Schofield of the University of London, a leading authority on the evolution of these disputes, provides an original and penetrating examination of these issues, including the dispute between Iran and the UAE over the islands of Abu Musa and the Tunbs. The author concludes that border disputes are increasingly being settled, due to growing territorial consciousness at the state level and the need to facilitate oil explorations.

Since 1994, the most serious domestic opposition movement against a local government has been unfolding in Bahrain, and this situation has led to questions of whether the crisis in that island-state will have a domino effect throughout the Gulf. The question is authoritatively explored by Munira Fakhro in "The Uprising in Bahrain: An Assessment." Dr. Fakhro, an expert on social welfare at the University of Bahrain, reviews the historical background and demands of the current reform movement and the role of external powers in manipulating events there. She considers whether Bahrain is an exception or whether, as she believes, it is the forerunner of similar developments in other littoral states.

Anthony Cordesman, perhaps the best informed and most widely respected military analyst of the Gulf states, provides a current snapshot of "Iranian Military Capabilities and 'Dual Containment.'" He provides an exhaustively referenced look at the facts and figures behind Iran's military expenditures and conventional arms buildup, its military manpower and program to develop weapons of mass destruction. The author, focusing on capabilities rather than intentions, finds that Iran poses serious potential challenges to the security of the Gulf. Since the debate over whether Iran poses a major threat or is evolving in a more moderate direction cannot yet be resolved, Cordesman believes it best to err on the side of military containment.

A chapter by Lawrence Potter on "Confidence-Building Measures in the Persian Gulf" seeks to apply techniques of tension defusion that have worked in other parts of the world. The article notes that Gulf states have a legacy of cooperation as well as confrontation. The CBM process is long overdue in the Gulf and, given some encouragement, the littoral states may be receptive to its introduction there. The author suggests the desirability of a regional forum in which all the Gulf states, including Iran and Iraq, can work out a program of regional security that could lead to the removal of outside forces.

Two chapters by experts on Islamic law and history at Harvard University address the religious dimension of Gulf affairs. In an original and theoretically sophisticated article, Frank Vogel writes on "Islamic Governance in the Gulf: A Framework for Analysis, Comparison, and Prediction." His article offers a subtle and perceptive framework for understanding Islamic legal systems, past and present, and searches for Islamic forms of governance that are capable of responding to the Western challenge. Vogel contrasts the "microcosmic" legal system of Saudi Arabia with the "macrocosmic" system of Iran and concludes that a major cause of political radicalization in the Islamic world today is the failure to establish modern political institutions on credible Islamic foundations.

In "The Islamic Movement: The Case for Democratic Inclusion," Roy Mottahedeh, one of the most knowledgeable and widely respected experts on Iranian history, and Mamoun Fandy, an expert on politics in Egypt and the Gulf, highlight the different forms Islamic revivalist movements have taken in the Middle East. In Iran, for example, where an Islamic movement holds power, the local cultural setting continues to strongly affect the way the country is governed. In the Arab Gulf states, the nature of Islamic opposition is partly determined by the willingness of governments to include them in the political process. This analysis is a useful corrective to generalized Western fears of Islamic resurgence; in reality, the Islamic revival has no central direction. While Islamic government is a goal for many Muslims, the authors note that the adjective "Islamic" explains very little and that agreement on its content is very limited.

The concluding chapter by Anwar Gargash, an independent scholar in Dubai, offers an overview of "Prospects for Conflict and Cooperation: The Gulf toward the Year 2000." Dr. Gargash explains the significant role that tension between the larger regional powers (Iran, Iraq and Saudi Arabia) plays in the politics of the region. He discusses differing perceptions of security of the regional states, including the evolving views of the GCC countries and the need for a U.S. presence. The cycle of mistrust among regional countries must be broken, he notes, to overcome obstacles to regional cooperation. This chapter is especially valuable as an evaluation by a seasoned observer from within the region on the future direction of Gulf politics.

Notes

1. As recognized by the United States Board on Geographic Names, the name of the body of water that lies between Iran and the Arab states of the Gulf Cooperation Council is the "Persian Gulf." For political reasons, Arabs often refer to it as the Arab or Arabian Gulf. That dispute will not be resolved in this book, which will use the terms "Persian Gulf" and "Gulf" interchangeably and without political intent. The phrase "Gulf region" as used in this book refers to the eight littoral states (Bahrain, Iran, Iraq, Kuwait, Oman, Qatar, Saudi Arabia and the United Arab Emirates) unless otherwise indicated.

2. Estimates of one million casualties (i.e., killed and wounded) have been carelessly translated by the media and some other sources into claims of one million military personnel killed. Mohsen Rafiqdust, the former head of the Iranian Revolutionary Guard Force, told Robert Fisk of *The Independent* (June 25, 1995) that 220,000 Iranians were killed and 400,000 wounded during the eight-year war. That is roughly consistent with Iranian official statements and with independent Western estimates. Iraq has never published any figures on its losses, but Amatzia Baram, a specialist on Iraq at Haifa University, estimated that 150,000 Iraqis were killed (*The Jerusalem*

Quarterly, no 49, Winter 1989, pp. 85-86). If the standard ratio of two wounded for every man killed is applied, Iraq may have had 300,000 wounded. Thus, an informed estimate of total losses on both sides would equal approximately 370,000 killed and some 700,000 wounded, which is imprecise but plausible.

3. The electronic library, hosted at Columbia University, assembled an extensive array of documentary information on contemporary developments in the Gulf and provided a forum for informed discussion. This membership service, which was offered without charge, was limited to individuals who had an established professional interest in the region. Within a few years, it had attracted Gulf specialists from five continents and become a major center for innovative analysis, commentary and research.

4. Of the twelve papers presented in this volume, three were not formally presented at the meetings. The paper by Gary Sick was written for this volume, drawing on the findings of several Gulf/2000 conferences. The paper by Lawrence Potter on confidence-building measures grew out of discussions in the second and third conferences. The paper by Roy Mottahedeh and Mamoun Fandy on Islamic movements was added in response to a consensus among the participants that the Islamic issue was under-represented in the original papers. It was rewritten for this collection.

CHAPTER 1

THE COMING CRISIS
IN THE PERSIAN GULF

Gary G. Sick

Throughout the second half of the twentieth century, and particularly after the British withdrawal in 1971, the Persian Gulf experienced a series of political and economic jolts: two major oil shocks that affected the entire international economic system; two regional wars that depleted local economies and engaged the international community and outside powers; an Islamist revolution that altered the political face of the largest regional power; and a series of smaller conflicts and external interventions.

Out of this accelerating tumult of Gulf politics, it might have been expected that the region would have been transformed. Instead, it emerged almost unscathed—at least on the surface. Thirty years after the British withdrawal, the Arab states of the Gulf region continued to be ruled by the same families, sometimes the same individuals, under the same traditional forms and within virtually the same borders that had been engineered by the British political agents as they departed.

The dire predictions of political observers in the 1960s and 1970s about the fragility of tribal monarchies and the inevitability of new political and social structures in response to wealth, education, travel, communications, industrialization, urbanization and the complexities of managing independent economic and foreign policies in a demanding international environment appeared to have underestimated the resilience of the Gulf plutocracies and their ability to translate oil revenues into political legitimacy and staying power.

The conventional wisdom of the 1960s and 1970s anticipated that these "family-operated businesses" would give way, under the pressure of either internal or external forces (or both), to political forms that more closely resembled the state-building experience of their neighbors in the Middle East or in the developing world more generally. Ironically however, the Middle Eastern states that experimented with local versions of socialism, nationalism, pan-Arabism, and other ideologies soon faltered or came to be perceived as politically bankrupt, while the oil principalities of the Gulf managed to sustain an impressive level of stability and domestic tranquility despite the wars and revolutions that swirled around them.

So, by the mid-1990s, the conventional wisdom had come full circle. The small states of the Gulf were seen as stable and reliably pro-Western, while the two large states, Iran and Iraq, had come to be seen, at least in the West, as implacably hostile and dangerous.

A CRISIS IN SLOW MOTION

Widespread agreement about the political realities of any set of countries always warrants a measure of skepticism, and that has been particularly true in the case of the turbulent waters of the Persian Gulf, where reassuring perceptions of stability have had an unpleasant habit of giving way to sudden and unpredictable political surprises. The Iranian revolution was preceded by a nearly universal belief that the shah, whatever his failings, was politically secure. Even the shah's bitterest enemies later confessed their astonishment at how quickly the seemingly impregnable facade of royal power eroded and crumbled in 1978.

Iraq's invasion of Kuwait in 1990 belied the overwhelming consensus that Saddam Hussein would never invade a fellow Arab state, that his troop movements were part of a bluff, and that his territorial objectives were limited to a few border territories at most. That view prevailed, even in Kuwait, until Iraqi troops were descending into the outskirts of Kuwait City.

Reassuring scenarios are frequently accurate, and the conventional wisdom is usually the product of more than wishful thinking. Yesterday, as generations of political observers have learned, is almost always the best predictor of tomorrow. Complacency, however, is justified only if present assumptions are measured regularly against changing political realities.

Much of the analysis of the Gulf region has focused on state conflict. That is justifiable in view of recent history, and many of the subsequent chapters in this volume will address the very important aspects of inter-state relations. Less attention has been devoted to domestic and essentially economic factors that are likely to shape developments in these states. Yet, the success of these states in resolving their internal contradictions will affect their perceived vulnerability to outside predators and their ability to respond to external challenges should they occur. Consequently, the following essay will attempt to provide a prognosis of the health of the Persian Gulf states, in full awareness of the limitations of generalizations about a set of eight different countries and recognizing that other factors may intervene, as they have in the past, to upset the domestic apple cart.

This paper briefly summarizes and examines the evidence that the eight states of the Gulf, as they approached the turn of the century, were experiencing a slow-motion crisis that had the capacity to transform their domestic politics, their relations with each other, and their relations with extra-regional powers. The evidence that such a crisis was brewing was omnipresent and widely reported, but it was no less widely discounted, because: (1) the symptoms were incremental and accumulative, rather than being a single dramatic threat; (2) the danger signals were largely associated with messy and ambiguous problems of domestic policy and governance, rather than a well-defined external enemy that could be confronted directly; (3) the cures for the problems were well known and prosaic, but also politically unpopular, so there never seemed to be an appropriate moment to take the kind of bold and painful action that was required; (4) the nature and urgency of the problems varied from one country to the next, so there was no agreement on a universal remedy or timetable; and (5) the states of the region had been living with these problems for decades, apparently without serious consequences, so their continuation for another day or week or year did not inspire a sense of urgency.

In short, the "crisis" did not appear to be a crisis at all. Instead, most observers saw only an accumulated series of background conditions that had come to be accepted as an integral part of the regional environment. Moreover, previous expressions of alarm about the fragility of relations between rulers and ruled in the Gulf had repeatedly proved to be unduly exaggerated or simply wrong. The burden of proof was on those who claimed that the sky was falling.

Perhaps most important of all was the perceptual dilemma. Acknowledgement of impending political and social change in the Gulf on a substantial scale would demand a corresponding reexamination of policies by both regional and external powers. That in turn would place at risk comfortable practices and relationships that had evolved over time, often with considerable effort and even sacrifice. Since those arrangements were frequently beneficial—politically and personally—to decisionmakers and governments alike, there was no incentive to take actions that might undermine them. On the contrary, there was reason to believe that undue emphasis on the dangers might prove to be a self-fulfilling prophecy. It was far from clear what actions policymakers could or should take that would not risk exacerbating the problems they were supposed to solve.

Policymakers, like other human beings, are not inclined to dwell on unpleasant consequences, especially when those consequences appear to be uncertain at best, far in the future at worst, and whose remedy risks being worse than the disease. Thus, officials inside and outside the Gulf were inclined to give lip service to the array of potential problems, contenting themselves with modest policy adjustments that pecked away at some of the most urgent symptoms but left the more stubborn structural issues largely unaddressed.

The slow-motion nature of the crisis provided an illusion of security. Despite persistent voices—many of them within the region—arguing that immediate action was required to halt an accelerating downward spiral, few policymakers were willing to break with established policies that had served them well for decades. The purpose of this paper is to heed those troublesome (and often tiresome) voices of dissent and to survey in brief compass the logic of apprehension, as the states of the Persian Gulf approached the year 2000.

It must be added that the urgency of the problems facing the states of the Persian Gulf was largely due to the catastrophic actions of one man. President Saddam Hussein of Iraq wrecked the comfortable status quo of the Gulf states at the same time that he wrecked his own country. His invasion of Iran in 1980 not only drained and weakened Iran but also absorbed some $35 billion in unpaid loans from Iraq's Arab allies. Bankers estimated that another $65 billion in hard currency reserves was siphoned away from Kuwait, Saudi Arabia and other GCC states to pay for the military operations that ejected Iraq's forces from Kuwait in 1991.[1]

The structural dilemmas of the Gulf states were not created by Saddam Hussein. They had been there almost from the start. But the immense costs of paying for his misadventures effectively wiped out the cushion of financial reserves that had been accumulated by the Gulf states from the oil boom of the 1970s, and brought the day of reckoning much closer than would otherwise have been the case.

Table 1.1
Oil Reserves and Population in Selected States/Regions

Location	Percent of World's Proved Oil Reserves*	Pop. (,000) Total**	No. of Pop. that are Citizens
Saudi Arabia	25.7	18,000	12,000
Iraq	9.8	21,000	21,000
United Arab Emirates	9.7	2,400	600
Kuwait	9.5	1,800	700
Iran	8.7	60,000	60,000
Oman	n.a.	1,900	1,400
Qatar	n.a.	500	140
Bahrain	n.a.	600	400
Persian Gulf states	64.9	106,200	96,240
North America	8.5		
Former Soviet Union	5.5		

BP Statistical Review of World Energy 1996
** 1996 estimates

THE MYTH OF WEALTH

Genuine security for a state may begin with military defense, but it is a mistake to define security solely in terms of military preparedness. Iran under the shah and the Soviet Union under the Communist Party were both superbly equipped to deal with almost any external military threat to the state. Yet those elaborate and expensive preparations offered no defense against—and may in fact have contributed to—the ultimate collapse of the regimes. In the words of a respected Arab observer: "We in Kuwait and many other Third World countries have yet to learn the lessons of the collapse of the Soviet Union and the shah of Iran, where the main reason for collapse was the lack of available financial resources for the reinforcement of other necessary national security issues, in comparison with what was spent on the military sector."[2]

The states of the Persian Gulf are anomalous in many ways, but their most distinctive characteristic in comparison with most other Third World states is their sustained access to very substantial financial revenues derived from the extraction and sale of oil. By an accident of geography and geology, the eight countries of the Persian Gulf, with a combined territory of 1.7 million square miles (about the size of the western United States) and a total 1996 population of about 106 million people (roughly equivalent to Nigeria), sit atop the largest underground pool of oil in the world, some 65 percent of the world's proven reserves.

This peculiarity of nature has inspired a number of myths. One is the myth of fabulous riches. Indeed, there are many individuals in the region who are wealthy almost beyond imagination, but the revenues of the eight Persian Gulf states are surprisingly modest by comparison to the developed world. All of these states have operated at a deficit since the mid-1980s, when the price of oil collapsed, and their combined gross domestic product is comparable to Switzerland, a country of fewer than seven million people. To put it in perspective, in 1994 the combined GDP of all the states of North Africa and the Middle East, from Morocco to Afghanistan, including Israel, was considerably less than half the GDP of France.

What is unusual is not the sheer magnitude of national revenues but the fact that most of these revenues are in the form of "rent" or royalties on the extraction and sale of oil. With the partial exception of Iran, these countries do not have a well-developed domestic industrial base.

STRUCTURAL DISTORTIONS

Unlike the industrialized states, the citizens of the smaller oil-rich countries are net consumers of national resources while contributing marginally— if at all—to revenues. Like inherited money, this "blessing" can be a curse in disguise. It produces a series of structural distortions that have troubling long-term implications.[3]

1. *Budgetary Uncertainties.* National budgeting is dependent on the vagaries of the international oil market. Despite their best efforts, these states have been unable to manage the price of oil. As a result, their annual budgets are based on estimates of a commodity market that can be buffeted by events over which they have little or no control. A political strike in the oil fields of Nigeria, an economic downturn in Southeast Asia, or advances in drilling techniques in the North Sea, for example, can all have a dramatic impact on national income and can produce an unexpected shortfall or a welcome surplus in any given year.

Many countries in the region have adopted the practice of budgeting for a price of oil substantially lower than their own official estimates. This may be prudent, but it demonstrates the uncertain nature of the entire process.

Table 1.2
Oil/Gas Revenues as a Percentage of Total Revenues

Country	1986	1991	1996*
Bahrain	58	60	65
Kuwait	43	30	73
Saudi Arabia	58	79	73
Qatar	n.a.	64	68
Oman	78	79	76
UAE	n.a.	83	84
Iran	40	51	65

* estimate
Source: The Petroleum Finance Co.

2. *Dominance of the Public Sector.* Typically, the state owns the important means of production, and a stifling public sector jealously preserves its prerogatives. The booming principality of Dubai, with a traditional trading culture, illustrates some of the potential benefits of free market economics, but even there the ruling family controls all the main sectors of the economy: real estate, banks, ports, heavy industry and the airline.[4]

The public sector is far more attractive to nationals, for a variety of reasons. According to a female computer graduate in the UAE, "Jobs in the public sector are more secure, more comfortable and, above all, better paid. In addition, the work load is easier and working hours more flexible." She noted that the Civil Service Law stipulates a generous salary for university graduates working in the public sector, plus a wide range of benefits that cannot be matched by the private sector.[5]

As a consequence, however, the public sector in most of these states has become bloated to the point of becoming a self-defeating obstacle and is no longer available as a reliable career prospect for young people graduating in increasing numbers from local educational institutions. Thus, of 16,259 Saudis who graduated from Saudi universities in 1994, only 5,570 were able to find jobs in the public sector.[6]

3. *Dominance of Foreign Labor.* The absence of a vibrant private sector inhibits job creation, and this problem is exacerbated by the overwhelming reliance on expatriate labor. The extreme case is the United Arab Emirates, a country of 2.4 million people, three-quarters of whom are non-nationals. In 1995, more than 50,000 jobs were created in the industrial sector of the UAE; of those jobs, only 30 were taken by UAE nationals—an all-time

low. In 1995, the total number of UAE nationals in local industries to-talled only 736, representing 1.5 percent of the labor force.[7]

The Arab Gulf states are unique in the world in their reliance on imported labor. In 1995, expatriates reportedly comprised 90 percent of the work force in the United Arab Emirates, 83 percent in Qatar, 82 percent in Kuwait, 69 percent in Saudi Arabia and 60 percent in Bahrain.[8] In the mid-1990s, up to 40 percent of Saudi Arabia's annual oil revenue was repatriated to other countries in the form of remittances for foreign labor.[9]

In the years after the oil boom, foreign labor was indispensable to create almost from scratch a full range of infrastructure and services. The Arab states of the Gulf found themselves in the 1970s with almost limitless financial resources, but their populations were too small and lacked the training and experience to undertake the massive and urgent tasks of nation-building. The importation of foreign labor was the necessary answer, and it was soon institutionalized on a formidable scale.

Over the following quarter of a century, the Arab oil states promoted population growth and offered unparalleled educational opportunities for their citizens, with the objective of becoming more self-reliant. However, as new generations of young citizens graduated from college, they did not move into private-sector jobs as anticipated. Partly this was due to lack of interest, as indicated by the young UAE woman quoted above. But their aversion was equalled or exceeded by those with jobs to offer. "Why would I want to hire a Saudi?" a Saudi businessman once exclaimed to me. "By law, I must pay them more, I must give them an expensive package of benefits, and if they turn out to be poor workers, I can't fire them. I can hire an energetic and well-trained Pakistani or Indian for far less money and no risk."

The logic was unassailable. Despite repeated government programs to "Saudi-ize" or "Bahrain-ize" the work force, foreign labor continued to dominate the economic scene and was actually on the increase in several Gulf states in the mid-1990s. The solution was as clear as it was painful: higher standards and more practical educational training for national students to make them more competitive; unrelenting reduction in the number of work visas awarded to foreign laborers; and a leveling of the wage/benefit disparity between nationals and non-nationals. Although such measures might ameliorate the problem in the long run, the short-term effects would be sectoral labor shortages, inflation, and outrage from the powerful commercial interests. None of the governments were willing to pay that price.[10]

4. *Unemployment.* As a result of the above conditions, burgeoning unemployment of nationals was becoming one of the most intractable and politically dangerous problems in the Persian Gulf in the 1990s. If idle hands are the devil's workshop, then that old villain was presiding over one of the growth industries of the region.

Although state and family support networks in the Arab welfare states served to alleviate the worst effects of unemployment and underemployment, a growing body of idle and disgruntled young people, many of whom had acquired a nominal university education, was a potentially troubling phenomenon that was steadily getting worse. The 1995 development plan for Saudi Arabia stated that 659,900 citizens (roughly 6 percent of the citizen population) would require new jobs over the following five years.[11] Some economists claimed that unemployment among Saudi nationals in 1996 was 20 percent and climbing.[12] In Iran, where 48 percent of the population was under the age of 18 in 1995[13] and where one million or more young people were expected to enter the labor force each year well into the twenty-first century, this problem was even more severe.

An independent Kuwaiti economist estimated that the GCC states alone needed to create 8 million jobs for their own nationals by the year 2010 in order to accommodate the growing numbers of young people entering the job market. "Planners and decision makers," he warned, "must . . . create enough jobs for the newcomers or face the alternative—severe unemployment with possibilities of social and political extremism. All available signs point to the latter happening."[14] Another respected Arab commentator in 1995 detected stirrings of potential unrest throughout the Gulf and argued that if existing problems continued to go unattended they could jeopardize the Gulf states' "political and social cohesion."[15]

5. *Inadequate Revenues.* Revenues in the Gulf states were insufficient to keep pace with the growing cost of entitlements for a burgeoning population. In the early days of the oil boom, most of the oil-producing states created a social welfare network that was the most generous in the world. Free medical care, free education, low-cost housing, extremely inexpensive domestic telephone and transportation, and the world's lowest prices for energy were among the benefits routinely provided to citizens of the region, often with no income tax.

At the same time, most of these states actively promoted population growth, creating a demographic explosion. In 1970, there were approximately 45 million people living on the shores of the Persian Gulf. By 1995, there were over 100 million people, and by the year 2010 there will be an estimated 162 million. Approximately two-thirds of the Gulf population is located in Iran, but the Arab Gulf states are steadily increasing their proportion of the total.[16]

Almost without exception, by the mid-1990s these states were facing budgetary demands that exceeded their resources and were faced with the unpleasant prospect of reducing subsidies and cutting services that their citizens had come to expect as their birthright. The financial reserves that had been accumulated during the boom years of the 1970s were severely eroded by the costs of the war against Iraq in 1990-91.[17]

The rapid increase in population, with no corresponding rise in oil revenues, pushed budgets into deficit and eroded per-capita earnings. Per-capita annual income in Saudi Arabia in 1996 was only $6,900, compared with some $19,000 in 1980 at the height of the oil boom. By the mid-1990s, the income of the average Saudi had declined to less than that of some developing countries, and below the World Bank's rich-poor median line of $7,620.[18]

Nemir Kirdar, president and chief executive officer of the Bahrain-based Investcorp, put it very bluntly in a speech to Gulf businessmen in Washington in late 1996: "Energy is not going to bring Gulf countries the wealth they enjoyed in the past. So the question is, how can these countries generate other sources of wealth?" There is, he added, "a decline in real per capita income and a growth in the public deficit. . . . To absorb their fast-growing population, the Gulf states need to create 200,000 jobs a year."[19]

Despite a temporary recovery of oil prices in the mid-1990s, all of the Gulf states continued to operate at a deficit, and there was no indication that revenues from oil and gas, even when combined with modest increases in non-oil earnings, would reverse this trend for the foreseeable future.[20]

6. *Absence of Popular Participation.* Because of the reliance on oil, the social contract in most of the states of the Persian Gulf is peculiarly unidirectional and distributive. The national leadership collects the rents from oil and allocates them to the citizenry, with little or no involvement by the populace. This is less true in Iran, where oil revenues are declining and where a popularly elected Majles (parliament) intervenes vigorously on issues of economic policy. The Kuwaiti National Assembly, which was reinstated after the war with Iraq, also exercises vigorous oversight on certain issues. But the general rule in the Gulf is a heavy-handed statism, with little or no popular voice in public policy.

In the absence of an elected representative body (except in Kuwait and Iran), and with all media tightly controlled by the state, there was no safety valve for these societies to let off steam or to aggregate popular dissent in a peaceful or systematic way. On the contrary, in monarchies such as Bahrain, any expression of disagreement with the ruling family, or even peaceful calls for restoration of the constitution and parliament that had been unilaterally suspended in the 1970s, were regarded as tantamount to treason and were punished by loss of employment, arrest, imprisonment or exile. The preferred response to political opposition in most of the countries of the Gulf under most circumstances was repression.

Although the suppression of dissenting voices successfully maintained a facade of stability and control, repressive policies also drove the opposition underground and increased the likelihood that frustrated elements would resort to clandestine methods and acts of violence, particularly in circumstances of shrinking revenues and growing unemployment. The most violent disturbances of the early 1990s occurred in Saudi Arabia and Bahrain, the two states that had virtually no representative institutions and that were the least tolerant of political criticism.

7. *Lack of Accountability.* The absolute control of state finances by the ruling families in the Gulf monarchies permitted no systematic accountability. This was not viewed as a serious problem so long as the pie was getting bigger and revenues were sufficient to cover public expenditures; however, demands for greater accountability began to be heard as these governments were forced to contemplate cuts in entitlements.

This was an embarrassment, since huge sums of money had been disappearing for years. Money derived from the sale of oil and duly reported in balance-of-payment statistics routinely failed to appear in the oil revenues reported in the state budgets. Between 1990 and 1994, the percentage of revenues missing from national accounts was considerable: 29.5 percent of total petroleum exports for Saudi Arabia; 29 percent for the UAE; 23.7 percent for Kuwait; 18.7 percent for Qatar; 18.4 percent for Bahrain and 8.8 percent for Oman.[21]

Some of these funds may have been earmarked for defense and other legitimate purposes that frequently went unreported in the state budgets, but the magnitude of the missing accounts was so great that it raised suspicions.[22] The personal nature of state bookkeeping was dramatically illustrated after the palace coup in Qatar in June 1995, when it was discovered that a substantial portion of the state revenues were held in private accounts in European banks in the name of the former amir and were inaccessible to his son, who replaced him.

THE CASE OF IRAN

Although the above comments were intended to apply in greater or lesser degree to most of the states of the Persian Gulf, it is important to remember that these states have their own histories and their own special political, economic and social conditions. No single generalization will do justice to them all. Iraq was not discussed at all, because at the time of this writing it was ringed with international sanctions and its future relied more on the fate of a single man—President Saddam Hussein—than on any combination of political or economic trends.

It is necessary, however, to draw a further distinction between the Arab states on one side of the Gulf and their Iranian neighbor on the other. Iran is by far the most populous country in the Persian Gulf, with a population of some 60 million in 1996. It controls half the coastline of the Gulf, including the northern shore of the vital Strait of Hormuz. It is the only regional state with direct access to three major bodies of water: the Caspian Sea, the Persian Gulf and the Gulf of Oman/Indian Ocean. It has its own distinctive culture, language and religious beliefs and has played a significant role in world history since at least the time of Cyrus the Great. Together with Egypt and Turkey—which are comparable in size, maritime access and historical continuity—Iran occupies one point of the core triangle that defines the enduring historical and cultural contours of the modern Middle East. It is the only country in the Middle East to have experienced a genuine popular revolution, the only state in the Gulf to permit universal suffrage in contested elections and the only state in the world to practice a unique blend of populist, constitutional and clerical rule.

Iran shares many of the dilemmas of the other Gulf states, particularly the reliance on oil as the source of most of its revenues. It is, however, the only country of the region to have a somewhat diversified industrial base. In addition to its exports of carpets and agricultural products, it manufactures steel, assembles automobiles, builds ships and small aircraft, and produces most of its own pharmaceuticals, plastics and many other basic goods. Unlike the other Gulf states, Iran derives nearly 20 percent of its state revenues from taxes, including an income tax.

In contemplating the possible trajectory of the Islamic Republic of Iran into the twenty-first century, should the primary analytical weight be assigned to the word "Islamic" or "Iran"? From the very beginning, the rulers of Iran were confronted with the need to choose between the dictums of Islamic theology and the interests of the state. For the most part, state interests won. The most dramatic example of the subordination of religion to the Islamic state was the astonishing declaration by Ayatollah Khomeini shortly before he died that the God-given mandate of an Islamic state was the "most important of the divine commandments and has priority over all derivative divine commandments . . . even over prayer, fasting, and pilgrimage to Mecca."[23]

In the first eighteen years of the Iranian revolution, government decisions in the areas of land tenure, birth control, divorce, labor law and banking, among others, came down in favor of pragmatism (or creative reinterpretation) over strict Islamic orthodoxy. The price, however, was a growing division between socially conservative factions favoring strict adherence to the revolutionary "line of Imam Khomeini," and reformist elements.

The revolution, the eight-year war with Iraq, declining oil prices, and profligate borrowing in the late 1980s left Iran's economy in perilous condition. The postwar binge of borrowing to pay for imports was one of the most costly errors that Iran made in the first two decades of the revolution. By 1996, Iran was saddled with a $23 billion debt and an annual payment schedule that amounted to as much as 25 percent of its anticipated oil revenues. This was further complicated by U.S. attempts to block foreign investment and trade.

Iran responded to this challenge in three ways. First, it adopted a program of fiscal austerity to bring spending into line with revenues, and combined that with vigorous import substitution. Second, it continued to pursue its rural development program, in order to retain the support of disadvantaged sectors of the society who were the backbone of the revolution, while initiating an aggressive policy of birth control. Finally, Iran began a systematic effort to develop new markets in Central Asia, the Far East, South Asia and East Africa, including the opening of a rail link from the ancient Silk Road to the Persian Gulf.

Iran's progress, however, would be determined by its ability to resolve the contradictions in its own political institutions and policies. The struggle for the soul of the revolution, which revolved around personalities at least as much as actual policies, had unhealthy consequences for civil society. Each faction sought to quash opposing views, often by resort to extra-legal means, and tried to outdo others in reaffirming loyalty to the revolutionary principles of 1979. The outcome promised to be messy at best, possibly paralyzing the economy and society, and risking the loss of the modest gains that had been made since the early days of the revolution.

SOLUTIONS

As is frequently the case with matters of public policy, the prescription is easier written than taken. Various international institutions, private institutions and policy analysts have examined conditions in the Gulf states, and their conclusions are much the same. The World Bank, in a report on the Middle East as a whole, said the region had suffered from falling oil prices, a failure to train workers, a lack of economic liberalization and privatization, excess bureaucracy and the waste of resources in inefficient state-owned enterprises. To reverse this, it noted, will take promoting non-oil exports, making the private sector more efficient, producing more skilled and flexible workers and reducing poverty by accelerating growth.[24]

The International Monetary Fund, addressing the relatively comfortable United Arab Emirates, recommended a strong fiscal reform program while "reducing government subsidies to the public and private sectors, cutting redundant labor in the civil service, rationalizing non-productive spending and introducing large-scale consumption taxes as well as taxes on income of individuals and companies."[25] Similar prescriptions could have been written for virtually any of the Gulf states.

A simple glance at the list of the structural problems outlined above would suggest a set of fairly prosaic fiscal and public policy correctives: stimulation of an energetic private sector capable of generating jobs; privatization of many state-owned businesses; reevaluation of the extraordinarily generous entitlements that were adopted in the 1980s; curbing population growth; gradual reduction of subsidies on goods and services; the introduction of taxes or user fees; improved education and training of citizens to make them more competitive in the private-sector job market; removal of the many legal and financial benefits that skewed the labor market in favor of foreign workers; and political reforms that would permit a greater sense of public participation in the political process and, most importantly, a measure of accountability by ruling elites. Various combinations of these and other remedies began to be proposed by regional and international observers almost as soon as the nature of the problems became clear.

Although some of these adjustments had the prospect of being inconvenient or mildly painful, they were no more stringent than comparable belt-tightening measures adopted by other Third-World states, and even by a number of highly industrialized states during the late 1980s and early

1990s. Moreover, as a result of the slow-motion nature of the crisis, there was time to introduce reforms gradually and carefully, with due regard to public concerns and the state of the social safety net. In reality, most Third-World countries would gladly have exchanged places with the Persian Gulf states, whose problems seemed small in comparison with the "real" world, where energy was a debit on the national ledger, not a credit.

PROGNOSIS

A number of adjustments were made by regional states in the early 1990s in response to the problems outlined above. Most states cut back on expenditures, slashed funding for wasteful or misguided programs, reduced foreign aid,[26] stretched (or in some cases simply stopped making) debt payments, modestly increased the costs of some government-owned services and experimented gingerly with advisory councils that included citizens outside the royal families.

Perhaps the largest single change was the sharp reduction in the purchase of military equipment. Total arms purchases by the Persian Gulf states dropped from $62.3 billion in 1988-91 to $37.3 billion in 1992-95, a reduction of more than 40 percent.[27] Although the Middle East in general, and the Gulf in particular, remained the most lucrative arms market in the world, by the mid-1990s it appeared that the days of the mega-deals were over, at least temporarily. This reduction in arms purchases, which had been predicted by Yahya Sadowski of the Brookings Institution,[28] was not the result of a reduced concern about military security. On the contrary, it could be attributed almost entirely to fiscal constraints. It remained to be seen whether the brief increase in oil prices in 1996 would give rise to a new burst of military spending, as had happened on several occasions in the past.

Despite improved oil prices and diminished expenditures on arms, the underlying contradictions in the political and economic structures of the Persian Gulf states went largely unattended as these countries approached the twenty-first century. The government of Oman, faced with dwindling oil and gas reserves, in 1995 initiated a comprehensive study that showed promise of rationalizing its investments and planning over the next quarter-century. Kuwait, chastened by the catastrophe of the Iraqi invasion and prodded by the only authentic legislative assembly on the Arab side of the Gulf, established a measure of accountability in the management of its national finances. Iran, saddled with foreign debt and the threat of U.S. sanctions, took some preliminary steps in the direction of serious economic reform, although internal political rivalry limited the government's ability to act, and constantly threatened to undo what had already been accomplished. Saudi Arabia instituted a series of monetary reforms to reduce its burgeoning public debt and budget deficit. None of the Gulf states, however, were willing to initiate the kind of far-reaching reforms that would address their fundamental structural dilemmas.

Very little, for example, was being done in any of the Gulf states to promote genuine entrepreneurism by relaxing the suffocating hand of the state. As a consequence, these states were steadily sliding into a condition of comfortable stasis at a time when the world economy on which they depended was undergoing a dynamic transformation. In one decade, the World Bank noted in 1995, the Middle East and North Africa region went from the second-highest performer on income growth to last among regions of the world.[29]

Rising unemployment was the dangerous symptom where economics and politics merged. If the Gulf states could not provide the necessary jobs for their own citizens, they were certain to confront social and political pressures that could threaten the security of their governments as surely as any military attack. Jobs could be generated only by unleashing the creative energies of their own capital and labor, but this prospect was regarded by the existing rulers with unconcealed suspicion and fear that it would upset the balance of power on which their continued rule was based. The result was an uneasy paralysis.

In reality, the Arab Gulf states were faced with a dilemma. If they maintained the paternalistic statism that had served them so well for half a century, they risked a domestic struggle over a dwindling body of resources, compounded by the insistent voices of reform from their younger citizens who were increasingly educated, unemployable and attracted to radical Islamic alternatives. If, however, they opened the system economically or politically, they risked setting in motion a set of vigorous new institutions that would almost inevitably challenge their ruling styles, if not their very legitimacy. Given this disagreeable choice, it is perhaps not surprising that the rulers' initial inclinations were to stay with the status quo, to reform only at the margin, and to clamp down hard on any signs of serious opposition. That would preserve the golden goose in the short and middle term, leaving the future to their hitherto quiescent populations, while gambling that the vagaries of the oil market would once again come to their rescue. This tendency was reinforced by a brief increase in oil prices in 1996, which diminished any sense of urgency.

Table 1.3
Foreign Direct Investment Inflows
(1994 total = $225.7 billion)

European Union	32.6 %
Asia	26.9 %
North America	24.6 %
Latin America	9.0 %
Central & Eastern Europe	2.8 %
Others	3.9 %
GCC states	0.2 %

Source: UN World Investment Report 1995.

The investment community, which voted with its own hard cash, was dubious. As indicated in Table 1.3, direct investment in the Gulf states was almost negligible in 1994. In fact, the estimated $250 billion in assets of wealthy Gulf individuals continued to flow out of the GCC states into safe havens abroad.[30]

A banker in the Gulf remarked that "Too much analysis leads to paralysis. . . . They have diagnosed the problems to death. What governments need is the courage to apply the therapy. . . . They have the money but they don't use it properly."[31] On this point, both the critics and the defenders of the Gulf states could agree. The problems were not overwhelming, and the resources existed to solve them. Where observers divided was on whether the rulers of these states would demonstrate the skill, the wisdom and the political will to use those resources effectively while there was still time. Their record of performance in the 1980s and 1990s provided little grounds for optimism, although most analysts agreed that the crisis could probably be postponed for many years.

It remained to be seen if the unprecedented blessing of Persian Gulf oil in the late twentieth century would become the curse of the twenty-first. If the vast resources that the countries of the Gulf inherited by virtue of a geological accident were harnessed, the welfare and domestic tranquility of these states could be insured well into the next century. If, however, this inheritance became a kind of drug, lulling governments into a false illusion of comfortable immobility, it could create the conditions for a level of social unrest and prolonged instability that could challenge the existing order and tempt forces within and outside the region to intervene out of fear or simple greed.

An Iranian woman reportedly commented that, "Iran will never be a happy place as long as we have oil. We could be Japan if we didn't have oil."[32] That was no doubt an exaggeration about Iran, and it was even more of an exaggeration if applied to the other Gulf states whose entire modern existence was a function of oil wealth; but it did capture the dilemma with admirable clarity.

At the end of the twentieth century, oil is almost universally seen as the *deus ex machina* for all political and social problems in the Gulf. In the twenty-first century, it might come to be regarded as the root of all evil.

Notes

1. Estimates as reported in the UAE Ministry of Information's *Daily News Digest,* October 19, 1996.

2. Dr. Jasem K. Al-Sadoun, Chief Economic Analyst and General Manager, Al-Shall Consulting Group, and adviser to the Kuwaiti parliament, commenting on the proposed defense budget (Reuters, March 12, 1994).

3. For a detailed examination of the problem of resource-rich countries' failing to live up to expectations, see Jeffrey Sachs and Andrew Warner, "Natural Resource Abundance and Economic Growth," report published by the Harvard Institute for International Development, October 1995, reported in "Ungenerous Endowments," *The Economist,* December 23, 1995.

4. Robin Allen, "A thirst in the desert states: Oil prices are low and Gulf countries claim they need capital, but foreign investors are being thwarted," *Financial Times,* January 30, 1996, p. 17.

5. Interviewed in the *Gulf News* newspaper, cited in the UAE Ministry of Information's *Daily News Digest,* May 1, 1996.

6. John Lancaster, "Young Saudis Find Job-Hunting a Real Chore," *The Washington Post,* January 3, 1995, p. 1.

7. Based on a report prepared by Dr. Soheir Elsabaa, cited in the UAE Ministry of Information's *Daily News Digest,* May 28, 1996.

8. Economist Jasem K. Al-Sadoun in the *Arab Times* newspaper, cited in Reuters, February 5, 1995.

9. Henry Azzam, chief economist at the National Commercial Bank of Saudi Arabia, said remittances totalled $15.3 billion in 1994, and estimated them to stand at $14.5 billion in 1995, compared with an estimated oil revenue of $39 billion in 1995 (Reuters, May 30, 1996).

10. In 1996, the United Arab Emirates instituted an amnesty program to permit all illegal aliens to leave the country without penalty. The resulting exodus of nearly 8 percent of the population altered the demographic composition of the country and created a sharp downturn in the construction industry due to severe labor shortages.

11. Henry Azzam, chief economist at the National Commercial Bank of Saudi Arabia, op. cit.

12. Reuters, September 17, 1996.

13. Alireza Mahjoub, Secretary-General of Iran's Labor House, as quoted by the Islamic Republic News Agency (IRNA), January 22, 1996.

14. Jasem K. Al-Sadoun, *Arab Times,* op. cit.

15. Muhammad al-Rumaihi, editor-in-chief, *Al-Arabi* magazine, Kuwait, writing in *Al-Hayat* newspaper, April 19, 1995, as cited in *Mideast Mirror,* April 19, 1995.

16. World Bank, *Social Indicators of Development 1995* (Baltimore: Johns Hopkins Press, 1996).

17. By most estimates, the Arab Gulf states spent some $35 billion to finance Iraq's war against Iran between 1980 and 1988 and nearly $65 billion for the liberation of Kuwait from Iraqi invasion forces in 1991.

18. Robin Allen, "Pressures Mount as Oil States Dither," *Financial Times,* November 8, 1996, p. 2.

19. Cited in Robin Allen, November 8, 1996, *op. cit.*

20. For a more detailed examination of this point, see Vahan Zanoyan, "After the Oil Boom: The Holiday Ends in the Gulf," *Foreign Affairs* 74 (Nov./Dec. 1995), pp. 2-7.

21. These calculations, by the Petroleum Finance Company of Washington, D.C., were provided by Vahan Zanoyan, Chief Executive Officer of PFC and a participant in two of the three Gulf/2000 conferences in 1994-95.

22. In the only case of its kind in the Gulf, the former Minister of Oil of Kuwait and four associates were under prosecution by the state in 1996 for allegedly amassing $36.7 million in illegal profits from a state-owned oil tanker firm in the 1980s (Reuters, September 4, 1996).

23. Cited in H.E. Chehabi, "The Impossible Republic: Contradictions of Iran's Islamic State," *Contention* 15 (Spring 1996), pp. 135-54, which also includes a perceptive analysis of Iran's religious/nationalist dilemma.

24. "Claiming the Future," (Washington, D.C.: The World Bank, 1995), pp. 4-8. A similar set of warnings and prescriptions can be found in "Sultanate of Oman: Sustainable Growth and Economic Diversification," World Bank Report No. 12199-OM, May 1994.

25. Cited in Agence France Press, January 28, 1996.

26. Foreign assistance by Saudi Arabia, for example, was $21.5 billion in 1980-84, $12.2 billion in 1985-89, and only $7.9 billion in 1990-94, a reduction of more than 60 percent in a decade (Arab Monetary Fund, March 23, 1996, cited by the UAE Ministry of Information's *Daily News Digest*).

27. Richard F. Grimmett, "Conventional Arms Transfers to Developing Nations, 1988-1995," Congressional Research Service, Library of Congress, August 15, 1996, p. 11.

28. Yahya M. Sadowski, *Scuds or Butter? The Political Economy of Arms Control in the Middle East* (Washington, D.C.: The Brookings Institution, 1993).

29. "Claiming the Future," op. cit., pp. 1-2.

30. Robin Allen, "A Thirst in the Desert States," op. cit., p. 17.

31. Ibid.

32. Quoted in Thomas L. Friedman, "Waiting for Ayatollah Gorbachev," *The New York Times,* September 8, 1996.

CHAPTER 2

THE NEW GEO-POLITICS
OF THE GULF: FORCES FOR
CHANGE AND STABILITY

Richard K. Herrmann and R. William Ayres

INTRODUCTION

The geopolitical scene in the Gulf is complex and hard to describe. While many people can agree that various trends in the global system are likely to affect the Gulf, there is substantial disagreement and uncertainty about the geopolitical consequences of these developments. Because trends in the global system can have diverse effects on the Gulf, it is useful to consider geopolitics at three levels. The first level is the effect global competition outside the Gulf can have on politics inside the Gulf. This may involve the effects of great power competition or of civilizational contests and new pan-state groupings. The second level pertains to the international relationships among Middle Eastern actors. The key players at this level include not only ethnic groups like the Arabs, the Turks, the Persians, the Kurds and the Israelis but also states such as the GCC monarchies, Iraq and Iran. The third level relates to domestic politics in the nations and states of the Gulf. Here the focus is on the effects domestic change may have on geopolitical relationships.

In the rest of this chapter, we look at geopolitics in the Gulf from each of these levels or perspectives. The next part concentrates on the broadest global perspective. Here the question is whether geopolitical contests out-side the Gulf will set the terms of geopolitical contest within the Gulf. We argue that this is unlikely. Part 3 concentrates on the regional perspective and argues that the confrontation between the United States, Israel and the GCC monarchies on the one hand, and Iran and Iraq on the other, has become the primary determinant of geopolitical dynamics in the Gulf. Part 4 looks at the geopolitics of the Gulf from the sub-state level, examin-ing the domestic contests in Gulf states and their implications for geopo-litical trends. We close the paper by considering the interaction and feedback produced by geopolitical trends at each level.

GREAT POWER CONTESTS AND GULF POLITICS

During the Cold War, the conflict between the United States and the So-viet Union played a large role in the geopolitics of the Gulf. Although neither Washington nor Moscow granted the Gulf the strategic priority they gave to Europe and North Asia, both saw it as important in the broader global contest. Because of West European and Japanese dependence on imported oil, the Gulf represented a possible Achilles heel of American containment strategy. If the Soviet Union gained control of the Gulf and denied access to the energy resources there, then Moscow could blackmail American allies in NATO and East Asia. The fear of a Soviet military move to choke off access to the Gulf motivated U.S. defense plans in the area for decades. It is possible that Moscow also saw the Gulf as related to its secu-rity, representing a land base for U.S. military encirclement and as a pos-sible pressure point the USSR could threaten in retaliation should Washington move against Moscow's interests in Europe or Asia. Both the United States and the USSR moved to secure allies in the Gulf, Washing-ton eventually settling on Iran and Saudi Arabia as pillars, Moscow align-ing with Iraq.

Soviet-American cooperation during the war over Kuwait and the collapse of the Soviet Union undermined almost entirely the logic of inter-preting Gulf affairs in Soviet-versus-American terms. With the Cold War over, the likelihood of a Russian-American global contest spilling over into the Gulf appeared remote. While Americans could still fear an Iraqi or Iranian threat in the Gulf, without the Soviet military component the geo-political scenarios were very different than those traditionally feared. Nei-ther potential regional hegemon represented more than a pale shadow of Moscow's traditional military threat; neither could hope to prevail militar-ily against the United States in any effort to deny access to the Gulf. Nor could either afford for long the loss of oil revenues should they singularly or together try to blackmail the world by constraining Gulf oil production.

Without the superpower conflict that defined the Cold War, the great power contests that might spill over into Gulf affairs are limited. Scenarios that pit a revived revolutionary Russia against the United States, China against the United States, China and Pakistan against India, and the United States against Western Europe and Japan have all been advanced. None of these scenarios are very convincing. Neither is a clash-of-civilizations argument. Nevertheless, a few words about each is necessary.

In the immediate wake of the collapse of the Soviet Union, Russian-American relations were cooperative. To a substantial degree, leaders in Moscow and Washington perceived little threat from each other and saw important areas of common interest. To some extent, this cooperation may have been a product of Russian weakness. Certainly voices in Moscow complained that Russia was going too far in granting cooperation with Washington highest priority.[1] While conservative critics of the Yeltsin-Kozyrev foreign policy often concentrated on issues related to NATO's expansion, the war in the former Yugoslavia and arms control, they also complained that Moscow should not abandon its interests in Iran and Iraq.[2] The Yeltsin government insisted that it was not sacrificing Russian interests to American demands and, partly to prove the point, stood behind Russia's agreement to build nuclear reactors in Iran.[3] By the time Yeltsin stood for reelection in 1996, he had replaced Kozyrev with Yevgeniy Primakov, a well-known Soviet Middle East expert, who many saw as likely to reassert Russian policy in the Gulf, and, at minimum, make fewer policy tradeoffs in an attempt to win U.S. favor.

While the parliamentary strength of Gennadi Zyuganov's Communist Party and the popularity of General Aleksandr Lebed, along with the shift in the Yeltsin administration toward Primakov, might forecast new tensions in U.S.-Russian relations, these are not likely to reproduce the sort of contest that the Cold War projected into the Gulf. Neither Yeltsin nor his opponents define Russian interests in ways that make the Gulf instrumentally important in terms of competition with the West. American leaders are likely to see Russian commercial relations with Iraq and Iran as contributing to the threat posed by Baghdad and Tehran more than to a geostrategic threat posed by Moscow.

By the end of 1996, nearly all leaders in Moscow agreed that Russian commercial relations in the Gulf could play a positive role in Russia's economic development. Because Washington was committed to containing

Iran and Iraq, pursuing commercial opportunities—especially in military and related industrial sectors—would bring Russian and American policies into conflict. In this regard, Russia's position is not entirely different from France's, Germany's or Japan's. It must calculate the tradeoffs between potential commercial gains in the Gulf, and Washington's possible retaliatory moves. The question in the Kremlin was not how the Gulf can help them to acquire leverage against Washington or even NATO expansion, as it might have been during the Cold War, but rather how they can make the most money. In the mid-1990s, Russia pursued commercial relations in the Gulf without much regard to ideology, and certainly without regard to the client's relationship to the United States. Iran figured prominently in Russian trade missions and military sales, but so did Kuwait and other GCC states—to say nothing of Israel.[4]

While pursuing commercial opportunities in the Middle East was not controversial among Russians, defending states like Iraq and Iran was. For some prominent Russians such as Kozyrev, the prevailing American view of these states as radical sponsors of terrorism was accepted almost completely. They opposed, and were embarrassed by, Russia's associations with Baghdad and Tehran. Others, such as Duma Foreign Affairs Committee Chairman Vladimir Lukin, took a different view, saying little about the Near East while arguing that the whole region was outside of Russia's most important concerns. For them, Russia had "to act selectively, very economically, without encumbering [themselves] with trifles or regions which we cannot handle."[5] Some military voices and communists took a different view, arguing that Russia needed to stand by its former friends, and that to not do so was humiliating.[6] In none of these views, however, was the issue at hand competition with the United States or even taking sides in regional disputes.

Primakov argued that Russia should not accept Washington's picture of Iran and Iraq, nor follow Washington's lead in this regard. For him the prevailing view in Washington was excessively simple and driven by narrow self-interests that Russia did not share. Moreover, following Washington's lead in attacking the traditional interests of Arab nationalists and the emerging interests of Islamic fundamentalists would put at risk Russian interests closer to home in the Caspian, the Caucasus and Central Asia. Where the United States focused heavily on Iraq and Iran's relationship vis-à-vis the GCC states and Israel, Primakov looked at Iran's behavior in Azerbaijan, Turkmenistan, the Caspian Sea projects and the wars in Chechnya and Tajikistan. Where the United States saw only radicalism,

Primakov saw restraint, moderation and realism. Moreover, while Primakov could understand why, for bargaining reasons, it would be in Israel's and the United States' advantage to keep Iraq and Iran as weak as possible for as long as possible, this was much less important to Russia. Russia sought good relations with Israel and the GCC but shared few of the vested interests in Israel and the Gulf monarchies that the United States had accumulated during the Cold War.

Russia and the United States may disagree on the details in Arab-Israeli negotiations. Primakov is more sympathetic to Palestinian desires and less willing to support some Israeli aspirations than are officials in Washington. Moreover, he has tried to inject Russian diplomacy into the Arab-Israeli dialogue in ways that countervail against the U.S.-Israeli preponderance. At the same time, however, Primakov, like all Russian officials, strongly supports the basic Gaza-Jericho compromise and the continuing peace process. This sharply separates Russian diplomacy from the posture of Iran, Iraq or the Palestinians in Hamas and Islamic Jihad. Russia may want to be treated with greater respect within the bargaining context of the Middle East, but accepts the stability of the basic strategic context in which this bargaining occurs. It has not endorsed the revisionist agenda of Islamic fundamentalists or Arab nationalists. It also has not sustained its military ability to project power into the area.[7] Russian access by land has changed in important ways due to the independence of former Soviet Republics in the Caucasus. The army has not succeeded in either Afghanistan or Chechnya and would face stiffer opposition still should it try to exercise coercive leverage in the Gulf. Russia's naval assets in the area were never sufficient to challenge the United States and have only deteriorated since the collapse of the Soviet Union.

Policies toward Iran and Iraq may be a source of disagreement between Russia and the United States, but strategic competition between Washington and Moscow is not likely to affect geopolitics in the Gulf. U.S.-Chinese differences could escalate but China's ability to project influence into the Gulf is more limited than Russia's.[8] Beijing has provided weaponry and technology to Iran and Pakistan. Part of China's motivation in these sales may be competition with Washington and New Delhi, but commercial motives appear to dominate for China as they do for Russia. Indians complain about Chinese encirclement and Beijing's naval ambitions in the Indian Ocean.[9] China's ability to project naval power to the Bay of Bengal, however, is very limited and its ability to sustain influence in the Gulf almost non-existent.

Pakistani-Indian tensions have led the two countries to seek contacts in the Gulf. Pakistan has developed economic and military relations with Iran, looking for strategic depth vis-à-vis India. It has also cooperated with Saudi Arabia, especially during the war in Afghanistan, and has expressed interest in relations with Iraq. India, meanwhile, has promoted new initiatives with the United States and Israel.[10] This has led some observers to see a Hindu-versus-Islam split leading to a new geopolitical scene in which India seeks support from the West while Islamic forces in the Gulf consolidate power and align with China.

This scenario requires cooperation on broad religious grounds among communities in the Gulf, cooperation which is complicated by ethnic and national differences amongst Arabs, Persians, Kurds and Turks, to say nothing of the divide between Shi'i and Sunni Moslems. While Islamic populist movements are evident in all the Gulf states, their domestic success vis-à-vis secular and cosmopolitan economic elites is uneven. In Turkey they appear to still be gaining strength. In Saudi Arabia and other GCC states they appear to be mounting more public and violent opposition. In Iran, they still control important instruments of coercion in the security forces and government but appear to be on the wane, if not thoroughly detested by large segments of the population. It is possible that the burden of having been in power for a long time and performed poorly will determine the fate of regimes in the area more than Islamic or civilizational trends.[11]

The clash-of-civilizations perspective also predicts conflict where cooperation has been possible. For instance, Iranian president Hashemi Rafsanjani had little trouble finding common economic interests with India during his April 1995 visit to New Delhi. Even the Hindu nationalist Bharatiya Janata Party wanted to pursue major commercial relations with Persians, as Hindus have for hundreds of years. Interested in deflating Pakistani efforts to mobilize support, and interested in oil, gas, and rail access to Central Asia, New Delhi courted Iran as much as it scolded it for promoting Islamic causes. Iran, equally interested in good relations with India, had decided earlier in 1995 to soften its position on Kashmir and was upset about Pakistani policy in Afghanistan.

Another geopolitical perspective, popular in parts of the Gulf, conceives of competition between the United States and other G-7 states. In this perspective, Washington is driven to establish hegemony in the Gulf to acquire leverage vis-à-vis economic competitors in Europe and Asia. Washington is interested in the amount of oil production in the Gulf and the resulting world price for oil. It is also interested in stable oil prices. These interests, however, are not antithetical to European and Japanese interests, but, to the contrary, are complementary. All states that consume oil in large quantities benefit from high levels of oil production and from stable prices. If the United States used its military or political influence to limit production or affect distribution in some type of blackmail strategy vis-à-vis economic competitors, it would face commercial retribution and undermine its own economic well-being. The U.S. economy is so heavily intertwined with European and East Asian production, trade and commerce that contributing to instability in those economies would quickly feed back into the U.S. economy in self-defeating ways.

Although U.S. competition with other G-7 states is not likely to spill over into Gulf affairs, there is little doubt that the United States does play a far larger role in the Gulf than any other non-Gulf state. In fact, in the absence of serious global systemic geopolitical competition, the politics of the Gulf have been affected largely by the contests between the United States and Iran and Iraq.

REGIONAL CONTESTS:
THE UNITED STATES VERSUS IRAN AND IRAQ

Leaders in the Gulf have no shortage of perceived adversaries. Saudi Arabia fears that Iran and Iraq harbor expansionist ambitions. Several GCC states may share these concerns and perceive Saudi Arabia's motives as hegemonic as well. Leaders in Iraq and Iran perceive the United States as the primary hegemonic threat in the region, working with its allies in Israel and the GCC to bring down the regimes in both Baghdad and Tehran. Leaders on all sides make no secret of their desire to limit the influence of their perceived adversaries. Saudis, Israelis and Americans advocate containing Iraqi and Iranian power.[12] Iranians call for the reduction of American influence in the area and advertise their sympathy for internal political change in GCC states.[13] Iraq, in the meantime, has invaded Kuwait in a blatantly expansionist move, and Saddam Hussein continues to condemn GCC regimes.[14]

In the 1990s, Washington's struggle against Iraq and Iran became the most important geopolitical trend in the Gulf. In the following analysis we start with Washington's "dual containment" policy. We look at both its logic and its implementation. We then look at Iraq and Iran's efforts to countervail against this containment, on both internal and international levels. Finally, we explore in more detail the nature of the dispute, examining the particular interests of the United States, Iraq and Iran that are at the root of the conflict.

The Reagan administration relied on a strategic balance of power between Iraq and Iran and Baghdad's and Tehran's preoccupation with war against each other to insure that no regional hegemon would emerge. Before the end of the Iran-Iraq war Washington "tilted" slightly toward Iraq, identifying Iran as the principal threat.[15] The Bush administration continued this policy, exploring the possibility of using relations with Iraq to contain Iran. After Iraq's invasion of Kuwait, the Bush administration, and later the Clinton administration, identified both Iraq and Iran as serious threats. To differentiate itself from the Bush administration, the Clinton administration introduced the slogan of "dual containment" to capture this strategic perspective.[16] The United States would not rely on local players to offset regional threats but use its own power to constrain the options available to Iran and Iraq.

Dual containment was launched with the explicit purpose of bringing down the regime in Baghdad and changing the behavior of the government in Tehran. United Nations sanctions imposed on Iraq during the war over Kuwait provided a strong foundation for the containment of Iraq. They constrained Iraq's commercial and military options. In addition to these international constraints, the United States denied Iraq free access to air space over its northern and southern regions. Operation Provide Comfort was launched to protect Iraqi Kurds and to limit Saddam Hussein's ability to reassert control; in the fall of 1996, Clinton demonstrated that opposing Baghdad's reassertion of influence in the north and undermining the stability of Saddam's government were the dominant objectives. Operation Southern Watch provided reconnaissance over Iraqi territory north of Kuwait and also denied Baghdad a free hand in reimposing control in the south. Since 1991, the United States has taken an active role in trying to coordinate anti-Saddam Iraqi elements outside of Iraq, albeit with limited success.[17] It has also encouraged coordination among anti-Saddam Kurds, also without much success.[18] Washington played a critical role in delaying the relaxation of UN sanctions against Iraq, relenting in 1996 only to a UN-supervised limited sale of Iraqi oil that was postponed briefly when Baghdad intervened on the side of Massoud Barzani in the Kurdish war in the north.

Clinton's dual containment policy did not initially call for a change in the regime in Iran but sought a change in Iran's policies, especially toward the Arab-Israeli peace process, nuclear proliferation and terrorism. With regard to Iran, the United States did not have UN-endorsed sanctions and found it difficult to engineer international agreement on constraining trade with Iran. American allies in Europe and Asia did not agree with Washington's policy, but preferred to pursue engagement and trade with Iran, arguing that change in Iranian behavior was more likely to result from detente and Tehran's integration into world commerce than from its isolation.[19] As the Clinton administration's investment in the Arab-Israeli peace process grew and Iran's behavior did not change, Washington's determination to bring about change in the regime, as well as in Iranian policy, appeared to harden.

Both international and domestic forces affected Clinton's policy toward Iran. On the international scene, allies complained that Washington called for constraints on trade and commerce with Iran while remaining Iran's largest oil client. Iranian opposition to Israel and the Gaza-Jericho agreement, and its association with militant organizations such as Hamas, Islamic Jihad and Hezbollah, stoked domestic demands for tougher U.S. policies as well. The response in 1995 was Clinton's decision to oppose a deal between the National Iranian Oil Company and Conoco. Although the political controversy alone led Conoco to back away from the deal, both presidential and congressional legislative action followed quickly. The president issued Executive Order 12957 which prohibited contracts between U.S. companies and Iran. During the rest of 1995, further legislative details fell into place that implemented a far-reaching ban on commerce with Iran. In 1996, legislative action extended these restrictions further, imposing sanctions on non-American firms doing more than $40 million worth of business in Iran.[20] At the same time, the Clinton administration identified Iran as the principal state supporting terrorism in the world, and claimed that it was militarily training Islamic radicals from Saudi Arabia and other Arab states. In December 1995, House Speaker Newt Gingrich pushed through a $20 million appropriation for covert activities in Iran designed to overthrow the clerical regime, although it was apparently never implemented.

In June 1995, the Clinton administration added military measures to its containment policies. It established the U.S. Navy's Fifth Fleet based in Bahrain, and pre-positioned substantial military equipment in Kuwait and Qatar. Roughly 5,000 American troops were already deployed in Saudi Arabia. Washington ran military exercises in the area and worked with GCC states to improve their military options. American troops in Saudi Arabia were twice attacked by terrorists in 1995 and 1996, but this only reinforced Washington's determination to establish secure military positions in the Gulf and heightened American suspicions about Iranian subversive behavior.

While the United States acted to contain and compel change in Iraq and Iran, the regimes in Baghdad and Tehran resisted. In Iraq, Saddam Hussein's options were few. His regime tried to delay and evade UN restrictions but with minimal success. United Nations inspections and dismantling of Iraqi weapons-development programs were delayed but not avoided. Baghdad appealed to the sympathies of Arabs elsewhere, playing on humanitarian concerns for the populace of Iraq, but did not succeed in persuading any major countries to abandon the UN sanctions regime. Although Arabs, Europeans and Russians expressed interest in resuming commerce with Iraq for both humanitarian and financial reasons, the United States was able to hold the sanctions regime in place. Iraq in 1996 managed to acquire UN approval for the sale of oil under strict UN supervision. After delaying the measure for months, the United States finally relented, evidently convinced that UN oversight of the revenues generated would provide Saddam Hussein's regime little sustenance.

While the regime in Baghdad managed to foil domestic attempts to oust it and survived in the face of repeated Western predictions of its imminent demise, it made little headway toward resuming a revisionist foreign policy in the Gulf. While a future Iraq could play a major role in Gulf affairs, Saddam Hussein's regime appears to be stymied. It currently treats mere survival as an accomplishment and has made little progress in recovering much of the capability base or international leverage it enjoyed before the war over Kuwait. While the war among Kurds allowed Saddam to recover some influence in the north, the conflict also brought about stiffer U.S. enforcement of no-fly zones and provoked new military attacks, further destroying Iraqi air defenses. Whatever political benefits Saddam may have gained internally from his arrangement with Massoud Barzani, they did not substantially change Baghdad's overall ability to reassert influence beyond Iraq's borders, which remained very constrained as long as the United States remained committed to the GCC states. Iran, on the other hand, while also unable to overcome U.S. military superiority, was far more effective in countervailing against U.S. containment.

In 1993-94, leaders in the Iranian regime argued about the wisdom of seeking to defuse the escalating spiral of hostility between Washington and Tehran. On one side were clerical hardliners who argued that the United States was unalterably hostile toward Islamic Iran. For the leader, Ayatollah

Khamenei, negotiating with the United States made no sense.[21] Only the Iranian acquisition of countervailing power would deter the United States from trying to impose its will. On the other side of the debate were leaders who argued that Iran needed to repair its relationship with Washington in order to promote economic recovery. Former Iranian delegate to the UN, Raja'i-Khorasani, for instance, suggested in the fall of 1993 that detente with the United States could possibly be achieved and that the prospect should be tested.[22] Although President Rafsanjani staked out an ambiguous position in this debate, it appeared in 1994-95 that he was willing to explore the Khorasani proposal.

When seeking an international partner for the National Iranian Oil Company, Rafsanjani chose Conoco over a French competitor, presenting the decision as a positive signal to Washington and as a test of the Khorasani thesis.[23] The uproar the agreement caused in Washington and the eventual collapse of the deal, coupled with the Clinton executive order banning commerce with Iran, effectively ended the public side of the internal debate in Iran. Hardliners saw it as confirmatory evidence of U.S. and Israeli hostility, while others concluded that dealing with the United States was not possible without making substantially greater changes in Iranian policy, changes they could not effect due to the balance of power in domestic Iranian affairs. Public discussion in Iran about policy toward the United States moved quickly toward a uniform position. Iran would try to countervail against U.S. containment by acquiring allies, alternative economic options and indigenous military capability.

Iran was not successful in acquiring military allies against the United States, but was able to establish beneficial commercial and military supply arrangements with Russia and China. The relationship with Russia was particularly important in this regard. Despite American complaints, Russia in 1995 and 1996 went ahead with new joint projects and contracts for oil development, military sales and the continuation of the nuclear reactor construction at Bushehr. While in the late 1980s Iran acquired substantial military hardware from China, in the 1990s Russia became Tehran's largest provider.[24] While neither the quantity nor the quality of these weapons allowed Iran to challenge U.S. military superiority, they nevertheless improved Iran's arsenal in important ways. At the same time, Iran continued to forge commercial and weapons supply relationships with China, Pakistan and North Korea.[25] The development of Iranian missile capability appeared to benefit particularly from these relationships.

Although Iran was able to acquire military hardware, it could not compete in an arms race with Saudi Arabia. In the 1990s Iran had limited resources to devote to arms purchases and had no great power patron prepared to give it weaponry for free. From 1990 through 1994, Saudi Arabia was able to import nearly $38 billion in arms, while Iran was able to buy only $6 billion.[26] Iran began with a larger arsenal but also had to recover from eight years of war. The difference in the rate of increase of weapons and the superior quality of the weapons available to Saudi Arabia severely limited Iran's ability to compete with countervailing power in the military arena. Unless the United States launched a direct attack on Iran, however, what mattered more to the regime in Tehran was its ability to find alternative commercial options. In that arena it had substantial success.

Despite American criticism, France, Germany and Japan continued to pursue trade and commercial opportunities in Iran.[27] The development of oil and gas in the Caspian Sea area connected Iran to European, Turkish and Russian partners despite U.S. efforts to block Tehran's participation. Iran also worked with Turkmenistan to promote increased interest in gas resources and helped to build a rail line connecting the Gulf to Central Asia through Iran. Iran's resources and its access to Central Asia made it an attractive trade partner for India and the Association of South East Asian Nations (ASEAN). As economic growth in South and Southeast Asia increased, so did Iran's alternative market options. Only days after President Clinton signed into law legislation extending sanctions to foreign firms doing business in Iran, Turkey's prime minister signed a $20 billion natural gas deal in Tehran.[28]

Although Iran was partly able to countervail against U.S. policy in the diplomatic and commercial arenas, Washington's containment no doubt cost Iran. While it did not change Iran's behavior or bring down the regime, it did make it harder for Iran to attract the commercial investment necessary for Tehran to modernize its oil and gas industries. Moreover, Iran remained militarily vulnerable. In this latter domain, Iran's options appeared twofold. It could pursue coercive options below the level of conventional force, and it could acquire weapons of mass destruction. If it used guerrilla terrorism as a weapon and was careful to avoid provocations that would unite world opinion around U.S. policy, then it could attack American interests in the area and control the risk of U.S. military retaliation. Iranians may have calculated that the evidence with regard to terrorist acts would remain ambiguous and limit Washington's ability to rally international consensus. This would leave Washington in the position of being able to attack Iran in limited military ways but only with the high cost of international criticism and the possible mobilization of nationalist sentiment in Iran. It is possible that Iranian leaders believed that a full-scale U.S. military action against Iran was unlikely as long as Tehran did not engage in a major military offensive on the scale of Iraq's invasion of Kuwait.

It is difficult to assess Iran's pursuit of the terrorist and guerrilla option. Iran makes no secret of its support for Hamas, Islamic Jihad and Hezbollah.[29] American intelligence sources report that Iran has provided military training as well as financial support to these groups and to dissident groups in Saudi Arabia. Whether Iran has orchestrated particular violent attacks in Saudi Arabia or upon Israel cannot be determined from public sources. The regime in Iran endorses the aspirations and causes of these militant Islamic groups, and no doubt these groups have carried out violent operations. These groups, however, have their own reasons for attacking U.S. troops, the Saudi regime and Israel. Moreover, these groups have relationships with different elements of the Iranian elite, as well as other wealthy people in the Middle East, who can mobilize impressive resources independent of the governments in Tehran, Riyadh and other capitals.[30] Without more detailed information about Iran's operational role in the violent activities of these groups, it is difficult to assess clearly the degree to which it relies on these allies as possible countervailing instruments.

It also is difficult to judge confidently Iran's policy with regard to the acquisition of nuclear weapons and other weapons of mass destruction. Certainly Iran is acquiring nuclear technology and know-how. It also has acquired missile technology, and the logic for its weapons acquisition is not hard to imagine. Iranian leaders see in Israel and the United States enemies that have nuclear options. Iran has no great power ally likely to extend a nuclear umbrella over it, and it cannot match U.S. conventional military force any better than did Iraq. Iranian leaders could believe that nuclear weapons would provide important leverage for them.

This logic and the acquisition of nuclear technology, however, do not equate to the development of nuclear weapons. Iran is a member of the International Atomic Energy Agency (IAEA) and has signed the Non-Proliferation Treaty (NPT). Agency inspections have not found violations of the NPT in Iran, and Iranian leaders deny they are pursuing nuclear weapons.[31] Just the same, Iran might be. The acquisition of infrastructure and experience with nuclear technology is a necessary step toward the acquisition of both nuclear energy and nuclear weapons. Where the acquisition process will stop is impossible to say. In addition, the IAEA's experience in Iraq demonstrates the limits of the inspection regime. Inspectors can assess the likelihood of activities that violate IAEA norms within the specified areas they are allowed to inspect, but they cannot assure the international community about activities that might be going on in other parts of the country. As with the terrorism issue, the U.S. government has claimed that Iran is moving in ways that suggest it is determined to acquire weapons of mass destruction. From the public sources alone, however, it is difficult to assess these claims.

To some degree U.S.-Iranian relations resemble a spiral conflict. Each side has sought to acquire leverage against the other and has stepped up the competition in the 1990s. On the other hand, the spiral model of escalation can be quite misleading in this case. Iran is so much weaker than the United States that it cannot fully compete in any symmetrical way. It has been careful to avoid direct confrontation with the United States and has not responded in publicly provocative ways to the escalation in U.S. commercial pressure exerted in 1995 and 1996. To the contrary, the Iranian leadership ignored and at times scoffed at the Clinton containment efforts and simply pursued other available commercial options.

The spiral model also implies that the two sides are afraid of each other and that mutual misperception drives the contest. Emotional stereotypical images of Iran as a rogue state affect U.S. policy just as stereotyped images of the United States as the great imperialist Satan affect Iranian policy. Even if these images could be set aside, however, leaders on both sides insist that vital issues still divide the two states. Some leaders on each side claim that the conflict is inevitable because it is rooted in deep cultural differences. Other leaders believe that national interests are incompatible for narrower political reasons. While it is never easy to identify the motives of states, it may be useful to discuss in more detail some of the interests that propel the U.S.-Iranian conflict. Three that deserve attention are shocks to the oil market, the stability of GCC regimes and the security of Israel.

Protecting access to oil is often identified as Washington's primary concern in the Gulf, but the situation is complicated. The United States, like all major consumers of oil, has an interest in stable world oil prices. Oil prices are affected by many factors, including supply. Iran and Iraq could affect supply by limiting their own production or the production in other Gulf states, or by interrupting the transit of oil. The ability of either Iran or Iraq to do this for long, however, is limited. None of the Gulf states have self-sufficient military industries or economies. They all need to sell oil to sustain revenue streams necessary for the purchase of everything from basic food stocks to advanced weaponry. Scenarios that feature Iran or Iraq acquiring decisive leverage over Gulf oil and blackmailing the world are not seen as credible by most leaders in Europe and Asia. Oil consumers and producers, after all, have substantial common interests, as is clear in U.S. relations with the GCC and in European and Asian relationships with Iran and (in the past) Iraq.

It is not Iran's threat to oil markets per se that divides it geopolitically from the United States. Even if Iranian hegemony in the Gulf did not disturb oil prices, or even if it made them a bit lower, Washington would be opposed to Iran's acquisition of new revenues and increased influence. The Iranian regime's hostility toward the United States and its policies in the Middle East drive U.S. concerns about Iran. Tehran's threat to disrupt oil is not as compelling a worry in Washington as Iran's ability to use oil revenues to acquire leverage with which Iran can challenge other U.S. interests, in particular the stability of GCC monarchies and Israel.

The United States has developed vested interests in the GCC monarchies. Initially the monarchs played an instrumental role in U.S. foreign policy. They represented a source of oil and contributed to the containment of communist influence in the Middle East. By the time the Cold War collapsed and Washington came to see GCC monarchs as threatened by Iraq and Iran, Americans had established large-scale commercial and personal investment in GCC states. While at the macroeconomic level, regime change in the GCC might not affect world oil markets for long, at the micro-firm level losses could be substantial. Moreover, if monarchs in the GCC were overthrown by revolutionaries that enjoyed the support of Iran or Iraq, then U.S. credibility could be damaged and the leverage of Iran and Iraq enhanced. At times, the GCC states are also seen in Washington as important because of the logistical facilities they can provide for the pre-positioning of U.S. military equipment in the Gulf. This pre-positioning, of course, is necessary not because the GCC states are valuable military allies, but precisely because they represent defense liabilities. Ironically, it appears at times that Washington is more worried about the security of the GCC states from external threats than are the monarchies themselves.[32]

The GCC states partially follow the American lead on dual containment but adopt complicated postures. While Bahraini leaders blame Iran for internal disturbances and U.A.E. officials confront Iran on issues related to off-shore islands, Kuwait and Qatar continue to develop rather positive relations with Iran.[33] At times, the U.A.E. also accommodates Iranian sensibilities, perhaps reflecting their sense that it is necessary to appease Iran because of uncertain U.S. policy and perhaps reflecting their disagreement with the American view of Iran as a highly aggressive rogue state. Saudi Arabia's relationship with Iran also includes dimensions of confrontation and detente. The Saudis criticize and constrain Iranian attempts to politicize the Hajj each year and provide land bases for U.S. military personnel. At the same time, Iranian leaders often imply or announce directly that the Saudi family are unworthy guardians of the Moslem holy cities and are unjust rulers.[34] On the other hand, the public direct evidence of Iranian interference in Saudi internal affairs is not strong. The Saudi regime has made some efforts to accommodate the Arab Shi'i in the east but has provided little evidence of Iranian activity there.[35] Likewise, Americans have voiced suspicions about Iranian involvement in terrorist attacks on U.S. military personnel in the kingdom, but hard evidence in the public domain is still not available.

While the United States may want to see the GCC monarchies survive and Iran may want them to disappear, neither may be able to determine the monarchs' fates. Iran's ability to subvert them is limited, and the United States' ability to protect them from internal change is uncertain. It is not the survival of the GCC regimes per se that drives U.S. policy, but rather the fear that their transformation could add leverage to hostile forces in Tehran or Baghdad. The security of the GCC, ironically, is as much an instrumental interest that derives from the U.S.-Iranian confrontation as it is a cause of their geostrategic conflict. After the war over Kuwait, Washington's geopolitical calculations concentrated on nuclear proliferation and the relationship Iran, and someday Iraq, might play in the broader Middle East, not just the Gulf. Here the Arab-Israeli conflict remains central to U.S. policy.

Regardless of oil or GCC monarchs, a strong Iran or Iraq that is hostile to Israel threatens U.S. interests. This is a concern felt more strongly in the United States than in Russia, Western Europe or Japan. Moreover, in these other states many leaders will differentiate, in ways leaders in Washington might not, between Iranian threats to Israel's existence and Iranian opposition to particular terms of settlement between the Israelis and Palestinians. American administrations have invested a great deal of prestige in the Gaza-Jericho agreements, and they interpret opposition to these terms as threats to peace. Additionally, they believe that the Gaza-Jericho deal was made possible partly because of the asymmetrical power relationship that resulted from the end of the Gulf and Cold Wars. If that power relationship, which favored the United States and Israel over the Arabs, shifted, then the prospects for further progress along current lines could erode quickly.

Israel and Washington can gain in the Arab-Israeli theater from Gulf relationships. GCC states represent Arab partners that can either further normalization between Israel and Arabs or lend financial and moral support to Arab rejectionism. Of course, to the extent that Arabs in the Gulf identify with Arab nationalist causes and are allowed to express populist sentiment, they constrain the monarchies' room for maneuvering. Iranian and Iraqi efforts to stoke anti-Israel Arab and Islamic sentiments within the Gulf states are seen in Washington as a threat to the process and to U.S. interests. Iranian support for Hamas and other Arabs who use force to fight for a different set of terms is also seen as a direct threat to peace and U.S. interests. Iranians, of course, see American and Israeli use of force to compel Arab acquiescence as a source of continuing conflict. They also see the U.S. and Israeli support for Arafat's suppression of Hamas as part of the problem and evidence that Islamists face a choice between capitulation from a position of weakness or resistance and struggle to acquire more compelling and competitive leverage.[36]

In the 1990s, Israelis and Americans have seen the development of their power and Iran's power in zero-sum terms. Whether this is related to a contest over bargaining terms or over the very existence of Israel and the Islamic Republic of Iran is more controversial. Clerics in Iran appear convinced that Israel and the United States are determined to destroy the Islamic regime and will settle for nothing less.[37] Israeli leaders have reached similar conclusions regarding the clerical Islamic desire to destroy Israel as a Jewish state.[38] In the early 1990s, Israeli Prime Minister Rabin came to identify Iran as Israel's most dangerous and immutable strategic enemy.[39] Uri Lubrani, Rabin's key advisor on Iran, outlined Israel's concerns and strategy in some detail. First, Israel faced Islamic opposition in the occupied territories and southern Lebanon. Hamas and Hezbollah threatened peace and the security of individual Israelis. These, however, were tactical threats attached to more important strategic challenges that could threaten Israel as a country. These strategic threats emanated from potentially powerful external enemies, such as Syria and Iraq and, in particular, Iran.

Beyond these strategic concerns about regional threats, Rabin's and Lubrani's focus on Iran was also connected to Israeli-U.S. relations. In the wake of the Cold War, many Americans were rethinking U.S. foreign-policy priorities and entertaining notions of retrenchment and downsizing. Israel's security is affected in important ways by U.S. support, which is the product of widespread domestic affinity for Israel in the United States and Washington's traditional forward policy in the Middle East. Without a Soviet threat, Washington's primary reason for projecting power to the Middle East lessened. A perceived threat from Iran, however, helps to sustain the American forward deployment and the budget priority granted to the Middle East. Military planners in the Pentagon who might have traditionally taken a skeptical attitude toward Israel's strategic suggestions could agree with the focus on the Iranian threat as it pertained to the GCC. After all, they had longstanding investments in the GCC and a need for new missions.

Certainly the rhetoric of U.S. and Iranian relations has become intensely hostile. Israeli and American leaders are highly critical of the clerical regime in Tehran, while Iranian leaders rail against Israel and the United States in extreme terms. The ferocity of the rhetoric makes it hard to recall that Iran and Israel were traditional allies, as were Tehran and Washington. Persians had not traditionally identified with Arab causes, and many still do not follow the Palestinian issue closely. For Islamic fundamentalists, Jerusalem is important and essential to the *ummah* (Islamic community). For Iranian nationalists, however, the issue is not very salient. President Rafsanjani in the past has been ready to follow President Assad's lead on Arab-Israeli issues, even though Ayatollah Khamenei typically takes a more fundamentally hostile view.[40]

While Assad has neither endorsed the terms of the Gaza-Jericho deal nor moved away from his demands regarding the Golan Heights, he has often spoken of a two-state solution. This may not convince many Israelis that room for negotiation exists, but it may signal that the question is not entirely one of existence. Should the Iranian regime drift in the direction of nationalist and technocratic concerns, it is possible that the adversarial relationship could change. In its policies toward Kashmir, Tajikistan and Chechnya, Iran has placed nationalist interests over messianic Islamic priorities. Moreover, in cities such as Tehran the emerging municipal political leadership often expresses technocratic and economic concerns.[41] It is possible that internal change in the Gulf may shift the geopolitical scene that is characterized by the United States and GCC versus Iran and Iraq in very fundamental ways. It is to the geopolitical consequences of internal change that we turn last.

INTERNAL CHANGE AND GEOPOLITICAL EFFECTS

All the major players in the Gulf want to see the regimes in other major states change. The Iranian regime would like to see the monarchs in the GCC replaced by anti-U.S. and anti-Israeli leaders and would like to see Saddam Hussein replaced by someone Iran could work with.[42] The conflict between the United States, on one hand, and Iran and Iraq, on the other, has generated some movement toward Iraqi-Iranian cooperation but it is very limited due to the legacy that Saddam Hussein's attack on Iran has left in Tehran.[43] The Iraqi regime would like to see the regimes in the GCC collapse and be replaced by pro-Iraqi Arab nationalist leaders, while leaders in the Saudi kingdom make no secret of their dislike for Saddam Hussein and the Baath in Iraq or the clerical regime in Tehran.[44]

Because religious, ethnic and national boundaries in the Gulf are not synonymous with state boundaries, geopolitical competition is easily transferred into domestic politics. Leaders in Iraq or Iran, for example, can appeal to broad Arab or Islamic identities among the populations in the GCC states and attempt to undermine the monarchical regimes. If people in these states see their rulers as abandoning important loyalties to Arab and/or Islamic brethren, then sustaining stable governance becomes more difficult. The revolution in mass communication technologies diminishes the ability of governments to control communication coming into and circulating within the state. Additionally, the globalization of the world economy provides new resources to independent elites and creates new populist pressures as jobs and opportunities become more competitive. The combination of demographic, economic and populist trends facing Gulf regimes have led observers on all sides to see momentum for both their dreams and nightmares. Some Americans, for instance, think Iran is on the brink of state implosion and the Iraqi regime is about to collapse any day. Meanwhile, they fear revolutionary change in Saudi Arabia. Conversely, Iranian clerics may take heart in the domestic disturbances in Saudi Arabia and Bahrain, while becoming increasingly anxious about the staying power of their own regime.

While other chapters deal with the internal politics of Gulf states, several large trends are worth considering in this discussion of geopolitics. The first is the promotion of state nationalism in the GCC members. Arab public sentiments that were revealed during the war over Kuwait appeared to alarm most of the GCC monarchs. Arab nationalist and Islamist sentiments appeared to be growing more serious as challenges to the legitimacy of the existing regimes. The monarchs have not been inclined to appease these populist sentiments either at home or more broadly in the Arab world. Instead they have moved to insulate their states by promoting a national sense of identity separate from Arab nationalism. If city-state nationalism in the small Gulf states and Saudi nationalism in Saudi Arabia could be established independent of popular identity with broader Arab and Islamic concerns, then the monarchies would have greater political room for maneuver in foreign policy.

In the mid-1990s, Bahrain was perhaps the most vulnerable GCC state. In it a Sunni monarch ruled over a Shi'i majority and allowed a substantial U.S. military presence and Western cultural enclave. Bahrain's troubles, like those of many GCC states, have economic forces at their roots. Following boom periods in the 1970s and 1980s, a sustained drop in oil prices and continued spending by the royal family combined to push Bahrain into a difficult financial situation with high government deficits and sharply rising unemployment.[45] As economic pressures mounted, the disparities of wealth between the general population and the privileged few—mostly members of the ruling Al-Khalifa family—became increasingly evident. It also became clearer that wealth divided the majority Shi'i from the minority Sunni, with the latter holding the advantage—a cleavage the government exacerbated by refusing to meet with opposition groups of mixed sects. Demands for economic and political change grew more strident, flaring into violent riots beginning in late 1994. Continuing disturbances were met with force and repressed by the Al-Khalifa monarchy, which enjoyed the support of Saudi Arabia and the United States.

Far more worrisome to Washington than trouble in Bahrain was domestic opposition in Saudi Arabia. Riyadh was undeniably the strategic lynchpin of U.S. policy, yet it faced demographic, economic, and populist trends that created mounting difficulties. Like Bahrain, Saudi problems were rooted in economic decline, perceptions of corruption and frustrations of a growing educated middle class. Unlike Bahrain, however, the risks in this situation could not be contained by confidence in an effective and decisive intervention from external allies should the situation escalate out of control. While Saudi Arabia could intervene in Bahrain and limit the geopolitical effects of internal change, no external state was likely or able to effectively intervene to stop change in Saudi Arabia. While the kingdom faced a variety of increasingly organized and sometimes violent opposition movements, the United States could only provide police assistance and quietly encourage reform.

Radical change in Saudi Arabia would have an escalatory short term impact on oil prices but in the long run market forces would stabilize and even a revolutionary Saudi Arabia would need to sell oil. The geopolitical consequences, however, would extend far beyond oil. Change could radically affect Iranian and Iraqi options and spell danger for Israel. Not surprisingly, leaders in the United States and Israel hope that the regime in Riyadh has more staying power than the regimes in Tehran or Baghdad, both of which face domestic problems.

In Iran, falling oil revenues, along with a sharp rise in population, corruption and mismanagement, have produced serious problems.[46] All countries in the Gulf have experienced losses in oil revenue in the late 1980s and early 1990s; Iran's losses are exacerbated by their outdated energy infrastructure, which received little attention during the 1980s. By 1996, Iran's oil income was down to one-third of its pre-revolution level. Simultaneously, Iran's population nearly doubled in the 18 years after the revolution. Unemployment rose to 30 percent or more; even official Iranian estimates put the number of Iranians living at or below the poverty line at 40 percent. Inequalities were compounded by an economic system riddled with bribes and payoffs, and a political system that by 1996 had become increasingly corrupt, intolerant of dissenting views and representative of a shrinking support base.

Change in Iran could come in several ways. There could be an evolution toward nationalist and technocratic economic priorities. There could also be a full-scale regime change. In either case the geopolitical consequences would be important. Nationalist priorities dominating Iranian policy could lead to rapprochement between the United States and Iran and between Israel and Iran. At minimum, they would produce changes in behavior that would likely heighten the willingness of other countries to deal with Iran. Many countries already perceive this trend as far along in Iranian behavior and have refused to abide by U.S. containment policy even as Clinton escalates the pressure to do so.

Finally, domestic change may come in Iraq. Many observers expected Saddam Hussein to fall long ago. The pressures for change created by the sanctions regime, international isolation and Saddam's failure in two wars would appear to be enough to topple even the brutal coercive apparatus employed by the government in Baghdad. There are different scenarios for how change might come. Baath and army elements might assassinate Saddam and crush his Takriti clique. Army elements outside the Baath might kill Saddam, seize power and crush the Baath, the Takritis and all remnants of the current regime. A confederation of opposition groups might do the same thing. The country could also devolve into ethnic and sectarian war, with the Kurds successfully completing their effort to establish independence in the north, Shi'i in the south claiming their own autonomy, and the residual Sunni Arabs either pursuing their own state or integrating with other Arab states.

Because there are many scenarios for domestic change in Iraq, the geopolitical consequences can also be diverse. Iraq as a unified Arab state, free of the albatross Saddam Hussein represents, could escape UN sanctions and begin economic recovery. It could align with Syria and strengthen Assad's leverage and in turn further stiffen Syria's hard line in negotiations with Israel. Assad, on the other hand, could join Arafat and Mubarak in opposing Hamas and any Arab nationalist alliance with Islamic populism. In this case, Iraq in alliance with Syria could strengthen a military-technocratic coalition of Arab states. This coalition could include GCC states and work cooperatively with Washington. It would strongly oppose Iran and Arab Islamists. Of course, Assad could instead continue on the course he has set for the past ten years—seeking an alliance between Arab nationalists and Islamic populists, despite their history of confrontation. In this case a new Iraq could quickly align with Syria and Iran, lending strength to a new anti-Israeli, anti-U.S. and anti-GCC coalition. It is also possible that Iraq could divide, with Israel and the United States backing an independent Kurdistan. Saudi Arabia might help finance such change, convinced that only a dissolved Iraq would in the long run be a safe Iraq. The foreign ministers of Turkey, Syria and Iran have met many times to announce their strong support for the territorial integrity of the Iraqi state and their strong opposition to any plans for dismemberment. It is possible that the collapse of Iraq could touch off a serious regional war as Israel, Saudi Arabia, Turkey, Iran, Syria and the United States competed for influence over the process of change.

CONCLUSIONS

While the structure of Gulf geopolitics is undoubtedly complex and fluid, several key points emerge from the overview presented here: (1) Gulf politics are influenced only minimally by contests between extra-regional great powers; (2) the main geostrategic contests within the Gulf are driven by an intense rivalry between the United States, Israel and the GCC monarchies, on one side, and Iran and Iraq, on the other; (3) this main rivalry is dominated primarily by the United States/Israel versus Iran axis, with varying levels of complexity among GCC states; and (4) domestic conditions internal to nearly all states within the Gulf have the potential to significantly change these conflict dynamics. To place Iran and Iraq on the same "side" of this conflict is, of course, a misleading simplification. As indicated above, the level of cooperation between these two states is still extremely low, despite their common enemies. Indeed, Iraq is likely to be contained so long as Saddam Hussein is in power; what role Iraq will play when it emerges from this period will depend on who replaces him.

The conflict between the United States, Israel and the GCC, on the one side, and Iraq and Iran, on the other, has several dimensions. First, the parties are struggling for influence and power on several levels. On the conventional military level, the United States has the upper hand. Iran, despite recent high-profile military purchases, has been unable to spend even at the level of its regional adversary, Saudi Arabia, and cannot amass enough conventional force to defeat U.S. military power in the region. Not surprisingly, Iranians appear to have concentrated their efforts to countervail against the United States in nonconventional military spheres. At the economic level, Iran has been successful in maintaining important commercial ties with most major countries in the world except the United States. European states, Japan, India, Turkey, Pakistan, China and others have continued to do business with Iran. These connections fall well short of alliances—in the event of a "hot war," they do not provide Iran with any assurances of help—but they do provide Iran with military goods, commercial trade and access to capital markets.

Washington's inability to isolate Iran completely has limited its ability to control Iran's access to non-conventional means of competition, such as weapons of mass destruction and sub-state subversion. While public evidence on Iran's activities in either of these areas is spotty and often far from compelling, the logic for Iranian acquisition of either nuclear, chemical or biological weapons is not difficult to see. Iran's continued access to international capital and technology markets constrain U.S. options for blocking proliferation should Iran elect to do so, although Washington's containment policies have complicated Iran's efforts in this direction and have made progress for Iran both slower and more costly than they might have been otherwise. The United States and Israel retain military options for prevention and preemption should Iran go further in the nuclear weapons direction. Iranian support for various efforts to undermine states from within, both through violent terrorist acts and by means of political agitation and moral support, is sufficiently inexpensive that Iran will likely have the means to pursue it for some time to come. The prevalence of this kind of conflict at the sub-state level makes domestic change all the more important in Gulf geopolitics. Internal change in any of the Gulf states could lead to significant changes in the relative balance of power in the United States/Israel versus Iran conflict. Because of this, and because of the relative stability of the conventional military and economic situations, it is at the domestic level that change is most likely. In this arena the actors involved can be small, diffuse and difficult to influence. Just the same, it is at this level that the future shape of Gulf geopolitics may be determined.

Notes

1. V. Isakov, "False Guidelines," *Sovetskaya Rossiya,* March 2, 1993, pp. 1, 3, in *FBIS-USR*-93-034, p. 19; Yuriy Batalin and Pavel Filimonov, "Will the Might of the United States Be Enhanced by Siberia?" *Pravda,* April 15, 1993, p. 6, in *FBIS-USR*-93-053, pp. 64-66.

2. Interview with Sazhi Umalatova, "The Lessons of Steadfastness: Sazhi Umalatova on Her Trip to Iraq," *Sovetskaya Rossiya,* October 10, 1992, p. 3, in *FBIS-USR*-92-143, pp. 72-74.

3. President Clinton tried in Washington in October 1995 and again in Moscow in April 1996 to persuade President Yeltsin to reverse the Russian decision to construct nuclear reactors in Bushehr, Iran, but was unsuccessful both times. See *Reuters,* April 20, 1996 and "Russia to spend $60 million on building a nuclear-power plant in the Iranian province of Bushehr," Interfax, June 4, 1996, in *FBIS-SOV*-96-109, p. 27. Also see Mikhail Rebrov, "The History of One Atomic Myth in Five Fragments," *Krasnaya Zvezda,* May 24, 1995, p. 3, in *FBIS-SOV*-95-101, pp. 12-15.

4. See Richard K. Herrmann, "Russian Policy in the Middle East: Strategic Change and Tactical Contradictions," *The Middle East Journal* 48, no. 3 (Summer 1994), pp. 455-74.

5. "Interview with Vladimir Lukin," *Moskovskiy Komsomolets,* February 6, 1996, p. 2; *FBIS-SOV*-96-026, pp. 20-21.

6. Statement by a Group of Russian People's Deputies, "For the Honor of the Navy and the Honor of Russia," *Sovetskaya Rossiya,* September 5, 1992, p. 3, in *FBIS-SOV*-92-175, p. 26, and "The Lessons of Steadfastness: Sazhi Umalatova on Her Trip to Iraq," op. cit.

7. Of the five major fleets in the Russian navy, only two—the Caspian and the Black Sea—are relevant to the Gulf region. The former cannot reach the Gulf

itself, is divided amongst four countries (Russia, Azerbaijan, Kazakhstan and Turkmenistan) and is relatively small (only two frigates, twelve patrol combatants, and a handful of amphibious vessels). The Black Sea fleet is likewise divided between Russia and Ukraine, and has been a bone of contention between the two countries; it has only about thirty ships that can operate beyond the Black Sea, none of which are aircraft carriers. Likewise, Russia's ground forces in the North Caucasus Military District number only about 58,000—small even by Gulf standards (*The Military Balance 1995/96,* International Institute for Strategic Studies, pp. 118-19).

8. See *The Military Balance 1995/96,* op. cit. pp. 177-78. Also see M. Dmitriyev, "China's 'Western Impromptu?'" *Zavtra,* May 19, 1996, p. 2, in *FBIS-SOV-96-125-S,* pp. 5-7.

9. K.V. Ramesh, "Naval Forces are Necessary," *The Pioneer,* December 9, 1994, p. 9, in *FBIS-NES-94-242* pp. 33-35, and Subhash Chakravarti, "New Star in the East: India's Ties to ASEAN Merit Serious and Determined Appreciation," *The Telegraph,* August 8, 1996, p. 9, in *FBIS-NES-96-157,* pp. 45-47.

10. "Commercial Relations With Israel Described," Hyderabad *Deccan Chronicle,* October 24, 1994, p. 11, in *JPRS-NEA-94-057;* "Air Force Delegation on 'Goodwill' Visit to Israel," *The Hindustan Times,* August 1, 1996, p. 10, in *FBIS-NES-96-150,* pp. 43-45.

11. See the discussion of "Internal Change and Geopolitical Effects" below.

12. For U.S. views, see Anthony Lake, "Confronting Backlash States," *Foreign Affairs* 73, no. 2 (March/April 1994), pp. 45-55; Warren Christopher, "Interview," *New York Times,* March 31, 1993, p. A3; and Martin Indyk, "Address to the Soref Symposium," The Washington Institute for Near East Policy, May 18, 1993. For Saudi views, see statement by Saudi Foreign Minister Sa'ud al-Faisal, Riyadh, Saudi Arabian Kingdom Radio Network, November 24, 1994, in *FBIS-NES-94-228,* p. 29.

13. Statement by H.E. Dr. Ali-Akbar Velayati, minister for foreign affairs of the Islamic Republic of Iran, before the Fiftieth Session of the United Nations General Assembly, New York, September 25, 1995; Speech by 'Ali Hoseyni Khamenei, leader of the Iranian Islamic revolution, in Gonbad-e Kavus, Tehran Voice of the Islamic Republic of Iran First Program Network, October 19, 1995, in *FBIS-NES-95-204,* pp. 60-62; Interview with Mohammed Javad Larijani, deputy head of the Majles Foreign Relations Committee, Tehran, Irib Television Second Program Network, February 1, 1996, in *FBIS-NES-96-024,* pp. 56-58.

14. Interview with Iraqi Foreign Minister Mohammed Saʻid al-Sahhaf, London, *al-Quds al-ʼArabi,* July 26, 1995, p. 4, in *FBIS-NES-*95-146, pp. 38-44; "Aziz Assails Saudi, Kuwaiti Rulers, GCC Communique," Baghdad, Republic of Iraq Radio Network, December 23, 1994, in *FBIS-NES-*94-247, p. 15.

15. See Bruce Jentleson, *With Friends Like These: Reagan, Bush, and Saddam, 1982-1990* (New York: W.W. Norton, 1994), and Lawrence Freedman and Efraim Karsh, *The Gulf Conflict 1990-1991: Diplomacy and War in the New World Order* (Princeton, NJ: Princeton University Press, 1993).

16. Lake, "Confronting Backlash States." See also Warren Christopher, "Interview," *New York Times,* March 31, 1993, p. A3.

17. Norman Kempster, "US to Back Iraqi Group Seeking to Oust Hussein," *Los Angeles Times,* April 30, 1993, p. A1; Robin Wright, "US Intensifies Efforts to Topple Iraqi Regime," *Los Angeles Times,* August 27,1995, p. A1.

18. Caryle Murphy, "US Directs Backup Aid for Kurds," *Washington Post,* November 16, 1992, p. A14; Laurie Mylroie, "Unfinished Business in Iraq," *Wall Street Journal,* April 20, 1994, p. A14; David Hirst, "US Seeks to Heal Iraqi Kurd Rifts," *The Guardian,* July 25, 1995, p. 10.

19. During the G-7 Summit in June 1996, Clinton was strongly criticized by the other six leaders over the issue of sanctioning non-U.S. companies doing business in Iran (Associated Press, June 29, 1996; "G-7 Leaders Criticize US Trade Bans," *Boston Globe,* June 29, 1996, p. 5). Earlier in the month, the European Union issued a similar criticism, charging that proposed U.S. legislation would violate the international principle of extraterritoriality (Dow Jones News Service, June 20, 1996).

20. The Iran and Libya Sanctions Act of 1996 provides for sanctions to be levied against any person or corporation investing $40 million or more in any way that "directly and significantly contributes to the enhancement of Iran's ability to develop petroleum resources of Iran" (House Resolution 3107, July 1996).

21. "After weeks of Hesitation and Contradiction Iran Decides to Play a Major Role Against the PLO-Israel Agreement," London, *al-Sharq al-Awsat,* October 24, 1993, in *FBIS-NES-*93-205, pp. 49-50; speech by Ayatollah Khamene'i, *FBIS-NES-*93-212, pp. 58-61; and statement by Ayatollah Khamene'i in Tehran, Voice of the Islamic Republic of Iran, February 25, 1994, in *FBIS-NES-*94-039, pp. 94-95.

22. "Translation of excerpts from an analytical statement issued by the Mojahedin of the Islamic Revolution Organization (MIRO) on relations

with the United States," in Tehran, *Kayhan International,* September 23, 1993, in *FBIS-NES*-93-212, pp. 63-72; and interview with Tehran Majles Deputy Sa'id Raja'i-Khorasani, Beirut *al-Safir,* November 29, 1993, in *FBIS-NES*-93-238, pp. 65-67. See also James A. Bill, "The United States and Iran: Mutual Mythologies," *Middle East Policy* 2, no. 3, (1993), pp. 101-2.

23. In an interview with *ABC News,* Rafsanjani indicated that the deal had been meant as a message to the United States that cooperation on some levels might be possible. Elaine Sciolino, "Iranian Leader Says US Move on Oil Deal Wrecked Chance to Improve Ties," *New York Times,* May 16, 1995, p. A6.

24. Richard F. Grimmett, "Conventional Arms Transfers to the Third World, 1985-1992," *CRS Report for Congress,* July 19, 1993, pp. 41-47; James Wyllie, "Iranian Rearmament," *Jane's Intelligence Review,* October 1, 1995, p. 449.

25. Iran has acquired both land-based and sea-based anti-shipping missiles from China, *Wall Street Journal,* January 31, 1996, p. A1. In October 1993, Iran and North Korea tested a jointly developed missile (Kevin Rafferty, "Iran and North Korea To Test Missile," *The Guardian,* October 26, 1993, p. 20).

26. *World Military Expenditures and Arms Transfers 1995,* Arms Control and Disarmament Agency, pp. 128, 142. This trend had been going on since the 1980s; from 1982-92, Saudi Arabia spent nearly $75 billion in weapons acquisition, far more than either Iran ($20 billion) or Iraq ($40 billion) for the same period (Richard Grimmett, "Conventional Arms Transfers"). From 1992 on, Iranian spending declined still further; by 1994, arms imports dropped to $390 million, and the CIA reported that in 1995 Iran spent only $250 million on arms. See "Iran Builds Biological Arsenal," *The Sunday Times* and *World Military Expenditures,* p. 128.

27. In 1994, Japan extended $2 billion in credit to Iran, while Germany extended $2.6 billion ("A Failure for Containment," *Kayhan International,* April 18, 1994, in *FBIS-NES*-94-078, pp. 49-50). When the Clinton administration proposed a trade ban on Iran, Britain, France and Germany all objected, arguing that sanctions were the wrong approach (Fred Barbash, "Clinton's Call for Boycott of Iran Draws Little Support Abroad," *Washington Post,* May 3, 1995, p. A27). See also Elaine Sciolino, "US and Germany at Odds on Isolating Iran," *New York Times,* December 2, 1993, p. A13.

28. "Turkey Sets Iran Gas Deal, Says It Doesn't Defy Ban," *Wall Street Journal,* August 12, 1996, p. A7.

29. In 1993, Iran openly received Dr. Fathi al-Saqaqi of the Palestinian Islamic Jihad in Tehran, and reportedly provided $10 million to Hamas in 1994. See *al-Shira,* December 13, 1993 p. 9, in *FBIS-NES-93-239,* p. 41; *al-Sharq al-Awsat,* October 24, 1993, in *FBIS-NES-93-205,* pp. 49-50; and Address by Ayatollah 'Ali Khamenei, Tehran, Voice of the Islamic Republic of Iran First Program Network, March 24, 1996, in *FBIS-NES-96-058,* pp. 79-82. See also "After Weeks of Hesitation and Contradiction . . .," *al-Sharq al-Awsat.* However, although Rafsanjani has made clear his support for the Palestinian and Lebanese Shi'i causes, he has denied significant Iranian involvement in terrorism. See Interview with President Akbar Hashemi-Rafsanjani, *Tehran Times,* July 10, 1995, pp. 1, 14-15, in *FBIS-NES-95-136,* pp. 73-79.

30. "Funds for Terrorists Traced to Persian Gulf Businessmen," *New York Times,* August 14, 1996, pp. A1, A4; "Telling Friend from Foe: A Bombing in Saudi Arabia Raises Questions About Ties to Terrorists," *US News and World Report,* November 27, 1995.

31. Hans Blix, IAEA Secretary General, has concluded that Iran "is using nuclear energy in a peaceful way" and does not intend to do otherwise (Reuters, April 20, 1994; and IRNA News Agency, April 19, 1994).

32. In 1995 the Saudi government refused to allow U.S. officials to arrest Imad Mughniyah, a leader of Hezbollah, while on a flight landing in Saudi Arabia (*Los Angeles Times,* April 21, 1995). Throughout that year Saudi officials repeatedly rebuffed U.S. requests to pre-position a brigade's worth of equipment on Saudi soil (*New York Times,* April 22, 1995). Even after the two bomb attacks in 1995 and 1996 on U.S. troops on Saudi soil, the Saudi government delayed accepting U.S. plans to relocate troops to safer areas until late July of 1996 ("Saudis OK US Troop Relocation, Will Split Cost," *Los Angeles Times,* August 1, 1996, p. A4).

33. Tehran *Hamshahri,* April 9, 1995, p. 8, in *FBIS-NES-95-073,* pp. 21-22; "President Rafsanjani meets Qatari Health Minister," Tehran Irib Television First Program Network, April 21, 1996, in *FBISNES-96-079,* p. 71; and "Interview with Qatari Foreign Minister Shaykh Hamad Bin-Jasim," Paris *al-Watan al-'Arabi,* July 26, 1996, pp. 38-41, in *FBIS-NES-96-146,* pp. 22-25.

34. Interview with Mohammed Javad Larijani, deputy head of the Majles Foreign Relations Committee, Tehran Irib Television Second Program Network, February 1, 1996, in *FBIS-NES-96-024,* pp. 56-58.

35. "Saudi Officials Reporting Accord with Shiite Foes," *New York Times,* October 29, 1993, p. A11.

36. Statement by Ayatollah Khamene'i in Tehran, Voice of the Islamic Republic of Iran, February 25, 1994, in *FBIS-NES*-94-039, pp. 94-95; and statements by Deputy Speaker of the Majles Hasan Rowhani, Tehran, Voice of the Islamic Republic of Iran, April 8, 1994, in *FBIS-NES*-94-068, p. 46.

37. Statement by Ayatollah Khamene'i in Tehran, Voice of the Islamic Republic of Iran, February 25, 1994, in *FBIS-NES*-94-039, pp. 94-95.

38. "Isolate Iran!" interview with Israeli Foreign Minister Ehud Baraq, Munich, *Focus,* May 25, 1996, p. 80, in *FBIS-NES*-96-104, pp. 43-44.

39. Interview with Prime Minister Yitzhaq Rabin by Sana' al-Sa'id in Jerusalem, Cairo, *al-Ahram,* September 10, 1994, p. 7, in *FBIS-NES*-94-177, pp. 39-41.

40. Interview with President Akbar Hashemi-Rafsanjani, *Tehran Times,* July 10, 1995, pp. 1, 14-15, in *FBIS-NES*-95-136, pp. 73-79. Rafsanjani's view has also been reflected in several statements by Foreign Minister Velayati; see for example "*Abrar* Interviews the Foreign Minister," Tehran, *Abrar,* July 17, 1996, p. 1, in *FBIS-NES*-96-145, pp. 44-49.

41. "Tehran Mayor Karbaschi: I Am Not a Presidential Candidate," *Resalat,* September 2, 1996, p. 13, in *FBIS-NES*-96-178; "The Letter of the Mayor of Tehran to Mr. Nateq-Nuri Regarding Attending the Majles to Reply to the Inquiry Report," *Jomhuri-ye Eslami,* May 23, 1996, p. 2, in *FBIS-NES*-96-106, pp. 68-69.

42. Interview with President Akbar Hashemi-Rafsanjani, *Tehran Times,* July 10, 1995, pp. 1, 14-15, in *FBIS-NES*-95-136, pp. 73-79.

43. Voice of the Islamic Republic of Iran, October 18, 1993, in *FBIS-NES*-93-200, p. 75; *al-Wasat,* March 1994, in *FBIS-NES*-94-042, pp. 38-39; interview with Deputy Foreign Minister Zarif, *al-Wasat,* March 21-27, 1994, in *FBIS-NES*-94-059, pp. 80-82; interview with Vice President Ramadan in *al-Sha'b,* April 1, 1994, in *FBIS-NES*-94-068, pp. 28-31; commentary, Voice of the Islamic Republic of Iran, October 18, 1993, in *FBIS-NES*-93-200, pp. 74-75; "Normalizing Ties with Baghdad," *Kayhan International,* in *FBIS-NES*-93-241, p. 52; and Makil Mansur, "Iranian Rulers are Treacherous Revanchists in the Service of Washington," *al-Thawrah,* March 2, 1994, in *FBIS-NES*-94-047, pp. 16-17.

44. Author's interviews with members of the Majles al-Shura, April 10, 1994, Riyadh. The Shura was established by King Fahd in December 1993; see *The New York Times,* December 30, 1993, p. A8. On Iraq, see "'Aziz Assails Saudi, Kuwaiti Rulers, GCC Communique," Baghdad Republic of Iraq Radio Network, December 23, 1994, in *FBIS-NES*-94-247, p. 15.

45. In 1995, the government budget deficit rose 65 percent from the previous year, to $323 million (Reuters, June 1, 1995). Bahrain's troubles are compounded by the fact that, among all GCC states, it has the smallest oil reserves, which are expected to run out early in the next century (Ian Black, "Bahrain Struggles to Keep a Lid on Unrest as Fat Years Come to an End," p. 12, March 1, 1996, *Manchester Guardian* Foreign Page.) The unemployment picture, too, is complicated by the presence of a large number of foreign workers in Bahrain; in 1995, nearly 60 percent of the Bahraini work force of 226,000 workers were foreigners (John Lancaster, "Bahrain Invents a Working Class," *Washington Post,* April 4, 1996, p. A21).

46. See Robin Wright, "Dateline Tehran: A Revolution Implodes," *Foreign Policy,* Summer 1996, pp. 161-174.

CHAPTER 3

THE POLITICAL ECONOMY

OF NATIONAL SECURITY

IN THE GCC STATES

F. Gregory Gause, III

WHAT SECURITY? FOR WHOM?

By a conventional definition of security, that is to say protection from foreign military attack, the states of the Gulf Cooperation Council (GCC) are more secure than at any time in their independent existence. The defeat of Iraq in the 1990-91 Gulf War reduced the military capabilities and the political capacity of one potential threat. Iran's military travail during its eight-year war with Iraq, its limited air power and nonexistent amphibious capability, and its own internal political and economic difficulties, render it an unlikely source of conventional military threat to the GCC states (the islands issue excepted). It seems unlikely that Yemen, so recently embroiled in its own civil war, is a serious military threat to its neighbors. Most importantly, the Gulf War demonstrated that the United States is willing to commit massive military force to protect the GCC states from foreign invasion, providing those states with a powerful and credible deterrent against attack. While Saddam Hussein declares that he "won" the Gulf War because he is still in power, it is hard to imagine any other leader who would want to experience a similar "victory."

Limiting a discussion of security to so narrow a definition, however, would miss much of the political dynamics behind decisionmaking in both foreign and domestic policy in the Gulf states. It is *regime* security, not simply state security, that animates decisionmakers in the region. The former includes the latter, as ruling regimes for their own interests do not want to be subject to foreign attack, but goes beyond the external dimension of security to include *domestic* political stability. For example, it is safe to assume that the bombings of American military facilities in Saudi Arabia in November 1995 and June 1996 were a more serious and immediate issue on the Saudi security agenda than a hypothetical attack by either Iraq or Iran on Saudi territory. Policies aimed at regime security might be good for the population as a whole; they might not be. The focus for understanding how policymakers confront choices in the Gulf is not some Platonic notion of "national" security or a limited understanding of purely military security, but the idea of regime security.

In most Third World countries, the most serious threats to the security of ruling regimes (with some notable exceptions, like Kuwait) emanate from within their countries' borders.[1] These domestic threats to regime security are frequently tied up with foreign policy issues, as opposition groups look for support abroad and as the regimes' dealings with the outside world (be it with the great powers, the International Monetary Fund, or international commercial and financial markets) materially affect their ability to manage their domestic societies and economies. Thus while no state in the international arena can ignore the possibility of a conventional military attack against it, the most immediate and salient threats perceived by state rulers to their own security are very likely to be domestic, or some combination of domestic and foreign.

In formulating their security strategies, the rulers of the GCC states have to face both the possibility of foreign attack and the need to maintain their domestic positions. Though I contend above that the likelihood of conventional military attack from their neighbors is now relatively low, these states live in a neighborhood that has seen two very destructive conventional wars in the Gulf, civil wars in Yemen, revolutionary upheaval in Iran and an armed insurgency in Oman. Even among themselves the GCC states have disputes over borders. They find themselves adjacent to the Arab-Israeli area, which has experienced five conventional wars, two civil wars (Jordan and Lebanon), and one sustained low-intensity conflict (the Palestinian uprising) since World War II. They cannot ignore conventional defense needs.

At the same time, the regimes confront the continuous task of maintaining the domestic bases of their rule: the provision of welfare benefits to the population as a whole, the maintenance of the economic interests of the ruling families and of the local groups with whom they are allied politically, and the care and feeding of the coercive apparatus—the regular military, police and secret services. In the 1970s and early 1980s, when money was no object, the GCC states could address all these demands with little need to set priorities. Now, in a more constrained revenue environment, they face difficult tradeoffs.

The point of this paper is to highlight how the choices the GCC rulers face in the security realm, broadly understood, interact with each other. None of the individual issues that they face—military security, fiscal problems, economic development, demographic growth, political demands—can be seen in isolation from the other issues. The choices made in one area will directly affect the regimes' ability to deal with other areas. More money for weapons purchases means less money for domestic social and economic purposes. Privatization of state-owned economic interests might relieve fiscal burdens and improve economic efficiency in the long term, but at the cost of price increases and unemployment. The imposition of taxes and the building of real citizen armies—two responses of state-builders throughout history to fiscal pressures and foreign threats—would place burdens on the citizenry that could call forth demands for political change. Reliance on the United States for external security is costly financially (big-ticket purchases for civilian and military purposes) and could have, over the long term, negative domestic consequences.

In their effort to maintain their regimes' security, the Gulf rulers face a number of what Marxist analysts used to call contradictions—conjunctions of circumstances in which the pursuit of one goal makes the achievement of other goals less likely, continuance of the status quo increases the pressures for radical change in the future, and difficult choices have to be made. This paper points to some of these contradictions. It makes no recommendations on how to deal with them. Those decisions are for people in the Gulf states themselves to make. Nor does it contend that the GCC regimes are unable to deal with these contradictions in ways that will preserve domestic stability and regional security. They have vast experience in navigating treacherous waters. They have ample, if reduced, resources—financial, ideological and coercive—with which to confront their problems. It simply points out the potential consequences of various choices they could make in dealing with these contradictions.

CONTRADICTION NUMBER 1: GUNS VERSUS BUTTER

This is the fundamental choice that any state faces in considering its security policy. What is unusual about the GCC states is that for most of the past twenty-five years, because of their vast wealth, they could have *both* as many guns and as much butter as they wanted. With each of the GCC states now facing budget deficits and fiscal stringency, those days are over. Money spent on arms now comes at the expense of other demands on state revenue, particularly domestic social and economic programs.

It should be pointed out that in our discussion of military strategy, the assumption is that the GCC states are seeking a purely defensive capability—to protect their borders from outside attack. That hardly limits the range of potential military contingencies that might confront them. Civil conflict in Yemen, naval tensions in the Gulf, a potential collapse of authority and descent into civil war in Iraq could theoretically tempt GCC states to deploy force beyond their borders. However, if the past is any indication, the GCC governments have neither the capability nor the political will to exercise military force outside their borders. The GCC states are focused on the least likely military threat to their security—direct attack by a regional state—and have little military capability to affect less direct but more probable security contingencies.[2]

The military strategy of the Gulf rulers (with the exception of Oman) has for the last twenty-five years been to invest enormous sums of money in expensive and sophisticated military hardware, such as airplanes and tanks (and the physical infrastructure of bases to support them), with comparatively less emphasis on developing large and well-trained citizen armies. This reliance on a capital-intensive defense strategy has been dictated by a number of concerns. First, the big-ticket items are meant to make up for the relatively small size of the armies compared with those of potential enemies like Iran and Iraq. There has been a belief that high-tech weaponry can make up for inferior numbers, both in terms of deterrence and in terms of actual combat.

Second, these weapons sales are in part an indirect way to pre-position equipment for foreign forces to use if the need arises. Desert Storm could not have been mounted without the extensive military base infrastructure that the Saudis built. Third, weapons purchases are seen as a way of solidifying the commitment of the seller to the security of the buyer. Having sophisticated American, British and French weapons—with the training and support they require—is a way to strengthen the West's commitment to defend the GCC countries and support their regimes. Finally, the financial interests of those in the GCC states who benefit from these large-scale arms deals cannot be ignored as a factor in explaining this strategy. The immediate costs of continuing this strategy, however, have become increasingly apparent. Since the Gulf War, Saudi Arabia has placed orders for approximately $35 to $40 billion in arms, at a time when the state foreign-currency reserves have been largely depleted, budgets are being cut, consumer subsidies are being reduced and the state's debt burden is growing. In Kuwait, defense spending is taking up a larger and larger proportion of the state budget at the same time that the need for fundamental economic change (privatization, taxation, budget cuts) dominate the political debate. Even in Oman, geographically distant from the theater of the last Gulf War, defense has remained a sacrosanct aspect of state spending at a time when the International Monetary Fund (IMF) has suggested stringent austerity measures (though the most recent Omani five year plan calls for reduced defense spending in 1997 and beyond).[3]

Citizens of the GCC states increasingly see that every riyal, dirham or dinar spent on arms comes at the expense of some other state spending project. Given the fact that high-tech weaponry neither deterred Iraq from invading Kuwait nor gave the GCC states the power to defeat Iraq, some now question the military usefulness of these kinds of arms purchases. In Saudi Arabia, Islamic activists called for the creation of a 500,000-man Saudi army to avoid reliance on outside forces for defense.[4] However, this alternative defense strategy—building larger citizen armies for conventional defense—raises numerous problems for the regimes.

One problem is simply a matter of numbers. The combined citizen populations of the six Gulf monarchies is, by the most generous estimates, no more than 18 million. Iran's population is 60 million. The inability of the GCC states to agree on a comprehensive, coordinated defense plan, as was suggested by Sultan Qabus during the 1991 GCC summit, exacerbates the problem of their small populations. They cannot effectively even pool their already-limited manpower resources for defense purposes. But numbers are not the whole story. The combined population of the monarchies is close to that of Iraq, but no one in 1990 suggested that they could themselves confront the Iraqi invasion of Kuwait. It is the political context of the states that renders a policy of self-reliance even less feasible than the numbers suggest.

The mobilization of citizen manpower into the armed forces would require obligatory military service, a very real demand of the state upon its citizens (one the United States, for example, has now chosen to avoid). A

ruthless and efficient authoritarian state like Iraq or Syria can extract a
large proportion of its manpower from society for military purposes. States
animated by revolutionary fervor like Iran was in the 1980s, or by democratic ties of loyalty between citizen and state like Israel (for its Jewish
citizens), can call upon the population for military service and receive enthusiastic answers. The Gulf monarchies lack these kinds of mobilizational
abilities.

That lack is attributable to the fact that the Gulf monarchies used
their oil resources to build a particular kind of rentier state: their social
contract rests upon the provision of benefits *to* citizens, not the extraction
of resources (taxes and service) *from* them. Instituting a national service
requirement would upset that implicit deal between state and society. In
the West historically, the need to mobilize citizen armies contributed to
pressures for popular participation in government. The ruling families in
the Gulf want to avoid exacerbating the already-growing demands in their
societies for greater participation. Moreover, from the perspective of rulers
who remember the prevalence of Arab military coups in the 1950s and
1960s, permitting into the military groups whose loyalty to the regime is
questionable would decrease rather than increase security.

Military recruitment strategies in all the Gulf monarchies reflect these
social realities. Only in Kuwait is there obligatory service, and before the
Iraqi invasion such service was easily avoidable. All the other monarchies
rely upon volunteer forces. Discussions in official Saudi circles immediately after the Gulf War about doubling the size of their armed forces,
which would probably entail some kind of draft or obligatory service, appear to have been shelved.[5] In Oman, where the rentier phenomenon came
latest, there is more prestige to military service—a result of both the Sultan's
very personal involvement in the command of the forces and the resources
he devotes to them. In the other monarchies, military service is not as
socially desirable a profession. With economic opportunities relatively plen-
tiful for better-educated, young male citizens of these states, the incentives
to join the military have been limited.

Shi'i in Kuwait, Bahrain and Saudi Arabia rarely join their militaries
and even more rarely advance in the officer corps, as a result of both government discouragement and social custom within those communities.[6]
In Saudi Arabia there are persistent reports, unconfirmed and unconfirmable
officially, that those who are not from Najd (Central Arabia) cannot advance in the military hierarchy and are barred from certain sensitive positions (such as fighter pilot). Needless to say, one-half of these states' human

resources, female citizens, are not available for military service. Taken together, these factors mean that the Gulf monarchies cannot and will not mobilize their resources for military purposes with the same efficiency as their neighbors. Demographic, social and political constraints combine to rule out a policy of self-reliance in security matters.

Another strategy that might reduce expenditures somewhat is simply to give up any idea of self-defense, and rely completely on foreign alliances—primarily with the United States—for security. Such a strategy would still be expensive, as Desert Storm and the October 1994 American "mobilization" to meet Iraqi moves near the Kuwaiti border proved. Arms would still have to be bought, for pre-positioning forces. But the political costs of such a strategy would far outweigh any economic benefits. There is no guarantee that the United States could or would use its military to protect the regimes from *every* contingency, particularly domestic threats, that they might face in the future. Moreover, a policy that publicly handed over security matters to Washington would leave the GCC regimes even more vulnerable than they already are to charges from domestic and regional opponents that they are nothing but figurehead rulers and puppets of the United States.

In the end, there are few realistic alternatives to the existing military strategy for the GCC states, short of drastic changes in their relations with their societies and with one another. At the same time, maintaining current levels of spending on arms puts enormous financial pressures on these states, particularly Saudi Arabia and Kuwait, at the same time that they are enforcing some measure of economic austerity domestically. Riyadh has recognized this dilemma in its efforts to renegotiate the payment schedules for some of its arms deals and to complete its recent purchases of commercial aircraft from Boeing and Macdonald-Douglas in stages over time.[7] The issue for the GCC regimes is whether they can rein in spending on arms and military security enough to permit them to maintain adequate levels of domestic spending in other areas. It is to that basket of issues that we now turn.

CONTRADICTION NUMBER 2:
DEMOGRAPHICS VERSUS THE WELFARE STATE

All of the GCC states have very large rates of population growth. Between 1985 and 1991, the lowest growth rate in the GCC was in the UAE (3.1 percent per year) and the highest in Qatar (4 percent per year). By comparison, total Asian population growth during this period was 1.9 percent per year, and total world growth was 1.7 percent per year.[8] Growth rates declined somewhat in the mid-1990s, but each of the GCC states is projected to double its current population within 40 years if current growth rates are sustained.[9] While some of this growth came from immigration, a large portion of it is accounted for by high birth rates and longer life expectancies. The age pyramids in the GCC states are heavily skewed toward the younger end of the population spectrum. Thus the governments of these states face growing demands on social services and the need to create employment opportunities for the graduates of the education systems the states themselves built.

The problems of dealing with a growing, increasingly young population are not unique to the GCC states. What is different about their conundrum is that these larger populations are putting enormous pressure on welfare states constructed in the 1970s and early 1980s, when populations were smaller and revenue greater. When the GCC states faced a decline in oil revenues in the 1980s, they maintained government spending levels by drawing down their reserves and, in some cases, by borrowing on the international market and relying on transfer payments from neighbors. Those expedients are no longer available.

The combination of maintaining high levels of social spending and supporting Iraq's war effort against Iran in the 1980s, with the vast expenses of Desert Storm, has removed the cushion of financial reserves for Saudi Arabia and Kuwait. Estimates of Saudi reserves vary, from less than $10 billion to approximately $30 billion (down from well over $100 billion at the beginning of the 1980s), but it is clear that the government cannot finance continued deficits from that reserve. Saudi Arabian Monetary Agency (SAMA) maintains a foreign currency reserve of about $20 billion to support the Saudi riyal; thus a large portion of existing reserves are "off limits" for meeting budget deficits.[10] Al-Shall Consultancy estimates that Kuwait's foreign reserves are around $35 billion (down from well over $100 billion at the beginning of the 1980s), and that its foreign debt is approximately $30 billion. It estimates that, if current expenditure patterns continue, the Kuwaiti Fund for Future Generations will be completely depleted by the turn of the century.[11]

Clearly, for Saudi Arabia and Kuwait, living off reserves is no longer possible. Oman has run up against the limit of the willingness of international capital markets to finance continued deficits. Bahrain, which relies in some measure on Saudi Arabia to help it cover its budget deficits, faces the waning ability of Riyadh to do so. Even Qatar and the UAE, with larger financial reserves and smaller population-to-resource ratios, are experiencing fiscal pressures. Given growing demand on social services and limited ability to pay, the GCC states face two options: cut services or raise revenues. The first path holds the risk of alienating large portions of their populations who have come to expect extensive welfare state benefits as their right as citizens. It seems unlikely that oil prices will increase substantially over the medium term, so raising revenues means, in effect, "taxing" the population. The same political risk as that involved in cutting services applies.

The GCC governments do realize that change is necessary, though not all have taken even the first steps to bring spending and revenues more into line. Saudi Arabia has gone the furthest in confronting its fiscal problems. Riyadh adopted a mid-course 19 percent reduction in its 1994 budget, which still ran a deficit of over $10 billion (US), and a further 6 percent reduction in the 1995 budget. The 1995 deficit was forecast to be $4 billion, as a result both of spending cuts and of state-mandated price increases on gasoline, electricity, work permits and visas.[12] Government subsidies for agriculture, particularly wheat production, were reduced.[13] With oil prices in 1995 running higher than budgeted, there was even hope that the deficit could be eliminated by the end of the year.[14] However, it seems that the 1995 Saudi budget deficit was slightly higher than forecast, despite oil earnings between $3.7 billion and $4.0 billion more than earlier estimates.[15] The Saudis used this cushion to pay off the remainder of their debt to foreign lenders and to begin to make good on late payments to local contractors and farmers.[16] The 1996 Saudi budget deficit was approximately $4.5 billion, once again despite oil prices much higher than anticipated when the budget was adopted at the end of 1995, nearly 9 percent of total spending. The 1997 budget forecasts a similar deficit of $4.5 billion, over 9 percent of total spending.[17] Even with a concerted effort, controlling spending is proving a difficult task for the Saudis.

The UAE raised fees in 1994 for health services and electricity, while keeping spending largely the same in its 1995 budget. Still, early estimates of the 1996 budget deficit put it at over 5 percent of the total federal budget.[18] Qatar's projected budget deficit for 1995-96 was nearly $1 billion in a budget of $3.5 billion, though it budgeted for a lower deficit, approximately $800 million, in 1996-97.[19] Amir Hamad bin Khalifa Al Thani, who deposed his father in June 1995, has initiated ambitious steps to increase Qatari gas production and to privatize parts of the economy, though the potential benefits of such steps can only be realized in the future.[20] While increased oil production reduced Oman's projected 1995 deficit, the government does not foresee a balanced budget until the year 2000, according to the most recent five-year plan.[21] Bahrain was able to reverse a trend of rising budget deficits in 1996 only because Saudi Arabia transferred its portion of the revenues from an off-shore oil field that the two states share to the Bahraini government.[22] Even with that new source of revenue, Bahrain projected a deficit of nearly $200 million in its 1997-98 budget, though that figure is much reduced from the deficit in the previous budget.[23]

In November 1994 the Kuwaiti government announced plans to reduce spending in the 1994-95 fiscal year, which began in July, by 25 percent in an effort to meet the expenses of the U.S. military mobilization mounted in reaction to Iraqi troop movements near the border in the fall of that year. The 1994-95 Kuwaiti budget adopted in July 1994 had a deficit of $5 billion in a total budget of $13.8 billion.[24] Members of the Kuwaiti parliament fiercely criticized the government's 1995-96 budget, which forecast a deficit of 1.6 billion KD ($5.3 billion), but the parliament adopted the budget nonetheless. Higher-than-expected oil revenues allowed the Kuwaitis to halve the deficit to 653 billion KD ($2.2 billion) when the books were closed for that fiscal year.[25] Kuwait's budget for 1996-97 had a projected deficit of $3.83 billion, 28 percent of the total budget.[26]

The increase in oil prices during 1996, of about $5 per barrel for the OPEC "basket" price, lessened the fiscal pressure on all the GCC governments. However welcome that windfall was, it did not change the structural pressures these states face in funding the extensive array of social services they took on in the 1970s. In fact, if this (possibly temporary) increase in oil revenues deflects the governments from pursuing efforts to scale back spending, its long term harm will far outweigh its immediate benefit.[27] The few efforts at belt-tightening already undertaken hardly encompass the universe of hard economic truths that the GCC states face. The governments will simply be unable to fund the generous and extensive social welfare policies they adopted in the 1970s at current rates of population growth. The state sector cannot absorb the growing number of job-seekers graduating from the local universities. An increasing number of children have to be educated in the state school systems. As life expectancy rises, the health costs of caring for the population will increase.

Two questions present themselves. First, can these efforts to cut spending and/or increase revenues bring the fiscal house of the GCC states in order when demand for social services will continue to increase? There is no hard evidence to answer this question, since much depends on the choices these states make in the future. However, there is certainly a sense that the austerity measures taken by some of the GCC states are the beginning, not the end, of what will be a prolonged readjustment period. It is unclear whether the governments will have the wisdom and the political will to use the cushion provided by the 1996 oil price increases to facilitate such a readjustment, or whether the increased revenue will lull them into a false sense of security.

Second, what will the political consequences of the new austerity, if it is that, be in states where the past twenty years (if not more) of politics has been based on an implicit social contract between rulers and ruled, in which the former receive loyalty (or quiescence) and the latter a vast array of social services? It is interesting to note that, while some GCC states have raised fees for highly subsidized services, none has taken what would seem to be the natural way to meet the fiscal crunch—imposing taxes. It is also interesting to note that the belt-tightening has been accompanied by efforts by the regimes to give at least the appearance of more institutionalized consultative mechanisms for eliciting the populations' views of politics. Oman, Saudi Arabia and Bahrain all appointed new *majalis al-shura* (consultative councils) since 1990. Kuwait restored its elected parliament in 1992. The new amir of Qatar has promised elections for municipal councils in 1997. Saudi Arabia and Bahrain in 1995 also made sweeping changes in their cabinets (though not in the "political" ministries that are the reserves of the ruling families), bringing in new faces to deal with their economic problems. It is clear that the rulers feel the need to make some gestures toward their populations as they enforce, or contemplate enforcing, economic hardship.

CONTRADICTION NUMBER 3:
THE "PRIVATE SECTOR" VERSUS STATE OBLIGATIONS

One of the ways that GCC governments hope to deal with the new financial realities they face (or at least one of the ways they talk about dealing with those realities) is through privatization of state-owned and -controlled companies. The belief is that privatization will give the states a one-shot revenue boost while relieving them of the long-term burden of maintaining inefficient companies and/or producing subsidized goods and services. (There is little talk of privatizing very successful operations, like the Saudi Arabian Basic Industries Corporation-SABIC.) Kuwait has moved the farthest in actual privatization plans, auctioning its stake in the National

Industries Company, the largest industrial firm in Kuwait outside of the oil sector, setting up a private sector company to own and manage gasoline stations belonging to the Kuwait National Petroleum Company, and divesting itself of its 12 percent stake in the Gulf Bank. Kuwait eventually plans to privatize sixty local firms and public utilities, of which seventeen have already been sold.[28]

Oman has adopted plans to privatize some concerns (like the state electric company) and opened up new projects in the energy sector to domestic and foreign private capital.[29] Qatar has also sought foreign investors in its plans to develop its massive offshore gas reserves, and plans to institute a domestic stock market and to divest at least some of the government's share in local companies through that market.[30] Leaders in both Saudi Arabia and Kuwait have spoken publicly about privatizing their national airlines. As of the end of 1996, there were more privatization plans than actual privatizations in the GCC, but it is increasingly seen as one relatively painless way to deal politically with the consequences of the new fiscal austerity.

The problem with privatization plans, however, is that they are not costless politically. If they are to work—if the privatized companies are to be able to compete in the market and be attractive assets for buyers—then those companies will no longer be able to provide the social goods that the governments have distributed through them. The most important of those social goods is jobs. The state sector has absorbed the vast majority of citizens in the work forces of the GCC states. Privatized companies would, presumably, look to improve efficiency and boost profits by reducing their payrolls. Thus privatization could lead very directly to increased unemployment, a new and dangerous sociopolitical phenomenon that has reached noticeable proportions in both Bahrain and Saudi Arabia, and could become an issue in Oman and Kuwait.

Privatization also means upward pressures on the prices of the goods and services provided by the companies. Privatization as a fiscal strategy makes sense only if the states can reduce or eliminate the subsidized inputs they provide the companies. But if the newly privatized companies have to pay market prices for their inputs, then they will have to raise prices to make a profit. If regional electric companies are privatized, as has been discussed in Saudi Arabia, consumers can expect electric bills much higher than now, even with the recent price increase. If Saudia, the national airline, is privatized, cheap domestic flights will go the way of the caravans.

While privatization certainly has some things to recommend it, the context in which it occurs will be extremely important for the economies, and thus for the politics, of the GCC states. The "private" sector in these states, particularly the large trading and manufacturing concerns, has lived for years within a protected economic space—protected from foreign and even local competition by the government, reliant on government contracts and state spending, and benefitting from state-granted monopolies, licenses and subsidized inputs. It is questionable whether the creation of a real and competitive private sector is in the interest of much of the Gulf business elite, which has benefitted enormously from the status quo over the last two decades. Real privatization would require a wrenching transformation in the Gulf business environment—the creation of a real private sector. That would entail: (1) a more limited regulatory environment, decreasing the importance of contacts inside the government in avoiding legal problems; (2) a clear and enforceable commercial code with a judiciary able to adjudicate commercial disputes and an executive willing to enforce judicial decisions; (3) the reduction if not elimination of subsidies; and (4) a more open and competitive system of bidding on government contracts and licenses. Without these kinds of changes, "privatization" could turn into a process in which the state continues to bear much of the financial burden of supporting these companies while the profits that accrue end up in the pockets of the privileged business and political elite.[31]

If there is a real move to privatize, as was mentioned above, one of the inevitable consequences will be increased unemployment among Gulf citizens, for whom the state sector has been the last, and frequently the first, resort in job-seeking. Combined with the demographic pressures discussed earlier, privatization could heighten what is already a serious problem in Saudi Arabia and Bahrain and what promises to be a more serious problem elsewhere.[32] It is difficult for outsiders to believe that there could be citizen unemployment in the GCC states, which are host to millions of foreign workers. The natural solution to the unemployment problem would appear to be replacing foreign labor with local labor. Some Gulf officials have indicated that their states are thinking along those lines, also.[33] The UAE in 1996 conducted a very public campaign to deport undocumented foreign workers, for example.[34] However, such moves run up against the desire of the GCC states to encourage greater private sector activity in their economies.

Gulf businessmen are unanimous (or nearly so) in their belief that their productivity and profitability depend to some extent on foreign

labor. The wage levels of foreign laborers are much lower than that of lo-
cals. The ability of employers to maintain discipline over foreign laborers,
who have no political connections and tenuous legal standings in the countries, is much greater than would be the case with citizen workers. Many
Saudi businessmen in particular complain that graduates of the Saudi school
system, particularly the religious track in that system, do not have the skills
necessary to do clerical and middle-level management jobs. In 1986, when
Saudi Arabia attempted to place an income tax on foreign workers in the
kingdom, the outcry from the business community was so great that the
king quickly withdrew the proposal.[35]

So the GCC states face a dilemma in dealing with the unemployment
issue. On the one hand, citizens without jobs are an implicit rebuke to
regimes that have taken great pride in providing lucrative and stable employment to their citizens. They form a potential audience for opposition
political movements. The riots in Bahrain that started in December 1994–
January 1995 were not caused by unemployment per se, but it seems clear
that high unemployment is a factor among others motivating discontent
in that country. On the other hand, adopting legislation (eg., taxes, much
larger fees for visas and work permits) that would equalize the costs to
employers of hiring local as opposed to foreign labor would be opposed by
a private sector upon which the governments are relying to help them
through their fiscal problems. Such steps would also hit at the economic
interests of those who earn handsome sums from their ability to grant visas
and work permits. To some extent there is no choice in the longer term for
the governments but to replace foreign labor with local labor, but the steps
necessary to get there will be difficult to take.

Thus the "private sector" is no panacea for the economic problems
facing the Gulf regimes. Giving it a greater role in national economic life is
in many ways inevitable, but how it is done will have enormous political
consequences. There is no easy way to shift the economic responsibility
that the states took on in the 1970s—to provide citizens with comfortable
jobs and subsidized services—onto the private sector.

Another issue that arises when considering the role of the private sector in economic reform in the Gulf is the place of the ruling families in
that sector. The families literally are a category of their own—public, in
that they ultimately control the state and draw on its revenue, but also
private, in that the state is now distinguishable from the family, not all
family members are officials of the state, and some family members are
pursuing careers outside the state. They inhabit a unique space in between

the public and private sectors. Without a doubt the families provide political services in these states—continuity, stability, tradition, staffing of many state offices. But any effort to address the demands on the state budget will have, eventually, to address that portion of state revenues reserved for the families. The political implications of enforcing hardships on the rest of society while the families maintain, or increase, their share of state revenues could lead to enormous resentment. Likewise the role of the families in the private sector must be defined, particularly if increasing amounts of these economies are privatized. If family members are given an automatic advantage in the business world (eg., preferential treatment by state authorities, an immunity from judicial proceedings), some of the benefits of privatization could be lost, and members of the business community could become alienated from the political system.

Defining the future relationship of the families to the state and to the private sector presents a real contradiction to the rulers. On the one hand, the family is their ultimate constituency and base of support. Moves that are seen as decreasing its wealth and its privileges could have very immediate and negative consequences for Gulf rulers. On the other hand, in the new atmosphere of economic austerity, for the family to been seen by the rest of society as immune from the hardships and burdens shouldered by others could create a political backlash that is harmful to the long-term political stability of the state, and the family's role in it.

CONTRADICTION NUMBER 4:
ECONOMIC REFORM VERSUS POLITICAL REFORM

It is commonplace for Western observers of the Gulf to argue that the difficult economic choices facing the GCC states require a much broader base of popular involvement in decisionmaking. Enforcing hardship is a trickier political task than distributing benefits. It requires the active solicitation of support from at least the most important and politically aware stratum of the population if it is going to work, if it is going to be accepted and implemented without causing instability and violent political opposition, or so the argument goes. As was mentioned above, the regimes themselves seem to appreciate this fact. Economic belt-tightening has been accompanied by the restoration of the elected Kuwaiti parliament and the appointment of *majalis al-shura* in Saudi Arabia, Oman and Bahrain.

While there are a number of reasons why institutionalizing avenues for citizen participation in the politics of the GCC states would be a good thing, facing difficult economic choices might not be one of them. There are plenty of cases around the world in which painful economic transitions, that left the country in the longer term better off, were carried out by authoritarian and even brutal dictatorships. The Chilean, South Korean and Taiwanese governments that brought their countries to their current prosperity were hardly democratic. At some point when prosperity was achieved all moved to liberalize politically, but during the transition phase of economic restructuring (eg., replacing import-substitution industrialization policies with export-led growth policies and reducing the political and economic clout of labor unions) these regimes moved to limit, not to increase, popular participation in politics. China, with the fastest growing economy in the world and profoundly dislocating market reforms, is maintaining a tight lid on political freedoms. This is not to say that brutal authoritarianism is either necessary or sufficient for economic reform. Democracies have taken steps to restructure their economies (eg., Poland, India); authoritarian regimes have driven their countries into bankruptcy (eg., the Philippines of Marcos, the FLN in Algeria). But these examples are enough to call into question the idea that greater popular participation would make the economic task of the Gulf states any easier.

If American politics is any indication, the people's elected representatives are just as likely to oppose "rational" economic policies that would impose immediate hardships on their constituents as they are to use their positions to convince their constituents to sacrifice for the greater good. In GCC countries where austerity measures have been taken—like the increase in consumer prices in Saudi Arabia—there is no evidence that consultative councils had a role in formulating the decisions. Bahrain's budget deficit was slated to increase in 1995 and 1996 over 1994 levels, despite the new presence of an appointed *majlis*.[36]

Having an elected parliament has not helped Kuwait face its difficult financial situation. The Kuwaiti government floated a proposal in October 1994 for a 10 percent income tax on civil servants and workers in the state sector, to pay for the American military mobilization of that month. It quickly became clear that parliamentary opposition to the proposal was so great that the government dropped it.[37] Despite the recognition by its speaker Ahmad al-Sa'dun that "Kuwait is on the verge of bankruptcy," the parliament instructed the government to restore a number of subsidies it had proposed to cut and to postpone fee increases it had proposed in the 1995-96 budget. The parliament then approved, with only one dissenting vote, a 1995-96 budget that had a deficit of $5.3 billion, slightly larger than the previous year's deficit.[38] Just before the adoption of that budget in

August 1995, the parliament also succumbed to government pressure and approved a plan to extend repayment times and lessen interest payments for Kuwaitis, whose debts had been assumed by the government after liberation, despite criticism that the measure benefitted a small number of wealthy Kuwaitis who had the ability to pay the loans back.

Efforts to expand *real* participatory opportunities thus might make it more difficult to implement difficult economic decisions that hit people in the wallet. Citizens might oppose policies that threaten their jobs and increase the prices of goods and services. Organized groups like the business communities might use their influence to maintain special privileges, protection from competition, subsidized inputs and guaranteed prices. Steps that might be in the long-term political interest of stability in the GCC states could therefore impede the necessary short-term sacrifices necessary to put their fiscal houses in order. But clearly the most dangerous course for the regimes to pursue would be to limit political participation *and* to avoid the hard economic choices they face. Such a strategy would leave them politically isolated when the economic problems of today become the crises of tomorrow.

One interesting factor about the relationship between economic policy and political participation about which little note has been taken is the strategies that the Gulf regimes have used to cover their budget deficits, once their reserves had been depleted. Kuwait has sold assets abroad and borrowed on the international market. Oman and Qatar have also relied mostly on international borrowing to meet their deficits. Saudi Arabia and, to a lesser extent, Bahrain, have relied more on domestic borrowing, by issuing treasury bills and government bonds, the purchase of which are reserved to local institutions and citizens.

International lenders care little about the domestic political arrangements of their debtors. They simply want the payments made. However, domestic debt holders are not just investors; they are also citizens. Holding government debt, and the willingness to buy more government debt, could give citizens and local financial institutions in Saudi Arabia and Bahrain a new kind of power in dealing with their governments. The cry of the American Revolution was "no taxation without representation." None of the Gulf governments seems willing to take the political risk that direct taxation entails. But if they do not tax, and cannot drastically cut spending, debt increases are inevitable. Perhaps domestic debt, not taxes, will be the economic leverage through which demands for a larger say in political decisionmaking are placed more forcefully on the agenda in the Gulf states.

CONCLUSIONS

It is much easier to point out problems than it is to suggest solutions; this paper has done much more of the former than the latter. Clearly the extent to which each GCC country faces these common problems differs. Bahrain, the first "post-oil" state in the Gulf, experiences the dilemmas of defense, demographics and the welfare state much more immediately than its oil-rich partners. It is the country in which the unemployment problem is the most serious, and it experienced more sustained social unrest than its GCC neighbors in the mid-1990s. Bahrain's economic difficulties, which are greater in degree but not that different in kind from the other GCC states, are exacerbated by a particular sectarian problem—a large Shi'i majority population governed by a Sunni ruling family—that is unique in the area. It is unlikely that the other states will experience the same kind of political problems in the same way that Bahrain has recently, but events in Bahrain provide a cautionary tale to other GCC leaders.

There are specific social and political circumstances in each state that add complicating factors to the issues set out above: sectarian tensions, though less serious than Bahrain's, in Kuwait and Saudi Arabia; the size and unique role of the religious establishment and its institutions in Saudi Arabia; the continuing effects of the Iraqi invasion on Kuwait; the Bahrain-Qatar, Saudi-Qatar and UAE-Iran border disputes. While the context is common, the particulars in each state are different, and the choices they make will be different.

While recognizing the differences among the GCC states, I have argued that they face a common agenda of problems in the area of the political economy of security. If serious financial crises are to be avoided, state spending must be brought into closer alignment with state revenues. There seems to be no prospect for a substantial and sustained increase in oil prices, so difficult choices of resource allocation must be made. There are no drastic changes that they can make in their defense strategies. They are committed to a relatively expensive strategy of acquiring high-technology weaponry both to offset manpower deficiencies and to tie the security interests of the United States and other great powers to their defense. At best they can trim defense spending at the margins and stretch out payments for major new weapons systems.

The two areas that no GCC state can avoid addressing involve the size of the welfare state and the role of the state in managing the economy. The demographic numbers have a stern inevitability about them. The question

GCC state leaders must face is how to convince their citizens that belt-tightening is in the long-term interests of everyone in the country, as well as of their children and grandchildren. A first step in that direction is to make sure, and to be seen to make sure, that hardships fall on every group, including the ruling families themselves. As of yet none of the ruling elites have been willing to impose fiscal discipline on their families in a public way. A second step is to involve a greater range of the citizenry in decisionmaking, though perhaps *after* the initial difficult economic decisions are made. Whether appointed consultative councils will fit that bill is one of the major questions in the political future of the Gulf states. Clearly where the population has had the experience of elected legislatures (Kuwait and Bahrain), appointed consultative bodies are not seen as a step forward in terms of popular participation in politics. In the other states, it is more difficult to tell both how the consultative councils will develop, and how the citizenry will view them.

While the political sensitivity of shrinking the welfare state is well understood by the GCC, it appears that the political consequences of privatization are, as of yet, not. The enthusiasm with which governing elites in the Gulf have adopted the rhetoric of privatization (if not yet the reality) indicates that many see it as a cost-free way of dealing with fiscal problems. Nothing could be further from the truth. Real privatization would require two extremely difficult political choices by the GCC governments: (1) a willingness to tolerate, at least temporarily, substantial increases in citizen unemployment, or to radically restructure the economic incentives that now lead employers in these states to hire foreign labor; and (2) a willingness to construct legal systems based on clear, impartial and enforceable commercial laws that treat all citizens—employers, investors and workers—equally. A real and competitive private sector, not based on insider contacts, sweetheart deals and protected monopolies, would be a new thing in Gulf economies, and a politically difficult thing to build.

I reiterate the point I made at the beginning: The fact that the GCC regimes face difficult choices in the realms of security and economics does not mean that they cannot meet these challenges and maintain domestic and regional stability. There are many paths open to the regimes in dealing with these issues, but they must be faced sooner or later. The choices they make concerning them in the next few years will determine the character of politics in the GCC states into the next millennium.

Notes

1. Much of the recent literature on security in the Third World has emphasized the central analytical role of regime security in understanding the foreign and defense policies of these states. See for example Steven David, "Explaining Third World Alignment," *World Politics* 43, no. 2, (January 1991); Mohammed Ayoob, *The Third World Security Predicament* (Boulder, Colorado: Lynne Rienner, 1995); Edward Azar and Chung-In Moon, "Legitimacy, Integration and Policy Capacity: The 'Software' Side of Third World National Security," in Azar and Moon, eds., *National Security in the Third World* (London: Edward Elgar, 1988); and Brian L. Job, "The Insecurity Dilemma: National, Regime and State Securities in the Third World," in Job, ed., *The Insecurity Dilemma: National Security of Third World States* (Boulder, Colorado: Lynne Rienner, 1992).

2. Current security threats in the Gulf are discussed at greater length by the author in his book *Oil Monarchies: Domestic and Security Challenges in the Arab Gulf States* (New York: Council on Foreign Relations Press, 1994). A number of the themes developed in the paper are treated in more detail in the book.

3. Andrew Rathmell, "Oman: Severe cuts in Sultan's defence," *Jane's Intelligence Review* 3, no. 7 (July 1, 1996), p. 6.

4. The author obtained copies of the Memorandum of Advice (*muzakkarat al-nasiha*) in Saudi Arabia. "The Army" was one of the sections of the Memorandum, and included the call for a citizen force of 500,000 men.

5. See *The New York Times,* October 13, 1991, pp. 1, 18; October 25, 1991, p. A9, for references to the Saudi proposals. Since that time there have been no moves to expand the size of the Saudi military.

6. In 1991 leaders of the Saudi Shi'i community sent a petition to King Fahd in which they raised four specific issues which they were "absolutely sure . . . would be taken care of by Your Excellency." One of the four was a request that the "quarantine" against the entrance of Saudi Shi'i into the armed forces be removed, because many in the community wished to "discharge our duty of defending the soil of this country." Practically identical English-language translations of this petition appeared in "Makka News," no. 7 (April 6, 1991) and in "Arabia Monitor" 1, no. 6 (July 1992). "Makka News" was published by the Organization of the Islamic Revolution in the Arabian Peninsula, an Iranian-supported exile group with an American post office box address in Bowling Green, Kentucky. "Arabia Monitor" was the monthly newsletter of the International Committee for Human Rights in the Gulf and Arabian Peninsula, published in Washington, D.C.

7. Ashraf Fouad, "Saudi may buy $7.5 billion airliners in phases," Reuters (on-line), September 17, 1995.

8. United Nations, *Demographic Yearbook –1991,* (New York: United Nations, 1992), Table 1, p. 103; Table 3, pp. 106-11.

9. Population Reference Bureau, *1995 World Population Data Sheet* (Washington, DC: Population Reference Bureau, Inc., 1995).

10. It is extremely difficult to find accurate and official figures on the liquid reserves of the Saudi government. *Middle East Economic Survey,* January 25, 1993, p. B3, puts usable Saudi government reserves at $7.1 billion at the end of October 1992, though other analysts involved in Gulf financial matters put the figure much higher, closer to $20 billion. *The New York Times* published a two-part series on the Saudi financial situation (August 22, 1993, pp. 1, 12; August 23, 1993, pp. 1, A6) in which they quoted an unnamed Saudi official as estimating the country's liquid reserves at $7 billion. In a response to these articles, then–Saudi Finance Minister, Muhammad Aba al-Khayl, wrote that the Kingdom had a $20 billion hard currency fund to support the national currency, and that Saudi banks had hard currency assets in excess of $15 billion. Part of Aba al-Khayl's response was published as a letter to the editor in *The New York Times,* August 26, 1993, p. A18. The full text of the letter can be found in *Middle East Mirror,* September 2, 1993, pp. 20-22.

11. See al-Shall reports reprinted in *al-Hayat,* January 28, 1995, p. 9; and February 25, 1995, p. 9.

12. *al-Hayat,* January 3, 1995, pp. 1, 4; *The New York Times,* January 3, 1995, p. A3; "Saudi wants to quickly balance budget-minister," Reuters (on-line), January 9, 1995.

13. Christine Hauser, "Saudi Arabia cuts back desert wheat farms," Reuters (on-line), July 2, 1995.

14. Steven Swindells, "Saudi oil price strategy may cut budget deficit," Reuters (on-line), August 31, 1995.

15. Ashraf Fouad, "Saudi 1995 budget deficit slightly above target," Reuters (on-line), January 15, 1996.

16. Diana Abdallah, "Saudi economy healthier, but more challenges ahead," Reuters (on-line), June 11, 1995; Diana Abdallah, "Saudi may pay all contractors' debt by end of year," Reuters (on-line), May 20, 1996.

17. Diana Abdallah, "Saudi 97 budget projects higher spending, revenue," Reuters (on-line), December 30, 1996.

82   F. Gregory Gause, III

18. "UAE approves '95 budget with 25 pct deficit cut," Reuters (on-line), January 30, 1995; *al-Hayat,* October 3, 1996, p. 9.

19. Youssef Azmeh, "Qatar confident after loan deal for huge gas field," Reuters (on-line), June 19, 1995; "Qatar aims to slash budget deficit," United Press International (on-line), April 4, 1996; Reuters (on-line), November 18, 1996.

20. Hilary Gush, "Qatar bourse seen soon, privatisation later," Reuters (on-line), July 12, 1995.

21. "Oman narrows budget deficit," Associated Press (on-line), January 15, 1996; "Oil prices push Oman growth in 1995," United Press International (on-line), August 20, 1996.

22. Christine Hauser, "Saudi aid will ease Bahrain budget squeeze," Reuters (on-line), April 15, 1996.

23. Reuters (on-line), September 22, 1996.

24. *al-Hayat,* November 11, 1994, p. 9.

25. Inal Ersan, "Oil prices cut Kuwait deficit, but reform needed," Reuters (on-line), December 8, 1996.

26. *al-Hayat,* May 30, 1996, p. 9.

27. Diana Abdallah, "Gulf coffers fill, economic reforms slow," Reuters (on-line), December 19, 1996.

28. "Kuwait auctions share of industrial concern," Reuters (online), June 22, 1995; "Kuwait outlines petrol station privatisation," Reuters (on-line), September 11, 1995; "Kuwait to sell 90 million Gulf Bank shares," Reuters (on-line), December 19, 1996.

29. *al-Hayat,* June 23, 1995, pp. 1, 6; Randall Palmer, "Oman may be overdoing expansion, economists say," Reuters (on-line), January 19, 1995; Steven Swindells, "Oman attracts interest of foreign oil explorers," Reuters (on-line), June 20, 1996.

30. "Qatar to sell off shares in two firms," United Press International (on-line), September 15, 1996.

31. For an excellent theoretical discussion of the problems faced by states looking to privatization and liberalization as solutions for their economic crises, see Kiren Aziz Chaudhry, "The Myths of the Market and the Common History of Late Developers," *Politics & Society* 21, no. 3 (September 1993), pp. 245-74. It is interesting to note that Chaudhry did extensive fieldwork in the

Arabian Peninsula and Iraq for other projects. A similar argument about the
obstacles to privatization in the Gulf states has been made by Vahan Zanoyan
of the Petroleum Finance Company. See his "After the Oil Boom," *Foreign
Affairs* 74, no. 6 (November/December 1995).

32. The problems presented by unemployment for the GCC states were
    highlighted in a recent address to a conference in Dubai on economic
    development in the region by Kuwaiti economist Jasim al-Sadoun. He said
    that current demographic trends indicate that by the year 2010 there will be
    8 million new entrants into the labor market in the GCC states. "Planners
    and decision makers must then attempt to create enough jobs for the
    newcomers or face the alternative—severe unemployment with possibilities
    of social and political extremism. All available signs point to the latter
    happening. . . . People think that because of the large number of expatriates
    it will not be difficult to replace them with national manpower. The reality
    is otherwise," he said. Quoted by Reuters (on-line), February 5, 1995, citing
    an article in *Arab Times.*

33. Oman has had an official policy of "Omanization" of the work force for years,
    though until recently it has remained little more than rhetoric. Particularly
    after the departure of most of the Palestinian community from Kuwait after
    liberation, there were serious plans mooted to reduce Kuwaiti dependence
    upon foreign labor, but recent figures show that foreigners still make up more
    than 75 percent of the Kuwaiti work force. Sharon Stanton Russell and
    Muhammad Ali al-Ramadhan, "Kuwait's Migration Policy Since the Gulf
    Crisis," *International Journal of Middle East Studies* 26, no. 4 (November
    1994), pp. 569-87. Bahraini officials are considering doubling the cost of
    work permits and renewals of such permits for foreign workers, in the wake
    of serious social unrest on the island at the end of 1994 and the beginning of
    1995. "Bahrain might raise work permit fees for foreigners," Reuters (on-
    line), September 23, 1995. Saudi Interior Minister Prince Na'if ibn Abd al-
    Aziz, whose country increased the cost of foreigners' work permits at the
    beginning of 1995, told the Saudi Press Agency that "replacing the expatriate
    work force by Saudi nationals is a strategic goal of the state" ("Saudi to replace
    expatriates by Saudis, Minister says," Reuters (on-line), July 20, 1995).

34. *al-Hayat,* October 3, 1996, p. 9.

35. See the account of that incident in Kiren Aziz Chaudhry, "The Price of
    Wealth: Business and State in Labor Remittance and Oil Economies,"
    International Organization 43, no. 1 (Winter 1989), pp. 101-45.

36. Reuters (on-line), November 30, 1994.

37. See *al-Hayat,* October 18, 1994, p. 4; October 24, 1994, pp. 1, 4; October 29, 1994, p. 10 for reporting on this issue.

38. *al-Hayat,* June 28, 1995, pp. 1, 6; July 9, 1995, p. 5; August 23, 1995, pp. 1, 6.

CHAPTER 4

OIL AND THE GULF:
ALTERNATIVE FUTURES

Paul J. Stevens

INTRODUCTION

This paper considers how oil may influence the nature of politics in the Gulf. It develops a framework to identify transmission mechanisms from oil policies to the politics of the region. The paper then develops views about the oil market. These views, in conjunction with the transmission framework, can be used to consider contexts which, through oil policies in the region, may influence Gulf politics. Finally, the paper considers how the Gulf countries are responding to the oil market and the implications of these responses given the range of possible futures.

Several limitations of the paper should be identified. First, there exists a serious problem of simultaneity. The paper postulates that the politics of the region are a function of oil. However, oil is also a function of the politics. While the emphasis will be on politics as the dependent variable, the obvious feedback loop will not be ignored. Where appropriate, implications of oil as the dependent variable will be considered. Second, the paper is not an attempt at a forecast. Its prime aim is to set out an agenda of possible sets of circumstances that can then be used to consider the impact of other variables or influences upon the politics of the region.

The Transmission Mechanism from Oil to Politics

The oil industry in the Gulf creates linkages that force the countries of the Gulf to interact. The interaction may be competitive, cooperative or both.

Oil also provides levers or instruments to influence that interaction and interactions in other areas unconnected with oil.

The Linkages

A number of linkages are created between producers of the region. Oil production from one country competes with production from another. The history of the international industry has alternated among the sort of damaging price competition that generated the 1986 price collapse;[1] the effective cooperation that generated the price stability of the 1950s and 1960s[2] and weak cooperation that provides a culture upon which the bacteria of political conflict can grow.[3]

Oil production from one country may also influence the price of oil enjoyed (or suffered) by others. The determination of oil prices is a complex and controversial subject.[4] In this author's view, it has been and remains a complex mixture of administration and market forces.[5] The key lies in the existence of excess capacity to produce crude oil. Whoever has control of that excess capacity has the power to make prices in the market. They can state a price target and then set production levels to ensure the price is accepted as plausible. During the 1950s and 1960s, it was the major oil companies that through their joint control of Gulf production determined prices. After the first oil shock of 1973, it was Saudi Arabia acting as swing producer that, with the support of the major oil companies, took over control. After the second oil shock of 1979-81, OPEC took over this support role.

Since the third oil shock of 1986, the analysis has become more complicated.[6] The pricemaker is now a rangemaker that tries to set its production level to approximate demand in the market. However, this creates a very wide range, arguably between $10 and $30, within which, in a world of imperfect information, any price can act as an "equilibrium" price.[7] The price that actually rules is determined by the beliefs of the various market players as they interact in an essentially competitive market. However, it is important to remember that the "competitive" market depends upon the rangemaker's successfully making the range to prevent a truly competitive price emerging. Without the constraint upon the excess capacity, price would collapse. The whole process of pricemaking has been further complicated because oil is being traded like any other commodity. Fund managers are operating in the oil market. Therefore, changes in the price of oil are just as likely to be linked to what is happening in the equity markets as to the supply and demand of oil. Since the liberation of Kuwait, Saudi

Arabia has been acting as rangemaker with reluctant support from the rest of OPEC.

The political implications of such linkages are clear since pricemakers and rangemakers can deliberately affect the revenue of the pricetakers. In October 1973, the Gulf states' decision to increase prices benefited all other oil exporters. In 1986, the Saudi decision to eschew the swing role damaged all other producers. A more recent example was the behavior of Kuwait in undermining prices, a role that was a major contributing factor in the Iraqi invasion. More recently, it has been suggested that the reason for Saudi Arabia's apparent willingness to accept low prices is that it maintains Iraq's exclusion from the oil market.[8] Also Iran clearly sees the low oil price as part of a deliberate plot to undermine its economic position.[9]

A revenue impact also occurs when Gulf countries are competing for markets. Volume gains from price shaving represent revenue loss to competitors unless they too shave prices. In that case, both revenues are affected.

Another linkage created by oil involves a demonstration effect. One country's oil policies are likely to have an impression on others because of the constituency that may be created. A good example of this was the erosion and eventual collapse of the General Agreement on Participation reached in October 1972.[10] The rejection by the Kuwait National Assembly of the initial 25 percent equity share forced other governments in the region, many of them against their better judgement, also to push for a greater share. Similarly, the use of oil as a leading development sector in the region in the 1970s was in part driven by such a demonstration effect.[11]

There are two other sources of linkage between oil producers. Oil as a fluid is no respecter of international boundaries and this can create problems.[12] If the oil field straddles the boundary, then a barrel of oil or cubic foot of gas lifted by one party is lost to the other. Examples of such linkages include the dispute between Iraq and Kuwait over the Rumaila/Ratga fields and the dispute between Iran and Qatar over the North Gas field. Furthermore, the possibility of oil or gas deposits suddenly makes border demarcation a matter of urgent national priority. Recent examples include the border dispute between Saudi Arabia and Yemen and between Bahrain and Qatar.[13]

Finally, a new source of linkage has emerged recently. As I will discuss, in the region, only Saudi Arabia has explicitly ruled out upstream involvement by foreign companies. The other countries, with various degrees of enthusiasm and urgency, are seeking to obtain foreign investment by international oil companies. Because of the sensitivity of such investment to the terms offered, the countries are competing for such investment.

Oil revenues have created significant economic linkages in the region. Oil revenues funded various financial flows as either aid, grants or investments. The oil-generated economic boom of the 1970s triggered the labor migrations from the low- to the (relatively) high-income countries. Such linkages have had an enormous impact on the region, strengthening political linkages and providing many sources of political conflict.

There may also be linkages whereby the producer supplies oil to the non-producer and creates a degree of dependency, especially if the oil is supplied on concessionary terms.[14] Such linkages become even stronger if the producer supplies gas, since the nature of gas transportation precludes the importer from switching easily to other suppliers.

The need for oil- and gas-export routes can also generate significant linkages. The economics of transit pipelines is fraught with difficulties and problems.[15] The building of such lines requires the negotiation of terms with the transit country—a form of linkage. Once the line is built, the owner has the option to use it while the transit country has the option to allow its use—another form of linkage. The region is also characterized by three potential choke points on export routes—the straits of Hormuz and Bab al Mandab, and the Suez Canal. Control of these points inevitably creates links with the exporters wishing to use them. The events of the Iran-Iraq conflict and the tanker war illustrate the point.

The Levers

Linkages force interaction. Each country, while pursuing its own goals, can seek to get others to support or at least not hinder those goals. To do this, any country has at its disposal a range of instruments or levers.

In the Gulf, oil has been an important source of such levers. Levers include oil revenue, crude producing capacity and export routes. Such levers can of course be used as instruments in areas of policy other than oil.

Revenues can act as a lever directly or indirectly. They can be used directly to buy political support at a national, regional or international level. At a national level they have been widely used to provide subsidies and free services. The most extreme example is provided by the GCC countries. At a regional and international level oil revenues have been used to provide aid, grants or investment flows. Examples include support for the "front-line states." Oil revenues can also be used indirectly to persuade or cajole. This pressure can range from arms purchases to funding dissident groups in another country.

Access to crude producing capacity also acts as a lever since its existence on any scale acts as a threat to persuade others. The Saudi control of
the market during 1975-78 was derived in part from its believed excess
capacity.[16] Similarly during the period 1982-85, when OPEC was struggling to defend prices, it was the threat of Saudi over-production that helped
hold the line, albeit rather shakily. Today, Saudi Arabia's potential to flood
the market still acts as a potent lever against other producers.

Production capacity is a lever by which pricemakers can determine
price levels. Saudi Arabia's willingness and ability to produce its excess capacity following the Iraqi invasion of Kuwait was the main reason that oil
prices were contained during the crisis and that they remained low after
the crisis. Similarly, it was the willingness of both Saudi Arabia and Iran to
contain their capacity that gave credence to the $18-per-barrel agreement
reached by OPEC in December 1986, an agreement that signalled the end
of the third oil shock.

Control of another's export routes is another obvious lever. Control
implies the ability to close the route. For example, much of the history of
relations between Syria and Iraq can be written through the history of the
ex-Iraq Petroleum Company transit line.[17] Iranian threats to the Strait of
Hormuz added an important international dimension to the Iran-Iraq war
and eventually influenced its outcome.

Conclusions

Clearly oil has been an important influence on politics in the region. Its
importance has varied depending upon the sensitivity of the linkages and
the magnitude of the levers. Linkage sensitivity was dependent upon the
state of the oil market. For example, potential over-supply made competitive links crucial and highly sensitized. Lever magnitude was also dependent upon the state of the oil market. For example, the oil price shocks of
the 1970s gave significant power to otherwise weak countries. Thus to
make any assessment of the future impact of oil on Gulf politics requires
some view on the future of the oil market.

THE FUTURE OF THE OIL MARKET?

Each oil market variable is considered individually and then collectively in a set of qualitative scenarios to discuss how the oil market and
the Gulf producers' position in that market may look in the future. The
final stage is to explore political implications in the light of current oil

policies in the region given the sensitivity of linkages and the magnitude of levers.

So long as OPEC meets to determine production levels, no matter how effectively, OPEC will continue to act as the rangemaker to the oil market whether it likes the role or not. This is because whatever excess capacity exists in the future will reside in OPEC. Within that group it is the Gulf producers who will dominate since they will control the majority of any excess capacity, as they have since the 1950s. Even if more were to follow Ecuador and Gabon's example and leave OPEC, a core would have to remain. If there was no control and hence no rangemaking, prices would collapse.

To determine the call on OPEC requires a view of global oil demand and non-OPEC supply. The next key variable is the producing capacity within OPEC. The greater the capacity compared to the call, the greater the need for control and hence the greater the sensitivity of linkages. If production were to match capacity, no constraint would be required. The greater the excess capacity, the greater the constraint. Similarly, the more dispersed the excess capacity within OPEC, the greater the need for cohesion and again the greater the sensitivity of linkages.

Consideration of these variables sets the context to determine the sensitivity of linkages and helps identify the strength and location of levers. How much excess capacity in the Gulf must be controlled? Who has most? How much unused quota is available for redistribution to the Gulf countries? How do the countries themselves perceive the situation, and how are they responding? All of these questions will influence the context in which current oil policies in the Gulf are being operated. They also set the context in which oil prices will be determined, and this in turn will eventually feed back into the individual variables, hence revising the context.

Demand

Global demand for oil will grow in the foreseeable future. During the 1970s, oil demand averaged 3.5 percent growth per year. In 1980-85 it declined at 1.4 percent per year and grew during 1985-95 at 1.5 percent.[18]

Demand could grow faster than it has recently. If the world begins to grow rapidly, oil demand could increase. In particular, the developing countries possess a huge potential demand for energy and, given problems with infrastructure, investment and transportation, oil still retains significant advantages over other forms of energy. It can be argued that developing countries' demand for energy grows in a step function and that recent economic reform in many countries puts them on the brink of rapid economic growth. It is worth remembering that during 1986-95, the six Asian

Tigers together added 2.9 million b/d to world oil demand. Equally, if the oil price were to collapse and stay there for any period of time, demand could be higher as dual firing capacity reverts to oil. The strong case for demand finds widespread support. For example, the International Energy Agency (IEA) has projected a growth in oil demand to the year 2000 of 2.2 percent per year and 2.0 percent thereafter.

Demand could also grow slower than it has recently. Consumer governments are increasingly dictating the oil price that really affects demand by their control of indirect taxation. Currently in Western Europe, on average less than 12 percent of the gasoline price at the pump is accounted for by the price of crude, including transportation.[19] Oil products are a taxman's dream. The existence of large-scale, easily identifiable suppliers makes collection costs low; widespread use creates a large tax base, and short run demand inelasticity invites a high tax rate. Furthermore, while such policies are driven by the need for revenue they can be wrapped up in the electorally popular rhetoric of environmental concern. Although global environmental concerns have slipped down on the political agenda of most countries, concern about air pollution from urban traffic grows and could provoke a California-type response.

As the forecast moves further into the future, uncertainty rises. The main determinant of oil demand is the stock of energy-using appliances, both in terms of the type of fuel they use and the efficiency with which they convert usable primary energy into useful energy—light, heat and work. The size and nature of the stock change slowly. Also, changes to the stock are driven by price expectations rather than by current prices, although the two tend to be strongly linked. For oil, a number of issues arise. First, there is undoubtedly a huge potential for improving appliance efficiency.[20] Second, there is an equally enormous potential for gas to push out oil, even in the road/transport sector. This arises from a combination of developments in technology coupled with greater gas availability. Third, oil retains considerable advantages over other forms of energy because of its fluidity and high energy content. Of particular importance is the fact that, unlike gas and electricity, oil does not require large pre-supply infrastructure investment. Its ability to be handled and sold in divisible batches remains a potent advantage in situations in which financial constraints rule.

Non-OPEC Supply

Non-OPEC supply outside of the former Soviet Union (FSU) will probably continue its inexorable rise into the next century, although the impact from current exploration activities before 2000 will be limited because of the lead times on upstream projects. The capacity that will come onstream by 2000 has already been discovered.

There is always the uncertainty of whether or not low prices will inhibit investment in developing capacity. However, several factors will mute the effect of low prices, even if these prices endure. General technology improvements collectively employed are having a dramatic impact on costs. The North Sea provides the best examples in which the levelized field lifetime costs, pre-tax at 10 percent rate of return, have fallen from $21 in 1980 to $12 in 1993.[21] In addition to lower costs, technical change in the area of sub-sea completion and offshore tanker loading are allowing the development of fields without the very heavy front loading and long lead times that characterized previous developments. This ability to secure a positive cash flow early in the project is of crucial importance in a world of increasingly tight finance.[22]

Lower prices are also muted by the fact that fiscal systems are becoming flexible. Systems are emerging that allow for rapid cost recovery and for the sharing of economic risk between the company and the government. Currently only a dozen or so countries have such a system. The remainder tend to take a fixed percentage (70 to 75 percent) of the cash flow. However, given the international mobility of company exploration budgets, countries that fail to allow flexible terms will find themselves excluded.

The view that non-OPEC supply outside of Russia will continue to rise receives widespread support. The IEA's latest view shows an upward trend of non-OPEC supply (including the FSU) of 0.8 percent per year.[23] A study by Peter Odell, the most optimistic seen by this author,[24] suggests an annual increase for non-OPEC (excluding former communist) countries of 1.5 percent between 1990 and 2000. History supports this view. Forecasts of non-OPEC supply peaking were widespread throughout the 1980s and were invariably wrong because of a neglect of technical change and fiscal flexibility.[25] During the period 1980-95, non-OPEC production outside of "communist areas" and North America averaged 4.5 percent annual growth. During 1965-70, the last period of poor price expectations, with prices lower than today in real terms, growth was 6.5 percent per year.

If patterns continue, there will probably be little change in Russia's net export position before 2000,[26] although there is much debate about this.[27] Political and economic uncertainty could continue to reduce consumption. Production is less likely to collapse given its crucial role as a hard currency earner, although, absent foreign involvement, it will probably continue to decline. If the economic and institutional situation improves, investment by foreign companies in existing fields could quickly increase production. However, it will be some time before such improved economic conditions increase domestic consumption given the existing inefficient use of energy. Thus current export levels are regarded as a minimum that might increase. Only a full-scale destructive civil war or a collapse in the infrastructure would cause a collapse in net exports.

As with demand, the further out the forecast for non-OPEC supply, the more uncertainty grows. Two opposing forces are at work. On the one hand, the quantity of oil-in-place in the world is fixed and finite. On the other, the ability to convert oil-in-place into producing capacity is continually improving through technical progress. Furthermore, the willingness to convert, driven by the desire for profit, also has a long way to go before it diminishes. There is still a great deal of economic rent in the oil price, which by definition can be removed without inhibiting investment in supply. While investors would prefer to take a $10 barrel in rent, purely by definition, they would still be happy to accept any number above zero. However, of crucial importance for the later analysis of this paper is the fact that it is the owners of the oil-in-place who will find themselves losing revenue. To date, conversion to capacity has more than overcome the implications of finite resources.[28] After 2000, this tendency is likely to be reinforced, if the current political and institutional uncertainties in the FSU can be overcome, to give access to what is without doubt huge hydrocarbon potential.

Iraq

The timing of Iraq's full return attracts continual speculation.[29] It seems probable to this author that while Saddam Hussein remains in power, U.S. domestic political considerations will prevent a full lifting of sanctions. The only qualification to this view is if a politically induced supply disruption causes oil prices to rise very sharply. At that point, if it is perceived that the higher prices could remain for some time, political expediency may overcome political sensitivities.

When Iraq is allowed a full return, the question is at what levels. On balance, given Iraq's reserve base and large-scale foreign investment, and assuming sympathy from the transit countries, it is likely that Iraq will build its output capacity very quickly.[30] The attitude of Iraq's transit partners—Turkey and Saudi Arabia—will of course be crucial. However, it is likely that their attitude would be favorable on the grounds that the lifting of sanctions would presage a major change in international attitudes to Iraq.

It seems sensible to assume that whatever Iraq can produce will be produced and that Iraq will de facto remain outside any OPEC quota arrangement, at least for the first few years, on grounds of need. This is reinforced if much of the output being produced by oil companies is equity oil that would be lifted first by any company in preference to arms-length sales. This assumption of course begs all the interesting questions and raises again the issue of simultaneity. It assumes a generosity on the part of other Gulf producers, including Iran, an assumption that may well be unrealistic. This is particularly relevant since even if Iraq left OPEC to avoid quota constraint, Saudi Arabia, by virtue of its control of the Iraqi pipeline across Saudi Arabia, could still impose constraints on Iraqi exports. Hence Iraq's ability to export will be very much influenced by the Gulf politics of the time.

OPEC Capacity

There exists much uncertainty over current and future levels of OPEC capacity. Present levels of capacity are politically sensitive because of the need to maintain a position in anticipation of the negotiation which will be required when Iraq fully returns. The problems associated with such a negotiation have been avoided so far by simply rolling over the quota agreement that was set in 1993. Countries have a vested interest in overstating their potential capacity, since whatever other basis is used, capacity will play a key role in the division required to accommodate the full return of Iraq. Furthermore, a number of countries are struggling to maintain existing capacity in a context in which admission of falling capacity would be politically unacceptable domestically. Hence there are many numbers and many claims and counter-claims with particular uncertainty over the Iranian position.[31] Future capacity is even more uncertain since it depends entirely upon the investment levels that governments are willing and able to make and/or the willingness of governments to involve foreign oil companies. The amount of investment required is also controversial, with various estimates being suggested.[32]

THE SCENARIOS

Three scenarios have been created although no probabilities are attached.[33] The time horizon of the scenarios is roughly up to 2005. Their purpose is to provide a context to discuss the oil policies of the Gulf producers and possible price paths when feedback loops can no longer be ignored.

Business as usual is an attempt to capture what many observers in the industry believe to be the most likely future. This involves moderate growth in both demand and non-OPEC supply, together with a full return of Iraq soon after 2000. In such a world, the call on OPEC rises relatively slowly in a moderately tight market with what excess capacity exists concentrated in Saudi Arabia. Implicit in this scenario is a price in the range of $16 to $18 per barrel.

Shortage postulates strong demand with weak non-OPEC supply, together with no Iraqi return. In this world the call on OPEC would rise strongly although it is assumed that capacity, while tight, would be sufficient to avoid actual physical shortage. Implicit in this scenario is a price in the range of $18 to $25 per barrel although this would depend very much upon what Saudi Arabia wanted with respect to prices, since they would have the ability to seek much higher prices.

Plenty postulates weak-to-moderate demand but high non-OPEC supply and a full return for Iraq before 2000. In such a world the call on OPEC stagnates at present levels and perhaps actually declines if Iraq's production is excluded. Implicit in this scenario are very weak prices in the range of $13 to $16 per barrel.

Several qualifications are required in the scenarios. The first is that no scenario includes a feedback loop from prices. Thus a high-price scenario might be expected to lower demand and raise supply, while a low-price scenario might be expected to raise demand and lower supply. While this derives from a desire to keep the scenarios simple, it is also a realistic view of the world between now and 2005. In general it is not the actual price that drives supply and demand for oil but the price expectations. Price expectations take a long time to change. Despite some price strength in 1996, current expectations are for continued low prices (compared to 1973-86) which are already embodied in the various cases for the supply and demand variables (i.e. around $18 per barrel in 1992 dollars).[34] On the demand side, two points insulate demand from crude prices. First, there is the inevitable time lag since the only way to reduce oil use, apart from a behavioral response, is to change the oil-using appliance, and this takes time. Second, as indicated above, consumer governments are increasingly isolating the final consumer price from the internationally traded price of crude oil. On the supply side, it is the increasing flexibility observed in fiscal systems that insulates development decisions from price levels unless prices were to fall to extremely low levels.

There is a second dimension to the lack of a price feedback loop that is extremely relevant. It is widely accepted that the current low levels of oil revenues compared to 1973-86 are causing extreme economic problems for the region.[35] If revenues remain at the low levels experienced in recent years, these economic problems can only worsen before the year 2000.[36] Such economic problems will inevitably feed into the political problems facing the countries of the region. It remains to be seen how many of the governments will be able to survive such problems. It is perfectly plausible to assume that if oil prices fail to rise, the region could suffer major political upheavals and a radicalization of the political basis of some governments.

There is no price shock scenario in which prices rise dramatically. There are several reasons for this exclusion. Historically, such price spikes occur when a politically induced supply disruption coincides with a situation of tight capacity. Currently, there is a depressingly long list of potential disruptions, including civil war in Russia, Algeria and other countries. Furthermore, as outlined above, the longer the oil price stays depressed, the larger the list of candidates becomes. However, the timing of such events is impossible to predict. Timing is further complicated by the potential availability of large amounts of Iraqi crude at very short notice. All that can be done is to identify points of vulnerability that could be defined as periods when OPEC capacity utilization becomes tight. This occurs only in the Shortage scenario.

Similarly, there is no scenario in which prices collapse to below $13 per barrel. This is because, for reasons already explained, the timing of such a collapse, which would be driven by a fundamental change in market belief, is impossible to predict. However, in this author's view such a collapse is plausible, and as explained earlier, contrary to most views, prices could stay low for a long time.[37] However, while this is not included in the scenarios, the possibility will be considered when the oil policies in the region are discussed.

THE RESULTS

Business as Usual

In such a world, there would appear to be an incentive for other Gulf states to expand their capacities, and there would probably be growing dissatisfaction with Saudi Arabia's revenue gains if prices were perceived to remain weak because of Saudi policy. However, in such a market, quota issues would prove much less problematic as the call on OPEC gradually rises. Indeed, there would be a small amount theoretically available for redistribution.[38] However, some of this would arise from Iran's inability to meet its share of the growing call, and it is inconceivable that Iran would acknowledge this. In short, the scenario presents a "muddling-along" to 2005.

Thereafter uncertainty grows. Iraq is only just beginning to produce in any volume and is gearing up to go higher. Similarly, the relative tightness of the market, despite the price weakness, might encourage the Gulf producers to push more determinedly to expand their capacity, presenting potential over-supply. In particular, Iran may well have been able to secure the foreign company involvement it requires and its capacity might be rising. In the meantime, oil revenues will have shown little improvement from recent years, which suggests growing political problems as the economies continue to fail to perform. There are two key issues after 2005. The first will be what happens to non-OPEC supply. If it falters, then the call on OPEC in general and the Gulf in particular could begin to rise, providing some relief in the form of higher revenues. The second issue is how the market perceives prices. With the degree of tightness suggested before extra Gulf capacity emerges, this could persuade prices above their $16 to $18 band. This is especially true if it were perceived that Saudi Arabia was encouraging a tight market in order to push prices higher.

Plenty

The world presented by the Plenty scenario is likely to generate significant conflict. Revenues would decline from levels that Gulf countries, notably Iran, are already finding difficult to accommodate. Furthermore, the potential for a price collapse grows rapidly as OPEC's capacity utilization returns to the sorts of levels that characterized the mid-1980s. Under this scenario, Iranian and Saudi production would fall, giving grave discomfort since Iraq could be producing over 5 million b/d. In such a world, much of the drive for additional capacity would lose impetus, as I will discuss. Furthermore, quota renegotiations would be required to maintain the range within which prices could be made. Their absence would threaten a price collapse.

After 2005, such a world would be unsustainable. Weak prices coupled with falling volumes would produce revenue levels that Iran certainly could not manage and that Saudi Arabia probably could not manage without slashing defense expenditure.

Shortage

The high-price world represented by Shortage is very different. The cake gets progressively larger with significant amounts of unused capacity to be distributed among the Gulf members. How much depends upon the success of non-Gulf OPEC members in attracting upstream foreign investment. Outside of Saudi Arabia and Kuwait, there is little or no under-utilization of capacity to generate grievances. Production and revenues would grow strongly. They would be far from sufficient to easily solve the financial and economic problems facing the countries, but they would allow the status quo to survive, and economic problems might be seen as less the responsibility of neighbors. There would be very strong incentives for the Gulf countries to push ahead with capacity expansion as rapidly as possible.

In such a world, the Saudi attitude to prices would become a central issue. The Saudis would be in a position, by use of surge capacity and new capacity investment, to maintain prices below $20 a barrel. If this were to happen, it could sour relations with all of the other Gulf states. In such a world of perceived growing shortage, U.S. interests in protecting the status quo in Saudi Arabia would be paramount, and the United States thus could be expected to protect against potential threats. Also the rising revenue might be able to buy off growing domestic dissension.

Beyond 2005, something would have to crack, and if capacity expansion in the Gulf were delayed, the crack would occur sooner rather than later. One probable consequence would be the return of Iraq. Certainly shortages would start to push price higher. However, this is unlikely to be a gradual process. Much more likely would be that perceived shortages causing prices to rise would create self-feeding behavior with prices rising very rapidly indeed. The result would almost certainly be a price shock which, given the level of U.S. import dependence, would have extremely serious consequences for the international economy.

The results of the three scenarios present a range of plausible outcomes. Each scenario can be used as a context to discuss the implications of the current oil policies of the Gulf countries. This first requires a discussion of those policies.

The Current Oil Policies of the Gulf Countries and Their Implications in the Context of the Scenario Results

Although there are many significant differences among the petroleum policies being pursued by the Gulf countries, a country-by-country approach would involve excessive repetition. Therefore a topical approach is adopted with major differences highlighted.[39]

Capacity

All the countries in the region are committed to maintaining their current sustainable capacity or, in the case of Iraq, the restoration of previous capacity. Other than Iraq, the country that faces the greatest problem in this respect is Iran. In the period 1977-78, a major plan was drawn up for secondary recovery for the onshore fields, the majority of which were beginning to suffer from serious decline problems. The events of the revolution and the subsequent war with Iraq caused this program to be postponed. Recently it has been revived. However, a serious constraint is a shortage of gas for reinjection. The plan envisaged gas from the development of the North Pars field, but the development of that field has now been delayed. The result is that there is growing skepticism about Iran's sustainable capacity. The official line is that sustainable capacity is 4.1 million b/d with surge capacity at 4.5 million b/d. In May 1995, in a demonstration for journalists, the government claimed that a one-week test suggested capacity was more than 4 million b/d, but skepticism was expressed by some observers.[40] The considerable fluctuations in Iranian export volumes tend to add weight to such skepticism.

With the exception of Saudi Arabia, all of the countries also have a clear commitment to increasing capacity.[41] In Iran, while there are no plans to expand onshore capacity, the intention was to increase offshore from 465,000 b/d in the May test to 600,000 b/d by March 1996 and to increase to 1 million b/d by 2000. By the end of 1996 progress on these plans was uncertain, but continuing production fluctuations suggested they were far from complete. In the current five-year plan (1995-2000) $6 billion has been allocated, the majority for 12 upstream projects. In the UAE there are plans to expand the capacity of Upper Zakum from 470,000 b/d to 550,000 b/d by early 1997. Kuwait currently has plans to increase from 2.3 million b/d to 3 million b/d in "the next decade." More recently, the oil minister claimed a target of 3.5 million b/d by 2005. The logic behind this is interesting and was expressed by Nader Sultan, deputy chairman and managing director of Kuwait Petroleum Company (KPC). His argument was that since the price of oil will not rise, "why leave it in the ground? . . . if we cannot anticipate an increase in revenue from crude prices then we have to consider the option of increasing volume."[42] Qatar also announced plans to reverse its capacity decline by increasing capacity from

420,000 to 500,000 b/d by the year 2000 with increased recovery factors through new technology's playing a key role. Oman too appeared to be seeking further expansion with exploration in new areas on the Eastern Coast.

Iraq of course is in a special situation. The official line from the oil minister is that after the full lifting of sanctions producing capacity would be 2 million b/d, which could be increased by 500,000 b/d "within a few weeks," reaching 3.2 million b/d within 14 months. As the humanitarian oil begins to flow, such targets become increasingly plausible. Thereafter, the plan is to increase capacity to 6 million b/d within five to eight years, based upon the development of 4.65 million b/d in 33 discovered and appraised oil fields of which 2.1 million b/d would come from the four giant fields—Halfaya, Nahr Umr, Majnoon and West Qurna.

In all cases there are three issues—the requirement for exploration, the sources of finance and the role of foreign companies. With the exception of Iraq, all other countries require discoveries before significant capacity expansion can be considered. This significantly increases the risk of the exercise. For this reason, coupled with existing financial constraints, the countries are seeking to get foreign company involvement. The UAE, unlike other countries in the Gulf, retained foreign company involvement following "participation." For the last three years Qatar has had an open-door policy allowing foreign company involvement on a production-sharing basis although the tendency to date has been to offer only small and difficult structures albeit on what are claimed to be attractive terms. Oman is expected to also attract renewed foreign interest when Petroleum Development Oman (PDO) relinquishes significant areas of acreage in the near future.

Kuwait is faced with a dilemma. The KPC would like to see foreign company involvement in developing capacity and indeed already signed management assistance contracts with British Petroleum (BP) and Chevron. KPC's logic is a concern to acquire the latest technology but arguably also to get around management constraints caused by the expulsion of so many "expatriates." There is also support within the government for the idea of locking foreign companies, especially U.S. companies, into the northern fields for obvious strategic reasons. However, it is sensitive in a Kuwait with an active and vociferous National Assembly. A 1995 proposal recommending production-sharing deals in the northern border areas failed to win the backing of the Supreme Petroleum Council. The council members argued that technical superiority arguments were not convincing and that the assembly members should present a stronger case. Opponents have argued that only service contract arrangements need be offered to attract foreign company interest.[43]

The Iranian government has invested much time and effort since 1991 to create a suitable climate to secure foreign company involvement not least in Iran itself. However, a major problem was the Iranian negotiators' failure to fully understand the new oil market situation with acreage on offer all over the world on extremely attractive terms. The result was that the relatively unattractive terms failed to generate agreements despite much negotiation and some letters of intent. This changed as Iran finally began to offer more attractive terms, beginning with the Conoco deal to develop the offshore Sirri A and B fields to produce 120,000 b/d. The deal was stopped by the U.S. embargo and picked up by Total. Future prospects for foreign company involvement in Iran will very much depend upon the progress and responses to the recent secondary boycott legislation in the United States.

Iraq has also made it clear that foreign company involvement is central to its post-sanctions capacity plans. Prior to the invasion of Kuwait, acreage was offered to foreign companies but on a contracting-only basis. As a result there was no company interest. However, now it is quite clear that Iraq is willing to offer production-sharing terms to develop the fields. At a meeting in Baghdad in 1995, the government announced that 33 discovered and appraised fields were available, with a potential capacity of 4.65 million b/d. Considerable interest has been shown by a number of companies with various rumors of deals having been struck.

The situation in Saudi Arabia is somewhat different. Following the dramatic expansion in capacity following the Iraqi invasion of Kuwait, it was generally believed that there were no plans to develop capacity beyond 10 million b/d since this would provide a significant cushion for some time to come. Given Saudi Arabia's growing financial constraints, it made little sense to invest scarce resources in capacity that would not be used for some time to come. However, in May 1995, Saudi Aramco announced that it would go ahead with the development of the massive Shaibah field, which has gone through a series of proposals and postponements since 1989. Once fully developed, Shaibah would add some 500,000 b/d to capacity. There are various explanations for this apparent *volte face*. One is that Shaibah is light low-sulphur crude that would serve to lighten and sweeten the Saudi barrel and make Saudi export blends look more attractive. However, given this is at the expense of shutting in perfectly good capacity, the argument rings hollow. A more plausible explanation is that Shaibah was "gifted" by a border agreement with Sheik Zaid of Abu Dhabi. While he lives the agreement will be honored but on his death it will certainly be challenged by his successor. On the basis that possession is nine-tenths of the law, the capacity is being hastily developed to make return extremely difficult.

Quite clearly from the above analysis, the prospects for future capacity are extremely uncertain although all appear to be betting upon a rising call for Gulf oil. However, only in the case of Shortage would this strategy provide a payoff before 2005. In Business-As-Usual and Plenty, if new capacity did emerge it would create problems by developing linkages that could lead to conflict. One possibility is that the capacity is simply shut in. However, insofar as the new capacity involves foreign companies, it is likely that any shut-in would have to apply to the capacity owned by the national oil company. Given the sort of terms being offered to foreign companies, this would make the revenue losses to government even greater.

If Saudi Arabia decided to produce over its current ceiling of 8 million b/d to take advantage of any small increase in the call for Gulf oil, if this caused others to shut-in to accommodate newly developed capacity, this could generate conflict. Another possibility is that if some countries fail to develop (or even maintain) capacity, their inability to make quota might be seized upon by those with greater success in developing capacity, thereby reviving the whole issue of quota division within the region. The most obvious example would be the perception by Iran that its market share was being threatened in the longer term by countries on the other side of the Gulf.

Production and Crude Marketing

In terms of OPEC and quota issues the situation is fairly clear. All are interested in securing higher quotas whether or not they are in any shape to use them. At the same time, none is prepared to reveal its view on how quotas should be adjusted to allow for full Iraqi reentry. This in part explains much of the uncertainty and misinformation about existing capacity levels.

Without exception, all Gulf producers are intent upon locking in market share. Initially this was in anticipation of Iraq's full return. More recently, as that return seems less immediate, fear of losing market share to non-OPEC supplies has become the driver. For Saudi Arabia, Kuwait and, to a lesser extent the UAE, this has been partly behind the drive to develop a downstream capability. Currently, where they have refinery capacity, it is treated as part of an operationally vertically integrated system.[44] Iran and Iraq have no such option. For Iran, the only currently viable option is to try to move back to longer-term contracts than the current three-month norm.

An alternative way to lock in market share is to develop a portfolio of term contracts with refiners. This is done by reducing sales to traders and replacing them with direct sales to refiners. Iraq has announced that it will be seeking such deals in the future. Similarly Kuwait has signed refinery deals with Singapore and South Africa to process Kuwaiti crude. This trend has led to a move towards the markets of Asia, where prices are higher and term contracts are easier to negotiate than in the highly competitive Atlantic basin markets.

Another growing driving force is a desire to increase the ability to respond flexibly to changed market circumstances. This involves the acquisition of access to storage, either onshore or floating. Saudi Arabia has been actively engaged in leasing or buying storage in the main markets, and Iran has been negotiating with the South African Strategic Field Fund over the storage of 15 million barrels of crude.

The significance of these moves in terms of the scenario results relate mainly to Business-As-Usual and Plenty. In these scenarios, the pressure to lock in markets will remain high, and more processing deals and long-term contracts can be expected. However, tying up crude outlets in this way will make it much more difficult to accommodate a full Iraqi reentry—a condition of both scenarios. If too much volume is already spoken for, the only method of entry will be significant price shading, which could in turn prompt retaliation. The more inflexible the market at the time of full Iraqi reentry, the greater the disruption.

Prices

All of the countries of the Gulf are, to lesser or greater degree, revenue-constrained. As a result, all would prefer to see prices higher than those ruling since 1991. There are two issues relevant for policy: How much higher do they want prices to be? What policies should and could be pursued to gain higher prices?

The division over price targets is epitomized by the differences between Saudi Arabia and Iran. Since the liberation of Kuwait, it has generally been accepted that Saudi Arabia has pursued a "low" price strategy, generally thought of as being an OPEC basket price of $18. However, as budgetary pressures have grown, prices above this level have begun to appear desirable. The formation of Saudi oil policy is usually a ponderous affair. The more reasons that can be found for any specific policy path, the more entrenched that policy. Several factors dominated the moderate price strategy. After the liberation of Kuwait, the Saudis were determined to ensure that the allies did not go "wobbly" over sanctions against Iraq. While prices remained low, there was little or no pressure to allow Iraqi oil back into the market. There was also the drive for market share. In the short term this would assist revenues and position Saudi Arabia for the inevitable negotiation when Iraq might return.

While these factors were influential, of greater importance was the longer term. The Saudi establishment still carried the scars of the two oil shocks of the 1970s. To be sure, they had generated much revenue, but the price of reduced oil demand was perceived to have been too high. Higher prices pushed oil out of the energy scene. The fear was that Saudi Arabia's huge oil reserves would simply lose any commercial value as oil continued to be backed out of the energy market. The "market share–low price" philosophy has been present since the mid-1980s (and for some technocrats much earlier). Thus "low" prices would encourage a return to oil (via increased demand and lower supply from high-cost areas) and guarantee a viable future for the Saudi reserves.[45] Furthermore, the key was not so much low prices as expectations of low prices. The Saudis correctly understood that it was price expectations that drove the key decisions in the oil market, affecting the energy-using appliance stock or supply projects.

There is another explanation for the Saudi strategy that must be addressed for the sake of completeness despite the author's own skepticism over its validity. This is the view that Saudi Arabia pursues "low" prices following pressure from the United States. Indeed, this is now part of a conspiracy-theory explanation of the collapse of the Soviet Union and the apparent end of the Cold War. The key weakness with this view is the assumption of a unified cohesive policy prevalent in Washington that wants "low" prices. No such policy exists. It is worth remembering that it was undoubtedly U.S. intervention in 1986 that persuaded the Saudis to again reverse their oil policy because prices were perceived to be too low.

Iran on the other hand has consistently been pushing for much higher prices since the early 1970s. It perceives the "low" prices of recent years to be the direct result of Saudi Arabia's efforts to undermine the Islamic Republic. However, alone it can do nothing to influence prices, short of seeking to influence those whom it believes can influence prices.

In reality, gaining higher prices is difficult because once the range has been made, the price is set by the beliefs in a competitive market. To be sure, hawkish noises could change belief and push prices up, but such a respite on its own would be temporary. One way to ensure sustained higher prices would be to keep the market very tight by constraining supply while clearly indicating a desire for higher prices. Thus the range would be made in a context in which players believe in higher prices. The main problem with such an approach is that it is not conducive to fine-tuning prices. There is no guarantee that prices would not over-shoot whatever the target price levels were. The experience of significant price fluctuations in 1996 supports this view.

The only other way to achieve a given price target would be to act as ex–post residual supplier and agree to supply at a fixed price. This gets around the problem of over-shooting. However, this approach also has problems. If more than one country was involved then the inevitable problem would be that of cheating. This would effectively leave either ex–post residual suppliers who did not cheat or no such suppliers if all cheated. The alternative is that one country alone takes on the role. The consequence, of course, would be that all other suppliers produced to capacity, leaving the sole pricemaker as swing producer. The danger of such an approach is that it would simply lead to a rapid erosion of market share. Currently however, there is no sign that any of the Gulf countries would be willing to take on such a role.

An important question involves the Gulf countries' own perceptions of the future path of oil prices and, by implication, their revenues. It would appear in general to be their view that despite current weaknesses, prices will begin to strengthen and, at the same, time volume gains will tend to push up revenue. Furthermore, it is anticipated that the price-strengthening will occur as the result of market forces rather than the result of any direct action. They are in effect expecting the future to resemble the Shortage scenario.

Several factors provide confirmation that this is indeed a widely held view on both sides of the Gulf. First, there are the attempts to expand capacity. Although, as explained above, some of the plans are posturing, many are genuine and involve the investment of real resources. Second, there is the refusal to tackle the basic fiscal problems that face all of the countries. While this reflects in part political constraints on reducing expenditure, it also reflects a genuine belief by many in the region that recovering revenues will solve the underlying fiscal imbalances. It is simply a question of hanging on until rising revenues gallop to the rescue.

All three scenarios would enable Saudi Arabia to continue a "low" price path. In Business-As-Usual and Plenty this would happen with little effort, provided no significant supply disruption occurred. Furthermore, this could be done without obviously raising opposition from other countries in the Gulf. Prices continuing below $18 could be seen as simply the result of market forces in a comfortably supplied (or over-supplied) market. Only in Shortage would a proactive response be required from Saudi Arabia to keep prices "low." This would require production of current excess capacity whenever prices appeared to be strengthening. Even then the strategy might not work because of the danger of over-shooting mentioned earlier. However, what is clear is that absent a politically induced supply disruption of some magnitude, prices much above $18 for any length of time can only occur if Saudi Arabia wishes. This creates a linkage of great potency for the region.

Downstream[46]

With the exception of Saudi Arabia and Kuwait, all the countries of the region face shortages of domestic refinery capacity that reflect either rapidly growing domestic demand or, more commonly, a severe imbalance in product demand towards the lighter end of the barrel. Therefore all are either seeking to expand existing capacity or to develop upgrading capacity. For example, the Abu Dhabi National Oil Company (ADNOC) has expanded the Ruwais refinery by 135,000 b/d and has added upgrading plants to Umm Al Nar. Similarly, in Iran a new 232,00 b/d refinery is due onstream at Bandar Abbas. Iraq has also announced plans to upgrade its existing capacity to accommodate a heavier crude slate.[47] However, these plans face the financial constraints that are general in the region; plans are constantly being postponed or deadlines revised.

Saudi Arabia and Kuwait remain net exporters of products although Saudi Arabia recently has also been facing shortages of gasoline. Kuwait is in the process of developing additional upgrading capacity and has finally decided to restore the Shuaiba capacity to its prewar level of 200,000 b/d. One logical consequence of these trends is a growing trade in oil products in the region although, given the flexibility in the oil product trade, this does not imply the development of dependency linkages.

There is still interest in Saudi Arabia, Kuwait, Abu Dhabi and Oman in developing downstream capacity abroad. Saudi Arabia continues its negotiations although with little apparent progress. Kuwait has also announced, in a policy reversal, that it is now willing to consider joint venture downstream projects abroad rather than single ownership. Both Abu Dhabi and Oman are considering joint refinery projects in the Asian subcontinent.

Downstream moves have significant implications for pricing policies. A financially vertically integrated oil company is less concerned about crude oil prices than a company that simply sells crude. Falling crude prices can be hedged against rising refinery margins and vice versa. Thus the fact that Iran and Iraq are not moving downstream while the others are flags a potential future division over pricing policy. It has been argued[48] that Kuwait's policy of cheating to keep crude prices low in 1989-90 was prompted by the fact that this kept both Iran and Iraq weak at minimal cost to Kuwait with its downstream hedge.

A further downstream development of significance in all the countries is growing policy measures to restrain domestic product consumption. Driven by the oil boom of the 1970s and highly subsidized prices, domestic consumption has been growing in spectacular fashion.[49] This is seen as an increasing threat to oil-export capacity. For example, currently in Iran some 1.2-1.3 million b/d of domestic production is taken for domestic consumption, a figure arrived at after an average annual growth rate in domestic oil consumption of 7 percent. Among the key policy measures have been an attempt to reduce price subsidies. However, throughout the region, prices are extremely low in international terms, and sharp increases face serious political constraints. In Iran in 1994, a doubling of the price of gasoline, gasoil and heavy fuel oil led to considerable unrest.

Arguably, such policies are only important in the Shortage scenario in two ways. First because domestic consumption at prices below border prices would represent a real and immediate opportunity cost to government revenue. In Business-As-Usual and Plenty, the existence of surplus would preclude export. Second, because investment in downstream domestic refining capacity could represent a diversion of funds from investment in much needed (and saleable) upstream capacity.

Gas

There are two types of countries in the region: those such as Saudi Arabia, Kuwait and the Northern Emirates of the UAE, which face growing difficulties with respect to gas supplies, and those such as Iran, Qatar, Sharjah and Oman, which have significant reserves of gas that they are seeking to exploit. The gas-rich countries are in the process of developing their capacity. All are facing constraints. The first concerns the mode of development. All three have considered various export options. Qatar has clearly decided on a Liquified Natural Gas (LNG) route although talk of pipelines recurs. Iran appears to be giving more attention to pipeline options with projects being considered to export to Turkey, Pakistan and India.[50] Oman is to go ahead with an LNG project to supply India, having dropped a pipeline option. Common to all three countries is the problem of raising the necessary finance. All are trying to secure foreign company involvement. For the LNG projects this is normal given the size of the projects and their technical requirements. Iran is seeking foreign company assistance to actually develop the gas fields and has been in discussions with a number of foreign companies for some time.

The deficit countries are seeking to secure alternative supplies although the only trade that emerged was the supply of Iraqi gas to Kuwait prior to the invasion.

In terms of the impact on linkages, levers and the oil market the following observations could be made. The impact on the oil market is only relevant in two situations. First in the case of Iran, access to gas for reinjection will be a crucial factor in determining the status of the onshore capacity. Failure to develop could seriously threaten sustainable capacity. Second, where gas is used as domestic energy, this can release oil for export. The most obvious case is heavy fuel oil from power generation and water desalination.

Arguably the logical first use of the gas is in regional trade. LNG projects face horrendous problems of technology, financing and contract obsolescence while pipelines outside the region face the familiar problems of transit pipelines. Insofar as gas trade develops between the countries this creates linkages associated with dependency on imported energy sources and dependence on export revenues.

Conclusions

No clear view has been given on the likelihood of each scenario. In this author's view, the balance of probability suggests that the oil market will remain relatively weak for the next few years with prices staying below $18 per barrel—a world of Businesss As Usual or Plenty. This is despite the unexpected strength of prices in 1996. However, the longer this continues, the greater the possibility that growing competition in crude markets will push down price as economic rent is squeezed out. This has been the experience of most other commodity markets and it is difficult to see why oil should be different. Such "low" prices (or even lower prices) coupled with slow increases in volume means the countries of the Gulf face poor-to-limited prospects for increased revenue over the next few years. This is likely to generate conflict. Such constrained revenue will threaten domestic economies, and this may encourage governments to distract domestic critics by aggression elsewhere. If the market weakness is perceived to arise because of the oil policy of certain states, this tendency will be reinforced.

In general, with the exception of those countries developing a downstream hedge, current oil policies do not appear to be addressing these issues, and even the downstream hedge is of only limited help. Realistically, the only effective solution lies in general macroeconomic policy to reduce government expenditure and to promote economic development away from the export of crude oil. The latter has been a longstanding ambition of the oil exporters of the Gulf since the 1960s. Achievement of that objective is no nearer today than it was in the 1960s.

Notes

1. Mabro, 1986.

2. Blair, 1976; Steven 1984a.

3. Stevens, 1990; Oxford Institute for Energy Studies, 1990.

4. Hartshorn, 1993; Mabro, 1992, 1992; Roeber, 1993.

5. Stevens, 1995, 1996.

6. Stevens 1995.

7. Whenever a figure is given for an oil "price" in this chapter, unless otherwise stated, it refers to the OPEC basket price.

8. Both examples, if believed, provide excellent examples of the simultaneity problem identified in the introduction to this chapter. In both cases, "oil" was only the policy instrument to affect politics. The objective behind the oil policy was political rather than oil-based. Thus the oil objective of low prices was triggered by a political desire to weaken Iraq.

9. Reuters, December 19, 1993 and January 7, 1994.

10. Stevens, 1975.

11. Kurbusi, 1984; Stevens, 1986.

12. Schofield, 1993.

13. Not all such disputes are driven by oil. Witness the recent dispute between Saudi Arabia and Qatar. Also the Saudi-Yemeni dispute has to do with more than oil.

14. Increasingly, producers are also supplying other producers with products. Constraints on the development of refinery capacity, especially financial, coupled with a relatively balanced demand patter for products, is leading to a significant growth in product trade in the region.

15. Stevens, 1984b; Stevens, forthcoming.

16. Stevens, 1981.

17. Stevens, forthcoming.

18. All data unless otherwise stated is from the British Petroleum Statistical Review of World Energy.

19. OPEC, 1994.

20. Huntington, 1994; Jaffe and Stavins, 1994; Metcalf, 1994.

21. Mitchell, 1994.

22. Kemp and Macdonald, 1995.

23. IEA, 1995.

24. Odell, 1991.

25. O'Dell, 1994.

26. Estimated by the IEA for 1996 at 2.6 million b/d.

27. Dienes et al., 1994; Lynch, 1995; Watkins, 1994.

28. Adelman, 1993.

29. In December 1996, the first contract for the export of Iraqi crude oil under UN Resolution 986 for humanitarian aid was approved. Under the terms of 986, Iraq can export $2 billion worth of crude over six months. At $18 per barrel, this amounts to some 700,000 b/d. The prospects for the continued operation of 986 or allowable expansion attracts much the same speculation and uncertainty as the full return.

30. This will be discussed in greater detail later.

31. CGES, 1993; Varzi, 1992.

32. Adelman and Shihi, 1989; Browne, 1991; CGES, 1993; Seymour, 1993; Stauffer, 1993.

33. These scenarios are qualitative rather than numerical. For example, growth rates will be described as weak, moderate or strong rather than as actual percentages.

34. Historically, all of the scenarios provide relatively low prices in real terms. In 1992 dollars, the scenarios give a price range of $14 to $26 per barrel. Between 1973 and 1985 the average price in comparable terms was $36.50 per barrel. Between 1960 and 1973, a period that many argued suffered excessively low prices, the comparable average was $7.88.

35. Khadduri, 1994.

36. The price strength of 1996 has provided some windfall revenue relief but it is extremely debatable whether this price strength can be maintained.

37. Stevens, 1996.

38. In practice this is unlikely to trigger a negotiation since a degree of cheating among members would tend to absorb the limited unused quotas.

39. Unless otherwise stated, the factual information contained in this section is drawn from various figures compiled from *Middle East Economic Survey*. The opinions and the analysis are the author's.

40. *PIW* 34, no. 22. It was claimed by the government that Parsi and Karanj fields could produce but were awaiting the completion of the gas injection program.

41. Oman has also announced that it intends only to maintain its 800,000 b/d capacity. However, to achieve this will require net additions to reserves of 200 million barrels per year.

42. *Middle East Economic Survey* (MEES) 38, no. 32.

43. A view that is almost certainly mistaken as the Iraqi experience before 1990 shows (as I will discuss).

44. Operational vertical integration occurs when affiliate crude moves through affiliate refineries and affiliate products move through affiliate outlets. Such a system requires financial vertical integration, in which the affiliates have a common holding company that exercises capital budgeting. Financially vertically integrated operations need not be operational integrated since the affiliates can obtain or dispose by means of markets.

45. This explains the vehement attacks by Saudi Arabia on proposals for carbon taxes. Such proposals completely undermine the Saudi long-term strategy.

46. Both the downstream and gas dimensions of oil policy are important. However, to allow for constraints of space, they will be dealt with briefly and only insofar as they represent a regional dimension.

47. It has also announced its willingness to enter joint venture deals to refine Iraqi crude abroad.

48. Stevens, 1990.

49. Paga and Birol, 1995.

50. The Pakistan-India project is currently on hold because the Pakistani navy has refused to allow access for seabed surveys, and the Pakistani government will not insist. Iran's most urgent objective is to develop gas for domestic use. Certainly oil-field reinjection is an urgent need, and the government has announced an official target to increase domestic gas consumption to 44 percent of primary energy use (currently 33 percent)—some 50 billion cubic meters.

Other Sources

Adelman, M. A. and M. Shahi. "Oil Development-Operating Cost Estimates 1955-85." *Energy Economics* 11, no. 1 (January 1989).

Adelman, M.A. *The Economics of Petroleum Supply: Papers by M.A. Adelman 1962-1993* (Cambridge: MIT Press, 1993).

Blair, J. *The Control of Oil.* (London: Macmillan, 1976).

British Petroleum. *British Petroleum Statistical Review of World Energy* (London: British Petroleum, 1995).

Browne, J. *Upstream Oil in the 1990s: The Prospects for a New World Order,* BP Speech Reprint (London: British Petroleum, 1991).

Centre for Global Energy Studies. "Expanding Capacity: A Dilemma for OPEC." (March-April 1993) *Global Oil Report.*

Dienes, L., I. Dobozi and M. Radetzki. *Energy and Economic Reform in the FSU.* (New York: St. Martin's Press, 1994).

Hartshorn, J.E. *Oil Trade: Politics and Prospects.* (Cambridge: Cambridge University Press, 1993).

Huntington, H.G. "Been Top Down So Long It Looks Like Bottom Up to Me." *Energy Policy* 22, no. 10 (October 1994).

International Energy Agency. *World Energy Outlook.* (Paris: OECD, 1995).

Jaffe, A. B. and R. N. Stavins, "The Energy Efficiency Gap." *Energy Policy* 22, no. 10 (October 1994).

Kemp, A. and B. MacDonald. "Cost Savings and Activity Levels in the UKCS." *Energy Policy* 23, no. 1 (January 1995).

Khadduri, W. "Impacts of Low Oil Prices." *Oxford Energy Forum* 17 (May 1994).

Kubursi, A.A. *Oil, Industrialization and Development in the Arab Gulf States* (London: Croom Helm, 1984).

Lynch, M.C. *Penetrating the Enigma: Predicting Energy Supply and Demand in the FSU,* Occasional Papers, no. 70. (Stockholm: SNS Energy, January 1995).

Mabro, R. (Ed.) *OPEC and the World Oil Market: The Genesis of the 1986 Price Crisis* (Oxford: Oxford University Press, 1986).

Mabro, R. *OPEC and the Price of Oil* (Oxford: Oxford Institute for Energy Studies, 1992).

Metcalf, G.E. "Economics and Rational Conservation Policy." *Energy Policy* 22, no. 10 (October 1994).

Mitchell, J. "A Long Look at Low Energy Prices." *Oxford Energy Forum,* no. 17 (May 1994).

Odell, P. "Spotlight on Middle East Dims." *Oxford Energy Forum,* no. 7 (1991).

O'Dell, S. "Prospects for Non-OPEC Supply." Paper presented to 13th CERI International Oil and Gas Markets Conference. Calgary, Alberta, 1994. Mimeograph.

OPEC *Facts and Figures* (Vienna: OPEC, 1994).

Oxford Institute for Energy Studies. *The First Oil War* (Oxford: Oxford Institute for Energy Studies, 1990).

Paga, E. and F. Birol. "Domestic Pricing of Petroleum Products in OPEC Member Countries—An Overview." *OPEC Review* XIX, no. 1 (March 1995).

Roeber, J. *The Evolution of Oil Markets: Trading Instruments and Their Role in Oil Price Formation* (London: Royal Institute, 1993).

Schofield, R. (Ed.) *Territorial Foundations of the Gulf States* (London: UCL Press, 1994).

Seymour, I. "Political Constraints on Oil Producers' Policy Options." *Middle East Economic Survey* 36, no. 31 (May 3, 1993).

Stauffer, T. "Crude Oil Production Costs in the Middle East." *Middle East Economic Survey* 36, no. 17 (January 25, 1993).

114

Paul J. Stevens

Stevens, P. *Joint Ventures in Middle East Oil, 1957-1975.* (Beirut: Middle East Economic Consultants, 1975).

————."Saudi Arabian Oil Policy: Its Origins, Implementation and Implications," in T. Niblock, ed., *State, Society and Economy in Saudi Arabia.* (London: Croom Helm, 1981) pp. 214-34.

————."A Survey of Structural Change in the International Oil Industry 1945-1984," in D. Hawdon, ed., *The Changing Structure of the World Oil Industry* (London: Croom Helm, 1984).

————."The Economics of Hydrocarbon Pipelines in the 21st Century." *Pipes and Pipelines International* 29, no. 5 (September-October 1984).

————."Arab Downstream Petroleum Exports—Problems and Prospects." In *Middle East Exports: Problems and Prospects.* Occasional Papers Series, no. 29. (Centre for Middle Eastern and Islamic Studies, University of Durham, Durham, 1986).

————."Oil and OPEC," in C. Davies, ed., *After the War: Iraq, Iran and the Arab Gulf* (Chichester: Carden Publications, 1990).

————."The Determination of Oil Prices 1945-95: A Diagrammatic Interpretation." *Energy Policy* 23, no. 10 (October 1995).

————."Oil Prices: The Start of an Era?" *Energy Policy* 24, no. 5 (May 1996).

————."A History of Transit Pipelines in the Middle East: Lessons for the Future," in G.H. Blake, M.A. Pratt, C.H. Schofield (Eds.) *Boundaries and Energy: Problems and Prospects.* (The Hague: Kluwer Law International, forthcoming).

Varzi, M. *OPEC's Production Capacity in the 1990s* (London: Kleinwort Benson, 1992).

Watkins, C. "Unravelling a Riddle: The Outlook for Russian Oil." *The Energy Journal* (Special Issue 1994).

World Energy Council. *Energy for Tomorrow's World—The Realities, The Real Options and The Agenda for Achievement.* (New York: St. Martin's Press, 1993).

CHAPTER 5

THE EMERGING PRIVATE SECTOR: NEW DEMANDS ON AN OLD SYSTEM

Karim Pakravan

PRIVATE SECTOR GROWTH AND ECONOMIC DEVELOPMENT

The rise of the private sector in developing countries could prove to be one of the most important economic and political trends of the 1990s. The phenomenon of privatization (defined in the broadest sense as the takeover of economic sectors and activity by independent private sector agents) is gradually putting an end to almost 50 years of state-dominated economic development ideologies. The search for alternatives to state-led and state-fed growth has its roots in a combination of factors: strapped public finances, globalization, financial market deregulation and the failure of the statist development models.

The privatization boom has been particularly marked in some countries of Latin America and Asia. However, the Middle East has not been immune to this trend. The coming of age of private economic agents in these economies is just beginning, and many of the trends are only emerging. Nevertheless, the process of privatization of these economies is irreversible and can only accelerate.

Based on the global experience, conditions for the emergence of a strong private sector in a developing country are: strong political and legal institutions, macroeconomic and financial markets' stability, a tradition of entrepreneurship, a free market environment, a stable and efficient regulatory framework and developing capital markets.

The process of privatization of an economy also has major social and political ramifications. It can be accompanied by high social costs as the economy moves toward greater efficiency. Moreover, the rise in the private sector represents a shift of political and economic power from the ruling elites, the bureaucracy and the often-large private interests tied to the state toward the new entrepreneurial classes and financial markets. Privatization, almost always accompanied by deregulation, also weakens the ability of the government to control the economy and submits its economic decisionmaking to much stronger market discipline.

Privatization also has a broad political dimension. As the economic power and independence of private interests increase, so do their demands for a greater political voice. In this context, the paternalistic and tribal political systems prevalent in the oil-rich Arab countries of the Persian Gulf or the Islamic theocracy ruling Iran have become increasingly inadequate to fulfill the demands for greater political participation. Moreover, the diminished capacity of the oil producers to maintain the high living standards of their populations puts increased pressure on the political and administrative system to become more open and accountable. We see the impact of these powerful forces of change in varying degrees throughout the Persian Gulf.

In this paper, I will contrast two countries, Iran and Saudi Arabia. While these two countries are at the opposite ends of the political spectrum, they have considerable economic and political weight in the Persian Gulf region. In each case the state, by virtue of its large oil revenues and its historic role in economic development, plays a major economic role. Yet, both can build on a long tradition of vigorous private sectors.

PRIVATE SECTOR DEVELOPMENT IN IRAN AND SAUDI ARABIA

Both Iran and Saudi Arabia can be characterized as mixed economies, in which strong and vibrant private sectors have played an important part in national development. However, in both countries, oil has made the private sector dependent upon the state. In both countries, the control of the economy translated into political power—in Iran for the Pahlavi dynasty and later the clerical leaders of the Islamic regime, and in Saudi Arabia for the royal family of the Al-Saud.

Iran: Revolution, War and the Withering of the Private Sector

From the Pahlavis to the Islamic Revolution. Prior to the Islamic revolution, the Iranian private sector coexisted with a large state sector (the latter mostly concentrated in heavy industry and mining, but with an important presence in commercial and financial services) and operated in a highly regulated environment. Moreover, the economic development model of the Pahlavi era, spelled out in the various economic plans, was clearly dirigiste and interventionist and envisaged a dominant role for the state.

Thus, the Islamic regime that overthrew the Pahlavis inherited a substantial public sector, which it expanded by massive expropriations of private and foreign interests. There was an ideological element to these expropriations, as they reflected the left-wing rhetoric of the revolutionary leaders, but most of the confiscations were politically motivated. Furthermore, the expropriations almost exclusively hit the modern conglomerates; the *bazaar,* which had played a prominent role in the overthrow of the shah, once again came to the forefront. These factors led to the development of a two-tier public ownership system: the *bonyads* or revolutionary foundations, and the state sector.

The Bonyads: A State within the State. The *bonyads* evolved from the confiscation of the assets of the Pahlavi dynasty and that of the political and business elite of the imperial regime. The first foundations to be established were the Foundation for the Oppressed (*Bonyad-e-Mostazafan*) and the Alavi Foundation. Later on, the two entities were merged under the aegis of the former institution. The *bonyad* system was greatly expanded during the Iran-Iraq War. From a hodge-podge of confiscated assets that included cash, jewelry, real estate, industrial and commercial interests and land, these institutions have evolved into powerful political and economic players. Simply put, the *bonyads* represent the economic pillar of the more radical factions of the revolutionary elite.

The foundations are controlled by the senior clerics and have so far beaten back any attempts by the government to bring them under its control. There is very little information about the *bonyads.* Secretive and shadowy, these institutions do not publicize their financial and operational information, except in a fragmentary form. They probably account for 25 to 30 percent of Iran's GDP and are actively involved in every major sector of the economy.

The *Bonyad-e-Mostazafan,* the biggest foundation, controls 1,200 companies with assets estimated at anything between $4 and $12 billion in a wide range of activities: agriculture, agribusiness, tourism, textiles, heavy industry, construction and transportation. This *bonyad* remains the key partner in most foreign joint ventures and large projects in Iran. It has also been criticized for investing in the luxury residential construction business and for allegations of widespread corruption. However, this *bonyad* is legally responsible only to Khamenei, the Supreme Leader, and has been shielded from any interference with its empire.

These quasi-governmental institutions have set the stage for a future struggle with technocrats on one hand and the *bazaaris* on the other. The technocrats, closely aligned with President Rafsanjani, see the *bonyads* as a major obstacle to a more open and free-market economy. The government managed to end the *bonyads'* preferred access to cheap foreign exchange and imports and end their tax-exempt status in 1992. Nevertheless, efforts to bring these institutions under government control and make them more transparent have failed so far. From the *bazaari* point of view, the *bonyads'* monopolistic control of key sectors and their preferred access to government contracts limit the opportunities of the private sector. The unfolding of this struggle will be an important element in Iran's future economic and political development.

The State Industries. The legal structure of the state sector has not significantly changed with the revolution. The bulk of the state-owned industries is grouped in a holding company, the Iran Development and Reconstruction Organization (IDRO). Its current portfolio includes about 80 factories, with a turnover of $1 billion. In addition to IDRO, the state owns large mining concerns, as well as all of the financial institutions.

What Role for the Private Sector? The private sector's role in Iran is restricted to light industry and services. Its role was further restricted with the nationalization of foreign trade and the wartime controls introduced by the government. Moreover, the revolutionary and wartime environment of the 1980s was not propitious to the further development of the private sector. Despite these adverse circumstances, the private sector continued to show a remarkable capacity for entrepreneurship and flexibility. Nevertheless, it as been weighed down by heavy taxation, institutional chaos and the withering of the financial institutional framework. In combination with revolutionary uncertainties, wartime constraints and a high degree of corruption at all levels of government, these factors have halted the further development of the private sector, pushing its energies into speculative activities and sheer survival.

The Rafsanjani reforms of the early 1990s included the privatization of state enterprises, the return of the managerial and technical class that had fled since 1979, and the opening of Iran to foreign investment by liberalizing the investment code and establishing free trade zones (FTZs). These policies seemed to bear fruit for a while, and the private sector was revived alongside the economy in the 1990-92 period. However, starting in mid-1993, falling oil prices and a rising debt burden caused a major financial crisis in Iran. The rial depreciated rapidly and Iran became one of the few countries that ever defaulted on its trade-related external debt. (This debt was eventually rescheduled.) Moreover, Rafsanjani's efforts to lure back the know-how and capital of the hundreds of thousands of Iranians in self-imposed exile foundered because of fierce opposition from radical Islamic factions. The rial crisis of April 1995 sounded the end of these reforms. Thus, the private sector has not fared well, even in the—temporarily—more free market–oriented environment of the past few years. The failure of Rafsanjani's policy relative to the development of the private sector has its roots in many factors, the most important ones being: the lack of institutional stability, the financial and debt crisis of 1993 and the recession that continues to plague the economy.

Nevertheless, the Iranian private sector is a force that has yet to be tapped, with formidable technical, managerial and financial resources both in Iran and abroad. The real issue is the ability of any government of the Islamic Republic to provide a propitious environment for its development.

Saudi Arabia: The Private Sector Comes of Age

The Pre–Gulf War Period. The private sector in Saudi Arabia dates back to the large trading families of the Hejaz province. This sector is essentially formed of four subsectors: construction and contracting, retail and trading, manufacturing and banking. Construction and contracting is dominated by large companies, while the other two non-financial subsectors are mostly formed by smaller firms. With the discovery of oil, the fortunes of the Saudi private sector followed the oil price cycle, and reached their peak during the oil bonanza of the 1970s, when tens of billions of petrodollars flowed back into the economy in the form of huge contracts and government purchases. However, the private sector that emerged was entirely dependent on the government, which provided it with a superb infrastructure, services, cheap credit and subsidies, and contracts.

Table 5.1
Saudi Arabia Nominal GDP Rates of Growth

	Oil GDP	Non-Oil GDP	Private Sector GDP
1991	7.7%	12.0%	6.6%
1992	4.9%	5.0%	6.0%
1993	-4.3%	4.2%	5.1%
1994	-1.0%	1.5%	4.0%

Sources: Saudi Arabian Monetary Agency, National Commercial Bank and author's estimates

The oil producers suffered a reverse oil shock in the 1980s, when oil prices fell from their highs of almost $40 per barrel in early 1979 to less than $10 per barrel in 1986. The resulting cutbacks on the Saudi private sector were devastating, as many well-known names, such as Shobokhsi and Redec, went bankrupt, while most other companies were forced to shrink and banks accumulated bad loans. The prolonged economic downturn of the 1980s resulted in a fundamental restructuring of the private sector, which emerged "leaner and meaner" from both operational and financial points of view, laying the ground for a new surge in the early 1990s.

By 1988-89, the Saudi economy was on the mend. Paradoxically, the Gulf War, which could have dealt a severe blow to business confidence, led to a new wave of optimism. On one hand, the quick Western response and the decisive allied victory over Iraq confirmed the Western commitment to Saudi security. On the other hand, the huge rise in war-related spending by both the Saudis and the allies and the acceleration of the multibillion Arabian-American Oil Company (ARAMCO) capacity expansion program provided a significant boost to private business.

The period that followed the Gulf War was one of rapid growth for the Saudi private sector. It also witnessed fundamental qualitative changes in the attitudes of the Saudi private agents and their economic relation with the government.

Firstly, the private sector became more of an independent source of economic growth. Over 1991-93, non-oil GDP rose by a cumulative 23 percent, while private-sector GDP increased by 17 percent, reflecting continued strong private sector output. Moreover, non-oil GDP continued to grow in early 1994, while the oil GDP stagnated.

Secondly, the relationship of financial dependence on the government experienced over the past three decades began to reverse itself as the private

Table 5.2
Saudi Banks and the Private Sector

	Total Assets (SR millions)	Private-Sector Lending (SR millions)	Private-Sector Loans/Assets (%)	Foreign/Total Assets (%)
1987	191	57.4	30.05	46.49
1989	233	69.3	29.65	43.29
1991	258	68.9	26.71	32.58
1994	318	118.0	37.1	17.0

Source: Saudi Arabian Monetary Agency (SAMA), Annual and Quarterly Reports, 1985-95.
$1=SR 3.75

sector and the banks became a major source of financing for both the external account and the budgetary deficits. In particular, the Saudi government, which started borrowing domestically in 1988, accumulated about $45 billion in domestic debt between 1990 and 1993. Much of the government securities were placed with banks and Saudi mutual funds, and thus ended up being funded by private Saudi companies and individuals.

Thirdly, the rapid pace of private-sector growth required increasing reliance on financing. Thus, bank credit to the private sector rose by 64 percent between the end of 1990 and September 1993, after stagnating in the 1987-90 period. Other key banking ratios reflect this shift in Saudi banking activity toward the domestic market.

This period also saw a rapid expansion of the Saudi stock market. The Saudi stock market is the largest in the Middle East, with a market capitalization of $38 billion (about 30 percent of GDP) in May of 1994. Despite its ups and downs, the stock market remains very active and attractive to both issuers and investors. From the beginning of 1992 to mid-1994, there were 12 new issues, which raised a total of $2.7 billion. Most of the new issues were bank stock, and all were heavily oversubscribed, reflecting strong investor demand.

Trading is carried out electronically under the close supervision of the Saudi Arabian Monetary Agency (SAMA), the central bank. Only banks are allowed to sell shares, and the market is closed to non-Saudis. Moreover, the procedure for obtaining a listing and issuing shares is very lengthy and complicated. Additionally, many of the shares are closely held by the company owners and most investors have long-term positions. For these reasons, despite its size, the market is relatively shallow, with a low trading volume and no more than 2 to 5 percent turnover of shares.

Table 5.3
The Saudi Stock Market

	Market Capitalization ($ billion)	Stock Market Index (1985=100)	Listed Companies	Value of Shares Traded ($ billion)	Number of Shares Traded (million)
1991	17.3	188.9	78	2.276	30.7
1994	38.0	128.3	67	6.632	152.0

Source: Saudi Arabian Monetary Agency (SAMA), Annual and Quarterly Reports, 1980-95.

Corporate finance and capital market development are held back by a very cautious SAMA. Yet there is tremendous potential for the Saudi capital markets to mobilize the considerable domestic and foreign savings of a wealthy corporate sector and population through the broadening and deepening of the capital markets.

Privatization: the Road to the Future

In most of the developing countries, privatization of state assets has been an important part of structural reforms since the early 1980s. At the same time, it has generally been a difficult process, technically complicated and politically sensitive. There is considerable potential for privatization in both Iran and Saudi Arabia. Yet, for different reasons, the potential has not yet been exploited.

Iran: A Failed Experience

In Iran, the privatization drive has met with failure. State-owned enterprises were burdened by heavy losses, over-staffing, under-capitalization and politicization. While about 60 of them were sold (either directly or through the revived Tehran Stock Exchange) by the mid-1990s, the sales were conducted at rockbottom prices and in most cases ended up benefitting the ruling clerical elite and their allies.

IDRO, the government-owned conglomerate, also acts as the privatization body, and is listed on the Tehran Stock Exchange. According to IDRO data, the holding company realized 240 billion rials (about $0.5 billion) from the sale of 50 factories over 1991-94. However, there are indications that most of the shares were purchased by state-owned banks or the *bonyads*, which runs counter to the basic idea of privatization. Another obstacle to privatization has been legislation passed by the Majlies (parliament) requiring a set-aside of shares of privatized companies for the veterans of the Iran-Iraq War and the families of war victims.

In a broader context, the conditions for successful privatization do not exist. The main obstacles have been institutional and have been discussed elsewhere in this paper. Nevertheless, the potential is there—public utilities, telecommunications, upstream and downstream oil, services, banking, industry and mining—and it could be developed under the right circumstances.

SAUDI ARABIA: STRONG POTENTIAL, BUT . . .

Saudi Arabia, on the other hand, meets many of the conditions required for successful privatization: a better-established institutional framework, strong demand from domestic and foreign investors alike, more developed capital markets, a sophisticated banking system and a more favorable macroeconomic environment.

There are compelling reasons for privatization in Saudi Arabia:

- Financing large budget deficits
- Expanding the limited development opportunities offered to the private sector
- Attracting foreign capital and financing the external accounts' deficits
- Creating new jobs and infrastructure for the rapidly growing population

The best candidates for quick privatization are telecommunications, SABIC (the heavy-industry holding company), domestic oil refining and distribution, the national airline (Saudia), ports, municipal services and public utilities. Based on international comparisons, this list alone could yield $20 to $30 billion in revenues.

The petroleum industry is a case apart. While there can be some privatization of downstream activities, upstream activities (exploration, development and production) are too politically sensitive. However, even in this area, joint ventures with foreign oil and gas companies are not out of the question.

Despite the strong potential, there are major obstacles to privatization in Saudi Arabia.

1. Privatization would mean a sharp rise in the heavily subsidized prices for utilities, public services and transportation, which are politically sensitive. However, the Saudi government recently broke this taboo by sharply increasing the price of gasoline and electricity. While the new electricity rates were not sufficient to interest private investors in the Kingdom's utilities, they represented a step in the right direction.

2. Privatization would inevitably lead to cutbacks in the bloated public payroll in the privatized firms. Once again, replacing the lost jobs for Saudis might prove difficult, as the private sector is generally unwilling to hire Saudi nationals.

3. The sale of public assets also has a political dimension, as it involves a shift of political power away from the state. Such considerations are not insignificant.

Nevertheless, the Saudi rulers have committed themselves to the privatization of the economy, and economic necessity will push them to do so sooner rather than later. In addition to outright privatization, we are likely to see an increase in what we can call "privatization-by-default," which I will discuss briefly next.

Privatization by Default. In the past two decades, the Saudi government (like the other oil-rich states in the region) has invested hundreds of billions of dollars to create an extraordinary economic and social infrastructure of cities, schools and hospitals, roads, transportation networks and telecommunications. However, such an infrastructure is increasingly expensive to maintain, replace and expand, particularly in the face of the needs of a rapidly growing population. There are clear examples of the strains put on this infrastructure: an aging telephone system; the inability of the cities to provide water, electricity and sewer hookups to the newest neighborhoods; and the overcrowding of schools. Thus, we see signs of the state's turning to the private sector to provide infrastructure and social services it can no longer afford to provide or subsidize. In one instance, for example, the government used the private sector to build schools under an Islamic financing leasing scheme. We are likely to see an expansion of this kind of activity. However, this will raise important issues such as regulation of utilities and fee-setting for public services.

A New Power Equation. The expansion of the role of the private sector and the increased reliance of the state on private resources has also changed the political dynamics in Saudi Arabia. Milton Friedman and other Chicago School economists have argued that demand for increased political power is a natural outcome of rising incomes. Furthermore, as the private sector and the middle classes see their economic power rise, they can devote more resources to promote these demands.

The beginning of such a trend can be seen in Saudi Arabia. With the Gulf War as a catalyst, it became increasingly clear that the paternalistic/autocratic political model was no longer adequate to fulfill the political and institutional needs of a rapidly modernizing economy. Encouraged by the relatively more open political atmosphere that prevailed briefly during and after the conflict with Iraq, various Saudi groups (women, business-men, Islamic traditionalists) started demanding a more open and account-able system of government, mainly through widely circulated petitions. These pressures led finally to the convening by King Fahd of the first (ap-pointed) National Consultative Assembly (*Majlis al-Shura*) in January 1994. These changes might have happened in any case, given the global trends. Nevertheless, the privatization of the economy and the shift of economic activity away from the government is likely to accelerate the process.

SUMMARY AND CONCLUSIONS

The themes of private sector development and privatization figure promi-nently in the economic policies of both Iran and Saudi Arabia, two major Middle Eastern countries that are often at odds over regional issues. While the conditions for a successful broad privatization exist in Saudi Arabia, the process is severely constrained in Iran.

More fundamentally, the nature of Iran's Islamic revolution limits the potential for success. In the short term, private sector development in the absence of meaningful economic institutions and with the existence of monopolistic *bonyads* can only result in a non-productive and speculative economic pattern-akin to what we see in Russia. In the longer term, the revolution was about power, and the clerics and their allies have accumu-lated an enormous amount of economic power in the past 18 years. Genu-ine economic reforms would include a rapid transition toward a free-market model, the privatization of the state enterprises and the dismantlement of the *bonyads*. But these changes would put the regime's power and its sur-vival in question, and that is a risk that none of its leaders has been willing to take.

In Saudi Arabia, an expansive and increasingly assertive private sector is looking for new investment opportunities. Such opportunities are avail-able not just in an expanding private economy, but also in areas tradition-ally reserved for the state. The economic case for privatization is very strong, but political factors are slowing down the process. In particular, turning over activities hitherto reserved for the state involves not only a loss in political and economic control and patronage for the Al-Saud family, but also requires a radical change in the paternalistic social compact between the Saudi rulers and their subjects. While there is a clear unwillingness on the part of the ruling families to engage in such changes, the tremendous financial needs of a developing country with a rapidly growing population make these changes likely to occur over the next decade or so, albeit in a halting and non-systematic manner. The success of the current Saudi leaders and their successors in delivering these changes will play a critical role in Saudi Arabia's growth prospects in the twenty-first century.

Other Sources

Amuzegar, J. *Iran's Economy under the Islamic Republic* (New York: I.B. Tauris, 1994).

Askari, H. *Saudi Arabia's Economy: Oil and the Search for Economic Development* (London: JAI Press, 1990).

Bank Markazi Iran (Central Bank of Iran). *Annual Reports* (Tehran: 1990-95).

International Finance Corporation. *Emerging Stock Markets Factbook* (Washington, DC: 1995).

"Funding the Saudi Private Sector: Local Banks Can Take the Strain for Now," *Middle East Economic Survey* 37, no. 25, (March 21, 1994) pp. B1-B4.

"Time to Take Gulf Equity Markets Seriously," *Middle East Economic Survey* 37, no. 32, (May 9, 1994) pp. B1-B7.

National Commercial Bank. "Small Industries in Saudi Arabia" (Jeddah: August/September 1993).

National Commercial Bank. "The Emerging Arab Stock Markets" (Jeddah: October 1993).

National Commercial Bank. "Economic Outlook in the GCC Countries" (Jeddah: January 1994).

National Commercial Bank. "Economic Outlook" (Jeddah: February 1994).

Saudi Arabian Monetary Agency. *Annual Reports* (Riyadh: 1990-95).

CHAPTER 6

BORDER DISPUTES IN THE GULF:
PAST, PRESENT, AND FUTURE

Richard N. Schofield

INTRODUCTION: PROGRESS TOWARD
THE FINALIZATION OF THE POLITICAL MAP

Never has the concern of the modern Middle Eastern state to possess precise and permanent territorial limits been more evident than in the mid-1990s. Certainly, this is how it seems, with tangible and significant steps having been taken recently toward the finalization of the political map in Arabia and beyond (see map).[1]

The catalog of recent progress:

- In February 1995, by concluding a Memorandum of Understanding (MOU) in Mecca, Saudi Arabia and Yemen reaffirmed the short, existing stretch of their international boundary from the Red Sea eastward to the high mountains of Asir—a territorial limit introduced by the May 1934 Treaty of Islamic Friendship and Brotherhood and demarcated by joint technical teams shortly afterwards. A procedural framework was also set up in the 1995 MOU for negotiating Arabia's last indeterminate territorial limit in the desert wastes further east.[2]

- Bahrain-Qatar disputes over the sovereignty of the Hawar islands, the Dibal and Jarada shoals and the status of the Qatari coastal settlement of Zubara are currently being treated by the International Court of

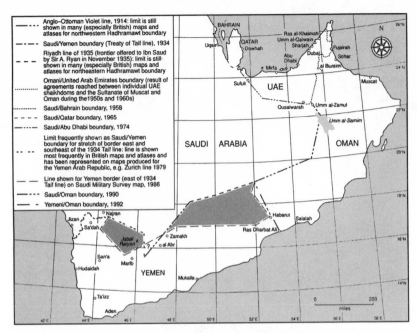

The contemporary status of boundaries in the southern Arabian peninsula.

Source: *R. Schofield, ed.,* Territorial Foundations of the Gulf States *(London: UCL Press, 1994), p. 58.*

Justice (ICJ), which in February 1995 confirmed that it possessed jurisdiction to try the case. This followed years in which Bahrain-Qatar maritime disputes had been effectively controlled by Saudi mediation but in which no real strides had been made to resolve the basic points at issue.

- In November 1994 the Iraqi government accepted unconditionally the verdict of the United Nations on its land and water boundaries with Kuwait, having previously denounced if not rejected outright this award for the previous 18 months.
- Progress toward finalizing the political map of southeastern Arabia continued. This was, in truth, little more than icing on a preexisting cake of settled boundary delimitations. Saudi Arabia and Qatar ostensibly remain committed to demarcating their land boundary delimitation of 1965. In 1993, following a negotiated adjustment to the 1974 Saudi-UAE border delimitation agreement, the United Arab Emirates was allowed to extend slightly its westernmost territorial limits on the Khawr al-Udayd at the expense of the Saudi kingdom. This relieved some of the lingering discontent felt by the UAE about the

way in which the original agreement had been reached. In 1995, Saudi Arabia registered the text of its 1974 border treaty with Abu Dhabi at the secretariat of the United Nations in New York.

- In the spring of 1993 the Omani foreign ministry announced that residual boundary disputes with the United Arab Emirates (but principally Abu Dhabi) had been "completely settled" following the signature of a "lasting agreement" between the two states.[3] Oman finalized its land boundary delimitation to the west with Yemen in 1992 and took the opportunity presented by the occasion to also make public the details of the border agreement it had negotiated in March 1990 with Saudi Arabia.

- The summer of 1995 witnessed rather lavish celebrations of the completed demarcation of the international boundary delimitation agreed between Oman and Yemen in an October 1992 treaty.[4] This was followed a month later by the high public profile given to a ceremony in Riyadh to commemorate the joint signature of a series of detailed, official maps of the Saudi-Oman border.[5] The texts of all Saudi boundary treaties are now publicly available in their entirety and registered at what the international legal community regards as the appropriate institutions.

- In October 1995 delegations from Kuwait and Saudi Arabia began discussions that will hopefully result in the announcement of a maritime boundary delimitation between the two states. There has been no indication of how the obstacle posed by the long-established, if low-key, dispute over the sovereignty of the islands of Qaru and Umm al-Maradim is to be broached in advance any settlement.[6] In May 1995, the Iranian Ambassador to Kuwait announced Tehran's preparedness to tackle the problem of finalizing maritime boundaries between the two states in the northern Gulf.[7] The Kuwaiti government confirmed during the autumn of 1995 that an agreement had been reached in principle to commence negotiations toward this end. These are dependent upon a successful conclusion of the ongoing negotiations between Kuwait and Saudi Arabia on maritime territorial limits.

Obstacles Ahead

It will not escape attention that much, though not all, of the above-noted progress involves member states of the Gulf Cooperation Council and Yemen. Moreover, strides recently taken in the Saudi-Yemeni and Bahrain-Qatar cases are merely promises of eventual territorial settlement, and many difficulties need to be overcome en route.

The text of the February 1995 Saudi-Yemeni MOU raised two important issues. First, the provision for recourse to arbitration (detailed in article three) was somewhat vague. Second, the two sides did not formally renew the May 1934 Treaty of Taif.[8] Instead, they "confirmed their adherence to the legality and obligatory nature" of the Taif treaty, in all of its provisions. Further consideration of such semantics was obviated by the formal renewal in June 1995 of the Taif treaty for a further twenty-lunar-year stretch.

The Saudi-Yemeni MOU and the subsequent renewal of the Taif treaty, however, can only be regarded as vague promises of a distant territorial settlement. Official talks on the boundary question have only been in train since July 1992, and progress in the rounds of negotiations held up to now has been painfully slow. Saudi Arabia and Yemen maintain quite different views of where their international boundary should run east of the 1934 Taif line, and historically there is a multiplicity of overlapping territorial claims along the southern rim of the Rub al-Khali.[9] It is not in the interests of either state to retract these claims. The fact that oil prospecting along the undefined borderlands has to date yielded disappointing results has, on the one hand, made negotiations easier to enter into—since the stakes have been lowered—but on the other hand has lessened the urgency of both states to arrive at a precise delimitation of sovereign territory. It seems most likely that settlement will ultimately be arrived at when there is an opportunity for a "political fix" from which both states can demonstrably gain.[10]

Living with the future ICJ verdict on Hawar *et al.* will be the acid test for Manama-Doha relations. In their awards of the last few years, both international arbitration tribunals and the ICJ have done everything possible to arrive at settlements from which both parties to a dispute can claim to have gained, or at least, not lost, everything. Yet the major problem in the Bahrain-Qatar case is that the former has almost everything to lose and the latter almost everything to gain from the award of the ICJ. This must be regarded as the reason that Bahrain dragged its feet throughout the early 1990s when it disputed the right of the ICJ to try the Hawar case and why, for the year or so after February 1995, it refused to take part in the case. Eventually, a disgruntled Bahrain submitted its memorial to the ICJ during the summer of 1996.

Notwithstanding the United Nations' final settlement of the Iraq-Kuwait boundary question in the spring of 1993 and Iraq's unequivocal acceptance during November 1994 of its findings, few experienced observers of Gulf affairs can confidently predict that the last has been heard of the plea by successive Baghdad governments for greater access to Gulf waters at the expense of Kuwait.

Iran's Exclusion from Such Progress

It will not escape the reader that one littoral state, Iran, is largely absent from this summary of recent progress. Yet Iran is confronted today with two of the region's most historically intractable disputes, one of which is alive and one of which holds the potential to threaten the territorial stability of the northern Gulf.

Iran's cyclical dispute with the UAE (and previously the Qasimi shaikhdoms of Sharjah and Ras al-Khaimah) over the sovereignty of the central Lower Gulf islands of Abu Musa and the Tunbs was reactivated during 1992 after a long period of relative calm. The classic positional dispute between Iran and Iraq over their international boundary along the Shatt al-Arab is not presently a burning issue, yet it must be regarded as dormant rather than permanently settled. The status of the Shatt al-Arab question is analogous to that of the Lower Gulf islands dispute before 1992 and therefore has a similar potential to be reactivated, only with more devastating consequences.

The irony is that both disputes are supposedly governed by legal instruments that are a model of their kind. The 1971 Memorandum of Understanding between Iran and Sharjah (by which the administration of Abu Musa was shared) was a highly imaginative and pragmatic arrangement, given the apparent insolubility of the dispute and the regional political realities of that time. The 1975 Algiers Accord and follow-up bilateral treaties between Iran and Iraq provided for the equal division of the waters of the Shatt al-Arab and contained every conceivable safeguard against future dispute over the course and status of the international boundary. The Algiers Accord package of agreements was technically well-conceived and comprehensive; in short, it remains arguably the most sophisticated legislation existing in international law to govern a divided river boundary.

It is the conviction of this author that the northern Gulf is a region in which territorial instability is endemic, and that Iran's territorial disputes with Iraq and the United Arab Emirates are always likely to be the focus of

Arab-Iranian rivalries. Since these disputes pose the greatest potential threat to regional stability, they will be the focus of this chapter.

Boundaries and International Relations

A different set of circumstances naturally will produce progress or deterioration in the territorial equation between neighboring states. It is well to remind ourselves of the three prevailing points of view concerning international boundaries and inter-state relations. Social scientists have long quibbled over whether there is such a thing as a good or bad boundary, or whether dissatisfaction with boundaries per se is a root cause of instability between states. The renowned French political geographer Jacques Ancel commented during the mid-1930s that there were no problems of boundaries, only problems of nations.[11] Another viewpoint contends that the shape and size of a state can give rise to genuine geopolitical and strategic problems—most notably, problems of access and communication.[12] One has only to look at the northern Gulf region in recent times to find evidence that supports both contentions. A third view, again applicable to the littoral states of the northern Gulf, is that states have difficulties in accepting and reconciling themselves to the very presence of an international boundary, especially in those instances in which external powers have had a large hand in its creation.[13]

MOTIVATIONS TO FINALIZE AND REGULATE THE TERRITORIAL FRAMEWORK

This chapter maintains that there has been a trend toward finalizing and crystallizing the territorial framework in the Arabian peninsula–Gulf region. Two possible motivations are briefly reviewed in this section: the increasing economic utilization of border regions in Arabia, and the increasing territorial consciousness of the populations of the states concerned. The role played by the Gulf Cooperation Council in promoting and regulating the finalization of the Arabian political map is also analyzed.

Oil Exploration in Arabian Border Regions

Beginning in the early 1990s, several Arabian states, notably Saudi Arabia, accelerated oil exploration and development close to their own (finalized or unfinalized) borders. Because of their politically sensitive location and general remoteness, these fields had generally been ignored prior to this point, but the economic imperatives of maximizing production in a flat oil market and of compensating for the maturation of older fields now came to outweigh such reservations.[14] Perhaps this development explains much of the progress made in recent years in finalizing border delimitations in southeastern Arabia. There is an argument that the Khafus incident of autumn 1992 on the Saudi-Qatar border was a consequence of this process, the case in question having been complicated by the absence of any demarcation of the boundary on the ground.

Difficulties have arisen in recent years in those instances where oil fields straddle international boundaries or where, in the case of Saudi Arabia and Yemen, no international boundary exists. Uncertainty concerning the precise position of the Iraq-Kuwait boundary and the geological configuration of the supergiant Iraqi Rumailah oil field contributed to tensions in the runup to the Iraqi invasion of Kuwait.[15]

In November 1992 Saudi Arabia decided to proceed with development of the Shaibah oil field (referred to as Zarara by the UAE), which straddles the kingdom's border with the principal shaikhdom of the UAE, Abu Dhabi.[16] Eighty percent of the field lies within Saudi Arabia and only twenty percent within Abu Dhabi, yet, according to the 1974 boundary treaty concluded between the two states, whose text has only recently been made publicly available, the Riyadh government had sole rights over the whole of the oil field. The slight westward shift of the UAE boundary in the Khawr al-Udayd in 1993 partially assuaged Abu Dhabi's sensitivities over the issue.

Forging a Territorial Consciousness at the State Level

Political scientists writing about the Arabian peninsula–Gulf region have tried to explain the increasing preoccupation of states with territorial definition in terms other than the appropriation of natural resources. It has been argued that the state is coming to be seen as belonging equally to its citizens. Importantly, this now applies as much to its territorial attributes as to the resources associated with that territory.[17] This tendency is probably easier to observe in those states in which a mass political consciousness is developed, that is, primarily Iran, Iraq and perhaps Yemen rather than the Arab states of the western Gulf littoral.

This might partially explain Iran's recent behavior over Abu Musa. It is a matter of debate as to whether Iran's action of denying access to the southern, Sharjah-administered part of the island to non-UAE nationals in 1992 was a local administrative blunder, a knee-jerk reaction to its exclusion from collective security arrangements for the Gulf or a calculated move designed to enhance its strategic position in the Lower Gulf. However, at a time when the Iranian public was being reminded that Iran was being isolated internationally by the United States' dual containment policy and denied a say in regional security arrangements, no Iranian was likely to demur at actions that could be perceived as upholding national rights in the region or that might serve as a reminder to its Arab neighbors that Iran was still a force to be reckoned with.[18] A history of the Gulf in which Iran has been dominant is an important article of faith for Iranian nationalism. As one American scholar recently commented, "Persians are deeply convinced that the Gulf has been a Persian lake ever since Cyrus the Great and the first Persian world empire. It is an article of faith deeply etched into the Iranian psyche, engendering deeply emotional responses toward the 'rightful dominance' of Iran over most of the Gulf. . . . A sense of the Persian Gulf, as an integral part of the realm of Persian culture and civilization, is an ineradicable part of the Iranian world view."[19]

That Kuwait rightfully belongs to Iraq is almost certainly still a prevailing view on the streets of Baghdad and elsewhere within Iraq. Ironically, it was probably much easier for President Saddam Hussein to recognize the United Nations verdict on the Iraq-Kuwait boundary than it would have been for Iraqi opposition groups. The UN decision on the course of the Iraq-Kuwait land boundary, announced in April 1992, was denounced not only by the current Iraqi regime, but also by the exiled opposition groups. As for the current Iraqi government's recent and unconditional recognition of the United Nations' ruling on the boundary, it is as well to recall that Saddam Hussein previously has given his unequivocal blessing to supposedly final boundary delimitations with neighboring states, only to disown them when the circumstances that drove him to make those territorial concessions no longer apply.[20] Kuwait must be only too aware of this.

THE REGULATION OF BORDERS AND TERRITORIAL DISPUTES IN THE ARABIAN PENINSULA–GULF REGION

As suggested earlier, the pragmatic consideration of delimiting state territory so that frontier oil exploration could proceed smoothly was the catalyst for much of the rapid progress made toward finalizing the political map of Arabia during the 1990s. There were certainly other motivations, not least the territorial insecurities fostered in the tiny emirates of the western Gulf littoral by Iraq's calamitous move on Kuwait. A reexamination of the territorial foundations of these states in the aftermath of Iraq's invasion serves as a reminder that they have always been vulnerable to the territorial acquisitiveness of their larger, more powerful neighbors in the region. Had it not been for Britain's decisive intervention at the height of the Jahrah crisis in 1920, the southern reaches of Kuwait would, almost certainly, have been subsumed into Ibn Saud's expanding Najdi domain. It should also be remembered that at the outset of the ill-fated Anglo-Saudi frontier negotiations in 1934, the Saudi state had recognized only the coastal settlements of Abu Dhabi, Doha, Muscat and Salalah—without their hinterlands—as independent of its own authority.[21]

As a result of the feeling of insecurity that Iraq's actions engendered in the smaller Gulf emirates, the Gulf Cooperation Council (GCC) felt obliged to take more concrete steps to entrench, regulate and institutionalize the prevailing framework of state territory. It was, after all, the only regional grouping that was capable of doing so. At the end of 1994 the council called for all outstanding disputes to be settled speedily and also expressed a preference for a certain mode of dispute resolution.

The Damascus Declaration of March 1991 (concluded among the six GCC states, Egypt and Syria) remains an important statement of policy, principle and intent as far as the regulation of state territory in the region was concerned. The following measures were promoted explicitly: greater regulation of existing borders, peaceful resolution of disputes, respect for international law, mutual non-interference and good-neighborliness.[22]

Following Iran's heavy-handed actions on Abu Musa in 1992, a further principle for maintaining the regional territorial framework would be added to those enunciated in the Damascus Declaration. The Abu Dhabi declaration issued at the thirteenth annual GCC summit in December 1992 laid great stress on the "inadmissability of the acquisition of land by force."[23]

The fifteenth annual GCC summit in Manama during December 1994 had seemed significant at the time for the articulation of policy toward territorial issues. Here, member states were urged to make every effort to resolve territorial disputes through bilateral negotiations within a twelve-month period. Furthermore, it was implied that the GCC itself would take an active role in promoting settlement should the requisite progress not have been made before the 16th annual summit meeting in Muscat. Time and events would soon prove that such directives had been given with the Hawar dispute primarily in mind—this was, after all, the only serious "in-house" dispute that remained to be settled. Also, it was and remains customary for pronouncements of GCC policy to promote the desiderata of the member state hosting the annual summit meeting, in this case Bahrain. In any event, the twelve-month timetable was not followed up at Muscat, where territorial issues barely figured. Could this have had something to do with the fact that Oman has no outstanding territorial disputes?

Perhaps the avoidance of territorial questions at the Muscat summit of 1995 also reflected the fact that the GCC states now believe they have done everything possible to get their house in order—the Hawar dispute excepted, as the GCC is somewhat uneasily awaiting the ICJ's verdict. Of Arabia's international land boundaries, only the eastern three-quarters of the Saudi-Yemeni border remains to be delimited. What can be said of the rush during the first half of the 1990s toward finally settled Arabian boundary delimitations is that the territorial framework has now evolved to the point where it must be regarded as final and permanent. Only five years ago, an experienced observer of territorial affairs in the peninsula had commented that Saudi Arabia's refusal to make boundary treaty texts public and to register them at the appropriate international institutions cast doubt upon whether the territorial arrangements were intended to be permanent.[24] The position has changed to the extent that Saudi Arabia can now point to the fact that it has renegotiated or modified all of the territorial understandings concluded between Ibn Saud and the British—or frequently imposed by the latter—during the early part of the century. Saudi Arabia's smaller and historically mindful Arab neighbors along the western/ southern Gulf littoral will also doubtless be reassured by the growing evidence that the territorial framework has evolved to a point of no return.

THE PERENNIAL SOURCES OF INSTABILITY: IRANO-ARAB TERRITORIAL DISPUTES, IRAQI ACCESS TO THE GULF AND OTHER REMAINING PROBLEMS

The previous two sections have tried to establish that the glass of fully settled Arabian boundaries has been filled as high as is currently possible. For the most part, this has been accomplished relatively painlessly. The remaining territorial problems that confront the Gulf and the Arabian peninsula are the same, serious challenges that have long threatened regional stability: the historically entrenched Irano-Arab territorial disputes over the Shatt al-Arab and Abu Musa and the Tunbs, the explosive question of Iraqi access to the sea, and the not-quite-so-explosive Hawar and shoals dispute. All of these have an important history that is rarely given sufficient weight in the literature.

This core section reviews in detail the evolution, current status and future prospects for the Iran-UAE dispute over the sovereignty of the islands of Abu Musa and the Tunbs, and the interrelated question of Iraq's problematic boundaries with Iran and Kuwait at the head of the Gulf. Though the Shatt al-Arab dispute currently lies dormant and the Iraq-Kuwait boundary has ostensibly been settled, these are long-established disputes that tend to recur every few decades. Seemingly intractable territorial disputes between Bahrain and Qatar have long embittered Manama-Doha relations, though they have ultimately always been kept in check by Britain, as colonial power in the region, and, in more recent times, Saudi Arabia. Brief summaries of this dispute and Qatar's other territorial problem with Saudi Arabia to its south are provided in this section. (The latter dispute contrasts strongly with the other three case studies, inasmuch as recent, very real strains between Doha and Riyadh have had almost nothing to do with the boundary itself.)

The Northern Gulf

Conflict and Territorial Instability in the Northern Gulf. The longstanding though currently dormant dispute between Iran and Iraq over the Shatt al-Arab seemingly provides a case in point for Ancel's argument (already outlined) that serious boundary disputes are symptomatic only of the poor relations existing at any one time between the governments of neighboring states. Over a period of 130 years (since the conclusion of the second Perso-Ottoman Treaty of Erzurum in 1847), the Shatt al-Arab had evolved from being an Ottoman river to being shared along the *thalweg* line between its riparians. In March 1975, on signing the Algiers Accord with Iraq, Iran secured a *thalweg* boundary delimitation (the line of continuous deepest soundings) to satisfy a longstanding demand that had been prosecuted with some degree of consistency for nearly fifty years. One of the most sophisticated river boundary treaties ever signed in international law, the Algiers Accord and follow-up bilateral agreements of June and December 1975 contained every conceivable safeguard against future dispute over the boundary. Yet, less than six years later, after the first few weeks of the 1980-88 Iran-Iraq War, the Shatt was blocked by the wreckage of burnt-out or abandoned vessels, and Iraq was in effect landlocked. As a prelude to prosecuting war, Iraqi President Hussein had unilaterally abrogated the river boundary agreement—he actually tore to pieces a copy of the document he had signed in 1975 before an Iraqi television audience. Iraq had perhaps sensed—wrongly as it turned out—that in the aftermath of the Iranian revolution circumstances were favorable for the restoration of the Shatt to its "rightful owner." Iraq had felt obliged to make the territorial concession in 1975 to quell the shah's support for the Kurdish rebellion in the north. It soon became apparent, however, that the Iraqi regime had not been at all convinced of the 1975 concession on the Shatt on its own merits and had only concluded it as a last resort. There is perhaps no more graphic illustration that the status of an international boundary is subject to fluctuations in the relationship between the neighboring states sharing that divide.[25] The fact that Iraq was apparently prepared, two weeks into its occupation of Kuwait, to recognize once again a *thalweg* delimitation along the Shatt, once more because of factors extraneous to the dispute itself, seemingly reinforces the case for an Ancelian interpretation.

Ancel's observation makes no provision for the way in which the positioning of a state's boundaries can disadvantage it strategically. Iraq's southern boundaries provide a good example. Because of the proximity of Iraq's international boundaries with Kuwait to the south and Iran to the southeast, separated only by the Faw Peninsula, a largely undevelopable mud flat, access to the sea has been an overriding concern for successive Baghdad regimes. One only has to glance at a map to realize that Iraq, with its minuscule shoreline on the Gulf, can be classified as a geographically disadvantaged state. It has long perceived itself as "squeezed out" of the Gulf.[26] Traditionally, this consciousness has stiffened Iraq's resolve not to make territorial concessions to Iran over the Shatt al-Arab. The insecure status of the Shatt al-Arab boundary has, in turn, encouraged Iraq, from the late 1930s onwards, to seek alternative port facilities to Basra, its principal dry-cargo port, at Umm Qasr on the Khawr Zubayr further west. In order to secure complete control over navigation in the Khawr Abdallah, the access channel that links this water inlet to the Gulf, Iraq has pressed, with remarkable consistency over the last half-century, for the cession or lease of the Kuwaiti islands of Warba and Bubiyan.

Though Umm Qasr port was developed by Iraq during the 1960s, Baghdad continued to insist that Kuwait make concessions over the islands if it wanted Iraq to reciprocate by agreeing to the final delimitation and demarcation of the land boundary further west, a longstanding Kuwaiti objective. For well over thirty years up to the Iraqi invasion of Kuwait in August 1990 (and notwithstanding an agreement of October 1963 in which Iraq recognized an independent Kuwait and its boundaries), the Iraq-Kuwait border and islands question in effect remained deadlocked. Iraq would not agree to the demarcation of the land boundary unless Kuwait first showed some flexibility on the question of ceding or leasing Warba and Bubiyan. Kuwait demanded the prerequisite of a fully demarcated land boundary in accordance with its description in existing official correspondence before any consideration of leasing Warba would be entertained. In truth, Iraq's demand for some sort of control over the islands was less of a territorial dispute than a plea that the existing boundary be adjusted (or Kuwait's effective sovereignty over the islands be substantively reduced) so as to improve Iraq's access to the sea, in acknowledgement of its disadvantageous position at the head of the Gulf. Traditionally, over the last half-century or so, Iraq has pressed Kuwait on the islands question when its relationship with Iran has been seriously strained over the status of the Shatt al-Arab.[27] Historically, successive Baghdad regimes have expected Kuwait to compensate Iraq for its geographic and strategic misfortune.[28]

Whether or not one accepts the thesis that dissatisfaction with existing boundaries is a genuine cause of inter-state conflict, it is clear that—nominally at least—the status of the Shatt al-Arab boundary and Iraq's preoccupation with gaining rights over Warba and Bubiyan were important factors in Saddam Hussein's respective decisions to prosecute war against Iran during the autumn of 1980 and to annex Kuwait during the summer of 1990. The fact that United Nations peace-keeping forces were stationed until January 1991 along the Iran-Iraq border and remain in position along the Iraq-Kuwait border surely underlines that the framework of state territory in the northern Gulf region remains unstable.

Iraq's Acceptance of the UN Demarcation of its Boundary with Kuwait. On November 10, 1994, Iraq's Revolutionary Command Council passed a decree that extended unconditional recognition to the UN Iraq-Kuwait border delimitation/demarcation.[29] For much of the previous two-and-a-half years Iraq's attitude had bordered on outright rejection of the demarcation team's decisions on the precise course of the boundary. The United Nations Iraq-Kuwait Boundary Demarcation Commission's (UNIKBDC) verdict on the course of the land boundary had first been announced in April 1992 and was demarcated by permanent pillar by the end of November of the same year.[30] The UN demarcation team announced a boundary for the Khawr Abdallah and Khawr Shetana (the water channels separating Iraq's Faw Peninsula from the Kuwaiti islands of Warba and Bubiyan) in March 1993. A list of geographic coordinates delimiting the whole boundary with precision was then released with UNIKBDC's final report when this was presented to the Security Council two months later, in May 1993.[31]

Despite much criticism, particularly in 1992, UNIKBDC appeared to adhere to its mandate in demarcating the land boundary. In April 1991 it was asked to settle along the line of the de jure Iraq-Kuwait boundary and, by extension, to ignore any de facto or temporary borders. As a result, the degree to which Iraq had extended its administration southward across the notional line of the de jure boundary in the three decades between the first Kuwait Crisis of 1961 and its invasion of 1990 was disallowed, if not unceremoniously cancelled, by the UN.[32] When it first became apparent that the southern portion of the modern Iraqi port of Umm Qasr was to be recognized by UNIKBDC as lying within Kuwait, widespread criticism appeared in respected quarters of the Western and Arab media since, in their opinion, the UN was reallocating Iraqi territory to Kuwait. Yet, all UNIKBDC had done was to establish as closely as possible the line of the de jure boundary.

UNIKBDC's March 1993 prescription for a median line delimitation along the Khawr Abdallah has left the principal navigation lanes of the water inlet, dredged and deepened by Iraq since the opening of Umm Qasr port in 1961[33], within Kuwaiti territorial waters. The future need for co-operation in the management of this stretch of the border is only too clear. UNIKBDC's nomination of the median line for the Khawr Abdallah, while not without its problems, was much less contentious than its ultimate con-clusion that a preexisting delimitation was there to be demarcated.[34] Of all Iraq's grumblings about UNIKBDC in the period before November 1994, those concerning the Khawr Abdallah seemed the most justified.

The acid test for the demarcated Iraq-Kuwait boundary will surely come at some point in the future, when UNIKOM (the United Nations Iraq-Kuwait Observation Mission) no longer polices the border zone and when relations with Iran next sour over the status of the Shatt al-Arab. The Shatt dispute could be resurrected at short notice. If and when it is, Iraq may seek to compensate itself by trying to expand once again at Umm Qasr on the Khawr Zubayr. This is not idle speculation but a proven his-torical pattern.

Territorial stability will probably come to this part of the world only when Iraq reconciles itself to its disadvantageous position at the head of the Gulf, when it perceives itself as no longer "squeezed out." For the long-term stability of the northern Gulf it is perhaps more important for Iraq to lose its negative consciousness surrounding access than for the Baghdad government to have demarcated boundaries at the head of the Gulf. Whether or not access is and has been a genuine problem is less important than the fact that successive Baghdad governments and, to an extent, Iraqi public opinion also, have always believed it to be so. Whatever line the UN had nominated to settle the border—de jure, de facto or otherwise—Iraq would still, almost certainly, perceive itself as a "big garage with a very small door."

The Hawar Islands, the Dibal and Jarada Shoals and Zubara[35]

There is at present only one serious "in-house" (inter-GCC) territorial dispute—that between Bahrain and Qatar over the sovereignty of the Hawar islands (lying off the west coast of Qatar), and the Dibal and Jarada shoals that lie to their northwest in the waters separating the two states. The International Court of Justice (ICJ) is expected to deliver its verdict on the sovereignty of Hawar and the shoals in the near future, probably in 1998. All of these features are currently occupied by Bahrain and have previously been recognized by Britain (in awards of 1939 and 1947) as belonging to the island state. On Britain's departure from the Gulf as protecting power in 1971, Saudi Arabia inherited the role of mediator. For the next two decades its mediating efforts could be deemed partially successful on two counts: firstly, for ensuring that the dispute never escalated into open hostilities; and secondly, by paving the way for a reference of the case to the international courts.

The early 1990s, however, witnessed a rather tedious dispute over the right of the ICJ to try the dispute, following Qatar's unilateral reference of the case to The Hague in the summer of 1991. Bahrain, which has everything to lose in the future ICJ decision on sovereignty, complained that the whole gamut of the case should have been agreed beforehand with Qatar and submitted jointly to the courts. The ICJ announced in 1994 that Qatar had been within its rights to submit the case to court as a consequence of agreements the emirate had concluded with Bahrain in 1987 and 1990, a ruling effectively confirmed in February 1995.[36] Qatar has prepared its legal claims to the features at issue, articulated in a memorial that was submitted to the ICJ in February 1996. At this stage, Bahrain had produced no such document of its own and had refused to attend court sessions. Ominously, the island-state had issued some fairly threatening rhetoric, letting it be known that should the ICJ award go against Bahrain, the islands and shoals would be handed over to Qatar "over its dead body."[37] Ultimately, the ICJ extended the deadline for submission of memorials until the summer of 1996, when the archipelagic state reluctantly complied. Nevertheless, Bahrain remains extremely unhappy with the ICJ's current treatment of the dispute. It refused to attend the GCC's seventeenth annual summit in Doha during December 1996 as a consequence.

An ICJ verdict on the case would have been guaranteed, however, with or without Bahrain's participation in court proceedings. It is ironic that the point at which the dispute is finally settled in international law could well constitute the most dangerous point in its entire history. Clearly, Saudi Arabia's traditional mediating role would prove critical to regional stability at the implementation stage, were the verdict to go against Manama—not that there is any indication that this is likely. A cursory glance at recent territorial awards made in The Hague, especially those introducing maritime delimitations, would suggest that the ICJ will endeavor to come to an arrangement with which both sides will not be totally dissatisfied. The specifics of this case give little room for flexibility, however, with Qatar standing everything to gain and Bahrain everything to lose in the impending award.

The Iran-UAE Dispute over the
Sovereignty of Abu Musa and the Tunbs

Iran and the UAE are currently engaged in a rather repetitive if occasionally heated war of words over the sovereignty and control of the Lower Gulf islands of Abu Musa and the Tunbs. Previously dormant or at least repressed by a pragmatic 1971 arrangement for the shared administration of the island, the dispute over Abu Musa was resurrected by the heavy-handed Iranian actions of twice denying access during 1992 to non-UAE nationals working in the southern, Sharjah-administered part of the island. The UAE reacted by calling for an end to Iran's twenty-one-year-long occupation of Greater and Lesser Tunb. In the period since the incidents of April and August 1992, the UAE has gained solid GCC backing and strong support within the wider Arab world for taking any peaceful measures it might deem appropriate to regain its sovereignty over the three islands. Usually these have involved suggestions that the disputes over the islands be referred to impartial arbitration or to the international courts for a judgement. Iran quickly admitted that it had made mistakes in 1992 and has consistently expressed its readiness to discuss Abu Musa bilaterally with the UAE. If public pronouncements are anything to go by, it still considers itself bound by the 1971 Memorandum of Understanding it concluded with Sharjah for the shared administration of the island. Iran considers, however, that its sovereignty over the Tunbs is non-negotiable.

In this section a few words will be said in turn about the origins and bases of rival claims to the islands, possible ways out of the dispute that have been suggested over the years, Iran's move on the islands following

Britain's withdrawal late during 1971 and, finally, the resurrection of the dispute during 1992.

Historical Background. Abu Musa is a well-watered island that has traditionally sustained a small but permanent Arab population in its southern reaches—in modern times this has generally been on the order of 600 people. The Tunbs, to its northeast, are drier and have never sustained a permanent population. Abu Musa lies on the Arab side of a median line drawn northwest to southeast through the Gulf, while Greater and Lesser Tunb lie closer to the Iranian coast. Rival claims by the Persian/Iranian state and the Qasimi emirates of Sharjah and Ras al-Khaimah (or Britain on their behalf and the UAE for the last two decades) have been maintained with great consistency for over a century.

Persian/Iranian Claims and the Early Phase of the Dispute. The Persian/Iranian claim to the islands has traditionally been based upon its boast to have controlled and administered them before Britain intervened in Lower Gulf waters during the first half of the nineteenth century to impose its own maritime order. For Britain, or British India to be more accurate, was concerned about the security of its trade routes and considered that much of the threat to these emanated from pirates operating from the Qasimi emirates of Sharjah and Ras al-Khaimah on the Trucial Coast and Lingeh on the Persian coast.

Iranians are often frustrated by the tendency of non-Iranian historical accounts of this dispute to begin with the nineteenth-century record maintained in the files of the British Residency. In Iran's view, this archival evidence tells only part of the story. Britain's late-nineteenth-century documentary record of human contacts with and initial claims to the islands must, they believe, be set within the broader context of Persia's earlier-established supremacy over the waters and islands of the Persian Gulf. Whether or not history affords Iran the right to claim such a hegemonic position—my own research would suggest that the Persian/Iranian claim to have been a continuously active and dominant player in Gulf affairs since ancient times needs to be treated with extreme caution[38]—has to be balanced against the fact that most influential Persians, from the nineteenth century onwards, believe that it has.

The problem Iran has faced when arguing that Britain displaced its administration of the Lower Gulf during the nineteenth century is that it has not yet come forward with any records of its own that display or document an earlier connection with the islands. Contemporary Iranian accounts of the dispute tend to make rather selective use of the British archives instead.[39] The British version of the origins of the dispute, as maintained in the British Residency files at the India Office Library and Records at Blackfriars, is patchy and disorganized but all that has been publicly unearthed to date.[40]

Evidence for ownership of the islands before the mid-nineteenth century barely exists. Political and territorial control in the Lower Gulf region before Britain's arrival on the scene (and for a good while thereafter) was marked by its fluidity. There had been a considerable degree of contact and interchange between the coastal communities of the Gulf, and Arab populations on both sides traditionally moved back and forth across this body of water. The economies of the coastal tribes were traditionally geared to the waters of the Gulf. Generally speaking, the inhabitants of the Lower Gulf littoral enjoyed appreciably more contact with their counterparts on the opposite shore than they did with, on the one hand, central authority in Persia and, on the other, the resource-poor Arabian interior.

During the mid-1840s, the Persian prime minister, Haji Mirza Aghassi, claimed all of the waters and islands of the Gulf as Persian.[41] Aside from reiterating this general, hegemonic claim, however, it would not be until 1877 that a Persian claim to the Tunbs was first formally entered and not until 1888 that Tehran did the same, though indirectly and informally, for Abu Musa. Up until 1873 the British Residency at Bushehr had generally believed that the Tunbs belonged to Persia, because of these islands' close connection with the southern Persian, though Qasimi-controlled, port of Lingeh. By the mid-1880s, however, Britain was increasingly of the opinion that the Qawasim of the southern littoral (or the Qasimi shaikh of Ras al-Khaimah on those fairly frequent occasions when the political unity of the southern Qasimi Federation was broken) ultimately held rights over the Tunbs, though it acknowledged that it was the Qawasim of Lingeh who maintained those few contacts that there were with the island. This followed the receipt of original documents from the Qawasim of the southern littoral, which showed that their counterparts in Lingeh may have been subordinate politically to Ras al-Khaimah.[42]

Persian/Iranian claims to the Tunbs rely strongly on the assertion that for ten years up until 1887, the Qawasim at Lingeh collected taxes from the islanders of Sirri and Greater Tunb and did so as Persian subjects. Persia claimed that the Qawasim at Lingeh, who had migrated to the northern Gulf littoral during the mid-eighteenth century, had acquired the status of Persian subjects before beginning their loose administration of Sirri and Greater Tunb. The British records would appear to lend partial support to these contentions. During the 1880s, certainly, the Qawasim at Lingeh had fallen under the increasing influence of central government in Tehran and paid tribute on request to the Persian governor-general of Fars Province. While taxes may well have been collected from Sirri island during this period, there is no evidence to suggest that they were collected from Greater Tunb, which was populated only seasonally, and even then very thinly. Persia also believed, wrongly but understandably, that the Qawasim of Lingeh also maintained contact with the island of Abu Musa. This had everything to do with a mistaken assertion contained within the first (1864) edition of the British Admiralty's *Persian Gulf Pilot*, which had erroneously made this very association. Persia's first informal claim to Abu Musa in 1888, which was more in the way of an indirect mention yet was still acknowledged internally by departments of British India, was based solely on the Admiralty's carelessness.[43]

Iran has also laid great stress historically on a British War Office map produced in 1886 in which Abu Musa and the Tunbs are shown clearly in Persian colors. This was presented to the Qajar shah as a gift by the British minister in Tehran during the summer of 1888 on the instructions of Lord Salisbury, British foreign secretary of the day.

In 1887 the Persian government banished the Qawasim at Lingeh to the southern Gulf littoral—their 130-year stay on the southern Persian coast was at an end. The Persian government also annexed the island of Sirri, a move to which Britain acquiesced since no great objections were voiced either at the time or thereafter.[44] Threats made at the same time to annex Greater Tunb were not acted upon until 1904, by which time the Qasimi flag flew on Greater Tunb and Abu Musa.

Qasimi Claims to Abu Musa Upheld by British India. Qasimi claims to Abu Musa are based upon the uninterrupted possession of the island by the ruling family of Sharjah over a long and continuous period. Sovereignty was gained, it is claimed, by a process of historical consolidation. Pearlers and fishermen visiting Abu Musa paid annual dues to the ruler of Sharjah from 1863 onwards. Britain has actively defended the claims of Sharjah to the island since the 1870s. While Sharjah's rulers would admit that the administration of Greater Tunb was effectively shared between the Qawasim of Lingeh and Ras al-Khaimah (especially for the crucial 1878-87 period referred to above) and that this island had more links with the northern than the southern Gulf littoral, they would strongly resist any suggestions that Abu Musa was anything other than directly administered from Sharjah itself during the eighteenth century. The weight of documentation in the

British archives would appear to confirm such a contention.[45] This is an important point since there has been a tendency to link the status of Abu Musa and the Tunbs historically—mainly because, for the twentieth century at least, the power that has held the Tunbs has also held Abu Musa and vice-versa. Linking the status of the islands is currently the explicit policy of the UAE federal government. Yet, as mentioned above, the nineteenth-century histories of Abu Musa and the Tunbs were not one and the same.[46]

In the late-nineteenth/early-twentieth century, Britain actively supported the claims of its protégés to any territory, such as Abu Musa and the Tunbs, that was deemed to possess a strategic or commercial value that might attract the attention of imperial rivals such as Germany, Russia and France. Following the Great War of 1914-18, the strategic threats to Britain's omnipotent position in Gulf waters had all but disappeared. Gone were the Ottoman Empire and Imperial Russia, while Germany was hardly in a position to reassert itself in the region. In this era before oil Britain sought to preserve the status quo and to do so needed only to come to an accommodation with Persia. Amongst the chief bones of contention that prevented Britain from concluding a broad package of agreements with Persia during the 1920s and 1930s on outstanding Gulf issues was the latter state's claim to Abu Musa and the Tunbs.

Various territorial trade-offs were debated during the period of the intermittent though ultimately unsuccessful Anglo-Persian general treaty negotiations. On several occasions during the 1920s and 1930s the Iranian Foreign Ministry offered to drop its claim to Bahrain if Britain would recognize its sovereignty over Abu Musa and the Tunbs. On other occasions Britain toyed with the idea of leasing Abu Musa and/or the Tunbs to Persia in a bid to move along the stalled general treaty negotiations. Sharjah steadfastly resisted any suggestions that Abu Musa should form part of these plans, however. Informally, Persia, or at least its minister of court, Abd al-Hussein Taimurtash, forwarded its own scheme, whereby Tehran would renounce its claim to Abu Musa in return for Ras al-Khaimah's dropping its claims to and administration of the Tunbs. Taimurtash had first raised such a possibility in 1930. Such speculation would survive his death three years later, for an individual within the Iranian Foreign Ministry added— again, informally—in 1935 that Iran would not only be prepared to drop its claim to Abu Musa, but would consider the possibility of extending leasehold rights over the Tunbs to Ras al-Khaimah—provided that these were first formally recognized as pieces of Iranian territory.[47] None of these potential trade-offs, though evidently much discussed, ever saw the light of day.

Britain tried unavailingly to refloat proposals for territorial trade-offs during the mid-1950s. Securing access to offshore oil reserves through the delimitation of maritime concession zones was obviously complicated by disputes over the sovereignty of islands, especially in those cases, such as Abu Musa and the Tunbs, where the features in question were located centrally in Persian Gulf waters. In 1955 Britain tried to sponsor an agreement that would have seen Sharjah and Ras al-Khaimah formally recognize Iranian sovereignty over Sirri (not, in truth, much of a concession since Persian occupation of the feature had earlier been accepted by Britain), Iran recognize Sharjah's ownership of Abu Musa and Ras al-Khaimah sell the Tunbs to Iran. Though the Trucial Coast rulers were apparently ready to agree to such a scheme, Iran proved unwilling to sacrifice its claims to Abu Musa. That at least is the British version of events.[48]

The Iranian Actions of 1971. The Abu Musa/Tunbs dispute burst into international prominence on the last day of November 1971, when Iran stationed troops on Abu Musa by prior agreement with Sharjah, but took the Tunbs by force as Britain vacated Gulf waters. Iran took these actions on the day before Britain terminated its treaty relations with the rulers of the southern Gulf littoral on December 1, 1971. On December 2, the federation of the United Arab Emirates was officially proclaimed. The Iranian action provoked sufficient anger in the Arab world for the issue to be brought before the United Nations Security Council.

On November 29, 1971, the ruler of Sharjah had announced that he had arrived voluntarily, if reluctantly, at an agreement with Iran some six days earlier by which the administration of Abu Musa would henceforth be shared, yet the respective sovereign claims of each state/shaikhdom to the whole of the island would be maintained. The initiative to reach this agreement had been launched from Sharjah in the face of the overt Iranian threat that the island would be taken forcibly. No such arrangements had been made with respect to the (uninhabited) Tunbs, with the result that the islands were captured by Iran on November 30, 1971. The ruler of Ras al-Khaimah had failed to accede to Iranian inducements for a peaceful transfer of sovereignty.

A protagonist in Iran's consultations with each of the Qasimi shaikhdoms in the period preceding the Iranian occupation has revealed the type of understanding that was in the cards for the Tunbs. It is clear that Ras al-Khaimah was given no option but to accede to Iranian demands for recognition of its full sovereignty over the two islands. Iran was apparently prepared to supply the shaikhdom with military and humanitarian support by way of compensation. Though the ruler of Ras al-Khaimah initially seemed disposed to accept Iran's compensatory offer of Western-built guns and armored vehicles plus an unspecified "humanitarian" component, he apparently later changed his mind, demanding a significant amount of money instead. Iran maintained that it could not possibly have entertained paying a huge amount of money for features that possessed no economic value.[49]

The value of the Tunbs and Abu Musa to Iran has, indeed, always lain in their strategic location. They are characterized as guarding the entrance to the Strait of Hormuz, and their control has traditionally been deemed vital by Iran for national security. In 1971 senior United States government officials appeared to accept this argument as new regional security arrangements were being drawn up to fill the vacuum left by Britain's withdrawal. Certainly, there were no great objections voiced in Washington, D.C. at the Iranian moves on the Lower Gulf islands.

Sir William Luce, British Resident in the Gulf during the mid-1960s, had been recalled to duty in 1970-71 to try, among other things, to arrive at some sort of understanding with Iran on the future status of Abu Musa and the Tunbs. Britain's hand was forced by the uncompromising if adroit attitude adopted by the shah at this time. He made it clear that Iran would not permit the existence of a federated Arab state on the southern Gulf littoral unless Iranian rights to Abu Musa and the Tunbs were admitted and satisfied. As such, the dispute over the Lower Gulf islands had, in the words of a former British diplomat in the area, assumed a "grossly disproportionate size."[50] There seemed to be little prospect of a formula that would retain Qasimi sovereignty over the islands, especially since Iran had by now officially recognized the desire of the population of Bahrain for independent statehood and dropped its historic claim to the archipelago. In a moment of understandable exasperation, as he perhaps realized that nothing was likely to preempt an Iranian move on Abu Musa and the Tunbs, Luce was reported to have commented, "The Iranians took Sirri in 1887 when we weren't looking—I sometimes wish they had taken the Tunbs and Abu Musa as well."[51]

As Britain's permanent representative at the United Nations would claim in the proceedings before the Security Council during December 1971, London had never been anything but honest about its inability to protect Abu Musa and the Tunbs against Iranian actions should no arrangements for their future administration have been made by the time Britain vacated Gulf waters. At the same forum, Britain stated formally that it was satisfied with the Iran-Sharjah Memorandum of Understanding. Perhaps this was a little surprising, given Britain's previous resolve to see Sharjah's claims to full sovereignty over the island substantiated and upheld. Yet surely this was a classic case of realpolitik. Iran had already been entrusted with the role of "Gulf policeman" (along with Saudi Arabia) in the so-called twin pillar policy for regional security following Britain's withdrawal from the Gulf.

The essentially pragmatic 1971 Iran-Sharjah MOU was most notable for the way in which it accommodated the claims of both Sharjah and Iran to Abu Musa. Its first clause read as follows: "Neither Iran nor Sharjah will give up its claim to Abu Musa nor recognize the other's claim."[52] By this agreement Iranian forces positioned themselves in key strategic areas (basically the range of small hills in the north of the island) defined on a map attached to the text of the Memorandum of Understanding. Within this designated area Iran possessed full jurisdiction, but outside it fell to Sharjah as before. Iran and Sharjah each recognized a territorial sea for the island with a breadth of 12 nautical miles in which nationals of both parties would enjoy equal fishing rights. The Buttes Oil Company would continue to exploit hydrocarbon reserves under the conditions specified in its concession agreement with the ruler of Sharjah—for as long as these were acceptable to Iran. Revenue from the field would be shared on an equal basis. Lastly, Iran was to give Sharjah £1.5 million annually in aid until such time as its oil revenue reached £3 million a year, which would take around three years.

Given the previous impasse in this dispute, an arrangement that allowed for the flying of each party's flag seemed, on the face of it, a fairly logical and sustainable compromise. The 1971 MOU withstood several challenges in the following two decades. In declaring war against Iran during September 1980, Iraqi president Saddam Hussein announced his intention to restore Abu Musa and the Tunbs to the Arab homeland.[53] During 1987 the regime for Abu Musa set up by the 1971 MOU was seriously infringed upon with an Iranian move into the southern, Sharjah-administered part of the island at the time of an attempted palace coup in Sharjah. By the time Iran realized that the attempt had been aborted, the Iranian military on the island had already lowered the Sharjah flag. They then hurriedly rehoisted it and returned to their allotted positions.

Iranian patrols into the south of the island had become an increasingly regular feature since 1983.

Until the spring of 1992 the status of the Abu Musa dispute seemed very similar to that of the Shatt al-Arab dispute: all was quiet though far from being finally settled, inasmuch as the 1971 MOU had completely ducked the question of sovereignty. Sharjah has not even felt obliged to construct its own deep-water landing facilities on the island, and it continues to use the Iranian landing facilities.

The Incidents of 1992 and the Resurrection of the Dispute. Perhaps the visit during February 1992 of Iranian President Rafsanjani to Abu Musa and other Lower Gulf islands signalled a change in Iranian policy. Yet well before this time and increasingly during the course of the 1980-88 Iran-Iraq War, Iran had expressed misgivings about the security situation of Abu Musa, justifying its own encroachments on the island since 1983 by pointing to the increasing number of visits made by non-Sharjah nationals. In January 1992 Iran requested that Sharjah agree to the Tehran government's issuing security passes to non-nationals visiting the island from the southern Gulf littoral.[54]

Then came the well-publicized incidents of April and August 1992, which seemed to suggest that the MOU was unworkable or, at best, in need of renegotiation. In April the Iranian authorities prevented a group of non-national employees of the emirate of Sharjah (a group comprised of Pakistani, Indian and Filipino laborers and technicians and, also, non-UAE—principally Egyptian-Arab teachers) from entering the Sharjah-administered part of the island. The dispute intensified with reports on August 24, 1992 that Iran had refused entry to a large party of over 100 third-party nationals. These were mainly Egyptian teachers and their families, many of whom had originally been denied entry to Abu Musa back in April. Iran had backed down on the first occasion, following strong representations from the UAE Federal Foreign Ministry, ostensibly so that pupils on the island could complete their exams in May-June 1992. It had apparently hinted, however, that the UAE and Iran would need to make strides in addressing the "security problem" before the beginning of the next academic year in September 1992. Attempts to resolve the resurrected dispute over Abu Musa through bilateral negotiations in the autumn of 1992 soon broke down when the UAE delegation demanded at the outset that Iran immediately end its military occupation of the Tunb islands.[55]

Following the August 1992 incident, Iran had been forced to endure a barrage of criticism from a hostile Arab media. It reacted at two levels.

On the one hand and perhaps slightly defensively, the Iranian government admitted some responsibility for the incidents on Abu Musa. Foreign Minister Velayati ascribed them to the misjudgement of "junior Iranian officials."[56] These comments followed the dispatch during September of an investigation team from the Iranian Foreign Ministry to the island. As a result of their recommendations, Iran's local naval commander was apparently sacked. On another level, Iran tended to adopt a "crisis, what crisis?" line on the whole affair.[57] Especially following the breakdown of negotiations in Abu Dhabi, the Iranian government was keen to make clear that it still felt fully committed to the 1971 MOU.

Tensions between Tehran and the Arab states of the Lower Gulf were rekindled, at least in a verbal sense, in December 1992 due to the closing statement of the thirteenth GCC summit in Abu Dhabi, which called upon "the Islamic Republic of Iran to cancel and abolish measures taken on Abu Musa island and to terminate its occupation of the Greater and Lesser Tunb islands, which belong to the UAE." According to the BBC, the Supreme Council also affirmed "its complete solidarity and absolute support for the UAE's position and [supported] all the peaceful measures and means it [the UAE] deems appropriate to regain its sovereignty over the three islands in accordance with international legitimacy and the principle of collective security."[58] Certainly, if these uncompromising words were taken at face value, the UAE's continued support for the 1971 MOU on Abu Musa seemed open to serious doubt. The statement provoked defiance from Tehran, with Rafsanjani underlining in no uncertain terms that Iran's presence on Abu Musa and the Tunbs was permanent and non-negotiable: "Iran is surely stronger than the likes of you . . . to reach these islands one has to cross a sea of blood . . . We consider this claim as totally invalid."[59]

The war of words continues to the present. Yet, at the local level, life returned to something approaching normal relatively quickly on Abu Musa. Quite soon after the incidents of 1992, the ferry was running to the island as normal from Sharjah. The oilsharing arrangements for Abu Musa had never been interrupted, even by the events of April and August 1992. Similarly, the Egyptian teachers at the heart of the August 1992 incident experienced no difficulties in returning for the start of the school year in 1993.

It would be a clear overstatement, however, to say that the MOU is fully operational at the local level. Sharqawis and their employees have experienced far more aggravation from Iranian officials than they did before 1992—spot-checks of documents are far more stringent and frequent than they were previously. There are reports that the Iranian military on

Abu Musa has been far more bullish in patrolling the divide through the island and that encroachments into the Sharjah-administered south continue unabated. The question of issuing security passes—the catalyst of the 1992 incidents—has still to be resolved.

Since the Abu Dhabi summit, the dispute has remained locked in the same war of words. Repeat pledges made by the GCC to employ all peaceful means to restore UAE sovereignty over Abu Musa and the Tunbs have been met with Iran's defiant words about crossing a sea of blood. There seems little reason to believe that the islands dispute will not continue to be the focus of Arab-Iranian rivalry in the Gulf for some time to come. Because of the geography of the dispute, with the waters of the Lower Gulf separating the disputing parties, there is also an element of safety in channeling rivalries in this manner. Assuming that there is no likelihood of the UAE's attempting to regain control of the islands by force, and presuming that Iran does not violate the terms of the 1971 MOU in a reckless manner, the dispute is likely to remain a war of words.

The United States has now taken the unusual step of departing from its avowed position of neutrality in the territorial disputes of the region. Then-Secretary of State Warren Christopher added his name to a joint communiqué issued by the foreign ministers of the GCC countries after a meeting in Jeddah on March 12, 1995. This read as follows:

> The ministers expressed their deep appreciation of the UAE's efforts to peacefully resolve the issue of the Iranian occupation of the three islands—the Greater Tunb, the Lesser Tunb and Abu Musa, which belong to the UAE. The ministers urged the Islamic Republic of Iran to respond positively to the initiative of the UAE and to agree to refer this dispute to the ICJ.[60]

The United States' overt support for the position of the UAE in the islands dispute followed its condemnation of Iran only a month earlier for having significantly remilitarized the northern half of Abu Musa island, and the Lower Gulf more generally. Chief among American concerns were the large number of Iranian ground forces periodically stationed on the island and the movement by the Iranian military of air-defense capabilities to Abu Musa and other Lower Gulf islands.[61] There can be little doubt that Iran has strengthened its military presence on Abu Musa considerably since 1995. The northern half of the island was used as the base for many Iranian military exercises in Gulf waters. Iran's mobilization has, of course, altered the status quo on Abu Musa. Whether it has contravened the express terms of the MOU must be open to considerably more doubt. Only by demonstrating that the territorial reality introduced by the MOU has been deliberately altered to its own permanent advantage by Iran could one claim that more than the spirit of the agreement has been broken. Despite frequent claims to the contrary, there is simply no evidence that Iran has brought areas of the southern, Sharjah-administered part of Abu Musa under its aegis.

Yet Iran's expansion of its unconventional arms, mine-warfare and submarine capabilities in recent years, its development of long-range missiles and air defense are, understandably, viewed nervously in the emirates of the southern Gulf littoral.[62] There has also been an escalation of war games in the Lower Gulf, with Abu Musa the center of many directed from Tehran. No doubt supporters of America's dual-containment policy in the region exaggerate the threat these developments—along with the remilitarization of Abu Musa—pose to the economically vital shipping lanes that pass through the Lower Gulf. Even the old, established but technologically defunct argument about Iran's ability to block the Strait of Hormuz has resurfaced in some quarters. The arrival on a more or less permanent basis in Bahrain of the United States' Fifth Fleet is a worrying prospect for Iran in the late 1990s. There always remains the distant danger that Abu Musa, the subject of a stalemated territorial dispute, might become the scene of an Iranian-American naval clash, over which the UAE would exert very little control.

A Way Out of the Stalemate? The stalemated nature of the dispute over the islands combined with the sobering prospect of the increasing militarization of the Lower Gulf had, by 1995, led to hints of frustration on the part of various emirates within the UAE federation. Privately, some prominent individuals began to bemoan a lack of strategy in the federal government's policy toward the islands and to question whether it was ultimately directed toward reaching a settlement with Iran. It is probably fair to say that Sharjah was not wholly satisfied with the conduct of the federal foreign ministry during the negotiations of autumn 1992. In February 1995, Crown Prince Muhammad of Dubai—admittedly, a man respected for his independent views—expressed the opinion that recent tensions over the islands had been "fabricated."[63]

In 1995, the GCC (or, more properly, its member states), moved to bring its policy toward the islands dispute more in line with directives issued at the December 1994 Manama summit for the resolution of territorial disputes between member states. Previously, they had been somewhat contradictory. Previous calls (from 1993 onwards) from the GCC for Iran to agree to the islands case being submitted immediately to the ICJ (International Court of Justice) for a ruling had contrasted rather starkly with its marked reticence to condone that same institution's current treatment of Bahrain-Qatar maritime disputes. So, in the summer of 1995, Iran and the UAE were urged to talk first and then—with the obvious expectation that such bilateral consultations would prove fruitless—refer the Lower Gulf islands dispute to the ICJ.[64] It was still, however, something of a surprise when bilateral talks recommenced after a three-year gap in Qatar during November 1995. As was the case back in 1992, it soon became apparent that a willingness to talk did not equate to a willingness to make the difficult compromises that would free the dispute from its deadlocked state. Unfortunately, the talks broke down every bit as quickly as they had during the autumn of 1992.

In its meeting with Iran, the UAE articulated and defended an agenda already published by the UAE government. This agenda was thoroughly consistent with officially-stated positions of the GCC throughout 1995. As had been the case back in the shortlived and unsuccessful negotiations of autumn 1992, the first item on the UAE agenda was a demand that Iran end its military occupation of the Tunb islands. Almost certainly—as was probably the case in the autumn of 1992—the talks broke down here. According to various Reuters reports, the UAE agenda for proposed talks was as follows:

  i. Iran terminates its military occupation of the Tunb islands;
  ii. Iran guarantees to abide by the express provisions of the 1971 Iran-Sharjah Memorandum of Understanding on Abu Musa and to cancel any measures which have violated or are violating this agreement;
  iii. the issue of sovereignty of Abu Musa should be settled;
  iv. the disputes should be referred to external arbitration should bilateral negotiations not produce a settlement within a specified time period.

It seems unlikely that Iran turned up with an agenda of its own. At least none was published. The Iranian government merely stated that it was going to bring up a few points of its own at the meeting.

In the wake of mutual recriminations over the breakdown of negotiations, the situation with respect to the dispute soon reverted to the position that had prevailed prior to the recommencement of the failed bilateral negotiations. That is to say that, compared to the late 1994/early 1995 period, some of the heat had been taken out of the dispute. The UAE and Iran recognize the need to talk but remain unprepared to relax their differing and opposing stands toward the islands question.

Early 1996 witnessed the most neutral commentary to date by Saudi Arabia on the Abu Musa and Tunbs dispute since its resurrection. In January the Riyadh government commented that Iran had valid claims of its own to the islands, and that these ought to be adjudicated by a submission of the case to the ICJ. At around the same time, members of the UAE negotiating team present at the 1995 shortlived talks privately blamed their failure as much on the conduct of the Qatari government as Iranian intransigence.[65] There can be little doubt, however, that the federal government in Abu Dhabi has effectively used Iran's regional and international isolation during recent years to internationalize the islands dispute and win support for its own territorial claims.

Successfully recruiting regional and international support for the UAE's claims has not, however, materially advanced the prospects of Abu Musa and the Tunbs' ever returning to UAE sovereignty. The UAE's diplomatic successes have only entrenched much more deeply the islands question as a national issue in Iran. The imprint of the Abu Musa/Tunbs dispute upon Iranian public opinion should not be underestimated. In the minds of most Iranians, these islands were taken by Britain in the nineteenth century and "rightfully" returned to Iran on Britain's departure from Gulf waters in 1971. For much of the past few years, they have assumed a far greater importance to the average citizen than other foreign-policy concerns such as the future of Palestine and relations with Iraq.[66] The islands question has become inextricably linked to regime legitimacy in Tehran. Logic dictates that a regionally isolated and defensive Iran simply cannot entertain requests from a small state such as the UAE that "Iranian" territory be handed over.[67] Iran continues to dig its heels in, on Abu Musa especially. In late 1996 there were reports that it was taking the sort of largely symbolic measures that states often resort to when trying to underline their control of a feature whose sovereignty is disputed. There are apparently plans for a university on the Iranian half of Abu Musa, while plans are in place to stage an international football match there.

Given the recent and very real progress made in the Arabian peninsula toward finalizing the political map, territorial arrangements that fall short of a final settlement of sovereignty questions are currently not in favor. Yet, the recent history of the Abu Musa dispute surely suggests that less-than-sovereign territorial arrangements have their place.[68] Whether or not the Iran-Sharjah MOU will prove workable in coming decades is open to question. However, it is difficult to conceive of an arrangement that improves upon the MOU's pragmatic accommodation of rival claims to the island. It is similarly difficult to envisage Iran ever relaxing its present hold on the Tunbs.

The Khafus Incident on the Saudi-Qatar Border

The rapid momentum toward finalizing the Arabian territorial framework received a severe jolt from an unexpected quarter in autumn 1992. An incident along the eastern stretch of the undemarcated though delimited Saudi-Qatar land boundary at the border post of Khafus resulted in three fatalities (two Qatari and one Saudi). At the time, the incident constituted the gravest internal challenge to have ever confronted the cohesion of the GCC. This land boundary had been settled in 1965, and there had been no indication since then that its alignment was a possible cause of dispute: maps and atlases produced in Doha and Riyadh showed an identical course for the territorial limit. It soon became clear that the two states were using the boundary to symbolize their political differences.

Following a brief suspension of diplomatic relations, Qatar and Saudi Arabia took the fairly obvious step of agreeing to demarcate the boundary at the end of 1992, following the mediating efforts of Egyptian president Hosni Mubarak. Yet, by the spring of 1996 the border remained undemarcated and continued to symbolize the fractious nature of Saudi-Qatari relations.[69] In the summer of 1996 Saudi Arabia and Qatar finally agreed to patch up their differences over the boundary but, by the end of 1996, there was still no confirmation that pillars had been lain down to make it a tangible feature. The problem has essentially been political, not territorial. Again, as with the Iran-UAE dispute over the islands, a basic consideration of geographical scale is involved here. Put crudely, large states are generally disinclined to admit the existence of problems with smaller neighbors.[70]

CONCLUDING REMARKS

Great progress has been made during the 1990s toward finalizing the political map of Arabia, and the number of minor disputes over the limits of state territory in 1997 is dramatically reduced from that obtaining only a decade ago. The speed with which the glass of settled Arabian territorial limits has been filled (from half to nine-tenths full) has been impressive, and the efforts of the states concerned are to be applauded. This process has been relatively painless, and no insuperable political obstacles have stood in its way. A clear and pragmatic motivation has fueled the recent rush to finalize the territorial framework—recognition of the need for final and precise boundary delimitations so that oil exploration and development might proceed smoothly and securely in border areas. GCC policy toward territorial questions to date has been rather fragmented and, above all, reactive. Nevertheless, as a result of recent regional crises, acknowledgement of the pragmatic incentive to settle and the tendency to pander to the territorial concerns of member states hosting GCC summits, a policy and a body of legislation has evolved that works for the maintenance of the current territorial framework and that advocates bilateral means to settle any residual disputes. For the present, the member states of the GCC probably reckon that they have done all that is possible to enact such a policy.

It is doubtful as to whether defense of national territory has become a politicized issue for the populace, except in those regional states where nationalist sentiment is highly developed. Though the UAE government has successfully elicited widespread regional and international support for its claims to the Lower Gulf islands, the issue has not become an increasing preoccupation of the average person on the street, as it has in Tehran. If anything, the development of a territorial consciousness among the populations of Iran and Iraq augurs negatively for the future conduct of the major disputes of the region. It severely restricts the Iranian government's room for any compromise that might free the Abu Musa/Tunbs dispute from its current deadlocked war of words. It must also hold implications for future Iraqi claims to Kuwait in the medium to long term, regardless of who wields power in Baghdad.

Whatever the explanation, the modern Middle Eastern state does seem more preoccupied than ever with territorial definition and the defense of national territory. The continuation of territorial arrangements, such as the Iran-Sharjah MOU, that fall short of a final settlement of sovereign rights, goes against the grain of finalizing precise limits to territory. Yet the institution of this arrangement and other measures taken in the past, such as the formation of neutral zones or joint-development areas between states, have generally been pragmatic responses to the peculiarities of any one territorial equation. Historically, the institution of non-state territory or the creation of zones in border regions, in which neighboring states have agreed to share or diminish their effective sovereignty, has often had beneficial political and economic effects in this region.[71] Perhaps Bahrain and

Qatar might have explored these options more fully in previous stages of their maritime disputes. The current climate is not conducive to the institution of such features, however.

Yet the major disputes of the region are really no closer to settlement in a real sense—that is, arriving at an irreversible position at which they no longer pose a threat to regional stability—than they ever were. If filling the glass of settled Arabian/Gulf boundary delimitations to nine-tenths has been reasonably painless, filling the last tenth remains a distant and problematic prospect. The absence of a Gulf-wide forum in which grievances (including territorial disputes) can be aired has resulted in the regional isolation of Iran. It is probably no coincidence that Iran's two main territorial disputes with its Arab neighbors—over the Shatt al-Arab and the Tunbs/Abu Musa—remain short of being finally settled, since there has been no opportunity for consultation on a region-wide basis.

The Khafus incident on the Saudi-Qatar border neatly illustrated Ancel's assertion that there are no problems of boundaries, only problems of nations. The roots of the problem seemed to be clearly political, for there had previously been no apparent problems with the alignment of the boundary. The same can probably not be said of the other disputes treated in this paper, disputes that have existed for most of this century and that have traditionally proved resistant—until very modern times, in the case of Iraq/Kuwait—to all proposals for their final settlement. Bahrain-Qatar disputes are deeply entrenched and have proven intransigent historically, though at least the prospects for their resolution have improved dramatically with their reference, finally, for a ruling by the ICJ.

Abu Musa will no doubt continue to be the focus of Irano-Arab rivalry in the Gulf, at least until such time as Iraq is reintegrated into the fold and the Shatt al-Arab dispute next erupts with Iran. It seems doubtful that the pragmatic compromise of 1971 for its administration can be improved upon, given political realities in the Lower Gulf. It would be a positive step, however, if the two sides could unlock the dispute from the current stalemated and rather predictable war of words. Notwithstanding the current dormant state of the Shatt dispute and the United Nations' final settlement of the historically explosive Iraq-Kuwait border question, Iraq's historical discomfort over access to the sea (or what it perceives as the lack of it) may in the medium to long term threaten the territorial stability of the northern Gulf. Ultimately it is up to all of the littoral states of the Gulf to cooperate closely enough to ensure that this does not happen. The integrated, or at least coordinated, economic development of the northern

Gulf seems to offer the best hope of future stability and the only probable means by which future Iraqi governments would ultimately come to terms with their restricted access to Gulf waters.

Notes

1. This chapter makes no attempt to chart the evolution of Arabia's international boundaries from a historical point of view. Those wishing to do so should consult Richard Schofield, "Borders and territoriality in the Gulf and Arabian peninsula during the twentieth century," in Richard Schofield, ed., *Territorial foundations of the Gulf states.* (London: UCL Press, 1994) pp. 1-77 (for a summary); and John C. Wilkinson, *Arabia's Frontiers: The Story of Britain's Boundary-Drawing in the Desert*, (London: I.B. Tauris, 1991) for much greater detail still.

2. For the translated text of the Saudi-Yemeni Memorandum of Understanding of February 26, 1995, see, *BBC Summary of World Broadcasts* ME/2238 MED/15-16, February 27, 1995.

3. Richard Schofield, "Borders and territoriality" in Schofield, ed., *Territorial foundations of the Gulf states,* pp. 56-57.

4. *Foreign Broadcast Information Service: FBIS-NES-95-111* (June 9, 1995), p. 35.

5. *Foreign Broadcast Information Service: FBIS-NES-95-133* (July 12, 1995), p. 28.

6. For a brief historical background to this dispute see Richard Schofield, "Borders and territoriality" in Schofield, ed., *Territorial foundations of the Gulf states,* p. 43.

7. *Foreign Broadcast Information Service: FBIS-NES-95-102* (May 26, 1995), p. 26.

8. This treaty, concluded following the Saudi-Yemeni war of the late spring of 1934, was much more than a boundary treaty per se—in point of fact only three of its twenty-three articles dealt with territorial questions. Unusually for a treaty defining and regulating international boundaries, the instrument requires renewal every twenty lunar years.

9. As a result of the first-ever articulation of a cartographically depictable territorial claim along the indeterminate borderlands by a San'a government in the summer of 1996, this degree of overlap has practically doubled.

10. For a detailed background to and analysis of the Saudi-Yemen boundary question, see Richard Schofield, "The Last Missing Fence in the Desert: The Saudi-Yemen Boundary," in *Geopolitics and International Boundaries* 1, no. 3 (winter 1997), pp. 247-99.

11. Jacques Ancel, *Les Frontières* (Paris: Delagrave, 1938).

12. Iraq's international boundaries on the Gulf are a case in point. See Richard Schofield, *Kuwait and Iraq: Historical Claims and Territorial Disputes,* second edition (London: Royal Institute of International Affairs, 1993).

13. It has been suggested that this has been the historical experience of Iran and Iraq. See Kaiyin Homa Kaikobad, *The Shatt al-Arab Boundary Question: A Legal Reappraisal* (Oxford: The Clarendon Press, 1988), p. 70.

14. For more information see David Pike, "Cross-border hydrocarbon reserves," in Richard Schofield, ed., *Territorial foundations of the Gulf states,* pp. 187-99.

15. Schofield, *Kuwait and Iraq,* pp. 133-36, 184-85.

16. Current plans aim for an output from Shaibah of 350,000 to 600,000 barrels per day (b/d) by 1997 through the drilling of up to 225 wells. See Pike, p. 190.

17. Shahram Chubin and Charles Tripp, "Domestic Politics and Territorial Disputes in the Persian Gulf and Arabian Peninsula" in *Survival* 35, no. 4 (winter 1993-1994), pp. 3-27.

18. Richard Schofield, *Unfinished Business: Iran, the UAE, Abu Musa and the Tunbs* (London: Royal Institute of International Affairs, forthcoming 1997), chapter five.

19. Graham Fuller, *The "Center of the Universe": The Geopolitics of Iran* (Boulder: Westview Press, 1991), p. 60.

20. Richard Schofield, *Evolution of the Shatt al-Arab Boundary Dispute* (Wisbech: Cambridgeshire, UK: Menas Press, 1986).

21. See John C. Wilkinson, *Arabia's Frontiers.* Also, Schofield, "Borders and Territoriality . . ." in Schofield, ed., *Territorial Foundations . . .* (1994).

22. For more detail see Schofield, "Boundaries, Territorial Disputes and the GCC States" in David Long and Joseph Moynihan, eds., *Gulf Security in the Twenty-First Century* (Abu Dhabi: The Emirates Center for Strategic Studies and Research, forthcoming 1997).

23. Ibid.

24. Wilkinson, *Arabia's Frontiers,* 1991, p. xi.

25. Schofield, "Borders and territoriality . . ." in Schofield, ed., *Territorial foundations of the Gulf states,* p. 4.

26. Richard Schofield, "The Kuwaiti islands of Warbah and Bubiyan, and Iraqi access to the Gulf" in Schofield, ed., *Territorial foundations of the Gulf states,* pp. 153-75.

27. Richard N. Schofield, "The Historical Problem of Iraqi Access to the Persian Gulf: The Interrelationships of Territorial Disputes with Iran and Kuwait, 1938-1990," in Clive H. Schofield and Richard N. Schofield, eds., *World Boundaries: The Middle East and North Africa* (London: Routledge, 1994), pp. 158-72.

28. For a comprehensive historical overview of the Iraq-Kuwait border dispute, see Schofield, *Kuwait and Iraq*; David H. Finnie, *Shifting Lines in the Sand: Kuwait's Elusive Frontier with Iraq* (Cambridge: Harvard University Press, 1992).

29. Its first two clauses read as follows:

  1. The Republic of Iraq recognises the State of Kuwait's sovereignty, territorial integrity and political independence (Arabic: *ta'tarif jumhuriyat al-iraq bisiyadat dawlat al-kuwait was salamataha al-iqlimiyah wa istiqlalaha al-siyasi*).

  2. In compliance with UN Security Council Resolution 833 of 1993, the Republic of Iraq recognises the international borders between the Republic of Iraq and the State of Kuwait, as demarcated by the UN Iraq-Kuwait Boundary Demarcation Commission, formed under paragraph 3 of Resolution 687 of 1991, and respects the inviolability of the above borders. Source: *BBC Summary of World Broadcasts:* The Middle East: Iraq's recognition of Kuwait: "RCC Decree Recognises Kuwaiti Sovereignty and Territorial Integrity," ME/2150, MED/1 (November 11, 1994).

30. There can be little doubt that UNIKBDC's 1992 award for the land boundary is what Britain had meant to introduce with its announcement of the vaguely described border in identical, unchanging terms on various occasions in the early part of this century: as the outer limit of Kuwaiti authority when concluding the unratified Anglo-Ottoman settlement of July 1913; the Cox-More exchange of notes of April 1923; and the Iraqi-Kuwaiti exchange of notes in the summer of 1932. In the words of someone close to the operations of UNIKBDC during the 1991-93 period, UNIKBDC's demarcation decision was effectively a "refinement" of Britain's earlier demarcation proposal of 1951, which had stood for nearly forty years as the most detailed existing interpretation of the vaguely defined de jure Iraq-Kuwait boundary, even though it was not capable of being mapped in detail.

31. For a detailed account of UNIKBDC's operations between 1991 and 1993, and of Iraq's reactions to them, see chapter seven ("The United Nations and its 'Final' Settlement of the Kuwait-Iraq Boundary") of Schofield, *Kuwait and Iraq*, 1993, pp. 150-98.

32. The precise extent to which Iraq encroached over the de jure border during this period has not been publicized by the government of Kuwait or by the United Nations.

33. By the end of September 1990, almost two months after the Iraqi invasion of Kuwait, European contractors finished deepening Umm Qasr's approach channels along the Khawr Shetana and the Khawr Abdallah to a new depth varying between 12.5 and 13.2 meters.

34. The old colonial definition of the boundary, UNIKBDC's delimitation formula, vaguely described a land boundary but did not cover the water boundary along the Khawr Shetana and the Khawr Abdallah.

35. For a detailed review of the historical background to Bahrain-Qatar maritime disputes and the curious saga over the status of the western Qatari settlement of Zubara, please see Richard Schofield, "Borders and Territoriality . . ." in Schofield, ed., *Territorial foundations of the Gulf states,* pp. 47-51. For a detailed review of developments through early 1996, see Richard Schofield, "Boundaries, Territorial Disputes and the GCC States," in David Long and Joseph Moynihan, eds., *Gulf Security in the Twenty-first Century* (Abu Dhabi: The Emirates Center for Strategic Studies and Research, forthcoming 1997).

36. It also observed, however, that the case as presented by Qatar had been less than complete, principally because it made inadequate mention of Bahrain's "historic interest" in Zubara. The two states were given five months to agree upon either joint or separate submissions of their respective cases. Three meetings produced no concurrence on a joint presentation, with the result that Qatar, alone, presented its articulation of the case to be adjudicated by the ICJ in a submission of late November 1994. The ICJ announced during mid-February 1995 that this would be the basis upon which the case would proceed, satisfied as it was that Qatar had enumerated all points of concern to Bahrain in its own articulation of the case.

37. "Round one to Doha" in *Middle East International,* March 3, 1995, pp. 14-15.

38. Richard Schofield, *Unfinished Business* (London: RIIA, forthcoming), chapters one and two.

39. Ibid.

40. Extensive selections from the British archives relating to the evolution of the Persian/Iranian-Qasimi dispute over the status and sovereignty of Abu Musa and the Tunbs are to be found in Patricia Toye, ed., *Arabian Geopolitics 2:*

The Lower Gulf Islands (Farnham Common, Buckinghamshire, UK: Archive Editions, 1993).

41. In the early part of the nineteenth century at least, British India was frustrated by the vague and prepossessing nature of the Persian claim. Elphinstone had been infuriated when confronted with it at the turn of the 1820s as British India tried to defend the Al Bu Said's rights to Qeshm island. He noted (unfairly in this instance) that the Persian claim to this island was based "solely on the argument that all the islands in the Gulf had once been Persian and they still were, regardless of what had happened over the centuries"— paraphrased in J.B. Kelly, *Britain and the Persian Gulf, 1795-1880* (Oxford: Oxford University Press, 1968), p. 185.

42. Schofield, *Unfinished Business* (forthcoming), chapter two.

43. Ibid.

44. Following the expulsion of the Qawasim from southern Persia in 1887, Britain developed the following, rather bizarre, explanation of the way in which the northern wing of the Qasimi federation had administered Sirri and possibly, by extension, Greater Tunb. They had governed Lingeh in their capacity as Persian officials but had maintained contacts with the Lower Gulf islands in their capacity as members of the Qawasim federation, answerable ultimately to their stronger southern counterparts in Ras al-Khaimah.

45. Schofield, *Unfinished Business* (forthcoming), chapter two.

46. India Office memorandum on the "Status of the islands of Tamb, Little Tamb, Abu Musa and Sirri" by J.G. Laithwaite, August 24, 1928. *India Office Library and Records, Political and Secret Files, L/P46S/18/B397.*

47. Schofield, "Borders and territoriality . . ." in Schofield, ed., *Territorial foundations of the Gulf states*, pp. 37-38.

48. Ibid., p. 38.

49. Ibid., pp. 36, 39.

50. Glen Balfour-Paul, *The End of Empire in the Middle East: Britain's Relinquishment of Power in Her Last Three Arab Dependencies* (Cambridge: Cambridge University Press, 1991), p. 127.

51. Schofield, *Unfinished Business* (forthcoming), chapter four.

52. Arab Research Centre, *Round Table Discussion on the Dispute Over the Gulf islands* (London: Arab Research Centre, 1993), p. 14.

53. Almost a year earlier, during November 1979, the Iraqi ambassador to Lebanon had called for Iran's evacuation of Abu Musa and the Tunbs. *BBC Summary of World Broadcasts:* The Middle East (November 2, 1979).

54. Sharjah refused, even though the request was unexceptional in the realm of contemporary Gulf affairs, on the basis that this might be the thin end of the wedge: requests for security passes might soon be followed by requests for visas, etc.

55. There remains some confusion about what actually happened in these negotiations. Informal accounts from various quarters in Sharjah sometimes contradict the official record released by the federal government in Abu Dhabi. This may demonstrate that the emirate of Sharjah was not entirely satisfied with Abu Dhabi's conduct in the short-lived and unsuccessful negotiations.

56. *Iran Focus* (November 1992), p. 2.

57. Nowhere was this illustrated better than in the following witty remark from Abbas Maleki, Iran's deputy foreign minister for research and education: "The volume of press coverage on Abu Musa is bigger than the island itself." Quoted in *Iran Focus* (November 1992), p. 2.

58. *BBC Summary of World Broadcasts:* the Middle East ME/1573/A/7 (December 29, 1992).

59. *Middle East Economic Survey (MEES),* (January 11, 1993), p. C3.

60. "Secretary-General Reads GCC Statement," in *Foreign Broadcast Information Service (FBIS-NES*-95-048), Daily Report on the Near East and South Asia, March 13, 1995, pp. 17-18.

61. See comments of General Binford Peay, Commander of U.S. Forces in the Middle East, to the Senate Armed Forces Committee in Washington D.C. as reported by Reuters (February 15, 1995).

62. Anthony Cordesman, "Defence: Spending Priorities," a paper presented to "Timewatch GCC: Economic Restructuring and Business Prospects," a conference organized by the Royal Institute of International Affairs, Queen Elizabeth II Conference Centre, London, November 15, 1995.

63. *Al-Hayat* (London), February 11, 1995, p. 8.

64. This new policy was articulated formally at the close of a meeting of foreign ministers of states signatory to the 1991 Damascus Declaration in July 1995: "The ministers renewed their support and backing to the UAE's sovereignty over its three islands, and urged Iran to hold direct talks with the UAE on the

status of these islands at the earliest opportunity. Meanwhile, they backed the UAE's call for referring the issue to the International Court of Justice if no agreement is reached through dialogue." Foreign Broadcast Information Service: *FBIS-NES*-95-131 (July 10, 1995), p. 4.

65. Confidential source.

66. Interview in New York with Mahmood Sariolgholam, Professor of International Relations, National University of Iran, Tehran, November 29, 1995.

67. Ibid.

68. For a persuasive articulation of this argument on a regionwide basis see Gerald Blake, "Shared zones as a solution to problems of territorial sovereignty in the Gulf states" in Schofield, ed., *Territorial foundations of the Gulf states*, pp. 200-10.

69. In April 1996, the governments of Saudi Arabia and Qatar announced that they had finally reached agreement on a procedure to demarcate their common land boundaries.

70. See Richard Schofield, "Mending Gulf Fences" in *Middle East Insight* 12, no. 3 (March/April 1996), pp. 36-41. For greater detail on this dispute see Schofield, "Borders and territoriality . . ." in Schofield, ed., *Territorial foundations of the Gulf states*, pp. 17-18 and Schofield "Boundaries, Territorial Disputes and the GCC States."

71. Gerald Blake, "Shared zones as a solution to problems of territorial sovereignty in the Gulf states" in Schofield, ed., *Territorial foundations of the Gulf states*, pp. 200-10.

CHAPTER 7

THE UPRISING IN
BAHRAIN: AN ASSESSMENT

Munira A. Fakhro

The uprising Bahrain has been experiencing since November 1994 has placed this island nation in the international limelight, and raises a number of questions: What are the reasons for this turmoil? Are there external forces manipulating the actions? What is the position of the Western powers (the United States and European Union)? What is the role of Gulf states, mainly Iran and Saudi Arabia? Further, does the Bahraini opposition outside Bahrain play a major role in the crisis; and is the current crisis a spillover from the Gulf War? Finally, should one expect a "domino effect" among the other Gulf states? This preliminary study will make an attempt to analyze this crisis within its historical perspective and within the context of current socioeconomic and political changes in the region.

HISTORICAL PERSPECTIVE

The current uprising in Bahrain is more or less a culmination of previous political movements that started at the beginning of this century, following the British-initiated administrative reforms of the 1920s. Since then, there has been a confrontation between those who were trying to push for modernity and a modern state, and those who were trying to maintain the status quo and who opposed any kind of reforms that would limit their power. One can divide the democratic movement into six phases:

1. Administrative Reforms (1919-29)

Bahrain has been ruled by the Al-Khalifa family since 1782. The British began contacts with the Al-Khalifa as early as 1820, when a "general treaty" was signed between Bahrain and the East India Company. Other peace and friendship treaties were signed with Great Britain in 1861, 1880 and 1892. These treaty arrangements strengthened the British role in Bahrain and secured Al-Khalifa rule there. At the same time these treaties allowed greater British involvement in the internal affairs of Bahrain. The British control of sea traffic in the Indian Ocean and the partial dependence of industry upon Eastern markets and raw materials made it necessary for Great Britain to tighten its grip on political affairs in Bahrain and to be more involved in local struggles for power. The opening of the Suez Canal in 1869 increased British involvement in the East and gave Britain an opportunity to expand its influence in that direction. In the same year that the Suez Canal was opened to international trade, the British directly intervened in Bahrain to end a family feud between Al-Khalifa claimants. After consultation with the prominent members of the family, they appointed Isa bin Ali ruler of Bahrain.[1]

In 1919, there was a shift in British policy beyond recommending reforms to the ruler and toward their more direct introduction. The British intended to introduce reforms through the civil courts, municipalities, schools and other modernizing institutions. Such reforms were opposed by many conservative groups, especially those of tribal origin led by the ruler's brother, who was considered a symbol of tribal power. However, in 1920 the British established a municipal council composed of eight members headed by the son of the ruler. Four members representing Bahrainis were appointed by the ruler, while the British Political Agent selected the other four to represent aliens residing in Bahrain.

In 1921, the British tried to eliminate tribal power by introducing administrative reforms. Such reforms became a major political issue in Bahrain and divided the people into two factions: the peasants and urban Shi'i, who suffered from the lack of standardized law, favored the reforms; the tribal groups and the merchants opposed them. The merchants feared the loss of privileges in trade, port facilities and custom duties, since many merchants paid very little or no tax on their imports. Local chieftains considered the reforms a threat to their influence. However, by 1929 the reforms were fully in operation.[2]

The administrative and bureaucratic reforms limited the power of tribal groups and the urban merchant class. In addition, the reforms reorganized public services and economic resources, including the pearl industry, palm cultivation, fish traps, imports and exports. The new specialized public services—which focused on the legal system, the state police and the various services and civil departments—later became specialized ministries after independence in 1971.[3]

In 1923 the customary council *(Al-Majlis al-Urfi)* was established and was given the right to deliberate on commercial matters and disputes including pearl fishing. Prior to that date, no form of administration existed; every shaikh ruled his estate and was responsible for the law and order within the estate, with help from a number of guards who collected taxes.

2. The Growth of Political Awareness (1938-52)

The pearl industry flourished in the 1920s, when the size of the Bahraini pearl diving fleet was at its peak and consisted of 2,000 sailing crafts *(dhows)*. In the 1930s, the pearl diving industry witnessed a rapid decline because of the world depression and the growth of the cultured pearl industry in Japan. The number of *dhows* dropped to 192 in 1945.

The discovery of oil in 1932 helped Bahrain to overcome its hardship. An oil refinery, the fourth largest in the world, was built, and it was supplied by crude oil from the Dammam fields in Saudi Arabia. Such economic developments diverted the local labor from traditional industries to the enterprise of oil. The labor force represented a spectrum of local ethnic, tribal and sectarian groups. Such groups had direct access to technical training and education, and this led to demands for better living standards. In 1938, these demands were manifested in widespread popular demonstrations and strikes, considered the first demonstrations in the Gulf area. However, the strikers were contained and quelled, and their leaders arrested. This political disturbance differed from previous ones in that both Islamic sects (Sunni and Shi'i) were unified in their demands. Furthermore, a new leadership emerged from students, merchants and Bahrain Petroleum Company (BAPCO) employees. This leadership introduced new ideas to the national movement. Beside supporting Shaikh Salman—the father of the present amir—as crown prince, they demanded the following:[4]

1. The establishment of a legislative body.
2. The introduction of reforms in the police department.
3. The coordination and classification of Bahraini laws.
4. The replacement of some of the judges.
5. Employment preference for Bahrainis in the Bahrain Petroleum Company.
6. The inclusion of three Sunni and three Shi'i in the legislative body.

These demands, however, never reached the authorities. Meanwhile the merchants withdrew, leaving the field to students and workers, who took charge and distributed leaflets that demanded reforms. The authorities arrested their leaders but later gave in to some of their demands.[5] In the early 1940s, during World War II, the forces of dissent were weakened due to the concentrated British military presence; the few educated individuals were absorbed by the British establishments that were operating in Bahrain during the war years.[6]

Soon after World War II ended, national movements began to gather strength and momentum. They were led by Bahrainis who identified their cause with pan-Arab movements in Cairo and Beirut, and expounded their views in the local press. During this period, many of the cultural and sporting clubs that had sprouted throughout the towns and villages were transformed into political centers in which debates and political views crystallized into movements.[7]

3. The Popular Uprising (1953-56)

After the introduction of bureaucratic and administrative reforms in the 1920s, labor protests and disturbances became frequent. The most prominent was the students' strike at Al-Hidaya School in Muharraq in 1928, followed by the pearl divers' demonstrations in 1932 and some Shi'i-led demonstrations in the same decade. These manifestations of dissent were arbitrary and lacked sophisticated organization and leadership. Khuri makes an exception in the case of the 1938 demonstrations, which led to the formation of a nucleus of the popular movement of the fifties.[8] Rumaihi reaffirms that the events of 1938 succeeded in proving the support for the popular movement and growth of political awareness among young students and workers.[9]

The beginning of the uprising was marked by sectarian clashes between the Sunni and Shi'i populations in 1953. Some leaders in the clubs and the press attempted to reconcile the two factions by calling a general assembly of leaders and dignitaries from both sides to end the dispute, but it was doomed to failure. This leadership, referred to as "the Network" by Khuri, held its meetings in secret and forged a new discipline and organization. It served to halt the civil clash, and then demand the reform rights. More than 100 candidates were selected to join the Network, and its members' names were kept secret in order to avoid government pressures. Their objective was to strengthen the bond between the Network and various popular sectors.

As the situation escalated, the Network called a popular meeting to declare the formation of a new political organization in opposition. One hundred twenty persons were selected to form a general assembly, which was to appoint a Supreme Executive Committee of eight members representing both sects. The committee immediately demanded the following of the ruler:[10]

1. The establishment of an elected parliament to be the sole voice of legitimacy in the country.
2. The introduction of civil and criminal law.
3. The formation of a court of appeal headed by judges with authoritative knowledge of the law.
4. The right to form trade unions and professional associations.

However, the ruler refused to receive the delegation that carried the petition, and announced his own counter-proposals to introduce some administrative reforms, such as the appointment of advisors in the law courts and the issuing of labor and penal laws. While the opposition grew in size and influence, the regime was making new preparations to quell the mutiny and restore the former situation. In 1955 the government established two appointed councils for health and education, with which the opposition refused to cooperate. Consequently, the opposition called upon the people to boycott the government councils and counteracted with the establishment of its own trade union, encouraging all to join. The opposition's main objective was to achieve formal recognition of a legitimate representative of the people, thus implicitly fulfilling the demands that called for a representative council and professional and trade unions.

The British were inclined to support the demands of the opposition for reform but did not favor the formation of a representative assembly and trade unions. This caused the leaders of the opposition to reduce their insistence on these two demands. According to Khuri, they thought it was possible to reconcile the principle of public representation with that of tribal dominance, insisting that a parliament and a labor union were meant not to weaken, but rather to strengthen the ruler's government.[11] Soon thereafter, splits within the ranks of the opposition became apparent, and this consequently hindered its stance. In 1956, Selwyn Lloyd, then the British foreign secretary, passed through Bahrain, and demonstrators pelted his motorcade with stones and smashed the windows of his car. Following this, the British authorities adopted a new more negative view toward the opposition. Since the government and the opposition could not agree between themselves, tensions grew between the two groups, and subsequently, members of opposition leadership were imprisoned for ten to fourteen years. Khuri comments on the failure of political dissent despite the arousal of a large sector of the Bahraini community to demand some political and civil rights. He reasons that the unity of demands and objectives does not automatically translate into a unity of organization and disciplined popular action. The opposition succeeded in mobilizing the masses toward political action, but failed to convert this mobilization into a permanent political organization.[12]

4. The Uprising of March 1965

The year 1965 witnessed a widespread strike at the Bahrain Petroleum Company (BAPCO) that escalated into a popular uprising, and culminated when students joined forces with the striking workers. The main demands of the strikers included the following: an end to all dismissals and the reinstatement of all those who were dismissed; a recognition of the right to organize labor unions; a lifting of the state of emergency, which had been in effect since 1956; a recognition of freedom of the press; the right to public assembly and freedom of expression and the dispensation of the services of British and other foreign employees of BAPCO.[13]

The uprising was nevertheless quelled within three months, and workers were forced to return to their jobs. Meanwhile, the strikers and other political leaders were detained, and some were exiled without trial. Despite the imposition of the state of emergency on the whole country, the government began to respond with extreme caution to some of the original demands. A press law was published, and a weekly newspaper was allowed to be established. Nakhleh comments that 1965 seemed like the beginning of a series of eruptions manifested in strikes and labor demands: 400 electricity workers struck in early 1968, demanding the establishment of labor unions, increased pay to compensate for rising living costs, and improvement in working conditions and safety regulations.

5. The First National Assembly (1972-75)

In his speech on the occasion of Bahrain's independence in 1971, the amir stressed the necessity of establishing a constitution. This gesture illustrated the determination of the regime to establish a legal foundation for its authority in addition to its rule by consensus and tradition. Bahrain proceeded in the steps of its northern neighbor Kuwait on the eve of its own independence in 1961, with some variations.[14] In 1972 the ruler called upon some of the well-known leaders and the representatives of the social clubs and societies to sound their views on the best ways to establish a constitution along the same lines as that of Kuwait. A constituent assembly was established in 1972 with twenty-two elected and eight appointed members. After many heated and elaborate discussions the assembly completed its task: a constitution for the country was established, and it called for a national assembly. The election of the assembly took place; it was made up of thirty male members over twenty-one years of age and no women. The government was represented by fourteen appointed ministers, including the prime minister. The cabinet members could cast a vote as equal members of the National Assembly. The percentage that voted was very high, reaching 80 percent to 90 percent of the total electorate.[15]

During the election campaign, three political groupings emerged: the people's bloc, the religious bloc and the grouping of the independent middle. An explanation follows of their social roots and ideological and political inclinations.[16]

a) *The People's Bloc.* This was comprised of the socialists, the communists and various Arab nationalist movements, including the Popular Front for the Liberation of the Gulf and Oman. This movement was distinguished for its struggle for labor and professional rights and the betterment of the general conditions of the working class. All of this bloc's candidates stood for the rights of labor to establish trade unions, earn higher wages and participate in decisionmaking. The power base of this bloc cut across sects and ethnicity.

b) *The Religious Bloc.* This was a rural Shi'i phenomenon made up of six members representing the rural constituencies. It was composed of two judges, one journalist, one religious leader *(mulla)* and two village school teachers. Their general academic background was a religious education at Najaf in Iraq. Their success was due to the support of religious upper echelons in their community. During the 1974 campaign, this bloc adopted a general manifesto supporting trade unions in order to attract votes. Some of their main slogans involved the banning of alcoholic beverages; the separation of the sexes in higher education and the exclusion of women from social clubs, mixed associations, and places of work.

c) *The Independent Middle.* Several of the National Assembly members belonged to the "Independent Middle." They were "independent" in the sense of not being bound politically to any bloc in parliament, and "middle" in the sense of fluctuating ideologically between the left (represented by the People's Bloc) and the right (represented by the Religious Bloc). The bloc fostered a neutral stance toward any known party or movement. They have been referred to as "service representatives," and came from the technocracy and the merchant community.

The first year of the National Assembly was an experimental period. The role of elected members was confined to raising peripheral questions rather than passing laws and policies. They were either engaged in discussion of economic projects introduced by the government or listening to complaints by the public regarding public services and general living conditions.

In 1974, the amir issued a new law granting government the power to arrest and imprison for three years, without interrogation or trial, any person posing a threat to the security of the state. Imprisonment was subject to further extension. This law was not presented to the National Assembly before it was issued, and this made most members take a hostile stand toward it. This matter became a *cause celebre* for many ordinary people, and was taken up by the local press, social and cultural clubs, and private groups. The more it was discussed, the weaker the government position became, thus strengthening the hand of the opposition. The Religious and the People's Bloc formed an alliance against this law, an act that worried the government. It appeared to the government that all attempts at compromise had failed. In August 1975, in accordance with the constitution of the country, the amir dissolved the parliament.

In addition to the previous reason, there are three important factors that could have contributed to the dissolution of the National Assembly:

1. All land owned by the state was at the disposal of the amir to grant to whomever he favored. The People's Bloc presented a bill to withdraw such a privilege and to revert all land to the ownership of the state. This emulated a similar move made by Kuwait, when their National Assembly passed a law in 1963 giving the state sole ownership of all common land.

2. The dispute between the government and the National Assembly over budget policy. In 1974, the parliament passed a bill granting the amir of Bahrain 6 million dinars ($15 million) yearly out of an overall annual government budget of 26 million dinars at that time. However, in 1975, after the sharp increase in oil prices, the amir preferred to have the upper hand over the government's share in the budget without the interference of the parliament.

3. The dispute between the government and the parliament over the rental of Juffair base to the United States. The "People's Bloc" opposed this agreement and presented a bill to end the American military presence in Bahrain. Consequently, the United States took a passive stand during the dissolution of the parliament.

6. The Shura Council (1992-present)

Since 1975, the year of the dissolution of the National Assembly, Bahrain has remained at the mercy of State Security Law. In December, 1992, the amir issued an order to form a Shura Council. The main function of this council is to express its opinion and advice on bills before they become law, on the general policy of the state, matters of general and municipal services and economic development. All such assessments are to be submitted to the cabinet for final approval. Furthermore, all members are appointed and have no legislative or supervisory authority; in other words, it is a powerless consultative body. The council is made up of thirty members appointed by the amir, most of them representing the merchant community and the private sector, and none belonging to any political movement. Fifteen members are merchants, three are building contractors, two are traditional religious preachers, two property landlords, one an academic, one from the workers committee of BAPCO, five professionals and one editor-in-chief of a local daily. The speaker, who is a Shi'i, is a former cabinet minister. The council is composed equally of the two sects. Two groups are excluded: the ruling family and fundamentalists from both sects. In 1996, the council was expanded to forty members.

The amir is empowered to dissolve the council if the interest of the state so demands. The subjects that the council has discussed since its establishment have not moved beyond the amendment of the labor law, unemployment, the completion of a sewage project, anti-smoking resolutions, and babies' milk (formula versus breast feeding).

There are signs of neither an increase in power of this council nor the preparation for democratic elections. On the contrary, the indications are that it is cruising in parallel with its sister councils in most of the other Gulf states, acting as a largely cosmetic emblem of democratic reform.

INTERNAL FACTORS

The total estimated population of Bahrain for 1996 is 600,000 people, of which some 230,000 are foreigners. The indigenous population is comprised of Sunnis, Shi'i and a handful of Christians and Jews. Ethnically, they are mainly of Sunni tribal origins, Sunni non-tribal, Sunni "Hawala" or émigrés from the Persian coast, Sunni of African descent, Shi'i Arabs and Shi'i of Persian origin. The latter segment of the population speaks Persian and Arabic, while being influenced by Persian culture. On the other hand, the Shi'i Arabs are culturally affiliated to the Eastern Province in Saudi Arabia and to southern Iraq. This Shi'i population (of both Arab and Persian origins) makes up more than 70 percent of the total population, while the Sunnis form the rest (30 percent). In 1941 the formula was different, the Shi'i constituting around half the population (52.5 percent). The balance has tilted over the past 50 years in favor of the Shi'i, who are a mostly rural community with social and religious traditions that allow polygamy and encourage early marriages and numerous children. This prolific aspect of the Shi'i is the main cause of their superiority in numbers. Another factor could be related to the discovery of oil in Qatar and the UAE in the mid-50s, an event that prompted a large number of Sunni (nearly 10,000), mainly tribal, to migrate to these states.

The small and constricted size of Bahrain, along with its sophisticated network of roads and other services, has caused extensive interaction among the island communities in both the urban and rural areas, leading to a phenomenon of inverse migration: the town has crept into the country. Unlike their counterparts in other third-world countries, Bahraini city dwellers spilled out into the open areas with their wealth and affluent way of life, and expatriates moved from the urban areas into residential compounds known as "gardens." This has posed a direct threat to the mainly Shi'i village dwellers with their conservative way of life and religious tradition. It has intensified the feeling of disparity between the two communities, causing the rural Shi'i to express a feeling of discontent at being disadvantaged in comparison with the "others."

Added to all this, the state's arbitrary building of residential townships has displaced many communities from their traditional areas, thus diluting the power of their leaderships. This was particularly systematic with the Sunnis, as the Shi'i leadership, both in towns and villages, put up a successful resistance to preserve their strongholds, such as the Ras Rumman and Mukhragah quarters in the capital. It is worth noting that the Shi'i religious leaders enjoy an economic independence through the sophisticated finances and administration of their Shi'i (Ja'fari) waqf (religious endowment), while their Sunni counterparts tend to be totally reliant on government salaries, and therefore under their control. For this reason the Shi'i clerics play a bigger role in their religious centers outside direct government censorship, while the Sunni preachers are confined by strict supervision by the state, risking the loss of their jobs for any violations.[17]

Unemployment and the increase in foreign labor has tended to accelerate the sequence of recent events. The official estimate of unemployment is 15 percent, but in reality this percentage likely exceeds 30 percent, which means that the unemployed number some 50,000 people. In the years between 1981 and 1991, foreign labor rose by 54,000, while the total addition to the local national work force, women included, went up by a mere 20,000. Such a disproportionate change in the labor force conspicuously weakened the call for a general strike by the opposition in April 1995 and led to its failure due to the presence of the foreign labor alternative.

There is another aspect to the influx of foreign labor that has added to the deterioration of the situation and that is not included in official statistics. This is the "free visa" worker, and estimates put them in excess of 30,000. Under the "free visa" program, each foreign individual pays his sponsor around $1,250 annually for his work and residence permits. This system is run and controlled by some senior bureaucrats and the elite who amass large fortunes from it.

Bahrain, like the rest of the Gulf societies, has undergone drastic social and economic changes in the last two decades since the sharp increase in oil revenues. This is especially true of the education sector. Bahrain instituted public education in 1919, earlier than any other regional state. Since then, the size of the school-enrolled population (those over three years in age) in all school stages increased from 500 males and 100 females in 1931 to 33,540 males and 27,332 females in 1976-77. In 1991, there were 67,931 male students and 66,750 females, a total of 134,681 students.

Like other developing countries, Bahrain is a nation of young people. The 1971 census indicated that nearly 60 percent of the indigenous population was under 20 years of age. This high percentage of growth is also reflected in the 1981 census, in which 65 percent of Bahrain's population was under 24 years of age. In 1991, this percentage decreased to 60 percent for the same age group. The substantial increase of youth under 24 years has added greatly to the strain on the educational system. Furthermore, the educational system in Bahrain is not well adapted to the needs of modern economic development, thus aggravating unemployment due to the discrepancy between the quality of training and education received and the requirements of the labor market.

Women played a significant role in the recent uprising. Prior to the discovery of oil in 1932, women in Bahrain were veiled and their role was restricted mainly to the home and child-bearing. With the new economic order and the expansion of education, women's roles began to change. Such change has been more visible in urban areas than in villages or in the poorer sectors of society, where women are still veiled and confined to their homes. Bahraini women constitute less than 10 percent of the overall labor force. Most working women are employed in different government agencies, where few hold high-level administrative positions; the majority of women work as teachers, secretaries and clerks. Most women in Bahrain and the Gulf are deprived of privileges granted to their male counterparts. Family Law remains the most pressing issue for women in Bahrain and the region. All the Gulf states except Kuwait still practice the old Sharia code, which ensures segregation of the sexes and discriminates against women in matters of inheritance, divorce, child custody and other family issues. The efforts of women's associations, in reforming laws governing women and pushing for progress toward equality between the sexes, is limited. Labor unions and formal political parties are banned. Hence, professional and cultural societies, as well as women's associations, are playing a major part in the social and political life in Bahrain and the Gulf states.

It is only indirectly, through the medium of non-political organizations and institutions, that political and social change can be channelled. There are more than 30 such organizations in Bahrain with a combined total of more than 6,500 members; professional societies form 70 percent of these, charity 15 percent and women's associations 15 percent. Furthermore, many women joined sports clubs, which were in the past exclusively for men. The role of such organizations is expanding, and this may lead to more involvement in political and social development in the future. Since the government is aware that such pressure groups might form a threat to its authority, it is trying to minimize their power by various means. In 1990, the government issued legislation limiting the role of all associations, including women's associations, and the new legislation grants absolute power to the Ministry of Labor and Social Affairs to dissolve any association without giving justification for such an act.

Such marginalization of women's activities created frustration and forced more women to join the present democratic movement in Bahrain. Many women joined the movement by signing a petition presented to the amir; nearly 20 percent of the 23,000 who signed the petition were women. Then another petition was sent to the amir in April 1995, signed by more than 300 women, mainly professionals and/or members of women's associations. This led to the summoning of 92 government employees among the signatories, from whom the government demanded written apologies and withdrawal of their signatures. Failing that, the petitioners would lose their jobs. The severity of punishment for those who signed the women's petition indicates that the government is aware of the impact women's collective action for change might have in the future.

At present, the opposition comprises four active groups:

1. *Bahrain Islamic Freedom Movement [Harakat Ahrar al-Bahrain al-Islamiyah].* This is mainly a rural Shi'i movement. One of their prominent leaders, Shaikh Abd al-Amir al-Jamri, is a former member of the 1975 parliament and was a member of the "Religious Bloc." The movement is considered the leading force in the uprising. One of its weaknesses is the lack of political experience and the ability to maneuver. Moreover, the members are not well organized inside Bahrain, while the opposite is true outside the country, the expatriate members being highly educated, sophisticated and well organized. This is due to their long stay in the West, which has allowed them to make connections with the media, human rights organizations, and parliamentarians in Europe and the United States.

2. *Islamic Front for the Liberation of Bahrain [Al-Jabha al-Islamiyah li-Tahrir al-Bahrain].* The movement was chaired by Hadi al-Mudarress who, in the early 1980s, had his headquarters in Iran. After a dispute with the Iranian authorities, many members of this movement fled to Syria, India and Bahrain. In 1982, the government accused the movement of plotting to overthrow the system in Bahrain. Seventy-two members were put on trial, and many were sentenced to life in prison. The movement is considered an extreme one, whose main objective is to overthrow the present system.

3. *The National Liberation Front (NLF) [Jabhat at-Tahrir al-Wataniyah].* This secular movement cuts across ethnic and sectarian boundaries and calls for the restoration of democracy. It is composed of former Marxists, socialists and Arab nationalists. After the dissolution of the parliament in 1975, the government arrested the movement's leaders and put them in prison, without any trial, for five to ten years. Consequently, their base was dispersed and fragmented. At present, the movement does not have a large power base, but its strength lies in its long experience in political activity.

4. *The Popular Front for the Liberation of Bahrain [Al-Jabha al-Sha'abiyah li-Tahrir al-Bahrain].* The movement emerged in 1971 out of the Popular Front for the Liberation of the Arabian Gulf, itself established in

1968. It has a wide power base among workers, students and intellectuals. The movement was crushed in 1973, and later modified its goal of overthrowing the present system to reforms through democracy.

At present, the two secular movements are in the process of merging to form one strong movement calling for reforms and the restoration of democracy. However, all four movements are working and coordinating actions with each other in the form of a loose alliance, which seems likely to strengthen over time.

The role of opposition outside Bahrain, headquartered in the United Kingdom, became more evident during the recent events. This was inadvertently caused by the government policy of sending into exile the most active dissidents. Most of those are Islamists, in addition to some liberal and Marxist elements. However, this group is a mere extension, not the major body, of the Bahraini Opposition movement, and indeed existed prior to the recently enlarged opposition within Bahrain

THE UPRISING OF 1994

In 1992, after the Gulf War, the Popular Front for the Liberation of Bahrain (PFLB) and the National Liberation Front (NLF) formed an agreement to cooperate and coordinate with each other. As part of this initiative, the two movements submitted a petition signed by 350 prominent citizens asking the amir for the restoration of democracy. Initially, the PFLB and NLF aimed to mobilize former parliament members to start calling for the restoration of the dissolved parliament, according to Article 65 of the constitution. This article states that if the amir has not called for a meeting of parliament within two months of its dissolution, the parliament goes back to its normal meetings regardless of the fact of the dissolution. The petition was handed to the amir's office, and the amir himself received representatives of the signatories on January 15, 1993, as the government was in the process of establishing a Shura Council. The opposition leaders were fearful at the beginning that a popular petition would not be successful. However, after meeting with the amir, their fear was reduced, and this strengthened the need for another popular petition among the people.

The first two years of the Shura Council neither brought any changes in legislation nor reduced the social and economic problems and the corruption that is rife in the public sector. The Gulf War apparently had no effect on the fundamental problems of political participation and Gulf unity. None of the problems, such as administrative corruption, unemployment and foreign labor, were dealt with either at ministerial levels or in policy programs. One opposition leader points out that the movement should have given the people the chance to realize by their own experience that it was impossible to replace a constitutionally elected assembly with an appointed one.[18]

In June 1994, unemployed workers demonstrated outside the Ministry of Labor and Social Affairs, but they were dispersed and told that the government would come up with a solution to their problem within two months. However, nothing came of this. Demonstrations resumed during the months of September and October of that year. In October 1994, a group of prominent citizens and religious leaders from both sects presented a petition to the amir, citing the unemployment situation, slackness in business, forced exile, restrictions on freedom of expression and subordination of the press to the government as examples of some of the problems Bahrain was facing. Nearly 23,000 citizens signed this petition calling for the restoration of parliament. The leading signers of the petition asked for permission to meet with the amir to present it but their request was turned down.

Following the arrest of three of the most prominent religious Shi'i leaders (Shaikh Ali Salman and two others), there were demonstrations in many Shi'i villages in December. A large number of arrests resulted, and that in turn led to more disturbances. The outcome was more than 30 killed, a few hundred injured and 3,000 to 5,000 people arrested, among them nearly 30 women and 50 children aged 12 to 15 years. All of those arrested were Shi'i. In addition, many schools and electric power substations were set on fire and destroyed. Since then, demonstrations and arrests have continued intermittently.

When we look into this situation, it is important to distinguish two different events without confusing them. The first was the petition that was signed by 23,000 citizens (men and women from both sects), the majority of which (nearly 70 percent) were Shi'i, and more than 20 percent women. This petition called for specific reforms, such as the return to democracy, an end to corruption, a reduction of unemployment and limitation of foreign labor. The second event was the series of street demonstrations and violence—in which only the Shi'i participated—that erupted in the capital and the villages after the arrest of the Shi'i cleric Shaikh Ali Salman.

It has been observed that the authorities and their media tried to confuse and combine the two events (the petition and the street violence). They were in fact separate, though parallel, matters, the main issue being a move toward peaceful political and civic reforms in which many leading members from both sects participated. The authorities played their part intelligently by dividing the movement and giving it a sectarian complexion, thereby concentrating on the Shi'i element and ignoring the Sunni participation. Not one Sunni was detained during the first year of the uprising. The first Shi'i leader to be detained (Ali Salman) was allegedly the one who played a major role in writing the petition and calling for a large number of signatories through his preaching in the mosques. He was also accused of instigating the villagers in an incident that sparked the whole uprising, when some marathon runners were stoned by villagers objecting to what they saw as the improper and indecent exposure of men and women wearing running shorts.

The authorities persisted in their accusations that there exists a Shi'i-inspired plot to overthrow the regime, and insisted that there is a Hezbollah underground organization in Bahrain. They also accused Iran of involvement in the plot by supplying the movement with arms and money. So far they have not produced the evidence to support the case.

The crux of the problem was the petition calling for reforms. The authorities had no wish to discuss the matter with anyone, especially where democracy was concerned. Admittedly, they played their cards cleverly by neutralizing the Sunni position and causing alarm among the other regimes in the region by indicating that the fire might spread in their direction. Furthermore, they aroused the U.S. suspicion that the Iranian influence might extend into the area should the requests in the petition be granted.

THE ROLE OF WESTERN POWERS
(THE UNITED STATES AND EUROPEAN UNION)

The United States policy of dual containment (vis-à-vis Iran and Iraq) contributed greatly to the successful handling of the recent crisis by the regime. It provided a plausible reason for outside interference by the Iranians. The Americans had to choose between two alternatives: (1) to support popular demands and urge the regime to restore democracy in accordance with declared American values throughout the world; or (2) to support a status quo in which the existing regimes are already committed to protecting American interests (for example, many of the assets of the Gulf countries and their citizens are invested in Wall Street and in U.S. treasury bills). Furthermore, the Gulf states on an ongoing basis buy various advanced weapons, at a time when the U.S. defense budget is sharply curtailed. The direct Gulf investments in the United States totalled $407 billion in early 1992. It is difficult to visualize a replacement of the regimes in the areas that commit such financial resources to the West in general and the United States in particular.[19]

It seems that the United States thought that free elections might bring in a majority of Shi'i fundamentalists, thus leading to a pro-Iran parliamentary policy. Added to this, the United States previously experienced the 1975 parliament, in which the "People's Bloc" opposed any U.S. military presence in Bahrain. Hence the pragmatic choice of strategic and commercial interests overruled democracy and human rights principles, causing the United States to stand by the regime. In March 1995, as the riots were raging, Defense Secretary William J. Perry visited the amir of Bahrain and made no public mention of the unrest, and Bahrainis interpreted this as clear support for the regime. It is worth noting that in addition to the military, there are 3,000 U.S. civilians working in Bahrain.

There is a growing concern over human rights conditions in the Gulf within the European Union. Some EU countries, namely France, Germany and Belgium, implicitly extended their support to the democratic demands by talking privately to the authorities. Britain, on the other hand— due to its large business interests and the presence of 7,000 of its citizens who work and live on the island—showed an attitude similar to that of the United States, supporting the current system and its policy toward any opposition. The new Labor government has expressed a more positive attitude toward self determination and democratization in Bahrain.

THE ROLE OF REGIONAL POWERS (IRAN AND THE GCC)

Regional powers, especially Saudi Arabia, have always influenced Bahrain's internal and foreign policies. During the days of the shah, Iran had demanded to annex Bahrain, until 1970 when it acquiesced in the verdict of a UN-administered referendum on the island's independence. From then on, Bahrain was rid of the persistent demands made continually by Iran.[20] However, Iran's religious influence has persisted among the Shi'i community, especially since the 1979 revolution. In 1982, the authorities uncovered a plot against the government, and accused Iran of being the prime mover of such a daring act. More recently, they pointed their finger again toward Iran as the inspiration of their current troubles. There is no evidence as yet of any Iranian organizational or material backing for the protesters, and the view among observers is that Bahrain's troubles are mostly homegrown. An interesting observation is that throughout the whole episode the Persian Shi'i community, which makes up 10 percent of the total population, remained neutral and silent (perhaps based on advice from Iran), and this enraged the ethnic Arab Shiʻi.

All GCC states have stood by the regime and supported all the steps taken to quash the uprising. In the early days of the troubles, the Saudi interior minister, who was in Bahrain at the time, announced that the security of Bahrain was inseparable from that of Saudi Arabia, thus enforcing the view that weaknesses in any of the Gulf states shall have a negative effect on the other regimes.

The GCC states, especially Saudi Arabia, play a major role in formulating political decisions in Bahrain for the following reasons:

1. Since the opening of the King Fahd causeway in 1986, the ties between Saudi Arabia and Bahrain have strengthened, especially since both expatriates and Saudis of the Eastern Province have started pouring into the island state for tourism and entertainment. On the other hand, the flow of Bahrainis in the other direction was encouraged by the availability of cheaper shopping and wider breathing space for motorists who take their families for weekend and evening drives.

2. Saudi Arabia has provided Bahrain with a major oil pipeline that carries crude oil directly from the mainland into Bahrain's refinery for eventual exportation. In addition, Bahrain receives the revenues of a Saudi-managed oil field north of Bahrain (Abu Safa) equal to 100,000 barrels per day.

3. The GCC states provide Bahrain with assistance for joint-venture and infrastructure project financing.

4. The general expectation is that oil may be fully depleted within the coming few years unless new fields are discovered. This would inevitably bring Bahrain closer to and make it more dependent upon the other states, as its financial resources dwindle.

5. Territorial disputes between Bahrain and Qatar over the Hawar islands, to which Qatar has laid claim (leading to arbitration at the International Court of Justice in The Hague), have required Bahrain to forge closer ties with the rest of the GCC members for support.

6. A continual increase in the population of Bahrain, with a corresponding increase in unemployment to 15 percent (unofficially estimated at closer to 30 percent), tends to worsen the situation regarding the training programs that cause a shortage of supply in the labor market. One of the alternative solutions would be to encourage an outward flow of labor from Bahrain into the other Gulf states.

CONCLUSION

In his National Day speech on December 16, 1995, the amir of Bahrain pledged continued firmness to guarantee security. "Over the past year," he said, "our country witnessed certain incidental adverse events aimed at disrupting the security of citizens, the nation and its prosperity. Such actions are, categorically, far from the nature and spirit of both this nation and various ranks and sectors of the people. The government dealt with them in accordance with the requirements of security, order and utmost interests of the country. It will continue to pursue the policy of firmness in order to maintain national security and to put into effect appropriate legal measures upon whoever violates it."[21]

The 1996 National Day speech did not include any mention of current disturbances; however, the amir emphasized the expanding base of the Shura Council. He added that he is proud of the unity of the loyal Bahraini people and their willingness to rally behind the leadership and overcome the challenges faced by the nation.[22]

This indicates that the attitude of the government is not to yield to people's demands to return to parliamentary life. Further, it gives no indication of its willingness to even negotiate the former issue. On the contrary, its response can be summarized as follows:

1. Suppression of disturbances with brute force, dispersal of demonstrations, detentions, and control of key points around trouble areas, as well as the presence of police controls on school grounds and university campuses.
2. Refusal to receive all delegates and their petitions, the most important of which were:
   a) The first petition of November 1994, with 22,000 signatories.
   b) The second petition of March 1995, signed by 110 prominent citizens from both sects.
   c) The women's petition of April 1995. Three hundred and ten women signed this petition, which was sent to the amir by registered post.
3. The selection of the new minister of education and the president of the University of Bahrain from the ranks of the military is another sign of the hard line toward any further student demonstrations.
4. The recent expansion of the Shura Council.
5. The introduction in 1996 of a system of provinces that links all public functions to the Ministry of the Interior.

It is noteworthy that the authorities acted in the same old-fashioned way as they did during the previous uprisings by not acknowledging the existence of any opposition. In fact, one can find some similarities between the present uprising and the previous ones, especially those of 1953-56. From the 1919 reforms until the present uprising, the system has been confronted with many challenges from new forces, such as students, BAPCO workers and underground political parties. They all demanded representation, power-sharing and a standardized code of justice. The government always reacted against the opposition; it arrested its leaders while sometimes later it gave in to some of their demands. The 1994 uprising signals for the first time women's extensive participation in an uprising.

The unrest has damaged Bahrain's service-based economy. The economic hardship Bahrain is witnessing today will worsen the political situation. The economy performed indifferently in 1995, with estimated real growth barely reaching 1 percent after stagnating in 1994.[23] Moreover, revenues were expected to fall to around BD 520 million ($1.38 billion) annually in 1996 and 1997, down from the BD 620 million received in 1994. Falling oil export revenues, which make up more than half the government's income, account for much of the reduction.[24] Consequently, the business community is expected to suffer more from such a shrinking budget, which might lead this community to side with the opposition in demanding political reforms. However, the influence of the Chamber of Commerce, which was established in 1939 and has played a significant role since then in the political life of Bahrain, is diminishing. This institution has proven its inability to solve the serious problems facing the business community that have forced a number of local merchants to declare bankruptcy. It is expected that the government will not yield to its demand for such reforms.

Finally, the vital question remains as to whether the case of Bahrain is an exception to the rule, or an indication of things to come in the rest of the Gulf. Each of the GCC member states has its peculiarities. As has been said previously, the birth of the education movement in Bahrain at the end of the nineteenth century, and the discovery of oil there earlier than in the other states of the region, led to a more advanced social awareness and political maturity as compared to the rest of the Gulf states, with the possible exception of Kuwait. This is offset by the increase in unemployment and bureaucratic corruption, and the depletion of oil revenues, the latter making Bahrain more dependent on Saudi Arabia.

Despite the conclusion that all the events in Bahrain are due to local internal issues, it is difficult not to envision similar developments in the other Gulf states. This view is reinforced by their collective reaction on many occasions, and at many levels, by the GCC commitment to aid Bahrain either with money or arms to suppress any future troubles. As an example, in 1994 Oman witnessed unrest amongst its youth. Some 2,000 people, including two under-secretaries, were arrested after being accused of sedition, public violence and unauthorized gathering.[25] Also in December 1995, a petition was sent to the amir of Bahrain on the first anniversary of the uprising, signed by 100 notable Kuwaiti citizens (professors, parliament members, lawyers, doctors, etc.). The petition called for the release of political detainees, the return of political dissidents who were forced to leave the country, and new parliamentary elections.

Furthermore, some observers stress the possibility of the turmoil's spreading to neighboring Saudi Arabia, bearing in mind that Bahrain is connected to Saudi Arabia by the King Fahd causeway. Saudi Arabia is experiencing similar conditions that have caused instability in Bahrain, including economic decline, uneven distribution of wealth and a disadvantaged Shi'i population in its oil-rich Eastern Province.[26]

It is doubtful, nevertheless, that this assumption is valid, since tiny Bahrain, which depends mainly on Saudi Arabia for its economy and security, cannot have a serious effect on events in Saudi Arabia. However, whatever happens in Saudi Arabia will have a great bearing not only on Bahrain but on the whole region.

Notes

1. F. Khuri, *Tribe and State in Bahrain: The Transformation of Social and Political Authority in an Arab State* (Chicago: University of Chicago Press, 1980), p. 22.

2. M. Rumaihi, *Bahrain: Social and Political Change Since the First World War*, 2nd edition (in Arabic) (Kuwait: Kadhma, 1984), p. 184.

3. F. Khuri, *Tribe and State in Bahrain: The Transformation of Social and Political Authority in an Arab State* (in Arabic) (Beirut: Arab Development Institute, 1983), p. 171.

4. Rumaihi, p. 212.

5. Ibid.

6. Khuri, p. 299.

7. Ibid., p. 265.

8. Ibid., p. 295.

9. Rumaihi, p. 221.

10. Khuri, p. 305.

11. Ibid., p. 311.

12. Ibid., p. 325.

13. Emile Nakhleh, Bahrain: *Political Development in a Modernizing Society* (Lexington, MA: Lexington Books, 1976), p. 79.

14. Ibid., p. 117.

15. Ibid., p. 177.

16. Khuri, p. 334.

17. Ahmad Al-Shamlan, *Al-Quds Daily,* issue no. 1917, April 28, 1995.

18. Ibid.

19. F. Gregory Gause, *Oil Monarchies: Domestic and Security Challenges in the Arab Gulf States* (New York: Council on Foreign Relations, 1994), p. 181.

20. Peter Waldman, *The Wall Street Journal,* June 12, 1995.

21. *The Gulf Daily News,* December 16, 1995, p. 1.

22. *The Gulf Daily News,* December 16, 1996, p. 1.

23. *Middle East Monitor* 6, no.1 (January 1996), p. 7.

24. Ibid., p. 7.

25. *Financial Times,* April 19, 1995.

26. *Wall Street Journal,* April 19, 1995.

CHAPTER 8

IRANIAN MILITARY CAPABILITIES AND "DUAL CONTAINMENT"

Anthony H. Cordesman

Iran poses serious potential challenges to the security of the Gulf and the flow of the world's oil. Iran can exploit significant conventional military strength, and is seeking to acquire weapons of mass destruction. Iran has major capabilities to execute unconventional warfare, carry out or support terrorist actions, and encourage extremist movements. Iran is also a politically unstable state whose future intentions cannot be predicted and in which any forces for moderation may be counterbalanced by voices for extremism.

Determining the best way to deal with Iran, and the potential threat it poses to the region and the flow of oil, has become a major policy issue. There is little consensus between the United States and its allies as to the seriousness of the Iranian threat, the nature of its actions, or the best way to structure policy toward Iran. The United States is now committed to a policy of "dual containment" that attempts to isolate Iran politically, economically and militarily. With the exception of Israel, most of America's allies inside and outside the region believe that the United States is exaggerating the Iranian threat and is pursuing policies that will make it more extreme, rather than encourage moderation.

Iran's leaders and intentions can change rapidly and without warning or evolve in one direction for years, and then change overnight. An aggressive Iranian military buildup might never lead to conflict. At the same time, a defensive military modernization might suddenly be used for aggressive war. Weapons designed for deterrence can be used for offensive operations. Moderate intentions can fail or change, and levels of conflict can rapidly escalate in the future in ways that leaders never anticipate.

Analysis can, however, provide some insights into Iran's military capabilities and strategic future. It can look beyond political rhetoric and examine the details of Iran's present and possible military capabilities and the role Iran can and cannot play in the Gulf. Such analysis cannot resolve any of the major uncertainties regarding Iran's future intentions, but it can provide a picture of the possible paths given types of regimes might follow.

IRANIAN MILITARY EXPENDITURES

There is no agreement within the U.S. government over the size of Iranian military expenditures. The U.S. Central Intelligence Agency (CIA) estimated that Iran spent $13 billion on defense in 1992, while the Arms Control and Disarmament Agency (ACDA) figures only total $3.9 billion. Similarly, U.S. government experts felt that Iran spent up to $8 billion on military forces in 1993, while ACDA estimated $4.9 billion.[1] Iran seems to have spent about 20 percent or more of its GDP on defense during much of the Iran-Iraq War, and over 50 percent of its central government expenditures. It seems to have spent 10 to 15 percent of its GDP on military forces and equipment since 1988.[2]

Iran's economic crisis in the mid-1990s forced it to make some painful choices between guns and butter. Its military spending remained sufficient, however, for Iran to continue to pose a significant threat to its neighbors.

THE IRANIAN CONVENTIONAL ARMS BUILDUP

The total value of Iran's arms transfers seemed to drop significantly after the Iran-Iraq War. At the same time, Iran's ability to import advanced arms and military technology improved, as its opposition to Iraq's invasion of Kuwait earned it new respectability and better access to the world's arms markets.

Iran lost 40 to 60 percent of its major land force equipment during the final battles of the Iran-Iraq War, and could not quickly re-arm after its defeat. Iran took delivery on only $8.6 billion worth of arms from 1986 to 1989, primarily from China, Eastern Europe and North Korea. Its arms transfers dropped again during 1990-93, when it took delivery on only $5.3 billion worth of arms, contrary to reports of a massive Iranian military buildup during this period. New Iranian agreements totaled $2.86

billion in 1990 and $1.9 billion in 1991. In 1992, when Iran's economy degenerated to a crisis point, Iran's imports suddenly plunged below $1 billion, and Iran's minister of defense reported a hard currency budget for 1993-94 of only $850 million.[3]

Cuts in the quantity of Iranian arms transfers, however, were offset by improvement in their quality. During 1990-93, Iran was able to get nearly $3.4 billion worth of deliveries from Russia, including first-line tanks like the T-72 and aircraft like the MiG-29 and Su-24. Iran also found it easier to obtain equipment and supplies for its biological and chemical weapons efforts, and got increased—if still limited—imports of high technology for its nuclear weapons program.

Iran's shift to arms imports from Russia had disadvantages as well. These imports meant that Iran had to convert to a third major supplier of arms in only 15 years, creating serious problems in conversion and standardization. Iran's force structure remained heavily based on Western supplied equipment, which was not interoperable with Russian and Asian equipment. Iran tried to deal with these problems by "cannibalizing" some weapons to keep others operating. Often, however, it could not obtain key parts or had to use spares obtained from Third-World suppliers that were worn or of low quality.

The cumulative effect of the Iran-Iraq War, the revolution, the lack of adequate technical training, and the low technical standards of some elements of the Revolutionary Guards led to steady equipment losses through age, wear and attrition. Iran was also forced to mix its aging Western-supplied equipment with equipment from non-Western sources. This lack of standardization created additional training, battle-management and logistical support problems.

Although Iran was able to buy some Western spares, upgrades, weapons systems and dual-use technologies on the black market, it made only limited progress in making its more sophisticated Western-supplied weapons fully operational and in giving them sustainability in extended combat. Further, the United States put heavy pressure on Russia, Poland, the Czech Republic and Germany to limit their arms transfers of dual-use items, and was joined in such efforts by Britain. The European Community strengthened its controls in mid-1993, and began to examine additional sanctions.

Iran also made progress in developing its military industries, shifting from an import strategy to one that emphasized self-sufficiency. Iranian plants manufactured ammunition, towed artillery, mortars, light anti-tank weapons, small arms and automatic weapons. Iran can rebuild armored weapons and a number of Western, former–Soviet bloc, North Korean and Chinese weapons systems. It also has the sophistication to rebuild the jet engines for many of its American fighters and helicopters, and to produce parts and modifications for some of its radars, missile systems, avionics, ships and armored personnel carriers. It can make multiple rocket launchers and long-range rockets and has made some upgrades to Iran's F-4s and F-14s—although with mixed success.

But Iran can only produce a sophisticated guided missile system or advanced conventional weapon by importing some of the major parts. It does not approach self-sufficiency in arms and military technology, and has no prospect of doing so in the foreseeable future.

IRAN'S MILITARY MANPOWER

Iran's current military capabilities are heavily influenced by its demographics and the size of its total military manpower. Iran is by far the most heavily populated Gulf state, with a total male manpower pool of about 14,382,000 (aged 15 to 49). The CIA estimates that 8,556,000 males are fit for military service, and that 601,000 reach military age each year.[4]

Iran does not maintain an active manpower base that is proportionate to its total population. Iran's active strength in the mid-1990s was about 513,000, including 120,000 Revolutionary Guards. This compared with 382,000 men for Iraq, which had less than one-third of Iran's total population. Iran had large numbers of Basij militia and 45,000 gendarmerie and border guards, but these paramilitary forces posed little threat to Iran's neighbors.[5]

THE THREAT FROM IRANIAN LAND FORCES

Iran's land forces were in a constant state of change from the end of the Iran-Iraq War. Iran's ground forces took far greater losses during the war than the Iranian air force or navy, particularly during the final battles. Iran's defeats during 1988 were so severe that they led to the disintegration of some elements of the Pasdaran and even Iran's main regular army units. These defeats also caused massive losses of weapons and equipment.

Iran later rebuilt some of its capabilities. According to the International Institute for Strategic Studies (IISS), the Iranian regular army had a strength of twelve division equivalents in 1995, and around forty maneuver brigades. These formations included four armored divisions (two with three brigades and two with four brigades, seven infantry divisions, and one special forces division with four brigades). Iran seems to have at least two, and probably has six, independent maneuver brigades. These independent maneuver brigades seem to include one to two airborne brigades and four special forces brigades, a surface-to-surface missile brigade, and a logistic brigade.

Iran had an inventory of around 1,245 tanks in early 1995—reflecting an increase of some 200 tanks over 1993 and 320 to 380 tanks over 1992. Iran's main battle tanks consisted of about 300 M-47s and M-60s, 135 Chieftains, 150 T-62s and 150 to 200 T-72s, 175 to 200 T-54s and T-55s, and 260 T-59s. Iran may, however, have taken delivery on 150 to 200 additional T-72s and 100 to 200 T-59s in late 1994, which would bring Iran's total inventory up to over 1,500 tanks.[6] Only part of this inventory, however, was operational. Some experts estimate that Iran's sustainable *operational* tank strength was only about 900 to 1,000 tanks. Further, Iran's Chieftains and M-60s are at least 16 to 20 years old.[7]

Iran had about 1,000 to 1,250 operational armored personnel carriers and armored infantry fighting vehicles, including 40 to 50 operational British-supplied Scorpions; more than 200 BMPs; some 150 to 175 M-113s and other Western APCs; and 500 BTR-50s, BTR-60s and BTR-152s. Iran has an unknown number of British Chieftain bridging tanks, and may have another 100 to 150 BMPs in the process of delivery.[8] Iran's BMPs are its only modern AFVs, and they total only about 20 percent of Iran's holdings of other armored vehicles. There were also significant problems in fighting from the vehicle, including limited night-vision capabilities and poor weapons system ergonomics and performance.

Iran had 2,000 to 2,500 medium- and heavy-artillery weapons and multiple-rocket launchers. This high total reflects a continuing Iranian effort to build up artillery strength that began during the Iran-Iraq War, when Iran used artillery to support its infantry and Islamic Revolutionary Guard Corps in their attacks on Iraq. Iran has had to use artillery as a substitute for armor and air power. Iran had some 2,000 weapons in 1994, of which approximately 1,200 were medium and heavy mortars. Iran had at least several hundred of its heavy mortars mounted in armored vehicles— many of which were U.S.-made M-106 mortar carriers sold to Iran during the time of the shah.

These artillery weapons gave Iran considerable ability to mass fire against relatively static area targets, but towed artillery is an anachronism in modern maneuver warfare operations, and Iran had only limited artillery fire control and battle-management systems, counter-battery radar capability, and long-range target acquisition capability (although it did have some RPVs) to support its self-propelled weapons. Most of its artillery units were only effective against slow-moving mass targets at ranges of less than 10 to 15 kilometers or in harassment and interdiction fire.

Iranian helicopter holdings are uncertain. According to the IISS, the Iranian army retains 100 AH-1J Sea Cobra attack helicopters; and 31 CH-47C, 100 Bell-214A, 20 AB-205A, and 50 AB-206 transport and support helicopters out of the total supplied by the West. Some experts feel these figures overestimate the number of attack helicopters and underestimate the number of troop-carrying and utility helicopters. Most experts agree, however, that the operational readiness of Iranian helicopters is low, perhaps only about 25 percent of inventory, and that Iran has little sustained sortie capability.

ISLAMIC REVOLUTIONARY GUARD CORPS

There are significant uncertainties regarding the organization and role of the Islamic Revolutionary Guard Corps (IRGC). Most sources agree that the IRGC was organized into 11 internal security regions in 1994. Some sources indicate that the Islamic Revolutionary Guard Corps forces were organized into 12 to 15 "divisions," although most such divisions had manning levels less than those of brigades in the Iranian regular army, and many had less firepower than Western combat battalions. The IRGC also had some 18 to 23 independent "brigades"—including armored, infantry, special-forces, paratroop, air-defense, artillery, missile, engineer and border-defense units.[9]

Most sources feel these IRGC land forces are now organized, trained and equipped largely as infantry, special-forces and internal-security forces. The IISS reports the IRGC has two to four armored "divisions," but it is unclear that the IRGC has any armored formations larger than brigade size, and these units seem to be far less heavily armored than Iranian regular army armored brigades. The IRGC seems to be the principal operator of Iran's land-based surface-to-surface missile forces. Both the Iranian regular army and IRGC have offensive and defensive chemical warfare capabilities.[10]

THE WARFIGHTING CAPABILITIES OF IRANIAN LAND FORCES

Iran is well-deployed to fight Iraq, and might be able to conduct limited armored offensives in the Iran-Iraq border area. Iraq should be able to defend against an Iranian invasion through the year 2000, but this defense will be heavily dependent on Iraqi unity and the willingness of Iraqi Shi'i to fight for the central government. Iraq is also likely to become significantly more vulnerable to an Iranian invasion after 2000 if Iraq does not begin to receive significant supplies of parts, munitions and new arms. Iran's land forces present only a limited threat to the Southern Gulf states, unless a change in a Southern Gulf regime should allow Iran to build up a significant military presence in the Southern Gulf.

It is also impossible to rule out a sudden or surprise Iranian attack in support of an uprising against a Southern Gulf regime that produced success out of all proportion to the size and effectiveness of the Iranian forces deployed. Iran has a number of land units that should perform well in unconventional warfare missions in support of any popular uprising. It could deploy brigade-sized forces relatively rapidly across the Gulf, if it was allowed to make an unopposed amphibious and air assault. It could intervene in a civil war in Bahrain, or another of the smaller Gulf states under these conditions.

Iranian land forces could easily defeat the Iranian Kurds or any other internal opposition force. They are also capable of intervening at the brigade and division level in a conflict such as the war between Azerbaijan and Armenia, or the war in Afghanistan. They have very limited capability, however, against the first-line force of Turkey.

It is far from clear that Iran's conventional land-warfare capabilities will improve faster than those of its neighbors, particularly if Iran's land forces remain split between the regular forces and those of the Revolutionary Guards. As a result, Iran may be more of an indirect threat to its neighbors and the West. Iranian land forces, particularly the IRGC, can already play a significant role in training, equipping and supporting guerrilla and terrorist forces in countries such as Lebanon, the Sudan and Bosnia. They can covertly project power in terms of supporting radical or extremist movements in other states, and all of these capabilities will improve as Iran builds up and modernizes its land forces.[11]

THE THREAT FROM IRANIAN AIR FORCE

While Iran had 85,000 men and 447 combat aircraft in its air force at the time the shah fell from power, it steadily lost air strength from 1980 to 1988. The air force suffered combat losses in the Iran-Iraq War, and many aircraft gradually ceased to be operational once Iran was cut off from its U.S. suppliers.

Iran's air strength improved significantly, however, after 1988. By early 1995, the Iranian air force and air-defense force had built back to a total inventory of around 260 to 300 combat aircraft in 18 combat squadrons, with a total strength of about 15,000 men, plus 12,000 more men in its land-based air-defense forces. Iran claimed that it was modernizing its F-14s by equipping them with IHawk missiles adapted to the air-to-air role, but it is far from clear that this is the case or that such adaptations can have more than limited effectiveness. Iran had a reconnaissance squadron with five to ten RF-5EIIs and three to eight RF-4Es; and it operates five P-3F maritime reconnaissance aircraft, RC-130s and other intelligence/reconnaissance aircraft, as well as large numbers of transports and helicopters. Iran also has 20 to 30 F-5B and F-5FII, 10 Tucano, and some Chinese F-6 combat-capable trainers.[12]

Force quality and readiness remain a major issue. Brigadier General Mansour Sattari, the chief of staff of the Iranian air force, claimed in 1994 that the air force had "reached self sufficiency in all fields, including pilot training, missiles, radar, air defenses, maintenance and repair, manufacture of parts and basic repair of facilities. . . . We constantly patrol the international waters and have a watchful eye on the moves of foreign warships there. . . . If the foreigners pose any threat, we will meet them with all our might."[13] These claims are little more than whistling in the dark. Many of Iran's operational aircraft had only limited operational capability. As few as 50 percent of Iran's U.S.-supplied combat aircraft may have been operational, and few of Iran's operational U.S.-equipped squadrons could long support sustained sortie rates higher than one per aircraft every three to four days. Some U.S.-supplied aircraft may lack the operational avionics necessary to properly fire air-to-air and air-to-surface missiles. Iran's most important source of new aircraft has been Russia. Iran's new MiG-29s and Su-24s are far superior in quality to the aircraft it has obtained from the Chinese, and Iran may have signed agreements that would give it a total of 50 MiG-29s, 36 Su-24s, and the necessary support equipment.[14]

Iran's purchase of Soviet aircraft had the major additional benefit of enabling the Iranian air force to use some of the Iraqi aircraft that fled to Iran during the Gulf War. There is some question about the exact number of aircraft involved, and how many are flyable. Some sources report as few as 106 combat aircraft, but Iraq has officially claimed that they total 139 aircraft.[15]

Iran by 1995 had already begun to fly Iraqi MiG-29s and Su-24s, had obtained Russian support in creating training facilities in Iran, and was in the process of absorbing all of Iraq's flyable MiG-29s, Su-24s and possibly its Su-20/Su-22s into its force structure.[16] This could give Iran up to 90 additional combat aircraft if it can obtain suitable support from Russia.

Iran probably cannot operate Iraqi Mirage F-1s effectively without French technical assistance, which currently seems highly unlikely. The eight to twelve Iraqi MiG-23s are sufficiently low in capability that Iran may be unwilling to pay for the training and logistical burden of adding this type to its inventory. The seven Su-25s are a more attractive option, since they are specially equipped for the close air support mission, but it would be very expensive for Iran to operate a force of only seven aircraft.

THE WAR-FIGHTING CAPABILITIES OF IRANIAN AIR FORCES

The Iranian air force can launch a limited number of squadron-level attacks on key military depots or bases. It can sustain limited numbers of daily attacks on hostile Kurdish camps and the bases of the People's Mojahedin. It can selectively attack shipping in the Gulf, and could assist the naval forces in limited operations in the Gulf, unless it met United States or Saudi resistance. It could assist Iran's land forces in any new fighting with Iraq. It might not be able to win air superiority over the Iranian border area, but could do a much better job of defending Iranian territory than it did in the Iran-Iraq War.

The Iranian air force is strong enough to deter offensive strikes from any Southern Gulf country's air force, except for the Saudi air force, and can probably penetrate the air space of all Southern Gulf countries except Saudi Arabia, at least to the extent of conducting selective slash-and-run attacks. It could probably execute at least one successful surprise attack on a Saudi target before the Saudi air force could fully organize its air defenses, although much would depend on the activity of the Saudi E-3A force and the readiness of Saudi F-15Cs. Iran will also continue to lag behind Saudi Arabia in its rate of modernization, and Iran has no foreseeable near to mid-term hope of challenging a combination of United States, British and Saudi air power.

The Iranian air force could, however, deploy quickly to a friendly air base in the Southern Gulf—in the event of a coup or other change in the political posture of that state—although it would take several weeks for Iran to deploy enough support equipment and stocks to support more than limited squadron-sized operations from such a base. While the Iranian air force could not compete with the Turkish or Pakistani air forces, it might be able to fly combat support and offensive missions over the territory of Azerbaijan, or the other former-Soviet republics near the Iranian border. Such operations would have to be squadron-sized and involve low sortie rates, but Iran has at least some capability.

The future capabilities of the Iranian air force are difficult to estimate. Much will depend on whether Iran can obtain modern combat aircraft from Russia, whether Iran can afford them in sufficient numbers, whether Iran can manage the complex conversion from United States to Russian aircraft efficiently and whether Iran fully understands and can accomplish the conversion from an air force organized to fight at the squadron or small-flight level to one that can conduct coherent force-wide operations and fight modern joint warfare. The problems Iran faces go far beyond modernizing its air order of battle, and require fundamental changes in its ability to conduct force or force warfare. It is far from clear that Iran can accomplish all these tasks in the near to mid-term.

THE THREAT FROM IRANIAN GROUND-BASED AIR DEFENSES

Iranian ground-based air defenses play a critical role in shaping Iranian willingness to take risks and use conventional military forces. As long as Iran is vulnerable to the kind of air offensive the UN Coalition conducted against Iraq during Desert Storm, it is likely to be restrained in the risks it will take. Much depends, however, on how Iran perceives its vulnerability to air attack and the attrition levels it can inflict on attacking aircraft. This perception will be shaped in part by Iran's ability to modernize its fighter forces. Iran has no near-term prospect of acquiring an airborne defense platform similar to the E-3A airborne warning and air control system (AWACS) operated by the Saudi and U.S. air forces, or match the West in airborne electronic warfare capabilities. Iran's success in modernizing its ground-based air defenses will, therefore, probably be as important in influencing its willingness to take military risks as its acquisition of aircraft.

Iran in early 1995 seems to have assigned about 12,000 men to land-based air-defense functions, including 4,000 to 6,000 regulars and 5,000 to 8,000 IRGC personnel. It is not possible to distinguish clearly between the major air-defense weapons holdings of the regular air force and IRGC, but the air force seems to have operated most major surface-to-air missile systems, and its total holdings seem to have included thirty Improved Hawk fire units (150+ launchers), fifty to fifty-five SA-2 and HQ-23 (CSA-1) launchers (Chinese-made equivalents of the SA-2), and twenty-five SA-6 launchers. The air force also had three Soviet-made long range SA-5 units with a total of ten to fifteen launchers—enough for six sites.

Iran faces serious problems in modernizing its air-defense system, many of which date back to the time of the shah. Although Iran bought modern surface-to-air missiles at the time of the shah, it never integrated these missiles into an effective land-based air-defense system. It had not made its air control and warning system fully operational at the time the shah fell, and had experienced serious problems in operating some of its largely British-supplied radars.

Revolutionary Iran has responded by obtaining the SA-2, CSA-1, SA-6 and SA-5 from the PRC, Russia and Central Europe. Iran has acquired some Soviet warning and battle management radars, command and communications equipment.[17] These transfers of surface-to-air missiles and sensors from Russia and the People's Republic of China have helped improve Iran's land-based capabilities, but they have not been not adequate to meet its needs. They give Iran improved capability against regional air forces without sophisticated jammers and anti-radiation missiles, but they scarcely give Iran a modern integrated air-defense system that can resist attack by a power like the United States.

THE WAR-FIGHTING CAPABILITIES OF IRANIAN LAND-BASED AIR DEFENSE FORCES

Further purchases of SA-2 and SA-5 systems cannot give Iran the range of capabilities it needs. The SA-2, CSA-1, SA-6 and SA-5 are highly vulnerable to active and passive countermeasures. The Improved Hawks in Iranian hands are nearly seventeen years old. If Iran is to create the land-based elements of an air-defense system capable of dealing with the retaliatory capabilities of U.S. air forces, it needs a modern heavy surface-to-air missile system that is part of an integrated air-defense system.

Russia is the only potential source of the required land-based air-defense technology. Russia, however, has not fully completed integration of the SA-10 and SA-12 into its own air defenses, has significant limitations on its air-defense computer technology and relies heavily on redundant sensors and overlapping different surface-to-air missiles to compensate for a lack of overall system efficiency. A combination of advanced Russian missiles and an advanced sensor and battle management system would still be vulnerable to active and passive attack by the United States.

An advanced land-based Russian air-defense system would, however, give Iran far more capability to defend against retaliatory raids from Iraq or any Southern Gulf air force. It would allow Iran to allocate more fighter/attack aircraft to attack missions and use its interceptors to provide air cover for such attack missions. It would greatly complicate the problem of using offensive U.S. air power against Iran, require substantially more U.S. forces to conduct a successful air campaign and probably greatly increase U.S. losses.

THE THREAT FROM IRAN'S NAVAL FORCES

Most Gulf nations have treated seapower as an afterthought, but the Iranian navy and the naval branch of the Islamic Revolutionary Guard Corps are likely to play a critical role in Iranian military action in the Gulf. Any Iranian intervention in a Gulf state that does not involve the cooperation of a Southern Gulf government, and free access to ports and air fields, would require some kind of amphibious operation. Naval forces are equally essential to a wide spectrum of other possible conflicts that affect the islands in the Gulf, control of the Strait of Hormuz, unconventional warfare using naval forces, attacks on coastal targets in Iraq and the Southern Gulf, and Western and Southern Gulf naval operations in the Gulf.

IRAN'S SURFACE NAVY

In early 1995, Iran's regular navy, naval portion of the Islamic Revolutionary Guard Corps, and marines totaled around 38,000 men—with about 18,000 regulars and 20,000 Iranian Naval Revolutionary Guard forces. While some sources list Iran as having three marine brigades, it is not clear how the marine units are structured, trained or equipped.[18]

While most Iranian major surface ships have limited operational capability, the combat strength of the Iranian navy was impressive by Gulf standards. According to various estimates, Iran's operational inventory included two destroyers, three frigates, ten missile combatants, thirty-three light patrol and coastal combatants, five mine-warfare ships (less one training ship), nine armed helicopters, and eight amphibious ships and craft. Iran had a small marine force and large numbers of naval revolutionary guards. Iran also had five to seven Silkworm (HY-2) anti-ship missile sites to defend its ports and cover the Strait of Hormuz.

Opinions differ as to how much of Iran's surface force is fully operational. Iran is clearly able to operate some of its British-made Saam-class fast-attack craft. According to some reports, it can also operate most of the weapons systems on at least one destroyer; two frigates; six to ten fast-attack craft (FAC); seven large patrol boats; forty coastal patrol boats; a maximum of fourteen Hovercraft; and fifty-seven amphibious assault ships, logistic ships and small patrol boats. If these reports are true, Iran has a total force of more than eighty vessels, although Iran would lack adequate air-defense and anti-ship missile capabilities for its major surface ships.[19] All of Iran's major surface vessels are obsolescent or obsolete, although they could be updated in Western shipyards.

IRANIAN MINE-WARFARE CAPABILITIES

Mine warfare, amphibious warfare, anti-ship missiles and unconventional warfare can offer Iran other ways of compensating for the weakness of its conventional air and naval forces. Iran's mine-warfare vessels include two to three shahrokh-class MSC 292/268 coastal minesweepers (one used for training in the Caspian Sea). The *shahrokh* and *Karkas* are known to be operational. They are 378-ton sweepers that can be used to lay mines as well as sweep, but their radars and sonars date back to the late 1950s and are obsolete in sweeping and countermeasure activity against modern mines. Iran has one to two Cape-class (Riazzi-class) 239-ton inshore minesweepers, and seems to have converted two of its Iran Ajar-class LSTs for mine-warfare purposes. Many of its small boats and craft can lay mines.

Both the Iranian navy and the naval branch of the IRGC are expanding their capability for mine warfare. While Iran has only a limited number of specialized mine vessels, it can also use small craft, LSTs, Boghammers, helicopters and submarines to lay mines. Iran has a wide range of Soviet, Western and Iranian-made moored and drifting contact mines. It is almost certainly seeking bottom-influence mines as well. If Iran does obtain modern mines, these could be placed in tanker routes, as they were during the Iran-Iraq War, placed near the Strait of Hormuz to deter commercial traffic, used to threaten warships in narrow zones of operation or placed in the Gulf of Oman—where sweeping and defensive coverage would be even more difficult than in the Persian Gulf. While such activity would be more a harassment than a war-fighting capability, it could be combined with the use of land-based anti-ship missiles, commando raids and submarine deployments. This would give Iran considerable leverage in terms of a cumulative threat to tanker and other shipping in the Gulf, and one that would be difficult to target, counter and destroy.

Iran has significant stocks of U.S. Mark 65 and Soviet AMD 500, AMAG-1 and KRAB anti-ship mines, and may have bought Chinese-made versions of the Soviet mines. It has claimed to be making its own non-magnetic acoustic free-floating and remote-controlled mines, and may have acquired significant stocks of non-magnetic mines, influence mines and mines with sophisticated timing devices from other countries. Such mines are extremely difficult to detect and sweep, particularly when they are spaced at wide intervals in shipping lanes. There also are reports that Iran has negotiated with China to buy the EM-52 rocket-propelled mine.[20]

Mines can be used throughout the Gulf, and in parts of the Gulf of Oman. The Southern Gulf states may develop effective mine-sweeping capabilities to sweep concentrated fields in limited areas, but Iran could use such mines throughout the Gulf, and tanker companies and captains are unlikely to take their ships into harm's way in the face of even limited risks. It is also difficult for even the most advanced Western mine counter-measure systems to detect and sweep modern mines. The U.S. ships damaged by mines during the Gulf War were all operating in waters that had supposedly been swept, and even the best trained and equipped mine-sweeping team has serious problems in sweeping non-magnetic mines, large areas with loose mines, and bottom mines or other mines that are timed to activate only after several ships have passed or at fixed intervals.

IRANIAN AMPHIBIOUS WARFARE CAPABILITIES

Iran has significant amphibious assets by Gulf standards, including four Hengam-class (Larak-class) LST amphibious support ships (2,940 tons loaded), 3 Iran Hormuz-class (South Korean) LSTs (2,014 tons loaded), and 1 Iran Ajar-class LST (2,274 tons loaded). Iran also has three 1,400-ton LCTs, one 250-ton LSL, at least 6 and possibly more than 129-ton LCUs, and about 50 small patrol craft. Each Hengam-class ship could carry 227 troops, 9 tanks, and 1 helicopter; each Iran Hormuz-class could carry 140 troops and 8 to 9 tanks. The Ajar-class could carry 650 tons, but were converted to mine-laying. These ships give Iran the capability to deploy about 800 to 1,200 troops, and 30 to 50 tanks in an amphibious assault, although Iran currently lacks the air and surface power to support a landing in a defended area or a movement across the Gulf in the face of significant air/sea defenses. Iran also would probably gain more from using commercial ferries and roll on–roll off ships to move Iranian forces across the Gulf to a friendly port.

IRANIAN ANTI-SHIP MISSILE FORCES

Iran has obtained at least 60 to 100 C-801 or C-802 (YF-6) anti-ship missiles from the Chinese and may be using these to refit its surface fleet as well as to equip some shore-based facilities and the naval branch of the IRGC. The C-801 anti-ship missile (also called the Yinji [Hawk] or SY-2 missile) is a solid-fueled missile that began test flights in 1986. It is roughly equivalent to the French Exocet, and can be launched from land, ships and aircraft. It has a range of approximately 74 kilometers in the surface-to-surface mode, and uses J-Band active radar guidance. It has a 512-kilogram warhead and cruises at an altitude of 20 to 30 meters. The CS-802 is an upgraded C-801 that was first exhibited in 1988. It has many characteristics similar to the C-801, but uses a turbojet-propulsion system with a rocket booster instead of the solid-fueled booster in the C-801.[21]

Iran has also sought to buy more advanced anti-ship missiles from Russia, North Korea and China, and possibly Chinese-made missile armed frigates. There is no way to know how many Iranian ships will acquire effective new anti-ship and anti-air missiles, or when any new types of missiles and ships might be delivered. Iran would have to make some such order by the late 1990s to keep up its existing strength, however, since its major Western-supplied ships cannot be made fully modern and operational without a comprehensive refit, which can only be done in Western shipyards.[22]

The naval branch of the Revolutionary Guards also plays a major role in Iran's anti-ship missile capabilities. The Guards have operated Iran's Chinese-supplied Silkworm surface-to-ship missiles since they were first delivered during the Iran-Iraq War. In 1995, the naval branch of the IRGC had three to five operational land-based anti-ship missile units with three to six Silkworm launchers each, and a total of fifty to sixty missiles. At least some of these units were deployed near Iran's naval base at Chah Bahar, Bandar Abbas, and at Khuestak near the Strait of Hormuz to cover the entrance to the Gulf. These units may be operated with the support of the Iranian navy. The Guards have formed at least one new unit using Chinese-supplied C-801 anti-ship and ship-to-ship missiles, and there are reports that Iran is seeking to acquire much-longer-range anti-ship cruise missiles from the People's Republic of China or the former Soviet Union.

IRAN'S SUBMARINE FORCES

Iran has attempted to offset the weakness of its major surface forces by emphasizing unconventional forms of naval warfare. It seems to have purchased or assembled one to three 27-ton midget submarines from North Korea in 1988. These submarines can dive to 300 feet, have a compartment for divers, and can carry two side cargoes of 5 tons or 14 limpet mines. It is unclear, however, whether Iran has been able to operate them successfully.[23]

Iran has also obtained two Russian Kilo-class submarines. The Kilo is a relatively modern and quiet submarine that first became operational in 1980. The submarines potentially give Iran a way of operating in the Persian Gulf and Gulf of Oman that reduces its vulnerability to air and surface attack, and its mini-submarines give it the potential to hide in the shallow depths and currents near the Strait. Submarines can be used to fire torpedoes or launch mines near ports or against slow moving tankers long before they can operate effectively against hostile combat ships. Iran has already shown that it can use its helicopters to communicate with its submarines using dipping sonars, and can improve its ability to target the submarines using its shore-based radars and patrol aircraft.[24]

Iran does, however, face significant problems in using such submarines in the Gulf. Many areas of the Gulf do not favor submarine operations. The Gulf's heat patterns disturb surface sonars, but they also disturb submarine sonars, and the advantage seems to be slightly in favor of sophisticated surface ships and maritime patrol aircraft. The deeper parts of the Gulf are noisy enough to make ASW operations difficult, and large parts of the Gulf—including much of the Southern Gulf on a line from Al Jubail across the tip of Qatar to about halfway up the UAE—are less than 20 meters deep. The Strait of Hormuz has a minimum width of 39 kilometers, and only the two deep-water channels are suitable for major surface-ship or submarine operations. Each of these channels is only about two kilometers wide. Further, a limited flow of fresh water and high evaporation make the Gulf extremely saline, and create complex underwater currents in the main channels at the Strait of Hormuz—complicating submarine operations but also complicating detection.

Submarines are easier to operate in the Gulf of Oman, which is noisy enough to make ASW operations difficult, but such deployments expose the Kilos to operations by United States and British nuclear-attack submarines. The effectiveness of the Iranian Kilos thus depends heavily on the degree of Western involvement in any ASW operation. If they did not face the United States or UK, the Iranian Kilos could operate in or near the Gulf with considerable impunity. If they did face United States and British forces, they might be able to attack a few tankers or conduct some mining efforts, but are unlikely to survive extended combat. This makes the Kilos a weapon that may be more effective as a threat than in actual combat. Certainly, they have already gotten the attention of the Southern Gulf states and convinced them that they must take Iran more seriously.

THE NAVAL BRANCH OF THE REVOLUTIONARY GUARDS

The naval element of the Islamic Revolutionary Guard Corps in 1994 was estimated to be 20,000 men, but the actual total could be as little as 12,000 to 15,000. It operated three to five of Iran's coastal defense sites, each armed with artillery and CSS-N-2 (HY-2) Silkworm anti-ship missiles. The naval branch of the IRGC also had training facilities and five bases in the Gulf, on the islands of Sirri, Abu Musa, Al Farisyah and Larak, and on the Halul oil platform. Most of these facilities appeared relatively small, although sources in the UAE claimed in early 1995 that the IRGC had fortified part of Abu Musa island, increased its troop presence there from 150 to several thousand men, deployed Silkworm anti-ship missiles and dug in tanks and artillery to support its fortifications.

The naval branch of the Islamic Revolutionary Guard Corps provides one of the largest unconventional warfare capabilities of any maritime force in the world. Iran had about 100 coastal patrol craft, 35 to 40 Boghammer 41-foot craft, 35 Boston Whaler 22-foot craft, and large numbers of river craft. The Naval Guards were definitely equipped with the Boghammer Swedish-built fast-interceptor craft, as well as small launches equipped with anti-tank guided missiles, and at least 30 Zodiak rubber dinghies to carry out rocket, small-arms and recoilless-rifle attacks. They were also armed with machine guns, recoilless rifles, and man-and-crew portable anti-tank guided missiles.

IRANIAN NAVAL WAR-FIGHTING CAPABILITIES

These new forms of sea power offer Iran the ability to tacitly and actively threaten the flow of oil through the Gulf, and the economic lifeblood of Iraq and its Southern Gulf neighbors. Iran could threaten or attack shipping near the Strait of Hormuz until decisive action was taken to destroy Iran's anti-ship missile units, mine-warfare capabilities, and submarines, as well as its ability to use smaller ships. Iran could also take advantage of the long shipping routes through the Gulf—and its ability to launch mines, naval or air strikes, and anti-ship missile strikes from positions along the entire length of the Gulf and the Gulf of Oman—to threaten or harass Gulf shipping. While strategists sometimes focus on "closing the Strait," a bottle does not have to be broken at the neck, and low-level mine and unconventional warfare strikes on shipping that are designed to harass and intimidate might allow Iran to achieve its objectives more safely than launching all-out attacks on the flow of oil.

Iran might also be able to exploit its buildup in Abu Musa, the Tunbs and other islands in the Gulf. While Clinton administration officials have emphasized the risk of an Iranian buildup in Abu Musa and the Tunbs, these are small islands and even Abu Musa would be difficult to use as a base for naval operations or sighting anti-ship missiles in the face of attacks by U.S. airpower. Further, while the three islands have a strategic position near the main shipping channels in the lower Gulf, Iran has long had anti-ship missiles deployed near the Strait that could attack any large vessels moving in and out of the Gulf, and has more developed bases at Sirri, Qeshm, Hengam and Larak—islands that are also capable of staging mining and Naval Guard operations. Iran seems to have deployed Silkworm anti-ship missiles on Qeshm and Sirri with ranges of up to 90 kilometers. There are at least some reports that Iran has also deployed advanced long-range anti-ship missiles, such as the Sunburst, on Sirri.[25]

Iran's surface force cannot hope to challenge the combined power of the U.S. navy and U.S. air power on a sustained basis, but Iran can use systems like anti-ship missiles, mines and submarines to at least threaten U.S. freedom of action and ability to deploy vulnerable high-value targets such as carriers in Gulf waters. As a result, it might take several weeks to decisively defeat Iran's ability to attack Gulf shipping once the United States deployed major naval and air forces, although much of Iran's naval power might be destroyed in a matter of days.

As for power projection, Iran cannot project power by land without crossing Iraq, but it can carry out small amphibious operations. This allows Iran to pose a tacit or active threat to the Southern Gulf states, particularly small vulnerable states like Bahrain and the UAE—although such capabilities are currently limited. Unless the Southern Gulf states and United States permit Iran to use ferries or commercial ships to conduct unopposed landings or transfers of troops, the Iranian navy and IRGC are very limited in capability. They can only conduct small landing operations, and these operations would be highly vulnerable unless they achieved total surprise. There is no way Iran could sustain them in the face of U.S. naval and air counterattacks.

As a result, Iran's present naval warfare capabilities can threaten and intimidate, and can cause significant initial or short-term damage to shipping in the Gulf, and offshore and coastal facilities in the Southern Gulf. Iran cannot, however, hope to engage in sustained naval warfare as long as the United States commits major naval and air forces and unless the Southern Gulf states are willing to provide bases and facilities and resist Iranian pressure.

IRAN AND WEAPONS OF MASS DESTRUCTION

Conventional threats are only part of the story. Iran has long sought weapons of mass destruction, and the means to deliver them—although its efforts have never compared in scale to those of Iraq. Iran has lacked the resources to finance such a massive worldwide purchasing effort, and its revolutionary turmoil has limited its access to foreign technology and limited the efficiency of its industrial base. Iran has, however, sought long-range missiles, produced chemical weapons, developed biological weapons and made efforts to acquire nuclear weapons.

IRAN'S LONG-RANGE MISSILE PROGRAMS[26]

Iran has steadily improved its long-range missile forces since the beginning of the Iran-Iraq War. These systems consist of the Scud B, North Korean variants of the Scud, and the Chinese CSS-8. Iran purchased an estimated 200 to 300 Scud Bs from North Korea between 1987 and 1992. Israeli experts estimated Iran had at least 250 to 300 Scud missiles, and at least 8 to 15 launchers, on hand in 1995—although some U.S. experts felt the total was much lower. All of these Scuds were obtained from other countries, and Iran's claims during the Iran-Iraq War that it was able to actually manufacture Scuds were false. Iran can assemble imported missile systems, but it has not yet demonstrated any capability to produce whole missiles or major assemblies like the booster.[27]

Many U.S. experts believe that China is now actively involved in giving Iran the technology it needs to produce either an extended range Scud or an M-9 class missile. The M-9 is a single-stage solid-fueled missile with a range of about 600 kilometers, a 500 to 600 kilogram warhead and a CEP of 600 to 1,000 meters.[28] Iran also bought 150 to 200 CSS-8 missiles and 25 to 30 launchers from the People's Republic of China in 1989. The CSS-8 has a range of approximately 150 kilometers (65 miles).[29] There are reports that Iran has at least two rocket and missile assembly plants, a missile test range and monitoring complex, and a wide range of smaller design-and-refit facilities.[30]

There is no way to reconcile the different unclassified estimates of Iran's current missile-production facilities. It does seem likely, however, that Iran's plants have the ability to rapidly assemble large numbers of North Korean- and PRC-supplied systems, or that Iran is developing the capability to build whole missiles, produce major components or allow Iran to design and produce indigenous designs.

Iran definitely succeeded in acquiring a more modern and longer range North Korean missile system—often referred to as a "Scud C"—although Iran formally denied this long after the transfer became a reality. Iran now seems to have 5 to 10 launchers for this missile, with several missiles each, and may have received four new North Korean TELs in 1995.[31] North Korea seems to have completed development of this missile in 1987, after obtaining technical support from the People's Republic of China. While it is often called a "Scud C," it seems to differ substantially in detail from the original Soviet Scud B, and seems to be based more on Chinese-made DF-61 than a direct copy of Soviet technology. It has a range of around 310 miles (500 kilometers), a payload of at least 500 kilograms, and relatively good accuracy and reliability. This gives Iran the ability to strike all the targets on the southern coast of the Gulf. It allows it to cover all of the populated areas in Iraq, although not the West. It can reach into part of eastern Syria and the eastern third of Turkey, and can cover targets in the border area of the former Soviet Union, western Afghanistan and western Pakistan.[32]

Some experts feel that Iran, Syria and possibly Pakistan are cooperating in acquiring and producing a longer-range North Korean missile called the No Dong 1. This missile is a single-stage liquid-fueled missile, with a range of up to 620 miles (1,000 kilometers) and a 1,200- to 1,750-pound warhead. The missile is about 15 meters long—four meters longer than the Scud B. It has an estimated theoretical CEP of 700 meters at maximum range versus 900 meters for the Scud B, although its practical accuracy could be as wide as 2,000 to 4,000 meters. It seems to be transportable on a copy of the MAZ to 543P TEL, although some experts question this. It has an estimated terminal velocity of Mach 3.5, versus 2.5 for the Scud B. This presents added problems for tactical missile defense.

The No Dong missile in 1995 seemed to be nearing final development in North Korea, possibly with substantial aid from military industries in the People's Republic of China. Iran may also be interested in the developmental North Korean IRBM, called the Tapeo Dong 1 or Tapeo Dong 2, which was detected by U.S. intelligence in early 1994. This missile has an estimated maximum range of 1,000 to 1,200 miles (2,000 kilometers).[33]

It is possible that Iran is developing a cruise missile with Chinese and other foreign assistance. While Iran has no capability to develop and deploy a missile as sophisticated as the U.S. Tomahawk, U.S. studies have indicated that Third-World nations such as Iran and Iraq may be able to build a cruise missile about half the size of a small fighter aircraft and with a payload of about 500 kilograms by 2000 to 2005. The technology for fusing and CBW and cluster warheads would be within Iran's grasp. Navigation systems and jet engines would be a major potential problem. Such cruise-missile systems could reach a wide range of targets. Such systems can also be programmed to avoid major air-defense concentrations at a sacrifice of about 20 percent of their range.

IRANIAN MISSILE WAR-FIGHTING CAPABILITIES

Even without such new ballistic or cruise-missile systems, Iran has the capability to launch missile attacks against Iraq, and to hit coastal area targets in much of the Southern Gulf. Iran is currently limited by its lack of sophisticated long-range targeting capability, and missile systems with the accuracy to attack anything other than area targets. It can pose a major threat in terms of intimidation and popular fear using conventional warheads and may be able to use missiles with chemical and biological warheads to destroy or incapacitate military area targets, paralyze warfighting capabilities or even attack large complexes of buildings and facilities. Such missile attacks would be vulnerable to point defense by the improved Patriot, and U.S. air power could probably break up large-scale attacks by strikes against Iran's missile-launch facilities. The United States, however, now has no way to prevent Iran from confronting it with the same "Scud hunt" problems it had during the Gulf War. It would be almost impossible for U.S. air units to hunt out and destroy enough of Iran's missile capabilities to halt all attacks. As a result, the United States might well be forced into deterring Iranian missile strikes by escalating its attacks on other high-value Iranian targets.[34]

Depending on how Iran chose to deploy its missiles, it could develop a significant launch-on-warning or launch-under-attack capability that the United States might not be able to preempt even in a surprise attack. It is doubtful that any "leakproof" defense system could be created to deal with such attacks, although a wide-area missile-defense system such as Theater High Altitude Air Defense (THAAD) or Aegis might have significant capability to degrade such attacks. This would place new emphasis on U.S. ability to deter Iranian missile strikes by escalating its attacks on other high-value Iranian targets, or by threatening the use of U.S. nuclear weapons.

IRANIAN CHEMICAL WEAPONS[35]

Both Iran and Iraq have signed the Geneva Protocols of 1925, which prohibit the use of poison gas. Both nations have also signed the Biological Warfare Convention of 1972, which banned the development, production and deployment or stockpiling of biological weapons. Nevertheless, Iran began a crash effort to produce chemical weapons in the early 1980s, in response to Iraq's use of chemical weapons against Iran. The Islamic Revolutionary Guard Corps, with support from the Ministry of Defense, was put in charge of developing offensive chemical agents, and Iran has covertly obtained substantial outside support. While Iran did not make extensive use of chemical weapons during the Iran-Iraq War, it had moderate-scale chemical weapons plants in operation at Damghan and Parchin by March 1988.

The exact status of Iran's current chemical war-fighting capabilities is unknown, but it is clear that Iran has established a significant chemical weapons production capability of 25 to 100 tons per year, including mustard gas and dusty mustard gas, phosgene gas and blood agents like cyanogen chloride or one of the cyanides.[36] This already gives Iran a significant capability to conduct a chemical war near its borders, to launch limited long-range air raids using chemical bombs, and to use chemical weapons in unconventional warfare.

While Iran's chemical warheads for its missiles are probably still of limited sophistication, it has had time to develop usable artillery, rocket warheads and bombs. It probably has storable binary weapons, or could soon introduce them into inventory, and there were indications that it was seeking to buy equipment to support its forces in conducting nerve gas warfare.[37]

Iran may have little practical experience in large-scale chemical operations, but chemical weapons do give Iran new capabilities to intimidate the Southern Gulf states and deter the West. Further, chemical weapons do not have to be delivered by missiles or aircraft. As is the case with biological weapons, devices can be smuggled into a target area. Agents can be dispersed by man-portable devices or even grenades. They can be used as terrorist or unconventional warfare weapons for delivery into any building with central air conditioning. A passenger airliner could be used to fly a line and disperse agents as an aerosol. Chemical devices could be smuggled into and detonated in commuter centers, stadiums or other crowded areas.

IRANIAN BIOLOGICAL WEAPONS

Iran seems to have begun developing biological weapons as early as 1982. Reports surfaced that Iran was working on the production of mycotoxins—relatively simple biological agents that require only limited laboratory facilities.[38] Some experts now believe the Iranian biological weapons effort is under the control of the Islamic Revolutionary Guard Corps, who are known to have tried to purchase suitable production equipment for such weapons. It is clear that Iran conducted covert operations in Germany and Switzerland that were linked to biological weapons research and production in the 1990s. Iran has also conducted extensive research on more lethal active agents like anthrax, hoof and mouth disease, as well as biotoxins, and has repeatedly approached various European firms for the equipment and technology necessary to work with these diseases and toxins.

Little is known about the exact details of Iran's effort to weaponize and produce such weapons. There are some reports that Iran has developed effective aerosol weapons and weapons designs with ceramic containers. Such uncertainties make it harder to determine the actual nature of Iran's current and probable future war-fighting capabilities than is the case with chemical and nuclear weapons. Iran may encounter continuing difficulties in developing effective ballistic-missile warheads using biological agents, but it should be able to meet the technical challenges in improving its targeting and finding effective ways to disperse agents from cruise-missile warheads and bombs. Iran may already have the technology to disperse agents such as anthrax over a wide area by spreading them from a ship moving along a coast, or out of a large container smuggled into a city or industrial complex. It also seems likely that Iran will be able to create a significant production capability for storable encapsulated biological agents by the year 2000.

Although biological weapons are fundamentally different in character from nuclear weapons, they can be as lethal as small nuclear weapons. The results of a study by the U.S. Office of Technology Assessment that compared the impact of a 12.5 kiloton nuclear weapon dropped in the center of Washington with the minimum and maximum effect of using a single aircraft to deliver 300 kilograms of Sarin and 30 kilograms of anthrax spores, indicate that the nuclear weapon would cover 7.8 square kilometers and produce prompt kills of 23,000 to 80,000; the nerve gas would cover 0.22 square kilometers and kill 60 to 200, and the anthrax spores would cover 10 square kilometers and kill 3,000 to 10,000. Such calculations depend on the scenario, time of day, and weather, and assume a sophisticated bomb or missile warhead. Such data are, however, a warning of the potential risks posed by biological weapons.[39]

IRANIAN NUCLEAR WEAPONS

Most Western experts do not feel Iran has been able to fund the kind of massive program that Iraq established, and Iran has often found it difficult to obtain nuclear technology. Few Western experts seem to support a recent report by a former member of the U.S. National Security Council staff that Iran had developed a $10 billion dollar plan to acquire nuclear weapons.[40]

Iran also does not have anything approaching Iraq's manpower base of several thousand nuclear technicians. Some estimates indicated that Iran had fewer than 500 nuclear physicists, engineers and senior technicians in the late 1980s—versus some 7,500 in Iraq. Most Western experts do feel, however, that Iran's revolutionary government at the time of the Iran-Iraq War revitalized the nuclear weapons program begun by the shah, and that Iran has engaged in many of the weapons-design and fuel-cycle activities necessary to build a nuclear weapon. The Iranian government apparently began to revitalize the shah's massive nuclear effort in the mid-1980s, after Iraq used chemical weapons on the battlefield, and strengthened the Atomic Energy Organization the shah had formed in 1974, providing new funds to the Amirabad Nuclear Research Center in Tehran, and forming a new nuclear research center at the University of Isfahan in 1984—with French assistance.[41]

Iran's efforts to acquire nuclear weapons accelerated in the late 1980s— although it is not possible to definitively separate such efforts from efforts to acquire nuclear power generating facilities. Iran's Yazd Province has significant uranium deposits (at least 5,000 tons) in the Shagand region, and Iran announced in 1987 that it had plans to set up a yellow cake plant in Yazd Province.[42] This facility was under construction by 1989, and Iran may have begun to build a uranium processing or enrichment facility at Pilcaniyeu.[43] It may also have opened a new uranium ore processing plant close to its Shagand uranium mine in March 1990, and it seems to have extended its search for uranium ore into three additional areas. Iran also may have begun to exploit stocks of yellow cake the shah had obtained from South Africa in the late 1970s, and obtained uranium dioxide from Argentina by purchasing it through Algeria.[44]

Iran later sought to buy large reactors. On July 4, 1994, Iran and the PRC announced they had signed an agreement for the PRC to build a 300-megawatt reactor near Tehran.[45] Since that time, Iran has expressed an interest in buying two 300-megawatt pressurized-water nuclear reactors from China similar to the Chinese plant at Qinshan in Zhejiang Province. At least one of these reactors would evidently be sited near Bushehr on the Gulf Coast.[46]

Iranian officials indicated in mid-May 1995 that Iran had already made an $800 to $900 million down payment on the deal with China. There are, however, uncertainties regarding such a deal. The Chinese nuclear industry is still in the developmental stage, and China has had serious problems in bringing some of its reactors on line and keeping them operating.

The reactor at Qinshan also uses a Japanese-made reactor vessel and German primary cooling pumps, and it is not clear whether these will be exportable to Iran.

Iran conducted similar negotiations with Russia. Iran began to seek nuclear reactors from Russia in the mid-1980s. Reports surfaced that Russia had signed a contract to sell two nuclear reactors to Iran in the late 1980s—although the existence of any such contracts was not made public, and no tangible steps seemed to follow. Negotiations continued, however, and on November 20, 1994, Iran announced that Russia had agreed to a $780 million agreement to complete a reactor at Bushehr that German companies had begun during the time of the shah. Iran signed this agreement with Russia on January 8, 1995.

The nuclear facility involved is about 730 miles south of Tehran, and 15 miles from the city of Bushehr. It is the site of two incomplete 1,200-megawatt reactors that Siemens began to construct in 1976. While it was halted in 1979—with the fall of the shah—Iran has long kept the facility active, and some 300 to 400 Iranians normally live on the site and maintain it. Facilities exist to house some 2,000 workers at the site and to support up to 2,000 more. As a result, Russia was immediately able to deploy some 150 technicians to the reactor site.

Russia was scheduled to complete work on the first reactor by the year 2000, although the project at Bushehr may be only the first step in a far more ambitious Iranian effort. Some U.S. experts believed that Iran was seeking to buy an additional four to five light water reactors from Russia at a cost in excess of $5 billion. These include two 1,000-megawatt reactors and two 463-megawatt reactors, and they are of a type that can be used to produce substantial amounts of fissile material for nuclear weapons. They also believed that Iran had aggressively sought to buy highly enriched and/or fissile material from the former Soviet Union, as well as the services of Soviet nuclear weapons designers.[47]

It is impossible to state categorically that Iran's reactor purchases would be part of a nuclear weapons effort. Russia is selling light water reactors, which are less suited to producing plutonium than the heavy water reactors Iran sought initially. Russia has indicated that it will take back the plutonium-bearing spent fuel in the reactor, and Mohammed Sadegh Ayatollahi, Iran's representative to the International Atomic Energy Agency (IAEA) has stated that, "We've had contracts before for the Bushehr plant in which we agreed that the spent fuel would go back to the supplier. For our contract with the Russians and Chinese, it is the same."[48]

At the same time, reactor sales to Iran present serious risks. Reactor-grade uranium and plutonium can be processed for weapons use, and Iran could reject IAEA safeguards once the reactor or reactors are complete and use such reactors to enrich its own uranium. The transfer of large-scale nuclear technology to Iran also will give it a nuclear technology base that many experts feel will allow it to build covert reactor facilities, centrifuge facilities and/or chemical-separation facilities even if it does comply with IAEA regulations and inspection agreements in operating its reactors.

Little other credible data is available on the size and nature of Iran's nuclear weapons effort and facilities, or the exact nature of Iran's imports of nuclear weapons-related and dual-use technology. Many Western experts believe that the fact Iran has clandestinely sought the material needed for a nuclear weapons effort for more than a decade is more important than the ability to target given facilities. They feel that Iran has repeatedly attempted to avoid Western controls on nuclear weapons technology since 1984, and that Iran made new efforts to buy nuclear weapons-related components in 1994. They believe Iran has bought extensive amounts of nuclear centrifuge technology from Germany—although it has denied it has done so—and that an audit trail of Iran's purchases indicates that it has bought a great deal of the specialized gear necessary to design and manufacture nuclear weapons, and simulate nuclear tests.[49]

There is also no way to estimate when Iran will get nuclear weapons. Some sources indicate that Iran may be able to build a weapon relatively quickly. Robert Gates, then-Director of Central Intelligence, testified to Congress in February 1992 that Iran was, "building up its special weapons capability as part of a massive . . . effort to develop its military and defense capability."[50] Press reports about the U.S. Central Intelligence Agency (CIA) National Intelligence Estimate (NIE) on this subject that was issued in 1992 indicated that the CIA estimated Iran could have a nuclear weapon by the year 2000. Reports coming out of Israel in January 1995 also claimed that the United States and Israel estimated Iran could have a nuclear weapon in five years.[51]

Other sources feel Iran may take substantially longer. United States intelligence sources denied the reports coming out of Israel and estimated that it might take seven to fifteen years for Iran to acquire a nuclear weapon.[52] Secretary of Defense William Perry stated on January 9, 1995, that "We believe that Iran is trying to develop a nuclear program. We believe it will be many, many years until they achieve such a capability. There some things they might be able to do to short-cut that time."[53] In referring to "short cuts," Secretary Perry was concerned with the risk that Iran could obtain fissile material and weapons technology from the former Soviet Union or some other nation capable of producing fissile material.[54]

At present, most experts feel that Iran has all the basic technology to build a bomb, but has only a low- to moderate-level weapons design and development effort.[55] They indicate that no major weapons material and production effort has yet been detected. In the late 1990s Iran seemed to be at least three to five years away from acquiring the ability to design a nuclear weapon that could be fitted in the warhead of a long-range missile system, and possibly five to nine years away from acquiring a nuclear device using its own enriched material.

IRAN'S WAR-FIGHTING CAPABILITIES WITH WEAPONS OF MASS DESTRUCTION

Weapons of mass destruction can radically change crisis behavior, perceptions of the risks of escalation, acceptance of new levels of conflict, and acceptance of given kinds of conflict termination. They alter perceptions, so decisionmakers and military commanders may have at best limited understanding of the technical capabilities and effectiveness of the weapons involved. They affect the transparency and predictability of war since neither Iran or Iraq have anything approaching the intelligence assets to obtain near-real time data on the actual impact of such weapons, and there is simply too little empirical data to predict either short-term or long-term damage effects.

The threat posed by Iran's weapons of mass destruction will become steadily more important as Iran acquires more effective chemical weapons. It would also be far more important if Iran acquired highly lethal biological agents, or even a few nuclear devices. Weapons of mass destruction produce unpredictable changes in the perceptions of both the attacker and defender in terms of political decisions and war fighting. While much of the discussion of such weapons focuses on casualty and physical damage effects, they have major psychological, political and tactical effects that may prove to be more important than lethality in a given contingency. Relative willingness to take risks and deal with the real-world outcome of uncertainty becomes critical. So does the relative value assigned to human life; to the predictability of weapons effects and the nature of retaliation; and to the protection of troops, civilians and potential target areas.

If Iran got a working nuclear device, this would suddenly and radically change perceptions of the military balance in the region. Iran could destroy any hardened target, area target or city within the range of its delivery systems, and Iran's neighbors are extremely vulnerable to attacks on a few cities. They are effectively "one bomb" countries: even one successful nuclear attack might force a fundamental restructuring of their politics and/or economy.

Iranian nuclear capabilities would raise major mid-term and long-term challenges to the Southern Gulf states and the West in terms of deterrence, defense, retaliation and arms control. It would almost certainly accelerate efforts to deploy theater missile defenses—although such systems seem more likely to be "confidence builders" than leak proof. It would almost certainly lead the United States to consider counter-proliferation strikes on Iran, and to work with its Southern Gulf allies in developing an adequate deterrent. Given the U.S. rejection of biological and chemical weapons, this raises the possibility of creating a major U.S. theater nuclear deterrent, although such a deterrent could be sea and air based and deployed outside the Gulf. If the United States failed to provide such a deterrent, it seems likely that the Southern Gulf states would also be forced to accommodate Iran or seek weapons of mass destruction of their own. Further, such Iranian possession would almost certainly trigger a major new Iraqi effort to acquire such weapons, and make any efforts at arms control meaningless for some years to come.

Future Threats and Military Scenarios

It is easy to generalize about Iran's future, and to use strategic rhetoric to support those who wish to "demonize" Iran and call it a major threat to its neighbors and the West, or those who wish to "sanctify" Iran and claim that it is evolving into a moderate state. The preceding analysis has shown, however, that there is no way to definitively resolve this debate. Iran has growing capabilities to threaten its neighbors, but it is far from clear that it will aggressively use such capabilities or that they will lead to war. Further, Iran faces a complex mix of military weaknesses and military strengths.

A Future of Military Limitations

Iran faces serious near-term and mid-term limitations on the military forces it can develop that no Iranian regime can overcome regardless of its intentions:

- Regardless of how Iran's political character and intentions evolve over the coming decade, any Iranian regime is likely to import significant numbers of major weapons and improve Iranian military capabilities in the process. It lost some 40 to 50 percent of its major ground force equipment in 1988, during the final battles of the Iran-Iraq War. Its navy suffered serious losses during the "tanker war." Iran has lacked effective military resupply and modernization for its Western-supplied land weapons, aircraft and ships for more than fifteen years, and maintenance standards were low and foreign-contractor dependent during the time of the shah. While Iran was able to make massive imports during the Iran-Iraq War, it not only lost much of this equipment during the fighting but many of its imports were aging Soviet-bloc systems or came from low-technology suppliers like China and North Korea.

- Regardless of how Iran's political character and intentions evolve over the coming decade, Iran faces severe limits on its ability to modernize and expand its forces. Both the shah and Iran's new religious regime systematically squandered Iran's development opportunities. Its large population has meant that it was particularly sensitive to reductions in oil prices. Regardless of the intentions of Iran's current and future regime, there are severe near-term financial limitations on its ability to fund a massive buildup of conventional capabilities of the kind that occurred under the shah.

- Regardless of how Iran's political character and intentions evolve over the coming decade, Iran faces powerful strategic constraints. Its Southern Gulf neighbors are modernizing and expanding their forces at a much faster rate than Iran. In spite of currently programmed force cuts, the United States retains the capability to decisively intervene in the Gulf. It can rapidly achieve naval and air supremacy, and while it cannot rapidly deploy land forces against Iran, it can carry out the kind of strategic-bombing campaign it carried out against Iraq. In spite of Iraq's defeat in the Gulf War, it is still a superior military power and still poses a potential threat to Iran.

- Regardless of how Iran's political character and intentions evolve over the coming decade, geography limits Iran's military capabilities in the Gulf. Iran has very limited amphibious capabilities, and little air-assault capability. Its only land route to the Southern Gulf is through Iraq, and its aircraft must fly relatively exposed routes over the Gulf to attack targets in the Southern Gulf.

- Regardless of how Iran's political character and intentions evolve over the coming decade, future Iranian regimes are likely to have to continue a low-level war with opponents of the regime. It is unlikely that anything other than coming to power will end the challenge the People's

Mojahedin poses in terms of bombings, assassination and attacks out of its bases in Iraq. Iran is likely to face low-level military challenges from extremist ethnic movements such as the Kurdish Democratic Party of Iran, and no regime is likely to entirely suppress internal and external violence over the issue of religion. Regardless of whether it is called terrorism, future Iranian regimes are likely to have to use their intelligence services, and sometimes their military forces, to deal with opposition movements.

These constraints are another factor that make it difficult to distinguish between "aggressive" and "defensive" Iranian actions. They also make it likely that many aspects of Iran's strategic future will look much the same as its present, regardless of the character and intentions of its regime. Almost any Iranian regime would attempt to modernize Iran's military forces because there is no alternative—other than to see Iran's military capabilities decay relative to those of its neighbors.

At the same time, future regimes will find it difficult to transform Iran's current process of military modernization into a massive military buildup. They will lack the resources to do so unless they can force Iran's population to make massive new economic sacrifices and unless they are willing to further mortgage Iran's economic development opportunities. Even if a regime arises that is willing to sacrifice Iran's people, Iran will not be able to achieve strategic hegemony in the Gulf unless the United States mysteriously withdraws from the region, and Iran will face significant geographic limitations on its ability to attack its neighbors.

Put differently, most types of future Iranian regimes are likely to feel that Iranian conventional military capabilities are marginal for at least the next decade. Instead of being able to create conventional forces that will give Iran hegemony in the Gulf, Iran faces a near-term decline in the capability of its surface fleet, and a combination of United States, other Western and Southern Gulf capabilities that can defeat it in a matter of days. Unless Iraq remains under UN sanctions for the next five years, or there is a major change in Iraq's political character, Iran's future leaders are likely to feel that Iran faces the continuing prospect of another Iran-Iraq War.

Unless the United Nations Special Commission (UNSCOM) is far more successful than it has been to date, they will also feel that Iran faces the prospect that Iraq will recover many of its chemical and biological warfare capabilities over the next five to seven years, and some of its missile-delivery capabilities. These trends, however, may lead a variety of different types of Iranian regimes to continue to seek weapons of mass destruction, and to see nuclear weapons and long-range missiles as potential equalizers in dealing with Iraq and compensating for Iran's conventional weakness.

A FUTURE OF MILITARY OPPORTUNITIES

At the same time, the preceding analysis has shown that there are important areas in which a given Iranian regime can either enhance Iran's defensive capabilities or acquire the capability to threaten and intimidate Iran's neighbors and the West:

- Iran can use unconventional warfare to attack its neighbors and the West. Regardless of whether the West chooses to call this "terrorism," Iran can conduct covert unconventional warfare against foreign officials, and use bombings and other unconventional means to attack military and civilian targets. It can also use its large Revolutionary Guard forces, particularly the naval branch of the Guards, to attack offshore oil facilities, plant mines, attack ships or attack critical facilities such as oil- and gas-loading ports and desalinization plants. Iran has already used such tactics during the "tanker war" of 1987-88, and in its war against the People's Mojahedin. It may have used them—at least in proxy form—against Israel.

- Iran can use proxies to achieve its strategic objectives. It can use the training and funding of extremist or terrorist groups to indirectly attack given targets. It can support Shi'i movements in Bahrain and Saudi Arabia. It can encourage the Hezbollah in Lebanon, cooperate with the Sudan in supporting given movements, provide funds for the "Afghani" training camps and movements, and support groups like the Hamas and Islamic Jihad.

- Iran can conduct "wars" of threats and intimidation. Iran can use the threat of military action to influence the behavior of neighboring and Western states without escalating the issue to overt military action, and try to force compromises or changes in the actions of other states. Iran has already acquired many such capabilities. It has built up large unconventional warfare forces, moved anti-ship missile sites to the Strait of Hormuz, deployed submarines, and purchased smart and deep water mines. It is building a port on the Gulf of Oman, and has conducted large-scale amphibious exercises. It has also strengthened its naval guard bases in the Gulf, and built up its military capabilities in Abu Musa.

- Iran can tailor its military capabilities to attack the vulnerable oil traffic through the Gulf. Rather than attempt to win a direct battle with the U.S. navy, Iran can develop a wide mix of capabilities for threatening or attacking tanker traffic through the Gulf—the most vulnerable link in the Gulf's economy and Western strategic interests. Once again, Iran already has many such capabilities. These include the unconventional warfare forces, anti-ship missile sites, submarines, smart and deep water mines, and naval guard bases in the Gulf described earlier.

- Iran can acquire and threaten to use, or use, weapons of mass destruction. Iran already has chemical weapons and has used them in limited amounts during the final phases of the Iran-Iraq War. It has conducted extensive research into biological agents, and is developing nuclear capabilities. It has Scud and Scud C missiles, and is expected to acquire a longer-range system such as the No Dong during the next three to five years. These weapons can partially offset Iran's limited conventional warfare capabilities—particularly if Iran can acquire and weaponize biological and nuclear weapons. They will enhance Iran's capabilities for intimidation, deterrence and war fighting—although they can also sharply raise the level of conflict and threshold of damage to Iran.

- Iran can seek to ally with Iraq or seek to divide the Southern Gulf. The military balance in the Gulf would change radically if Iran and Iraq could agree on an alliance, or if Iran could exploit religious divisions in a state like Bahrain and acquire a "base" in the Southern Gulf. There seems to be only a limited probability Iran would, or could, reach an alliance with Iraq or divide the Southern Gulf, but it is at least a strategic possibility, and one Iran could explore at relatively little cost.

- Iran can seek to exploit U.S. vulnerabilities by attempting to attack a key U.S. facility, and inflicting high casualties—similar to the attack on the Marine Corps barracks in Beirut. It can also attempt to engage the United States in costly deployments and politically complex conflicts in which the United States may choose to not pay the cost of prolonged engagement.

- Iran can seek counter-balancing strategic relationships. Potential relationships could include economic and military relationships with Russia, which could ease many of the problems in Iran's military buildup and give Iran a potential counterweight to the United States.

They could expand Iran's relationship with the new Asiatic republics to the north, or create stronger economic and military relations with Turkey. They could include creating a strong relationship with an Asian state to acquire weapons of mass destruction—candidates could include China, North Korea and Pakistan.

- Iran can seek counter-balancing economic relationships. It seems doubtful that Iran will have any near- or mid-term incentive to pursue common oil and economic policies with its Southern Gulf neighbors. Any probable effort to maximize Iran's oil exports and export earnings is likely to be at least partially dependent on limiting the exports of its southern neighbors. Iran can, however, attempt to develop strong economic relations with key trading partners such as Germany and Japan. Such relations would not enhance Iran's military strength, but they could undercut any efforts at containing Iran.

Few of these "opportunities" or options are mutually exclusive. Iran can exploit several of these options at the same time. It is also important to point out that none of these options require a radical change in Iran's regime. A truly radical religious regime might be isolated from options that require cooperation with other states, and counter-balancing strategic relationships, but the Rafsanjani government has already shown that a pragmatic religious regime would encounter few problems in dealing with Turkey and Russia, and might well be able to compromise with Iraq. Accordingly, either a secular or religious Iranian regime could pursue most of the strategic opportunities open to Iran.

It is again difficult to label the pursuit of some of these "opportunities" as "aggressive" or "defensive." A future Iranian regime might well see pursuing such "opportunities" as a necessary defensive measure to compensate for Iran's military problems and weakness, as a means of deterring or defending against Iraq, or as a defensive reaction to U.S. strength in the Gulf and the buildup of Southern Gulf military forces.

Any future Iranian regime that actively pursued a wide range of such options, or that pursued any option that directly challenged another state would obviously be more threatening than a regime that did not. At the same time, it seems doubtful that any future Iranian regime will fail to pursue at least some of these "opportunities" in the future. Further, such a regime might pursue such "opportunities" even while it attempted to establish a rapprochement with the United States, Europe and its Southern Gulf neighbors.

"Dual Containment": Dealing With the Threats and Non-threats From Iran

There is no easy way to transform this mix of Iranian strengths and weaknesses into firm conclusions about policy. They do not support either the "demonization" or "sanctification" of Iran.

While some of Iran's actions and rhetoric have been more moderate since the death of Khomeini, the preceding analysis has shown that many of its actions and rhetoric have not. Iran has not been openly aggressive, but it has taken actions that threaten its Southern Gulf neighbors. Iran has taken a hard-line rejectionist stand that denies Israel's right to exist. Iran has provided at least indirect support to Islamic extremists in the civil war in the Sudan, Algeria and Egypt. Neither the West nor the Southern Gulf states have any reason to build up Iran's forces as a counterbalance to Iraq. Regardless of the Arab proverb, the enemy of our enemy is rarely a friend.

As a result, it may be best to err on the side of military containment. The West and Southern Gulf may be able to expect Iranian pragmatism but they cannot count on Iranian moderation. Iran's actions are likely to be heavily dependent on whether the West maintains strong power-projection forces, whether the Southern Gulf builds up its military capabilities and cooperation with the West, and whether continuing efforts are made to limit the more threatening aspects of Iran's military buildup.

There seems to be good reason to discourage destabilizing arms transfers to Iran, particularly modern armor, long-range attack aircraft, advanced anti-ship and surface-to-surface missiles, submarines and amphibious ships. There are also good reasons to control "dual-use" technology transfers to Iran. Regardless of any safeguards short of constant inspection, all dual-use technology may be put to military use whenever this is to Iran's advantage, and virtually every item of nuclear, chemical, biological and aerospace technology Iran can use in advancing its acquisition of weapons of mass destruction will be put to that use.

At the same time, the preceding analysis does not indicate that Iran is so extreme that the West and the Southern Gulf should extend "containment" from limiting Iran's military forces to attempting to isolate Iran in political, cultural or economic terms. Iran's threatening actions should be treated as threats, but the West and the Southern Gulf should encourage stronger economic ties to Iran, and encourage any Iranian political initiatives that can be accepted as moderate or as serving mutual interests.

Notes

1. Central Intelligence Agency, *World Factbook, 1992,* pp. 160-63; Arms Control and Disarmament Agency, *World Military Expenditures and Arms Transfers, 1993-1994* (Washington, DC: GPO, 1995).

2. Author's guesstimate. Iran claimed in February 1992 that it was spending only 1.3 percent of its GNP on defense (*Washington Times,* February 20, 1992, p. A9).

3. See Richard F. Grimmett, *Conventional Arms Transfers to the Third World, 1983-1990* (Washington, DC: Congressional Research Service, CRS-91-578F, August 2, 1991, pp. CRS-53-72); *Conventional Arms Transfers to the Third World, 1984-1991,* CRS-92-577F, July 20, 1992, pp. CRS-57-72; *Conventional Arms Transfers to the Third World, 1985-1992,* CRS-93-656F, July 19, 1993, pp. CRS-56-70.

4. CIA, *World Factbook, 1994,* pp. 160-63. *See also* International Institute for Strategic Studies (IISS), *Military Balance, 1994-1995,* pp. 127-31.

5. IISS, *Military Balance,* 1994-1995, pp. 127-31.

6. *New York Times,* May 17, 1995, p. A3; *Los Angeles Times,* May 18, 1995, p. 8.

7. *Jane's Defense Weekly,* January 7, 1995, p. 4; February 25, 1995, p. 4.

8. Based on estimates by Israeli and U.S. civilian experts, and the IISS, *The Military Balance, 1993-1994,* (London: IISS, 1993), pp. 115-17, and *The Military Balance, 1994-1995,* pp. 127-29.

9. Division, brigade, regiment, and battalion are Western terms applied to Iranian and Iraqi formations. Actual unit strengths and organization often have nothing to do with the titles applied in Western reporting.

10. Adapted from interviews with U.S., British and Israeli experts, and Iranian exiles. Anthony H. Cordesman, *Iran and Iraq: The Threat from the Northern Gulf* (Boulder: Westview, 1994); John W.R. Taylor and Kenneth Munson, "Gallery of Middle East Air Power," *Air Force* (October 1994), pp. 59-70; the IISS, *The Military Balance, 1993-1994,* (London: IISS, 1993), pp. 115-17; *The Military Balance, 1994-1995,* pp. 127-29; *World Defense Almanac: The Balance of Military Power,* XVII, Issue 1-1993, ISS N0722-3226, pp. 139-42; Anoushiravan Ehteshami, "Iran's National Strategy," *International Defense Review,* (April 1994), pp. 29-37; and working data from the Jaffee Center for Strategic Studies and the *Washington Times,* January 16, 1992, p. G4; *Washington Post,* February 1, 1992, p. A1; February 2, 1992, pp. A1 and A25; February 5, 1992, p. A19; *Financial Times,* February 6, 1992, p. 4;

Christian Science Monitor, February 6, 1992, p. 19; *Defense News,* February 17, 1992, p. 1.

11. See James P. Wootten, "Terrorism: U.S. Policy Options," Congressional Research Service, IB92074, October 6, 1994, pp. 6-7; Kenneth Katzman, *Iran: Current Developments and U.S. Policy,* Congressional Research Service, IB93033, September 9, 1994, pp. 5-7; *Christian Science Monitor,* March 22, 1994, p. 6; and June 28, 1994, p. A1. *Time,* March 21, 1994, pp. 50-54. *Washington Times,* December 19, 1993, p. A3; February 19, 1994, p. A8; March 9, 1994, June 22, 1994, p. A14; June 24, 1994, p. A1; June 27, 1994, p. A22. *Washington Post,* January 1, 1994, p. A15; February 4, 1994, p. A14.

12. Based on interviews with British, Israeli, and U.S. experts, and on Anthony H. Cordesman, *Iran and Iraq: The Threat from the Northern Gulf* (Boulder: Westview, 1994); *Wall Street Journal,* February 10, 1995, p. 19; *Washington Times,* February 10, 1995, p. A19. IISS, *The Military Balance, 1993-1994* and *1994-1995;* and working data from the Jaffee Center for Strategic Studies. U.S. and Israeli experts do not confirm reports that Iran has ordered and taken delivery on 12 TU-22M Backfire bombers. There were some indications that it may have discussed such orders with the USSR.

13. *Philadelphia Inquirer,* February 5, 1994, p. A18.

14. *Jane's Intelligence Review,* Special Report no. 6, May 1995, p. 23; *Washington Times,* January 16, 1992, p. G4. *Washington Post,* February 1, 1992, p. A1; February 2, 1992, pp. A1 and A25; February 5, p. A19. *Financial Times,* February 6, 1992, p. 4; *Christian Science Monitor,* February 6, 1992, p. 19; *Defense News,* February 17, 1992, p. 1; *Jane's Defense Weekly,* February 1, 1992, p. 159.

15. Based on interviews with British, Israeli, and U.S. experts, and on Anthony H. Cordesman, *Iran and Iraq: The Threat from the Northern Gulf* (Boulder: Westview, 1994).

16. *Jane's Intelligence Review,* Special Report no. 6, May 1995, p. 23.

17. *Defense and Foreign Affairs,* no. 1, (1994), pp. 4-7. There have also been reports from the Czech Republic that it might sell Iran an advanced mobile air surveillance system called Tamara. The manufacturer of this system—Tesla Pardubice—has claimed it is capable of tracking stealth aircraft. Tamara, however, seems to be a signals-intelligence system with some air-defense applications, and its claims to special advantages in detecting "stealth" aircraft seem to be nothing more than sales propaganda. *Defense News,* July 12, 1993, p. 1; *New York Times,* December 27, 1993, p. A17.

18. This analysis draws heavily on U.S. Naval Institute, *The Naval Institute Guide to the Combat Fleets of the World, 1993, Their Ships, Aircraft, and Armament,* (Annapolis: Naval Institute, 1993); *Jane's Fighting Ships, 1992-1993* and *1994-1995*; IISS, *The Military Balance.*

19. Adapted from the IISS, Annapolis, and JCSS databases, and the *Washington Times,* January 16, 1992, p. G4. *Washington Post,* February 1, 1992, p. A1; February 2, 1992, pp. A1 and A25; February 5, 1992, p. A19; *Financial Times,* February 6, 1992, p. 4; *Christian Science Monitor,* February 6, 1992, p. 19; *Defense News,* February 17, 1992, p. 1.

20. *Defense News,* January 17, 1994, pp. 1, 29.

21. Teal Group Corporation, *World Missiles Briefing,* 1995.

22. Dr. Anoushiravan Ehteshami, "The Armed Forces of the Islamic Republic of Iran," *Jane's Intelligence Review,* February 1993, pp. 76-79; Gordon Jacobs and Tim McCarthy, "China Missile Sales—Few Changes for the Future," *Jane's Intelligence Review,* December 1992, pp. 559-563.

23. The submarines are based on World War II designs. They can lay mines, have a five man crew, have a maximum range of 1,200 miles, and have a speed of 6 knots. Iran claims to have built one of the submarines. The first underwent trials in 1987. The second was delivered in 1988. These ships are difficult to use in mine-laying and often require frogmen to place the mines. *Jane's Fighting Ships, 1992-1993* (London: Jane's Publishing, 1994); Naval Institute database.

24. *Defense News,* December 6, 1993, p. 1.

25. *Jane's Defense Weekly,* March 11, 1995, p. 2; and March 18, 1995, p. 5.

26. For additional details, see Anthony H. Cordesman, *Iran and Iraq: The Threat from the Northern Gulf* (Boulder: Westview, 1994), and Roger C. Herdman, *Technologies Underlying Weapons of Mass Destruction,* Office of Technology Assessment, U.S. Congress, OTA-BP-ISC-115, Washington, GPO, December 1993, pp. 197-255.

27. Details of the Iranian missile program are taken from W. Seth Carus and Joseph S. Bermudez, "Iran's Growing Missile Forces," *Jane's Defense Weekly,* July 23, 1988, pp. 126-31; Dr. Anoushiravan Ehteshami, "The Armed Forces of the Islamic Republic of Iran," *Jane's Intelligence Review,* February 1993, pp. 76-79; Gordon Jacobs and Tim McCarthy, "China Missile Sales—Few Changes for the Future," *Jane's Intelligence Review,* December 1992, pp. 559-63; *Jane's Intelligence Review* 4, no. 5, pp. 218-22; *Jane's Intelligence Review* 4, no. 4, p. 149.

28. *New York Times,* June 22, 1995; *Baltimore Sun,* June 23, 1995, p. A9; *Defense News,* June 19, 1995, p. 1; *Insight,* February 27, 1995, p. 13; *Jane's Intelligence Review,* Special Report no. 6 (May 1995), pp. 16-18.

29. U.S. State Department press release, "Joint U.S.-PRC Statement on Missile Proliferation," Washington, DC: October 4, 1994; Robert Shuey and Shirley A. Kan, *Chinese Nuclear and Missile Proliferation,* Congressional Research Service, IB92056, October 4, 1994; *Jane's Intelligence Review,* Special Report, no. 6, May 1995, pp. 16-18.

30. See "Iran's Ballistic Missile Program," *Middle East Defense News* 6, no. 6, (December 21, 1992).

31. Some U.S. experts believe Iran has fewer than 100 missiles (*Jane's Defense Weekly,* May 13, 1995, p. 5).

32. *Jane's Intelligence Review,* Special Report no. 6 (May 1995), pp. 16-18.

33. *Jane's Defense Weekly,* March 19, 1994; May 7, 1994, p. 1; January 15, 1994, p. 4. *Washington Times,* 4, February 25, 1994, p. A15; *Jane's Intelligence Review,* Special Report no. 6 (May 1995), pp. 16-18.

34. The technical content of this discussion is adapted in part from the author's discussion of the technical aspects of such weapons in *After the Storm: The Changing Military Balance in the Middle East* (Boulder: Westview, 1993) and *Iran and Iraq: The Threat from the Northern Gulf* (Boulder: Westview, 1994); working material on biological weapons prepared for the United Nations, and from Office of Technology Assessment, *Proliferation of Weapons of Mass Destruction: Assessing the Risks,* United States Congress OTA-ISC-559, Washington, D.C., August 1993; Kenneth R. Timmerman, *Weapons of Mass Destruction: The Cases of Iran, Syria, and Libya* (Los Angeles: Simon Wiesenthal Center, August 1992); Dr. Robert A. Nagler, *Ballistic Missile Proliferation: An Emerging Threat* (Arlington: Systems Planning Corporation, 1992); and translations of unclassified documents on proliferation by the Russian Foreign Intelligence Bureau provided to the author by the staff of the Government Operations Committee of the U.S. Senate.

35. General references for this section include "Chemical and Biological Warfare," Hearing Before the Committee on Foreign Relations, U.S. Senate, 91st Congress, April 30, 1969; Department of Political and Security Council Affairs, *Chemical and Bacteriological (Biological) Weapons and the Effects of Their Possible Use,* Report of the Secretary General, United Nations, New York, 1969; unpublished testimony of W. Seth Carus before the Committee

on Governmental Affairs, U.S. Senate, February 9, 1989; W. Seth Carus, "Chemical Weapons in the Middle East," *Policy Focus,* no. 9 (Washington, DC: Washington Institute for Near East Policy, December 1988); unpublished testimony of Mr. David Goldberg, Foreign Science and Technology Center, U.S. Army Intelligence Agency, before the Committee on Governmental Affairs, U.S. Senate, February 9, 1989; unpublished testimony of Dr. Barry J. Erlick, Senior Biological Warfare Analyst, U.S. Army, before the Committee on Governmental Affairs, U.S. Senate, February 9, 1989; unpublished testimony of Dr. Robert Mullen Cook-Deegan, Physicians for Human Rights, before the Committee on Governmental Affairs, U.S. Senate, February 9, 1989; Elisa D. Harris, "Chemical Weapons Proliferation in the Developing World," *RUSI and Brassey's Defense Yearbook* (London, 1988), pp. 67-88; and "Winds of Death: Iraq's Use of Poison Gas Against Its Kurdish Population," Report of a Medical Mission to Turkish Kurdestan by Physicians for Human Rights, February 1989.

36. *Journal of Commerce,* January 6, 1993, p. 5A. *Washington Post,* January 6, 1992, p. A22; September 3, 1993, p. A33. *Washington Times,* August 14, 1993, p. A2; *New York Times,* August 9, 1993, p. A6; *Defense News,* September 27, 1993, p. 23.

37. Based on discussions with various experts, the sources listed earlier, and working papers by Leonard Spector. *Observer,* June 12, 1988; *U.S. News and World Report,* February 12, 1990; *FBIS-NES,* March 23, 1990, p. 57; *Defense and Foreign Affairs,* November 20, 1989, p. 2. *New York Times,* July 1, 1989; May 9, 1989; June 27, 1989. *Financial Times,* February 6, 1992, p. 3; *Washington Times,* January 8, 1995, p. A9.

38. Such reports begin in the SIPRI Yearbooks in 1982, and occur sporadically through the 1988 edition.

39. Office of Technology Assessment, *Proliferation of Weapons of Mass Destruction* (Washington, DC; GPO, August 1993), especially p. 53.

40. According to one report by Zalmay Khalilzad in *Survival,* Pakistan was deeply involved in this $10 billion effort, as was China. U.S. experts do not confirm these reports (*Washington Post,* 17 May 1995, p. A23).

41. *Jane's Intelligence Review,* Special Report no. 6 (May 1995), p. 14.

42. The agreement made under the shah would have given Iran about 250 to 300 metric tons of uranium enriched to 3 percent. During 1980-90, Iran refused to accept the material or pay for it. When Iran did ask for the material in

1991, France used the fact that Iran's option to obtain enriched material for its investment had expired to deny Iran shipment of the material guaranteed under the original terms of the Iranian investment. *Washington Times,* November 15, 1991, p. F-4; David Albright and Mark Hibbs, "Spotlight Shifts to Iran," *Bulletin of the Atomic Scientists* (March 1992), pp. 9-12.

43. *Washington Post,* April 12, 1987, p. D1; James Bruce, "Iraq and Iran: Running the Nuclear Technology Race," *Jane's Defense Weekly,* December 5, 1988, p. 1307; working papers by Leonard Spector; JPRS-TND, October 6, 1989, p. 19.

44. *El Independent,* Madrid, February 5 and 6, 1990; *FBIS-Middle East,* December 1, 1988; *Jane's Intelligence Review,* Special Report no. 6 (May 1995), p. 14.

45. *Washington Post,* November 17, 1992, p. A1; April 18, 1995, p. A13. *Wall Street Journal,* May 11, 1993, p. 14; Robert Shuey and Shirley A Kan, *Chinese Missile and Nuclear Proliferation,* Congressional Research Service, IB92056, October 4, 1994, pp. 6-7. *Nucleonics Week,* September 24, 1992; October 1, 1992. *New York Times,* May 27, 1993; *The Middle East,* July/August 1994, pp. 9-10.

46. *New York Times,* February 23, 1995; May 16, 1995, p. A1; May 18, 1995, p. A11. *Washington Post,* April 18, 1995, p. A13; May 8, 1995, p. A22; May 18, 1995, p. A22. *Nucleonics Week,* February 13, 1992, p. 12; October 14, 1993, p. 9; December 16, 1993, p. 11. September 22, 1994, p. 1; October 6, 1994, p. 11. *Washington Post,* February 14, 1992; February 12, 1995. *Nuclear Fuel,* March 14, 1994, p. 9; March 28, 1994, p. 10. *Nuclear Engineering,* April 1992, p. 67; November 1994, pp. 4, 10. UPI, November 21, 1994; Reuters, November 20, 1994.

47. *Khaleej Times,* January 11, 1995, p. 1; *New York Times,* January 5, 1995, p. A10.

48. Leonard S. Spector, Mark G. McDonough, and Evan S. Medeiros, *Tracking Nuclear Proliferation* (Washington: Carnegie Endowment, 1995), pp. 119-123. *Washington Post,* March 3, 1995, p. A32; April 4, 1995, p. A19; May 4, 1995, p. A17; May 5, 1995, p. A29. *Washington Times,* February 21, 1995, p. A13; *Iran Business Monitor IV,* no. 6 (June 1995), p. 1; *Newsweek,* May 15, 1995, p. 36; *New York Times,* May 5, 1995, p. A8.

49. For more background, see the author's *Weapons of Mass Destruction in the Middle East* (London: Brassey's, 1992) and *Iran and Iraq: The Threat From the Northern Gulf* (Boulder: Westview, 1994). For later reporting see *U.S.*

News, November 14, 1994, pp. 87-88 and *New York Times,* December 27, 1994, p. A17.

50. *Los Angeles Times,* March 17, 1992, p. 1.

51. *New York Times,* November 30, 1992, pp. A1 and A6; January 5, 1995, p. A10; *Washington Times,* January 6, 1995, p. A15.

52. *New York Times,* January 10, 1995, p. A3.

53. *Khaleej Times,* January 10, 1995, p. 31; *Washington Times,* January 19, 1995, p. A18.

54. Although the possibility is a real one. *Financial Times,* January 30, 1992, p. 4; *Agence France Presse,* January 26, 1992; *Sunday Times,* January 26, 1992; *Der Spiegel,* July 20, 1992, p. 117; Patrick Clawson, *Iran's Challenge to the West, How, When, and Why* (Washington, The Washington Institute Policy Papers, no. 33, 1993), pp. 63-65; *U.S. News and World Report,* November 14, 1994, p. 88.

55. *Washington Times,* May 17, 1995, p. A15.

CHAPTER 9

CONFIDENCE-BUILDING
MEASURES IN THE PERSIAN GULF

Lawrence G. Potter[1]

In recent years political relations among the states of the Persian Gulf, and between some Gulf states and external powers, have been marked by tension and misunderstanding and the region has undergone the ordeal of two major wars, one between Iran and Iraq and one between Iraq and the U.S.-led alliance. Although the Desert Storm campaign succeeded in ending the Iraqi occupation of Kuwait, it did not put an end to regional problems. Saddam Hussein remains in power, border disputes periodically flare up and a dangerous race to acquire ballistic missiles and possibly weapons of mass destruction continues. The Arab states of the Gulf Cooperation Council (GCC) have sought U.S. protection, while Iran, the country with the longest Gulf coastline, opposes the presence of U.S. forces. Instead of becoming a zone of peace, the Persian Gulf has in fact remained a zone of tension more typical of the Cold War era than the new age that is now unfolding.

It does not have to be this way. At a time when the need for cooperation and mutual understanding among the littoral states has never been greater, these states should benefit from the lessons learned in other parts of the world about how to reduce tensions and prevent conflict. Over the past two decades, confidence-building measures (or CBMs) have played an important role in reducing tension between East and West. Although specific CBMs that have been adopted in Europe are not necessarily transportable to the Middle East, the underlying ideas and concepts are. However, so far the diplomatic and military techniques of confidence-building have not been applied to this area.

The Persian Gulf states are now lagging behind other regions in actively attempting to reduce tensions and prevent war. It is time for them to catch up, for in the post–Cold War world, countries at odds with each other can no longer depend upon the superpowers to resolve their conflicts. The comfortable notion that someone else must be to blame for their troubles is giving way to a realization that many problems are self-inflicted. Although oil prices rose markedly in 1996, future prospects are uncertain, and governments throughout the region must concentrate on strengthening economies. Simply stated, political tension and insecurity are bad for business.

What are confidence-building measures, and what can they accomplish?[2] CBMs are generally regarded as part of the arms-control process. Their goal is to make military activities more predictable and transparent though not, as in the case of arms control, to actually reduce armaments or military size. Transparency—that is, greater openness—can help prevent misunderstandings that could escalate into armed conflict. (The danger admittedly exists that transparency on the part of a weak state may invite aggression.) Confidence-building measures have been most highly developed in the context of East-West relations, and have gone through several phases. The first CBM referred to as such was the "hotline" established between the United States and the Soviet Union after the Cuban Missile Crisis in 1963, and since then such communication links have proved to be an essential tool. In 1975 in Helsinki, Western and Soviet-bloc nations agreed to a number of new, voluntary CBMs. Measures agreed to included advance notification of large-scale military maneuvers (over 25,000 troops) and the invitation of observers to witness such maneuvers.

In 1986 in Stockholm, more advanced measures, now dubbed "Confidence and Security-Building Measures," were adopted that were mandatory, not discretionary, for participating states. These included on-site inspections of military activities, prior notification of major military maneuvers and the invitation of observers to all exercises involving more than 17,000 troops. A third generation of CBMs was adopted in 1990 in Vienna, calling for extensive exchanges of information, increased constraints on conducting large-scale exercises and the creation of a Conflict Prevention Center. Further agreements were reached in 1992, including the Open Skies Treaty, which provided for mandatory overflights.

These confidence-building measures, negotiated incrementally over a long period, were instituted in an atmosphere of greater trust between East and West that facilitated the end of the Cold War. They have also been employed elsewhere: in the 1980s, CBMs helped end the nuclear race between Argentina and Brazil.[3] CBMs are the key tool for security in non-European regions in the 1990s, according to Michael Krepon, president of the Stimson Center in Washington, D.C.[4] They are uniquely appropriate to the Middle East and the Persian Gulf, where no serious attempt has been made to defuse longstanding problems.

What are some of the techniques of confidence building?[5] They include measures providing for information, communication, observation, notification and constraint. The first step may be simply a declaration of goals or obligations a state will undertake. The cooling of rhetoric, by both political leaders and the media, is important. States are inclined to take inflammatory words seriously, even if they are meant only for domestic consumption. This is a particular hazard in the Middle East, where "most regional leaders have an interest in emphasizing only the most provocative acts of their neighbors, not the acts that demonstrate restraint."[6]

The exchange of information about military forces and capabilities is essential to begin breaching the wall of suspicion. Communications links, such as the original hotline, can clarify intentions in times of tension, and can prevent the misinterpretation of an exercise as a surprise attack. Prior notification of military maneuvers makes their occurrence more predictable. Measures of constraint, such as limitations on armaments and manpower, may or may not follow later.

Why would a state want to reveal military data to an adversary? The answer is that CBMs are designed to help military professionals do their job better by clarifying information about another state. By correcting misperceptions, they help address the psychological dimensions of security, while not requiring structural changes. Confidence-building measures still allow for secrets to be kept, but they provide for a reciprocal and controlled exchange of information on subjects upon which they have mutually agreed. A key to success is that obligations for transparency be mutual and reciprocal.

All of the above measures are included in the repertoire of CBMs developed in the context of the East-West conflict. It must be emphasized that these are voluntary measures that require countries to cooperate—they cannot be imposed by outside powers. Third parties can, however, play an important role in negotiating and implementing CBMs. Typically,

CBMs are first employed following some major development such as a war or international incident. Less ambitious than CBMs are conflict-avoidance measures, which help to separate parties that do not trust each other, for example, hostile forces on cease-fire lines.

Confidence-building measures are not designed for countries that are enamored of each other. They are modest steps designed to reduce suspicions between countries experiencing continuing hostility. Low-risk and inexpensive, CBMs can be reversed, although they seldom are. They cannot work in the absence of an atmosphere of rapprochement: some level of trust must exist between the parties that have made a political decision to begin the process of cooperation. To be effective, words must be followed by deeds; if they are not, credibility will be lost. This has hindered their implementation by India and Pakistan.[7]

CBMS IN THE MIDDLE EAST[8]

The Madrid Peace Conference in the fall of 1991 between Israel, the Palestinians and Arab states launched the CBM process in the Middle East. Bilateral negotiations between Israel and the Palestinians, Jordan, Syria and Lebanon were accompanied by five multilateral working groups on issues of general concern to the region's future. One of these is the Arms Control and Regional Security (ACRS) talks, which began in January 1992.[9] As Jill Junnola notes, "While confidence-building measures have been employed rather extensively in the Middle East on a bilateral basis over the last several decades, the ACRS talks represent the first sustained *multilateral* effort to establish a confidence-building regime in the region."[10] The countries that have participated include the parties to the bilateral talks (except Syria), and Bahrain, Egypt, Oman, Qatar, Saudi Arabia, Kuwait, the United Arab Emirates, Yemen, Algeria, Mauritania, Morocco and Tunisia. Iran (along with Iraq and Libya) was not invited to participate. Although Iran probably would have refused, it would have been reassuring to Iranians to have outside powers seek to include, rather than exclude, them from a regional agreement.

The main obstacle holding back the multilateral talks is that progress in them is supposed to follow, not precede, that in the bilaterals, and by early 1997, the bilaterals had all but broken down. The greatest progress to date has come on maritime CBMs, with general agreement reached in March 1995 on the texts of two measures, relating to the prevention of incidents at sea and search-and-rescue cooperation.[11] At the same time an interim regional communications network was established in The Hague, with an end-user station installed in Qatar. It was subsequently decided to establish a regional security center in Jordan, with regional subcenters in Qatar and Tunisia. The ACRS talks eventually foundered over issues that existed outside their mandate, namely normalization of Israeli-Arab relations and the Israeli nuclear preponderance. Since September 1995, the formal ACRS process has been dormant, despite informal efforts to keep it going. With the faltering of the peace process following the election of the Likud government in Israel in May 1996, prospects seemed dim for the resumption of the ACRS talks.[12]

A PERSIAN GULF SCENARIO

There are admittedly some problems in applying CBMs in the Gulf. These include huge variations in the size and wealth of countries: for example, at the end of 1996, Iran had over 60 million people,[13] the United Arab Emirates, 2.4 million. In terms of per-capita income, their roles are reversed, with that of the UAE (estimated at $16,500 for 1995)[14] many times that of Iran.[15] There are also wide variations in military capabilities, with the GCC states generally reckoned no match for Iran or Iraq. In these circumstances, it is sometimes hard for the large countries to take the small ones seriously. There is also a tendency in the area to see political negotiations as a zero-sum game, in which one side must win and the other lose.

The security concerns of the various states differ. Saudi Arabia has reason to fear Iraq and Iran, and traditionally has asserted primacy over the smaller states on the Arab side of the Gulf. Both Iran and Iraq would like to be the regional hegemon, as Katzman has pointed out, and "because each strives constantly to dominate the Gulf, the balance of power is continually destabilized."[16] The smaller GCC states fear bullying by their larger neighbors: Kuwait is primarily worried about the Iraqi threat, while Iran is the chief concern of Abu Dhabi (because of the islands issue) and Bahrain (because of suspicion Iran is promoting unrest there and has even tried to overthrow its government).[17]

The level of distrust between Iran and the Arab Gulf states should not be underestimated. Iran regards them as dangerously dependent upon the West and, until recently, too ready to deal with Israel. "Due to the low level of diplomatic exchange, political dialogue and even elite-level communications between Iran and the Arab world, there are scant prospects of minimizing threat perceptions between Iran and the Persian Gulf states," according to Mahmood Sariolghalam, Professor of International Relations at the National University of Iran.[18] Hussein Sadeghi, the Iranian Foreign

Ministry's director general for the Persian Gulf region, admitted in October 1996 that for the time being there was no mutual confidence among the Persian Gulf states.[19]

The rhetoric of Tehran indicts the United States as the greatest threat to regional security, and demands a withdrawal of its forces. Iran believes that it rightfully should dominate the Gulf and is prevented from doing so by the United States. "Neighboring states should not provide an excuse for the presence of foreigners who only seek their illegitimate interests," in the words of former president Rafsanjani.[20] There is no guarantee, however, that the Gulf would be any more secure in the wake of the troops' removal. In reality Iraq, with which Iran has not signed a peace treaty, poses the major future challenge.

Still, the Persian Gulf states would be well advised to begin to negotiate and implement confidence-building measures, even if conditions are not yet in the state of "ripeness" required for CBMs to take hold. The idea may be gaining that coming to an agreement is better than not doing so. The people of the littoral states, having recently experienced war, are keenly aware that cooperation is better than conflict, and that peace must prevail for economic conditions to improve. Indeed, CBMs can help foster investor confidence and promote economic growth. This is increasingly recognized in Iran. Facing a U.S. trade embargo, large debt repayments and high inflation, Iran cannot afford any military confrontation in the Persian Gulf.

There are several factors that make the Persian Gulf a logical place for CBMs. For a start, it constitutes an integrated region historically characterized by constant interchange of people, commerce and religious movements. Before the modern era, peoples of the region shared a maritime culture based on pearling and the long-distance trade, and many tribes moved freely back and forth. The period of British hegemony that lasted for some 150 years until 1971 established a pattern of outside involvement in which the Persian Gulf was not dealt with as a whole, but rather divided into its constituent parts to make it easier to govern. Jurisdiction was split between the government of India, with responsibility for the Arabian side of the Gulf, and the Foreign Office in London, with responsibility for the Persian side. States, some artificially created, developed closer ties with Britain, and later the United States, than they did with their neighbors on the other side. This longstanding failure to conceptualize the Gulf or devise policies for it as a whole has worked against the establishment of an effective security regime.

Actually, there is a legacy of regional cooperation and shared interests to draw on. All states, for example, benefit from higher prices for gas and oil and the security of their export. States on occasion have agreed to share sovereignty in order to conclude agreements. This applies in particular to border disputes, which, with some notable exceptions, are increasingly being resolved.[21] The agreements to dissolve the neutral zones between Saudi Arabia and Kuwait (1965) and Saudi Arabia and Iraq (1981) are examples of creative diplomacy. The Algiers Accord of 1975, which "settled" the boundary on the Shatt al-Arab, was "one of the most sophisticated river boundary treaties ever signed in international law," according to expert Richard Schofield.[22]

The delimitation of marine boundaries in the Gulf, necessary for oil and gas extraction, has also been largely successful. Back in 1958, Saudi Arabia and Bahrain came to the first agreement in the world to share revenues from seabed resources.[23] The 1971 Memorandum of Understanding (MOU) between Iran and Sharjah over the island of Abu Musa was also a pragmatic response to a longstanding problem. By agreeing to share the administration of the island and to not relinquish either's claim to sovereignty, a way was found to defuse tensions that worked well for two decades.[24]

Written agreements, though, like confidence-building measures, depend on good will. When this evaporates, they lose much of their value. Twice in recent years Iran has signed agreements with neighboring states only to have them repudiated. Thus on the eve of the Iraqi invasion of Iran in 1980, Saddam Hussein unilaterally abrogated the Algiers agreement. The fact that he switched positions suddenly after invading Kuwait and accepted the Iranian demand to observe the *thalweg,* or midpoint division of the river, was gratifying to Iran but may not be indicative of Iraq's attitude in the future.

The disputed islands of Abu Musa and the Tunbs have been a focus of considerable tension in the Gulf since 1992. Iran's militarization of its part of Abu Musa since late 1994 has certainly changed the facts on the ground and caused fears in the UAE that missiles deployed there are aimed southward. However, so far Iran apparently has not challenged the right of Sharjah to administer the southern portion of the island, as provided for in the MOU. Iran has repeatedly called for dialogue on the issue,[25] as has the UAE, which claims that Iran's "occupation" of the islands threatens regional security.[26] The UAE has suggested that it might take the issue to the International Court of Justice in The Hague.[27]

THE NEED FOR INCLUSION

For over a century in the Persian Gulf, external powers—first Britain and later the United States—have taken responsibility for providing security. But as a result the regional countries have been precluded from reaching their own accommodation. The U.S. policy of dual containment, which seeks to isolate and punish both Iran and Iraq, continues to discourage the Gulf states from working together. The United States has now signed bilateral defense agreements with a number of Arab Gulf states. Should the United States draw back from its military commitment in the future, the regional states' need to create a mechanism for conflict resolution would become urgent.

The greatest need at present is for a forum, either official or unofficial, that includes all the Persian Gulf states.[28] As it is, states' contact with each other is sporadic. The formation of the Gulf Cooperation Council in 1981 by six states of the Arabian peninsula came in belated recognition that at a time when their two larger neighbors, Iran and Iraq, were at war, they needed to band together. However, after the ceasefire of 1988, the continued exclusion of Iran and Iraq meant that still no region-wide forum existed. The resentments and miscalculations of Iraq soon plunged the region into another war. Following the Desert Storm campaign, the GCC states plus Egypt and Syria issued the Damascus Declaration, which envisioned a new grouping of "6 plus 2" that could provide Persian Gulf security.

This, however, has proved illusory. Iran rejected the Damascus Declaration and the attempt by others to exclude it from a regional security agreement. Iran also resents the Damascus Declaration states' repeated affirmations of UAE sovereignty over the contested islands. For example, a strongly worded statement by these states (including Syria, supposedly an Iranian ally) in December 1996 demanded an Iranian withdrawal from the islands and condemned Iran for deploying missiles on them.[29]

Likewise, Iraq's exclusion from regional affairs, due primarily to UN sanctions, has created an unnatural situation. With the resumption of Iraqi oil exports in December 1996 and the eventual lifting of sanctions, Saddam's government may push for a more active regional role. But Iraq's participation in CBMs is problematic. "Too much has passed between Iraq and its neighbors during the past twenty or so years for any trust to exist that in a collective security arrangement, the other parties would have the security of Iraq or of the Iraqi regime at heart . . . it would be extraordinarily difficult for an Iraqi government to surrender any power of decision or arbitration to an organization that it does not itself dominate in some form," concluded analyst Charles Tripp.[30]

Lately there has been greater recognition by regional leaders of the need for inclusion. Qatar's foreign minister stated on February 1, 1997, "Qatar attaches high importance [to] Iran's principled efforts to develop peace and security in the sensitive and strategic region.[31] Shortly thereafter, Prince Sultan, the Saudi defense minister, observing that "rapprochement and cooperation are not created by force, but by mutual respect," urged Iran to settle the islands issue with the UAE.[32] Even the UAE acknowledged that Iran had the right to participate in Gulf security arrangements, once it had given back the islands.[33]

For its part, the Iranian government has expressed greater interest in confidence-building measures than any other regional state.[34] Former president Rafsanjani, in remarks at the conclusion of the conference of the Institute for Political and International Studies on December 18, 1995, specifically endorsed the idea of confidence-building measures. He said, "The policy of the Islamic Republic of Iran is to refrain from any threat. We know we cannot resolve anything with threat of force." He emphasized that "no country should be afraid of each other" and "we should try to promote trust and confidence-building."[35] At the same time in Doha, Qatar, Hussein Sheikoleslam, deputy foreign minister for Africa and the Middle East, announced Iran's readiness to sign a non-aggression treaty with all Persian Gulf states.[36]

Iranian officials have continued to promote this idea. Even the presence of U.S. forces need not slow down Iran's cooperation with regional countries, according to Abbas Maleki, Iran's deputy foreign minister for research and education.[37] A senior Iranian foreign policy official, Ambassador Kamal Kharrazi, has even suggested that the United States could facilitate confidence-building between the GCC states and Iran.[38] In an address in Switzerland in June 1996, Foreign Minister Ali-Akbar Velayati noted that because of the instability in the Gulf the promotion of CBMs had become a priority: "it is essential to forge vigorously [ahead] with the adoption of confidence-building measures in this region with a view to reinforcing the concept of predictability."[39]

There were indications in the spring of 1996 that Iran had in effect initiated the CBM process by suggesting military cooperation with some Persian Gulf countries. (Iran has conducted joint exercises with the Pakistani navy and probably that of Oman.[40] In June 1995, an Omani warship

visited the Iranian port of Bushehr for the first time since the revolution.[41])
According to an Iranian Foreign Ministry spokesman, Iran has proposed
holding joint military exercises with Kuwait and other Gulf states.[42] This
offer was evidently declined but an agreement was reached between Iran
and Kuwait for cooperation in marine transportation, shipping facilities
and the prevention of sea pollution.[43] In May 1996, Qatar declined an
Iranian offer of a bilateral defense pact, but the following month, two Iranian navy ships made the first friendly port visit to Doha in 17 years.[44]
Cynics, however, believed that this was evidence of an Iranian effort to
develop bilateral security relationships with members of the GCC states at
a time when relations were strained over Bahrain and Abu Musa.

The apprehensions of the Arab Gulf states are stoked by contradictory actions and words on the part of Iranian authorities. Thus in March
1997, Iranian Foreign Minister Ali-Akbar Velayati made a tour of all six
GCC states professing friendship and promoting the idea that Gulf security is the responsibility of the littoral states. He emphasized Iran's readiness to enter into negotiations with the UAE over the three islands, and
suggested that the existing MOU could be the basis for a settlement.[45] But
critics suggested that the real reasons behind Iran's "charm offensive" were
to curry favor with Islamic states so they would agree to attend the meeting
of the Organization of the Islamic Conference in Tehran planned for December 1997, and to deflect possible U.S. retaliation should Iran be impli-
cated in the bombing of the American compound in Dhahran, Saudi Arabia,
in June 1996.

In late April 1997, shortly following Velayati's goodwill tour of the
Gulf, more than 200,000 Iranian Revolutionary Guards staged the largest
wargames ever in the area. Land, sea and air exercises took place along the
entire coastline, with landings on the islands of Qeshm and Hengam to
repel "enemy forces."[46] The head of the Revolutionary Guards was quoted
as saying that the wargames aimed to display the might of Islam while
conveying a message of peace and friendship to neighboring countries.[47] It
is such mixed messages from Iran that keep its Arab neighbors on edge.
Given the existence of multiple power centers in Tehran and the likelihood
of a continuing power struggle there, reassurance for the Gulf Arab states is
not likely to come soon.

It is becoming increasingly obvious that any agreement or grouping
that does not include all the littoral states is doomed to failure.[48] A better
idea is the concept of "security by inclusion" formulated by former UN
negotiator Giandomenico Picco. Thus Iran and Iraq should be included in

regional arrangements: the alternative, he fears, is "security by confrontation," which would be the best recipe for the proliferation of weapons of mass destruction. Picco suggests that the United Nations, perhaps through the Office of the Secretary General, might promote a "Charter of the Gulf" along the lines of the Helsinki Charter.[49] Because in the past security was guaranteed by external rather than regional powers, there could be a future UN role to help negotiate, monitor and verify confidence-building measures.

A number of suggestions have been made on how to get a "peace process" started in the Gulf. Dr. Jalil Roshandel of the University of Tehran has suggested that Gulf countries adopt a strategy of "non-offensive defense" which would include signing a pact affirming principles all can agree on—such as respect for states' territorial integrity and independence, non-aggression, respect for human rights, and opposition to drug trafficking—and institute greater transparency in military and defense budgets.[50] Dr. Peter Jones of the Stockholm International Peace Research Institute (SIPRI) has proposed initiating the CBM process with maritime measures, such as exchanging information on naval procurement and major exercises, inviting observers to selected exercises or bases, refraining from potentially provocative actions while at sea, and, ultimately, reaching agreements to not attack civilian shipping or oil-production facilities.[51]

Given the role of the Soviet Union as the co-sponsor of the Madrid talks, Russia may be willing to assume a similar responsibility in the Gulf. Mr. S. V. Kerpichenco of the Russian Foreign Ministry has highlighted the necessity of setting up a regional security system beginning with confidence-building measures, such as the refusal to use force or threaten to do so; strict compliance with international obligations; close cooperation with the UN, especially the Security Council; and refraining from obtaining weapons of mass destruction and missile technology.[52]

What practical steps might be taken in the Persian Gulf area to help build confidence? Declarations of peaceful intent on the part of regional leaders and the exchange of basic information would be positive and reassuring. Better communications also are easy to install. The easiest CBMs to agree on are maritime ones, and these will likely be the precursor to others. Regularly scheduled consultations among military forces could help allay suspicions and allow military leaders to get to know one another. Such personal interaction is key. The annual conferences hosted by The Institute for Political and International Studies in Tehran and the Emirates Center for Strategic Studies and Research in Abu Dhabi can help speed the process of understanding among the peoples of the Gulf countries. "Track

242 Lawrence G. Potter

two" diplomacy, consisting of unofficial and informal meetings, can be the precursor of formal agreements. The Gulf/2000 Project has demonstrated the success an informal forum can have. Written agreements are, indeed, not necessary—informal agreements may be easier to reach and can be just as effective.

Iran has already demonstrated that it is willing to accept intrusive inspections of its nuclear facilities by outside observers of the International Atomic Energy Agency, who have found Iran in compliance with the Nuclear Non-Proliferation Treaty. This attitude bodes well for the CBM process, in which concessions must be made by both Iran and the Arab Gulf states to allow for verification and inspection.

CONCLUSION: TAKING RISKS FOR PEACE

The process of confidence-building in the Persian Gulf can start with small measures, and CBMs there are likely to take a different form or sequence than those in Europe, or even in other parts of the Middle East. (For example, in Europe, mutual recognition of borders preceded the negotiation of CBMs, but this may not be the case in the Gulf.)[53] Modest measures of conflict avoidance may be all that can be hoped for at present, especially when leaders are very averse to risk-taking. CBMs must be built on trust—and verification—and in the Gulf states trust in neighboring countries is notably lacking. Measures to increase communication and information may be feasible; measures that would limit forces might not be. Verification and transparency are keys to success but will take time to negotiate. The arms race has been a major factor fuelling regional insecurity, and in 1996 defense spending among Gulf countries rose, due to the stronger price of oil.[54]

The attitudes of external powers, especially the United States, will be important in fostering a climate of regional peace. (The UAE, for example, assured of U.S. backing, has been emboldened to raise the islands issue at every opportunity with Arab states.) For the foreseeable future U.S. forces will remain in the Gulf, although over the long term it is likely that due to domestic reasons their numbers will be much reduced. By continuing to exclude Iran and Iraq from regional affairs, tensions and suspicions are exacerbated and the atmosphere of trust necessary for CBMs cannot be established. A major uncertainty is the future course of relations between the United States and Iran. Whether they will improve during the second Clinton administration and following the inauguration of a new president in Iran in the summer of 1997 is unclear. Given present circumstances, and the opposition of both Iran and Iraq to the presence of U.S. forces, it is preferable that the U.S. government not take the lead role in security discussions. It is important for regional states to move at their own pace and not feel they are being pressured to implement an agenda set by outsiders.

The political decision must be taken by governments in the Gulf to institute CBMs. Iran has already proclaimed its willingness to do so, although the Gulf Arabs insist that words must be followed by deeds. Iraq is another matter, since in the near term it likely will remain isolated, subject to severe UN sanctions and preoccupied with its own problems.

Seven years after Iraq invaded Kuwait, the ACRS process had stalled, and few would argue that the atmosphere in the Persian Gulf seemed propitious for confidence-building measures. Yet the atmosphere can change due to many reasons, and when it takes a turn for the better, CBMs will be needed. People in the countries of the Persian Gulf need to start thinking about CBMs. If the political climate does not seem favorable to introduce them, this is all the more reason to do so. Unquestionably, the need to alter mutual perceptions will take time. The important thing to keep in mind is that attitudes and public opinion, even if negative, can change. (The visit of Egyptian President Anwar Sadat to Jerusalem in November 1977 and the handshake of PLO Chairman Yasir Arafat and Israeli Prime Minister Yitzhak Rabin on the White House lawn in September 1993, vividly demonstrate how public opinion about old adversaries can change. However, in the absence of continued progress, the mood can later sour.) The CBM process, once begun, can actually contribute to a transformation of views. The Middle East is not an area of exception that is immune to the forces shaping the post–Cold War world. The peoples of the Persian Gulf states have a common historical legacy and, for better or worse, in the future the fate of each will be linked to that of the others. Hopefully, the region really can become a zone of peace. As President George Bush once said, "good will begets good will,"[55] and never was this more needed than in the Persian Gulf today.

Notes

1. This chapter is based on a paper presented at a conference on "The Persian Gulf and the Changing Structure of the International System" held by The Institute for Political and International Studies (IPIS), Tehran, December 17-18, 1995. Revised versions were subsequently published in *Middle East Insight* 12, no. 2 (January–February 1996) and *The Iranian Journal of International Affairs* 8, no. 2 (Summer 1996). The author would like to

extend his appreciation to Dr. Peter Jones, Ms. Jill Junnola, Ambassador Mohammad Jafar Mahallati, Dr. Seyed Mohammad Kazem Sajjadpour and Dr. Gary Sick for comments on earlier drafts.

2. George D. Moffett III, "Confidence-Building for Peace," *The Christian Science Monitor,* September 24, 1992.

3. Lisa Owens, "Confidence Building in Latin America: Nuclear Controls between Argentina and Brazil," in *Regional Confidence Building in 1995: South Asia, the Middle East, and Latin America,* Jill R. Junnola and Michael Krepon, eds., (Washington: The Henry L. Stimson Center, December 1995): pp. 37-59.

4. Michael Krepon, "The Decade for Confidence-building Measures," in *A Handbook of Confidence-building Measures for Regional Security,* 2nd edition, Michael Krepon, ed., (Washington: The Henry L. Stimson Center, January 1995): pp. 1-10. For a contrary viewpoint that regards faith in CBMs as misplaced, see Marie-France Desjardins, "Rethinking Confidence-Building Measures," in *Adelphi Papers* 307 (December 1996).

5. Johan Jorgen Holst, "Confidence-building Measures: A Conceptual Framework," *Survival* 25, no. 1 (January-February 1983), pp. 2-15.

6. Aaron Karp, "The Demise of the Middle East Arms Race," *The Washington Quarterly* 18, no. 4 (Autumn 1995), pp. 30-31.

7. Michael Krepon, "South Asia: A Time of Trouble, A Time of Need," in *Regional Confidence Building in 1995,* pp. 1-9.

8. For an excellent overview of the subject, see Jill R. Junnola, "Conflict Avoidance and Confidence Building in the Middle East," in *Regional Confidence Building in 1995,* pp. 11-36. See also Gabriel Ben-Dor and David B. Dewitt, "Confidence Building Measures in the Middle East," in *Confidence Building Measures in the Middle East,* Gabriel Ben-Dor and David B. Dewitt, eds., (Boulder: Westview Press, 1994), pp. 3-29; and Admiral Robert Hilton, Peter Stein and Caroline Ziemke, "Confidence- and Security-Building in the Middle East: Past, Present and Future" (Alexandria, VA: Institute for Defense Analysis, September 13, 1993), unpublished and unclassified draft.

9. Ariel E. Levite and Emily B. Landau, "Confidence and Security Building Measures in the Middle East," *Journal of Strategic Studies* 20, no.1 (April 1997). Also see Joel Peters, *Building Bridges: The Arab-Israeli Multilateral Talks* (London: Royal Institute of International Affairs, 1994).

10. Junnola, "Conflict Avoidance and Confidence Building," p. 30.

11. Peter Jones, "Maritime Confidence-Building Measures in the Middle East," in *Maritime Confidence Building in Regions of Tension,* Jill R. Junnola, ed. (Washington, DC: The Henry L. Stimson Center, May 1996). See also his "Maritime Confidence and Security-Building Measures in the Persian Gulf Region," in *The Iranian Journal of International Affairs* 8, no. 2 (Summer 1996), pp. 368-92.

12. Peter Jones, "Arms Control in the Middle East: Some Reflections on ACRS," *Security Dialogue* 28, no. 1 (March 1997), pp. 57-70.

13. According to the national census conducted in October 1996, as reported by the Iran Statistics Centre, in Reuters (on-line), January 13, 1997.

14. Figures for the end of 1996 from the UAE Ministry of Information's *Daily News Digest,* January 25, 1997.

15. The figure for Iran is problematic; for a recent estimate see "Children of the Islamic Revolution: A Survey of Iran," in *The Economist,* January 18, 1997, p. 4.

16. Kenneth Katzman, "Beyond Dual Containment: Towards a Persian Gulf Peace Process," *Middle East Insight* 12, no.1 (November-December 1995), p. 25.

17. Reuters, June 3, 4 and 5, 1996.

18. Mahmood Sariolghalam, "The Future of the Middle East: The Impact of the Northern Tier," *Security Dialogue* 27, no. 3 (September 1996), p. 314.

19. Islamic Republic News Agency (IRNA), October 19, 1996.

20. Reuters, September 24, 1996.

21. Richard Schofield, "Border Disputes in the Gulf: Past, Present, and Future," in this volume.

22. Ibid.

23. Gerald Blake, "Shared zones as a solution to problems of territorial sovereignty in the Gulf states," in *Territorial foundations of the Gulf states,* Richard Schofield, ed., (London: UCL Press, 1994), p. 205.

24. Richard Schofield, "Borders and territoriality in the Gulf and the Arabian peninsula during the twentieth century," in *Territorial foundations of the Gulf states,* pp. 39-40.

25. For example, see Reuters, December 11, 1996, quoting the official Iranian news agency IRNA: "The Islamic Republic of Iran once more stresses that it does not pose any threat to any neighbors in the region and further it invites

[the Gulf Arab states] to take an initiative in bringing about a joint security arrangement of the nations of the region to guarantee stability, regional security and help the Islamic Republic of Iran safeguard its vast territorial waters . . . in the interest of all."

26. Reuters, December 1 and 2, 1996.

27. UAE Ministry of Information, *Daily News Digest,* December 14, 1996.

28. In the aftermath of Desert Storm, Secretary of State James Baker III declared that both Iran and Iraq could play an important role in the future security of the Persian Gulf. See his testimony to the Senate Foreign Relations Committee of February 7, 1991.

29. Reuters, December 30, 1996.

30. Charles Tripp, "The Future of Iraq and of Regional Security," in *Powder Keg in the Middle East: The Struggle for Gulf Security,* Geoffrey Kemp and Janice Gross Stein, eds., (Lanham, Maryland: Rowman & Littlefield Publishers for the American Association for the Advancement of Science, 1995), p. 157.

31. Reuters, February 1, 1997.

32. UPI, February 22, 1997.

33. Reuters, March 17, 1997.

34. Eric Arnett, "Beyond threat perception: assessing military capacity and reducing the risk of war in southern Asia" in *Military Capacity and the Risk of War: China, India, Pakistan and Iran,* Eric Arnett, ed., (Oxford: Oxford University Press for the Stockholm International Peace Research Institute, 1997), pp. 16-17.

35. As reported in the Tehran newspaper *Ittila'at* (in Persian), 28 Azar 1374/ December 19, 1995, p. 1; also (with slight variations) in "Text of the speech of His Excellency Mr. Hashemi Rafsanjani, President, in the meeting with guests of the Persian Gulf Seminar, 27 Azar 1374" (in Persian).

36. *Iran News* (English) and *Ittila'at* (Persian), December 17, 1995; also in *Iran Focus* (January 1996), p. 13. This was the first such public offer. Unfortunately it went unnoticed, as the press secretary to the Iranian Mission to the UN lamented in a letter to *The New York Times,* January 13, 1996.

37. According to concluding remarks he made at the IPIS conference, Tehran, December 18, 1995.

38. George Moffett, "Iran's UN Envoy Blames Sour Relationship on US" [interview with Kamal Kharrazi], *The Christian Science Monitor,* March 20, 1996.

39. Dr. Ali-Akbar Velayati, "The Security of the Persian Gulf," address to Crans Montana Forum, Switzerland, June 20-23, 1996.

40. *Jane's Military Exercise and Training Monitor,* October-December 1995, p. 12. The UAE, on the other hand, has carried out naval exercises with India (ibid., p. 1). I am grateful to Dr. Peter Jones for calling this to my attention.

41. Agence France Presse, March 10, 1997.

42. *Iran Digest,* March 27, 1996 and Reuters, April 16, 1996. The commander of the army, Ahmed Dadbin, confirmed that Iran was ready to hold joint military exercises with neighboring states (Xinhua, on-line, May 30, 1996).

43. *Iran Digest,* April 8, 1996; *Al-Sharq al-Awsat,* July 12, 1996, interview with the Kuwaiti defense minister.

44. Reuters, May 7, 1996 and Xinhua, June 5, 1996.

45. Reuters, March 16 and 21, 1997.

46. Agence France Presse, Tehran, April 25, 1997; Reuters, Dubai, April 24, 1997.

47. Reuters, April 23, 1997.

48. This point regarding Iran is developed by Hooshang Amirahmadi, "Persian Gulf Stability Hinges on US-Iran Dialogue," *The Washington Report on Middle East Affairs* (April 1996).

49. Giandomenico Picco, "Political and Economic Cooperative Measures Available to the Gulf States," paper presented to the Gulf/2000 conference on "Security Issues in the Gulf," Abu Dhabi, March 27-29, 1995.

50. Jalil Roshandel, "Confidence-Building Measures in the Persian Gulf," *The Iranian Journal of International Affairs* 8, no. 3 (Fall 1996), p. 627-42.

51. Peter Jones, "Maritime Confidence and Security Building Measures in the Middle East."

52. S. V. Kerpichenco, "On the Concept of [a] Regional Security System in the Persian Gulf Zone," abstract of paper delivered at IPIS conference, December 17, 1995.

53. Cathleen S. Fisher, "The Preconditions of Confidence-building: Lessons from the European Experience," in *A Handbook of Confidence-building Measures for Regional Security,* 2nd edition, p. 33.

54. Andrew Rathmell, "The Gulf Arms Bazaar," *Gulf States Newsletter* 547 (December 1996).

55. President George Bush in his Inaugural Speech, January 20, 1989, as
    reported in *The New York Times,* January 21, 1989.

CHAPTER 10

ISLAMIC GOVERNANCE IN THE GULF: A FRAMEWORK FOR ANALYSIS, COMPARISON, AND PREDICTION[1]

Frank E. Vogel

Islamic governance, whether exercised by regimes now in power or projected by oppositional Islamic political movements, is a matter of crucial international importance. This article offers a framework for a comparative legal analysis of both the present practice and the future prospects of Islamic governance for the Gulf countries (excluding Iraq).

Issues of Islamic governance arise in four contexts: first, Islamic political movements calling for the reinstatement of Islamic law *(shari'a)* and the establishment of "Islamic states;" second, the regimes established by such movements where they have gained power—in Iran, the Sudan, and now perhaps Afghanistan; third, the states of the Arabian peninsula, which, relatively unaffected by colonial power, still apply traditionalist Islamic political and legal norms; and fourth, the remaining Muslim countries, which under colonial tutelage adopted systems modeled legally and politically on the West but which enshrine Islamic law in their constitutions and codes to some degree.

The first context—the Islamic movements—has been much studied,[2] but remains poorly understood. Despite an initial impression of a monolithic threat to established order, these movements show considerable doctrinal and geographical variety, ranging from pietist movements uninterested in politics to violent, revolutionary groups. Confusion about them reveals itself in free-floating nomenclature. The terms *moderate, radical, liberal, reactionary, modern* and *traditional* have proved notoriously misleading. While media rely on the vague, alarmist and disapproving term *fundamentalist,* scholars increasingly use the term *Islamist,* which suggests both the shared doctrinal core of these movements and the conscious, constructed and variable manner in which they evoke that core. That term will be used here to refer to movements engaged in political activism to replace an existing regime with an "Islamic state."

The remaining three contexts of Islamic governance also have not been studied adequately. For example, have existing states adopted new political, legal or administrative forms constituting innovations or developments in the Islamic art of governance? Candidates exist for such an honor, such as the Iranian Council of Guardians, various Gulf countries' new consultative *(Shura)* councils, and Saudi Arabia's "Board of Grievances," framed after both a medieval Islamic tribunal and the French Conseil d'État. A great many Muslim countries mention Islam and *shari'a* in their constitutions, codify laws taken from *shari'a,* and confer authority on their courts to fill gaps in West-based codes using Islamic precepts. Scholars have generally ignored the question (albeit more important for Muslims than for others) of whether such arrangements are validly Islamic.

Since attention tends to focus on the radical Islamist movements (and on the regimes they found), the role of Islam in politics tends to be identified with "fundamentalism," an error that serves the interests of both radical Islamist movements and their arch opponents, the supporters of secularization and Westernization. Western observers often assume that calls to Islam are irreducible and irrebuttable: pious Muslims automatically support any call for an Islamic state or for the application of Islamic law; if they do not, they have turned from God to secularism. Such a position misrepresents how Muslims feel about political change. Although in the absence of elections or free expression we know little about how Muslims react to Islamist movements, clearly many seek civil rights and freedoms (for women as well as for men), economic opportunity, honest government and a fair distribution of wealth and privilege, and consider those to be Islamic goals. Many reject Islamist movements as harsh, ideological or violent, and oppose the harnessing of Islam to any narrow political agenda. Failure to appreciate the possible range of religious attitudes toward Islamist movements (and the governments they create) causes observers to overstate the short-term significance of Islamist politics and understate the long-term legal, constitutional and political significance of Islam.

Islamic politics poses a notorious challenge to the proposition that the whole world is destined to be completely secularized, and even Westernized.[3] Those who predict that economic development will doom Islamist oppositions must contend with the fact that they gain strength in rich countries as well as in poor ones. Some Muslim governments hope to defeat Islamists through repression—Algeria and Egypt have virtually declared war on them—but few outside those regimes expect their strategy to succeed, and many fear that violent repression—for example, in Egypt, Algeria, Tunisia and Saudi Arabia—will radicalize Islamist opposition and root it more deeply. For all these reasons, it seems vain to suppose that Islamic norms are losing their relevance to public life, even now, a century-and-a-half after wholesale Westernization began. The choice may rather be between two different Islamic futures: one exclusive and authoritarian; the other inclusive, pluralistic and democratic.

Whatever the situation elsewhere, in the Gulf countries the future of governance seems unlikely to be anything but Islamic. All these countries strongly identify themselves with Islam in political matters. As the home of the two holy places, Saudi Arabia assumes a responsibility to adhere to pure religious practice and to zealously uphold Islamic law; Iran regards itself as the font of revolutionary Islam and contemporary Shi'ism. All the countries in the Gulf Cooperation Council (GCC) replicate traditional Islamic political and social structures and practices long after they have disappeared elsewhere, and in all of them *ulama* (a term by which we mean religious scholars of largely traditional training) remain influential in both society and government. With the exception of Iran, all have escaped pervasive Westernization under direct or indirect colonial domination. Even in Iran the government has for eighteen years cultivated independence from imported Westernized attitudes. These countries all possess wealth, political autonomy and cultural confidence, and awareness of the many choices that lie before them. Given these facts, one fully expects that, even if governments in Algeria or Egypt quell their Islamist oppositions, politics and governance in the Gulf countries will remain markedly Islamic. If extensive secularization and Westernization are ruled out, and these polities are to develop at all, they will be forced to evolve forms of governance that are both indigenous and Islamic.

Despite its worldwide appeal, Islamic governance is in crisis. As it is presently practiced, both Muslims and non-Muslims often view it unfavorably, for not altogether different reasons. Virtually all existing Muslim regimes face ardent political opposition on both secular and Islamic grounds. A great many Muslim countries have poor records on freedoms and human rights, and nearly all of them remain outside the world's widening circle of democracies and nascent democracies. The West considers the two most ideological Islamist states, Iran and the Sudan, international pariahs, condemning them for widespread human rights abuses and for fomenting international terrorism.

As to its theoretical development also, Islamic governance is in crisis. Much of the vehemence of the Islamist call reflects frustration with achievements so far. The failure to ground modern political institutions on credibly Islamic foundations is one of the major causes of political radicalization in the Islamic world. A priori the result is surprising, since Islamic law is impressively endowed with stirring political ideals, many of them startlingly modern in their connotations. It is easy to find in the revealed texts a foundation for popular participation in government *(shura, nasiha),* the social contract and the consent of the governed *(bay'a),* the rule of law (the sovereignty of God and of the *shari'a),* the right to petition for redress of grievances *(nasiha, mazalim),* the sanctity of individual life, liberty and property and their protection from state interference, equality of all before the law, office as a public trust *(amana),* prohibitions of embezzlement *(ghulul)* and bribery *(rishwa),* and other basic political ideals. From the standpoint of these texts it is easy to assert that evils like tyranny, intolerance, corruption and denial of human rights offend Islam, and doing so allows Muslims to distance themselves from events of their past and present of which they disapprove.

What, then, are the obstacles to the theoretical development of Islamic governance? One, overwhelmingly important, is colonialism, direct and indirect, which installed Western-derived legal and political arrangements in nearly every Muslim country and interrupted any natural sequence of adaptation to modern and Western influences then underway. Since imposed Western institutions have operated by default for a long time in most of the Muslim world, it has become habitual to consider governance exclusively in Western, not Islamic, terms. Questions posed assume a Western frame of discourse: Are democratic institutions (such as elections in Kuwait) consistent with "Islam"? Should members of Shura Councils, such as in Saudi Arabia, Bahrain or Oman, be appointed or elected? Outside the Muslim world, Western opinion, most obviously in the media, often treats Western political forms as if they were universally valid or the only possible expression of fundamental human values. Any role played by religion in politics is seen as by definition fundamentalist and reactionary.

Political forces combine to stifle thought and experimentation in Islamic governance. Internationally, Islamic countries cannot hope to evolve polities on their own terms, in cultural and political isolation. Inside the Muslim world, governments oppose Islamism with arrests, torture and killings. Regimes usually tolerate Islamic innovation or experimentation only in the most innocuous, state-controlled forms, fearing opportunism, demagoguery or encouragement of radical Islamism.

Other obstacles to the theoretical development of Islamic governance arise from within Islamic political thought and traditions. Islamic history reveals how states consistently offended Islamic political ideals and continued to be accepted as legitimate. This has its reflection in classical Islamic law (*fiqh*[4]) itself, which elaborates no institutional structures for constraining power comparable to the modern legal and constitutional devices of separation of powers, checks and balances, review of administrative action, and objective or impersonal conceptions of office. Indeed, a basic tenet of the faith is that believers must be loyal even to an evil-doing tyrant, if the only alternative is civil unrest.

Lacking sufficient concrete material with which to build, Islamic political thought slips into apologetics: Muslims have tended to evaluate Islamic doctrines and institutions, whether favorably or unfavorably, in terms of Western ones.[5] This line of thought has to its credit spread knowledge about Islamic political ideals and inculcated certain beliefs about their relevance to modern institutions. For example, Muslims seem now to agree, as they would not have a hundred years ago, that an Islamic political system must be democratic in the sense that it systematically solicits and responds to the views of the people. But apologetics have proved unable to identify substitutes for Western conceptions or models that are authoritatively Islamic, whether these are identical to their Western counterparts, different from them in details, or divergent from them completely. Even the new ideas it has engendered among Muslims become at once controversial when attention shifts to their implementation, and none seems to have generated religious loyalty to actual political institutions. An inevitable weakness in apologetics is that, in a climate of culture and thought perceived as inauthentic, arrangements adopted from the West, even when they seem just and beneficial, can neither be finally accepted as Islamic nor purposively modified. This leaves as the most convincing answers Islamically those that reject Western imports.

Muslims thus face a quandary: innovation of Islamic legal and political institutions is both difficult and unavoidable. What specific positive political, legal and constitutional measures should Muslims adopt to fulfill Islamic political ideals and stem the tide of such evils as tyranny, corruption, religious intolerance, social and economic inequality, and denial of human rights? If the classical legal corpus does not yield specific answers, then only three possibilities remain. One is that Islamic law abandon the attempt to constrain politics toward the enactment of God's order in the world, and simply rely on virtue of leaders.[6] Viewed purely as doctrine, classical Islamic law approximates this stance. The second possibility is that Islamic rulers and scholars have mistaken the teachings of the Quran and the Prophet's Sunna for most of the last 1,400 years. There are advocates of Islamic reform who so argue, but they have not yet convincingly derived from the revelation a new more efficacious political theory. Viewed in an idealized light, and shorn of their later history, the earliest texts offer general guidance and inspiration, but few specifics for implementation, leaving the reformer to confront Western models with only the apologetics mentioned above. The third possibility is that Islamic societies struggled and continue to struggle (successfully and unsuccessfully) against political evils, and that Islamic constitutional, legal and political history affords Muslims a rich empirical social and political "commentary" on the earliest texts and traditions, supplementing what is found in learned writings. Even outsiders may detect in that history typical patterns or tensions reproduced whenever political actors have taken the Quran and Sunna as God's literal commands.

Here we shall develop the third alternative as the most likely to yield solutions, and offer a framework by which to lend structure to the resulting Islamic historical-legal-sociological inquiry. This framework, used as a tool for comparison, seeks to identify aspects of Islamic legal systems past and present that offer degrees of congruence—of function, not content—with Western political ideals and institutions. It may also provide categories by which to classify modern Islamist movements that are more useful than those developed so far.

In looking for congruences, we shall focus on the most important Western political institutions and ideals, those of democratic liberalism, such as the rule of law, religious tolerance, civil rights and freedoms, pluralism and individual autonomy. In particular, we consider how Muslims who wish to advance the liberalization of their political and social orders might do so.[7]

A Framework for the Comparative
Study of Islamic Governance

The framework we propose emerges from the idea of *ijtihad*.[8] The fundamental legislative principle in classical Islamic law, *ijtihad* is the law's response to a peculiar dilemma posed by the Quran. The Quran tells the believer **both** that divine revelation provides a ruling for each and every human act for all time, **and** that one should rely exclusively on the divine revelation to know what the divine ruling is, turning away from all that is merely human, arbitrary and uncertain. But how can the revelations of the Quran and Sunna—finite in size—contain explicit divine rulings for an infinity of acts? The answer to this conundrum is called *ijtihad* (individual striving). Through *ijtihad,* humans discover the divine value for each action which, though God revealed it in the texts, can be discovered only through effort. *Ijtihad* forms an immediate and continuous link between the actions of each individual believer and divine revelation. The believer feels that he or she responds directly to the divine command, or that God's sovereignty applies directly, of its own force. This is, of course, the ideal; limitations in piety, intelligence, learning and time demand that in daily life the ideal be stepped down through many intervening doctrines and institutions. But *ijtihad* remains the dominating conception throughout the law, like the vanishing point toward which everything inclines.

Islamic legal thought does not assert that *ijtihad* yields divine truth, or that its verdict is the divine law. It is not represented as ritual or charismatic, but as scholarly and moral. Whether an *ijtihad* attains truth is known only to God. The doctrine is summed up in the saying of the Prophet, "If a judge judges, and practices *ijtihad,* and attains the truth, he has two rewards. If he practices *ijtihad* and is in error, then he has one reward."[9] It is possible to find the true divine ruling for a particular case, since finding it earns a special reward; truth is accessible and not otherworldly. But because finding truth is difficult, the sincere striver is rewarded even if he fails to find it.

The practitioner of *ijtihad* first consults the Quran, and then (because the Quran so commands) the Prophet's Sunna. If these yield no clear answer, then two further sources—*ijma'* (consensus) and *qiyas* (analogy)— are consulted as aids in interpreting the first two. Again, these further sources are considered only because the first two sources, the Quran and Sunna, are read as so requiring. Islamic law takes its textualism seriously, striving for epistemological rigor in interpretation and seeking to exclude as much human distortion as possible.

Since *ijtihad* is based rigorously in texts, those who have the greater knowledge of the texts automatically gain the greater authority. But Islamic sources make clear that to a degree *ijtihad* is a duty borne by every person. First, each Muslim is obligated, through his own reasoning, to attain certainty that God exists, that he reveals his commands through messengers, and that these commands must be obeyed. These beliefs are not *ijtihad* but a foundation for it. Second, every believer must determine God's ruling independently if a more learned person is unavailable. Third, even when one relies on one more learned than oneself, one must first decide who is most qualified to be followed, and this is a sort of *ijtihad.* Fourth, some scholars, like Ibn Taymiyya, urge that the laity learn as much as they can about the revealed proofs for legal rulings and make use of that knowledge. For Ibn Taymiyya *ijtihad* is in degrees, and all must practice it to his or her own capacity.[10] Finally, however one comes to know the governing legal ruling, that ruling is still general and abstract to a degree. How to apply it to one's own actions requires a judgment, inevitably the individual's to make.

Four points about *ijtihad* deserve emphasis. First, it involves no institution, council, hierarchy or church that can answer questions with certainty or exclusivity on behalf of God. *Ijtihad* ultimately resides in each individual's response—in his or her conscience—to the divine command. But, as a second point, *ijtihad* is not individualistic, in the Western sense of individual autonomy. From the description so far, one might think one person's *ijtihad* could never be imposed on another—doing so would intrude on the other's moral autonomy. But *ijtihad* generates law, not morality alone, and does so in a fashion obligatory not only on oneself but also on others. Since everyone's acts affect others' interests, everyone to that extent rules over others. A saying of the Prophet holds: "Each of you is a shepherd, and each of you is responsible for his flock."[11] Other texts enjoin that in ruling over others, one acts justly by applying only God's law and no other. If one fails to do so, one is punished in the Hereafter. Suddenly, the stakes on the accuracy of one's *ijtihad* increase: one bears the awesome responsibility of discerning a divine judgment determining, not merely one's own duties, but also the rights of others—and this under conditions that by definition exclude certainty. This particular dilemma—the crux of the judge's (*qadi's*) function—is the crucible in which the concept of *ijtihad* is forged. Notably, the sayings of the Prophet that define *ijtihad* all involve judging, not mere individual action.

As a third point, *ijtihad* offers an epistemological criterion for the legitimacy of all actions. In an Islamic state, power or authority is legitimate only when a warrant in ultimate truth for its exercise can be shown. This conception has in practice provided the chief limitation of power throughout Islamic history. Legal scholars *(ulama)* and the body of law they created (the *fiqh*) usually dominated legislation and legitimacy. In fact, the degree of the *ulama's* success is striking, given that rulers possessed not only material power but their own source of Islamic legitimacy—that of right guidance by the caliph as successor to Muhammad.

A fourth point about *ijtihad* requires a longer discussion. The objective of *ijtihad* is not finding general laws, but finding God's will in a particular situation, or discerning and applying God's law to a concrete act. Ideally, each and every act of obedience involves an *ijtihad,* a fresh conscientious drawing of truth from the divine texts. Thus, one capable of *ijtihad* cannot follow another's opinion in any matter, but must derive his own law independently. If a judge decides a case, and then faces a second factually identical case, he is not bound by his prior opinion. Even if he still holds his old opinion, he should perform *ijtihad* a second time. If a judge belongs to a particular legal school but is convinced that the view of another school is correct, he must give judgment according to his conviction; if he does not do so, his ruling must be reversed by a later judge, even if the latter judge believes the first judgment correct. Even apart from the problem of determining the applicable law, a judge needs to practice *ijtihad* to determine the factual situation before him in order to know which ruling applies. Finally, if a scholar advises a lay person on the law, his opinion *(fatwa)*, because it is general and abstract, is not binding but only advisory. The individual must decide whether to accept it and how to apply it in his concrete circumstances.

In its ideal conception, then, *ijtihad* has two crucial characteristics. First, it is an act bound to a concrete case (we might call this "instance-law," or law that pertains to a single concrete event, in distinction to "rule-law," law applying to a class of events). Second, it issues from an individual conscience (of the judge or other legal actor), and not a worldly collectivity or institution. (We might call such laws "inner-directed," in the sense that the substratum for justification is the inner conscience responding to divine revelation, as opposed to "outer-directed," meaning that the justification issues from an institution or collectivity.) Thus, *ijtihad* is individual or atomic in two senses: (1) it concerns a particular, concrete act or problem;

and (2) it is the product of a unique individual conscience. It need not be individual in a third sense, however, namely that its impact is on only one person. Rather, the conception involves a case in which one's decisions legally bind others. *Ijtihad* therefore diverges from any conception that would separate moral from legal, or individual from social.

This extraordinary sort of law-making—inner-directed instance law—we call "microcosmic law-making" to capture its atomic or monadic quality, both as regards the lawmaker and the event to which the law is applied. Its opposite, "macrocosmic law-making," then is outer-directed rule-law.[12]

Microcosmic law-making has certain advantages. It is particularly suitable for ethical judgments, since it responds to all the circumstances of a case. It models, as a legal and interpretive practice, the religious conception by which God observes and judges each human act. As noted above, it portrays the believer as responding directly, without intermediary, to the divine command, and creates a vital, immediate, continuous link between the individual believer and the divine revelation. It conveys a vivid sense that God's sovereignty is direct, operating by its own force. It accounts for much of the religious quality of Islamic law, past and present.

Macrocosmic law-making, on the other hand, also has advantages. Since it relates to the collectivity and to conditions in general, it alone can deal with the collective aspects of human existence, by which society is more than the sum of its parts. Wherever law seeks to advance human welfare, whether in this world or the next, by collective means, this law-making is essential. Ethically, this law-making addresses issues generated by life in classes or groups.

The clearest example of macrocosmic law-making is legislation issued by the legislature of a modern secular state. In the secular West not only statutory law, but even judge-made law, is increasingly conceived of in macrocosmic terms. Microcosmic law-making when practiced, as by a jury, is seen as arbitrary and unpredictable. By contrast, in *fiqh*'s internal conception of historical Islamic legal systems, it was macrocosmic law-making that was grudgingly acknowledged. When practiced by the ruling establishment, it was represented by the *ulama* as exceptional, ad hoc, contingent and dictated by necessity. Formal general laws or legislation were, to an extent odd to modern eyes, rarely practiced in fact and even less understood in theory.

Thus, the microcosmic/macrocosmic distinction offers a fundamental contrast between Islamic and modern Western legal systems, one perhaps capable of lending more precise and functional meaning to the obvious sense in which one is religious and one is secular. Its usefulness increases still more to the extent that, as we show next, it reveals a tension latent in Islamic legal systems themselves. It is precisely the distinction's double significance, that it measures tensions both within the Islamic legal system and in that system's confrontation with the West, that enriches its use for analysis and comparison.

Using this microcosmic/macrocosmic distinction we can elaborate the desired framework for the analysis of Islamic legal and political systems and their comparison across time and with other systems.[13] To do so we associate the distinction with two other distinctions central to historical Islamic legal systems. The first is a distinction between such systems' chief legal actors (chief from the perspective of the formal system of governance): the ruler and the *ulama*. Microcosmic law-making or *ijtihad*, though ideally open to all, associates naturally with those most knowledgeable in the texts—the *ulama*. Macrocosmic law-making, on the other hand, rises naturally to the summit of the legal system, the ruler, who has knowledge of the collectivity and the power to impose rules across the board. The ruler also benefits from macrocosmic sources of legitimacy rooted in the Quran and Sunna, in such conceptions as the community of the believers (*umma*) and of the need for a leader of that community (*khalifa, amir al-mu'minin, amir, sultan*) to wield power for its benefit.

A second distinction in medieval Islamic systems is between two acknowledged sources for legal judgments: *fiqh*, or the jurisprudence developed by the *ulama*, and *siyasa* (policy) administered by the ruler. As understood by the *ulama*, the ruler possesses authority under *siyasa* doctrine to act freely to pursue the welfare of the *umma* as he understands it, as long as he offends no fixed rule or principle of *shari'a*. Since this theory permits the ruler to gauge actions by general utility first, consulting texts only as a limit, *siyasa* is the inverse of *fiqh* and is the obvious category for macrocosmic law-making. *Fiqh*, on the other hand, uses microcosmic methods operating on texts, treating arguments from communal utility as subsidiary. Since they are complementary in function and method, the two bodies of law tend to divide legal subject matters between them. The *fiqh* and *ulama* are concerned first with ritual worship, then with family, then with contract, then with criminal law, and least of all with state administration and constitution. *Siyasa* operates on the same spectrum but in reverse, its coverage being most intense at the public end. Similarly, each of the two bodies of law developed its own courts and systems for enforcement.

Although *siyasa* and *fiqh* seem neatly complementary, in practice their coexistence within a single legal system has been continually competitive, and the border between their jurisdictions in contention. The *ulama* struggled to subject legal systems to the divine law, which to them meant the *fiqh* itself. Carried to its conclusion, their approach would demand that they be constantly consulted in the exercise of power. Such a vision inevitably clashed with that of rulers who, if they showed concern for Islamic legitimacy at all, sought legitimacy by exerting physical might (for example, *jihad*) to advance the *ummas* macrocosmic ends, such as justice or prosperity.

To counter the rulers' power and claims to independent legitimacy, the *ulama* employed four basic strategies. First, in their writings on *fiqh*, they adopted the strategy of unrelenting ambition, asserting the universality of their own legal methods and of their jurisdiction. *Fiqh* rarely acknowledges either the division of jurisdictions between the ruler and the *ulama* or the extent to which their functions are naturally complementary. For example, *fiqh* constitutional or public law portrays the exercise of rule in microcosmic terms, as requiring the application of *ijtihad* to every act of state. *Fiqh* propounds rules for matters of public law such as taxation, the election of caliphs, or land tenure, though these rules are sparser than in private law, since the available revealed sources are fewer. Often these provisions show little concern for practicality.

Second, *fiqh* writings on public law lay down idealizing qualifications for a legitimate ruler. An example is the requirement that the ruler be a scholar adept at *ijtihad*. Most rulers fell short of these qualifications and therefore of *fiqh* legitimacy. *Fiqh* writings often condemn actual rulers as impious and unjust.

The third strategy was to liberally delegate authority for public functions to the ruler. Unlike the first two strategies, this one increased rulers' power. *Fiqh* represents communal functions not as formal, positive macrocosmic institutions, but rather as so many burdens on the ruler's religious conscience. The person of the ruler becomes the font of all government. Because his *siyasa* authority is so broad and unstructured, so long as the ruler does not counter *shari'a* principles, he may do whatever advances the general welfare. The ruler must be obeyed, even if he is personally an oppressor or sinner, so long as he "establishes prayer" and so long as removing him would entail social unrest, which, in medieval times, it almost always did.

This last strategy, as is clear in these examples, seems inconsistent with the first two, in appearing to undo all *fiqh* constraints on the ruler, but in fact it is not. The first two strategies claimed for *fiqh* power to regulate the ruler's behavior and laid down a web of rules that most rulers could not or chose not to observe. The net result was to deny actual rulers *fiqh* legitimacy, maintaining them only as an unfortunate necessity, as a last resort compelled by the decay of Muslim society (*fasad al-zaman*) since the Prophet's time. The third strategy delegated authority to rulers, but, after the operation of the former two strategies, only at the level of mere contingency, not proper doctrine. The very breadth of this delegation avoided involving the *ulama* normatively in pragmatic questions of rule, and also avoided the emergence of formal institutions capable of competing normatively with the *fiqh* and the *ulama*. Hence the much-noted absence from *fiqh* doctrine of corporate institutions and personality or of positive institutionalizations for the conceptions of advice or petition (*nasiha*), consultation (*shura*), and oath of loyalty (*bay'a*). Politics is left as the moral obligations of individuals.

The fourth and last strategy of the *ulama* was to stabilize microcosmic law-making by creating their own macrocosmic social and legal institutions. Having excluded the ruler from partnership in legal legitimacy and having strategically exaggerated the microcosmic nature of *fiqh*, the *ulama* needed to develop macrocosmic means to stabilize and apply their law. Importantly, however, they refrained from enshrining any of these innovations in *fiqh* doctrine, since, again, doing so would dim the microcosmic ideal; the innovations were in that respect latent or covert. Examples of this phenomenon are the linked conceptions of legal school (*madhhab*) and the "closing of the door of *ijtihad.*" These obliged rank-and-file judges and jurists to follow fixed written doctrines of a single school (i.e, to practice *taqlid,* or the following of another's opinion without question). Yet *taqlid* was never explained as anything but a contingent necessity, never as doctrine: it arose, scholars said, simply due to the absence of qualified persons.

By these four strategies *ulama* sought a wide application for their law and legal vision. In fact, much legislation and adjudication—as well as other vital social functions—did fall within their control and outside the control of the ruler. Circumscribing the role of the ruler was an essential part of their scheme. In Marshall Hodgson's words, in referring to the central Islamic regions between approximately 950 and 1500 C.E.: "the role of the state was as far reduced, especially in the basic sphere of law, as it ever has been in citied high culture."[14] The balance of power between ruler and *ulama*, the product of competition and cooperation between them, shifted over time and place but was never superseded.

Because the *ulama* never embodied their program to check arbitrary rule in explicit, positive or formal doctrines or institutionalizations, it becomes difficult to trace. One can read the *fiqh* itself as written, consciously and unconsciously, with an eye to defending and advancing this particular vision of law. But to gain a complete picture of the theory and practice of the Islamic legal system, to grasp the Islamic constitutions of the past, to weigh their successes and failures in particular respects and at given periods, we need to supplement *fiqh* writings with other sources revealing the history and sociology of Islamic legal systems.

If for this article we confine ourselves to examining *fiqh*, we find that its doctrines reflect the pervasive tension between microcosmic and macrocosmic visions of the law. On many issues, especially those that affect the constitutional balance between ruler and *ulama*, *fiqh* harbors many opinions that can be arranged across a spectrum with respect to whether their content advances a microcosmic or a macrocosmic vision of law (an issue distinct from whether their legitimation is microcosmic, as it usually is). Presumably the *ulama* benefited from this range of opinions in modulating their encounter with the state.

Starting at the highest or most ideal level, the *fiqh*'s "theory of sources" *('ilm usul al-fiqh)*, we find that on a single doctrine *fiqh* may offer a number of conflicting views ranging from the microcosmic to the macrocosmic. (The discussion will be confined to Sunni theories, but comparable observations apply in Shi'i thought.) For example, *ijma'*, or consensus, meaning the unanimous agreement of all scholars capable of *ijtihad* at a given time on a point of law, renders the rule in question divine law and true as a general and abstract proposition. *Ijma'* seems macrocosmic in the sense that it permits a group to enact binding general rules. But there is much difference of opinion about *ijma'* among the schools and the scholars. A spectrum of views can be found ranging from those that make *ijma'* rare and virtually metaphysical (enhancing the microcosmic tendency) to those that make it flexible, frequent and legislative (enhancing the macrocosmic). Points in debate include the size and concreteness of the agreeing group (scholars of the entire *umma*, past and present, at one pole of a spectrum, local scholars of a single Sunni school at the other), the extent of agreement required (unanimity versus a majority), and the evidence demanded for the fact of agreement (for example, an express statement from each scholar versus the mere absence of a report that a scholar dissents). *Ijma'* is rare if it demands the explicit, unanimous, historically demonstrated agreement of every scholar of the *umma* (which is impossible to show and assumed only for points that are wholly uncontroversial anyway, such as the timings for the five prayers); it is common when it is the tacit agreement of a majority of the scholars of a single school. As *ijma'* becomes more common and applicable, the scope of freedom of opinion declines and law-making increasingly adheres to the consensus of an actual community, or rather of that community's *ulama*. This relatively macrocosmic pole of the doctrine enabled the maintenance of legal systems without recourse to state legislation. At its microcosmic pole, on the other hand, a narrowed, restrictive *ijma'* permits greater innovation in judgments and autonomy of the legal actor.

It is often not recognized that *ijma'* harbors principles of freedom and pluralism; or alternatively, that *ijma'* defines a zone within which difference of learned opinion, freedom of *ijtihad*, is unassailable. As long as an *ijtihad* does not contradict the Quran, the Sunna or an *ijma'*, only God knows whether or not it is false. Interestingly, in the *'usul al-fiqh* texts, in which their epistemological bent got free play, *fiqh* scholars state that the only *ijma'* capable of overruling all difference of opinion and constraining belief is one that meets the requirements of all scholars (i.e., one that meets the most rigorous requirements and is most rare). In other words, canonical doctrine concedes status as ultimate truth only to the most microcosmic *ijma'*. Other *ijma'*s have only partial, not universal, followings. They thus persuade only those who acknowledge them, yielding even then only presumptive, not absolute, proof. Thus members of a school may be bound by a partial *ijma'* of the type accepted by that school, while those capable of independent *ijtihad* or belonging to other schools remain free to reject it. Such *ijma'*s constrain the rank-and-file of the *ulama*, not the elite. The everyday *ijma'*s in actual use—of schools, localities, religious communities—were of this order.

This example shows a mode of thought typical of *fiqh*—a certain nesting or telescoping of doctrines on a single issue. At one extreme of a spectrum appears a doctrine that is universally accepted but also highly microcosmic in its effects; ranged across the rest of the spectrum are doctrines less authenticated, less universally acknowledged, and also more macrocosmic in their effects. In such nested sets, the various doctrines usually co-exist as valid doctrine, without being authoritatively reconciled. Scholars, modern and classical, benefit from this plurality of doctrine, since they can shift by various means from one view to the other, sometimes even to suit a particular circumstance; indeed, this is a characteristic feature of the microcosmic patterning of law.

As an example, consider the doctrines that define who, by word or action showing unbelief, commits a crime and deserves punishment (usually death). Obviously, freedoms of religion, expression and belief are limited by these doctrines. We find that the doctrines inhabit a scale from microcosmic to macrocosmic. First in the series is apostasy *(ridda),* which punishes backsliding from religion. Apostasy in turn is defined by a sub-spectrum of definitions of a Muslim, of which the most widely accepted definitions occupy the microcosmic pole. At that pole apostasy is shown only by the accused's leaving the religion openly, refusing to attest to Islam or asserting a doctrine contradicting the rare *ijma'* that no scholar denies exists. Even then, most schools allow the offender to repent by renouncing his position within three days. Historically, cases of apostasy were rare apart from conversion to another religion. (To narrow the crime of apostasy further would require departing, as some modern scholars have, from classical *fiqh* altogether, for example by reinterpreting the Quranic verse "No compulsion in religion."[15])

As one moves toward the macrocosmic end of the spectrum, punishments for expressing unbelief shift away from apostasy toward blasphemy and then treason, becoming more and more political in nature. Thus, the *zindiq,* or the "concealed heretic," is usually punished not as an apostate but rather under a more political Quranic provision (5:34-35) criminalizing "waging war on God and the Prophet" and "spreading corruption in the land." Next in line is the crime of insult to the Prophet, the Quran, the angels, etc. (*sabb al-nabi,* etc.). Some scholars punish it as apostasy, but most treat it as a separate offense arising from separate textual sources, in which the crime is simply uttering the insult. The absence of any element of belief is shown by the refusal to consider repentance or the excuse of innocent intent (e.g., joking). The tendency to ignore repentance and intent increases as we move along the spectrum. Doctrine on the crime of "the propagator of innovation" *(da'i bi-al-bid'a)* is still more clearly political, punishing not false belief at all, but the spreading of disapproved ideas harmful to the Muslim body politic. What the offender believes is irrelevant. Finally, at the end of this spectrum comes the Quranic crime of *baghy,* or revolt by Muslims, the punishment of which is essentially countervailing warfare by the state. This forms the limit of our concerns, since the perpetrators are conceded to be Muslims and since the only false expression is rebellion against the Islamic state. As we move along this spectrum the crimes become progressively more constitutive of an actual polity, more harsh (as in excluding repentance), and more restrictive of freedom of belief (penalizing a broader and broader spectrum of beliefs, even ones within Islam). Note also how a single act can be penalized under a number of these at once, especially when they are expansively interpreted.[16]

The overlapping and vagueness observable in these doctrines reflects two seemingly contradictory characteristics of the Islamic state. First, the Islamic state, thought of as being built on a loyalty not solely of this world, must face situations in which the religious dissent of individuals or groups is considered not merely a matter of opinion but disloyalty or treason. For example, the law declares the apostate a civil and political outlaw. But since Islam possesses no synod or pope who, supplanting God, defines a baseline of belief, not only loyalty but the test for it is ultimately transcendent, lending the issue of religious citizenship a peace-preserving ambiguity. These doctrines serve to mediate between these two characteristics, balancing the political and the transcendent to permit the community to maintain both worldly solidarity and its transcendent origin.

Turning to doctrines governing the law's application, we find these also, when tested against a microcosmic-to-macrocosmic spectrum, reflect the phenomenon of graded series of positions. Here even more clearly the spectrum displays simultaneous declines from textually legitimated doctrine to rulings legitimated merely as expedient or contingent (for example, as compelled by "the [increasing] corruption of the times" [fasad al-zaman]). While it thus condones other measures, fiqh makes constant obeisance to the ideal, holding it alone to be true doctrine.

For example, texts on adjudication require that all qadis and muftis be perfect practitioners of ijtihad, but they also briefly and grudgingly acknowledge that actual persons occupying these posts no longer meet this standard. Taqlid is thus presented, not as doctrine, but as an unpleasant fact. Ignored in theory, in practice taqlid pervaded the day-to-day functioning of the legal system. The ideal of ijtihad meanwhile stands pure and pristine, powerfully justifying the entire system. In similar fashion, usul al-fiqh texts condone various non-textual grounds for decision, but only as subordinate to the four primary sources. These grounds include necessity, community welfare, avoidance of harm, and custom. Yet, as classical scholars sometimes acknowledged, in practice the subsidiary sources can loom largest, since on many issues, new or old, the influence of the relevant texts has already been exhausted in shaping the available choices.

Fiqh public or constitutional law contains many instances of these graded spectra of views. Having few revealed texts to work with, *ulama* built up a body of works on public law based largely on past events, many of which fell afoul of the doctrines the *ulama* would have liked to assert. For example, *ulama* declared that succession to the caliphate is by election by influential persons, followed by the ruler's concluding a contract with each of his subjects (the *bay'a*). These doctrines are impressively anti-authoritarian, egalitarian and individualistic, and seem to prefigure modern ideas. But then the *ulama* went on to condone practices falling short of these norms. For example, they approved an early practice by which a ruler chose his own successor, usually a relative. Later scholars even validated rulership gained by force.

The following table summarizes a number of doctrines that occur in telescoping sets of positions from microcosmic to macrocosmic, taken from both procedural and substantive law. The table represents them at only three points: the first column states the ideal; the second column names evils into which pursuit of the ideal can fall in practice; and the third column shows compromises made by way of avoiding the evil while still approaching the ideal.

Using our emerging framework, the practice column represents the more macrocosmic doctrines, which are stepped down considerably from the ideal nearly always on grounds presented as temporal and contingent and with weaker authority from the revealed texts. The general theorem or generalization that results is that the doctrines that are most microcosmic in their vision of society tend to be those that enjoy the most microcosmic proofs, and those that have the most microcosmic proofs are those that enjoy the highest degrees of authentication or legitimation in traditional *usul al-fiqh*. In other words, the soundest doctrines tend to be the most microcosmic in their vision of society. Thus, to the extent that one cleaves to the microcosmic in method, one strengthens elements of *ijtihad,* individual autonomy, tolerance, universality and pluralism, and weakens authoritarian or totalitarian versions of Islamic political order, reducing the sway of the state and eventually even that of the *ulama*. Microcosmic principles, by constructing events atomistically, intrinsically raise moral, legal and intellectual obstacles to collective or social action, and thus tend to "privatize" legitimacy. Systematic emphasis on the more microcosmic and ideal doctrines in these spectra (and others throughout *fiqh*) could shift the balance of political life in these directions.

SOME IMPLICATIONS OF THE FRAMEWORK

Implications for Modern Islamic Movements

The system sketched above has many implications for contemporary efforts to establish Islamic states. Insofar as Islamic states and Islamist movements invoke the classical *fiqh*, they take a law written for one set of legal and social institutions, abstract it from its context, and attempt to apply it literally in a wholly different system. Doing so they inevitably reproduce, often unknowingly and often with distortions, many of the consequences of the *siyasa / fiqh* distinction in both ideal and practical realms.

For example, if modern activists take their political theory from the *fiqh*, they will tend to idealize the Islamic state for which they agitate. They will embrace delegation to the state of a power to act that is constrained only by basic principles of *fiqh*. But even that constraint is meaningless without the *ulama's* (doctrinally covert) macrocosmic institutions that projected and defended the *fiqh's* authority. When these movements seek power, their assertions of *fiqh* ideals such as *shura* or economic justice against existing "godless" regimes are no doubt sincere and attractively democratic-sounding. But after one of these movements gains power, if the religious activists assume power themselves, their doctrines will easily admit of oppression and arbitrary acts. Oppression in the name of literal religious legalism can be particularly intrusive and ruthless. If the end—for example to establish or preserve the Islamic state—is seen as sacred then all means may become lawful; the check of highly general *shari'a* principles easily evaporates. This is a reason for human rights abuses rampant in Iran and Sudan since the Islamists took control,[17] and the unbounded authority seized by Ayatollah Khomeini after the Islamic revolution and preserved in the constitution of the Islamic Republic. A particularly vivid illustration is Ayatollah Khomeini's *fatwa* of January 1988 holding that an Islamic state, since it rules by divine sanction, could, in the interests of the community, supersede not only specific rulings of *fiqh* but even the five pillars of the faith.[18] If instead of gaining power for themselves, the activists serve as the ideological wing of a regime run by the military (another view of events in the Sudan), then they will find scant authority in *fiqh*, and even fewer institutional means, to rein in abuses.

Table 10.1
Ideal / Practice Tensions in (Sunni) Fiqh Governance Doctrines

The Ideal	The Evil to be Avoided	The Practice
Politics		
shura, nasiha / consultation, advice	fitna / civil war	ta'at za'ir / obedience to an evildoer
insan, mu'minun, umma / unity of humanity, believers, the Islamic Community	'asabiyya / tribal solidarity, division by worldly groupings	dawla, muslimun / regime, Muslims
imama / caliphate, religiously legitimate rule	zulm, fawda / oppression, chaos	sulta, sultan / authority of de facto power
Legislation		
ijtihad / independent reasoning	bid'a, jahl / heresy, ignorance	taqlid, sadd bab al-'ijtihad / scholarly conformism, closing of the door of ijtihad
ikhtilaf mujtahidin / diversity of opinions all based on ijtihad	niza', shudhudh / conflict, bizarre opinions	ijma' madhhab aw al-madhahib / ijma' of a school or of the 4 Sunni schools
siyasa shar'iyya / broad legislative authority in the ruler	awamir sultaniyya / sultanic commands	ilzam bi-madhhab, qanun, tashri' / imposing a single school as binding, human law, legislation
Executive		
siyasa shar'iyya / legitimate siyasa	siyasa zalima / unjust	siyasa, fasad al-zaman, darura / siyasa, corruption of the times, necessity
maqasid al-shar' / the objectives of the shari'a	masalih khassa / welfare of particular persons, elites	masalih al-dawla, al-nas, etc. / utilities of the state, of the people, etc.
jihad / just war	hazima, khudu', fawda / defeat, subjugation, chaos	quwwa, sulta, 'izza / power, authority, might, glory

Table 10.1—continued

The Ideal	The Evil to be Avoided	The Practice
Judiciary		
ijtihad al-qadi / judgment by *ijtihad* of qadi	*hukm min al-hawa* / arbitrary or self-interested judgment	*taqlid, ilzam bi-qawl, qanun, taqlid,* requiring a qadi to follow a particular legal view, state legislation
ijtihad la yunqad / *ijtihad* cannot be reversed on appeal	*tahakkum, fasad, jahl* / arbitrariness, corruption, ignorance	*ri'asat al-qada', tafaqqud al-qudah naqd* / authority of chief qadi, appeal, reversal
al-ijtihad shart wilayat al-qadi / *ijtihad-*capability as a condition of appointment	*jahl* / ignorance	*ta'yin al-aslah fa-al-aslah* / appointment of whoever is the best person, whether or not duly qualified
Community		
islam man ashhad bi-allah wa-rasulihi / all who recite the shahada are Muslims	*kufr, zandaqa, tawa'if, fitna* / unbelief, heresy, sectarianism, civil strife	*islam man ma khalaf al-ijma'* / all are Muslim as long as they do not differ with *ijma'* (in its various degrees)
amr bi-al-ma'ruf wa-nahy 'an al-munkar / moral correction exerted only for doctrines with categorical revealed proofs	*fasad, hawa, nifaq* / decadence, passion, hypocrisy	*takfir, ilzam bi-ra'y* / calling others infidels, making mere opinion obligatory

All this follows if one accepts *fiqh* as the full statement of the *shari'a*, ignoring its classical institutionalization. One doubly misunderstands *fiqh* if one also takes it in its weaker, less authenticated, more expedient form (*taqlid, madhhab* loyalty, submission to ruler legislation, acquiescence in abuses of power), and neglects its ideal doctrines rooted in the microcosmic response to revelation (individual *ijtihad,* or, politically, ordering the good, *shura, nasiha* and *bay'a*). Again, the former doctrines reflect accommodations within a legal and political system that is now dismantled; in a new and different system their impact on *fiqh* and its objectives cannot be predicted.

If instead Islamist groups tried to effectuate microcosmic ideals, and to call on citizens to participate in implementing them, this might succeed in tapping Islamic legitimacy at its roots, and in mobilizing individuals on a plane that the *ulama* have too long monopolized for themselves. It might awaken something like the individual autonomy of meaning, the transcendent dimension of the self, that attended the birth of liberalism in the West and without which, many now argue, it is incoherent. Not surprisingly, innumerable Islamic reformists call for the reawakening of a spirit of *ijtihad,* even among the unlearned. The parallels to the Reformation are obvious,[19] especially if one accepts the view of Muslim apologists who say that Islam needs no reformation because it has no clergy and no church.[20]

If, instead of appealing to the microcosmic impulse, innovation is pursued by importing Western democratic institutions, these institutions present themselves as belonging to the public, macrocosmic sphere. The link to *shura* or other microcosmically grounded notions, as these are now understood, is insufficiently convincing to arouse religious loyalty. Despite the heavy reliance Muslim reformists place on such doctrines to legitimate Western imports, these imports have not so far engaged Islamic thought and loyalty beyond the doctrinally weak, contingent level of *siyasa*. They remain little more than limitations the state voluntarily imposes on itself. Moreover, these institutions are associated with secularism, which, in a Muslim country, means alien to the religion. The idea of secularism does not, as it does in the West, evoke microcosmic values potentially harmonious with prevailing religion, such as rationality, individual civic duty, social contract or the transcendence of truth entailing tolerance and freedom of belief. Since they are not rooted in Islamic microcosmic principles, Westernizing innovations may have an effect opposite to that intended, and simply shift the balance of power all the more toward the macrocosmic principle—which, once again, the classical doctrine can only weakly constrain. If, in contrast, these institutions were to grow up naturally in support of the microcosmic principle, as the now-eroded *ulama* institutions once did, they might both survive and strike lasting roots. In all this are indications of a possible blind-spot in Western observers' common deprecations of Islamists' politics as "meta-" or "transcendent."

Importing either classical Islamic law and politics or Western law and politics into new Islamic states in ignorance of age-old traits in Islamic systems can, therefore, be disastrous. To compare Western and Islamic political systems merely by their outward rules and institutions is to take the problem as one-dimensional, when, because it involves the history and institutionalization of both sets of systems, it is far more complex.

Paradoxically, genuine innovations in Islamic governance are unlikely where *siyasa* principles apply, whether administered by *ulama* or by rulers, because their *siyasa* origins so radically dilute their *shari'a* legitimacy. An example is the current status of the numerous Arab law codes drawn up using European models, which, even after more than a century, are still denounced as foreign, anti-Islamic imports.[21] Rather, advances will be found where *ijtihad* shapes action—even action that seems merely pragmatic, or civil rather than political. The *ijtihad* involved may be implicit, as it is when, thinking matters settled and not consulting *ulama*, Muslims take action in the belief that they are following divine revelation. We must look for lessons of this sort, for the "public" sphere, in the innumerable mundane elaborations of explicitly Islamic institutions in the states where they exist (for example, the Islamic courts of Saudi Arabia, Iran or the Sudan), or in the acts of municipal governments under Islamist control (for example, municipalities controlled by the Algerian Front Islamique du Salut [Islamic Salvation Front] or the Turkish Welfare Party); or, for the "private" sphere, in the numerous voluntary, private Islamist organizations (for example, mosques, clinics, schools, or the new Islamic banks and insurance companies) or in private clubs devoted to religious inspiration, business, society or education (such as social clubs in Bahrain, *diwaniyyas* in Kuwait, chambers of commerce).[22] Explored using the above framework, all of these could yield useful case studies for how *ijtihad* functions in Islamic governance.

Implications for Reforms of Islamic Law

Muslim efforts to reform Islamic law have so far emphasized those Islamic texts and doctrines that correspond most closely to Western ideas. For example, discussions of democracy focus on the Islamic conception of *shura* and *ijma'*. Apart from the fact just noted that imports of Western notions can lead to unintended results, this approach has likely achieved as much as it ever will. If the crime of apostasy or the ban on interest has not given way yet, if *shura* has not yet led to Islamic democracy and if women are not yet accorded equal status, it is not because any textual stone has been left unturned.

So far modern Islamic legal reform efforts have all lacked three things. The first is a convincing methodology. Many have realized this, but as yet no method capable of competing with classical *usul* has emerged. While *ulama* and non-*ulama* offer ideas for new interpretive methods, none of these has gained widespread authority or been made the criterion for any major action.[23] Often proposed changes in *usul,* like changes in substantive doctrine, are readily dismissed as concessions to, or ready imitations of, the West, or as ungrounded or undemanding in textual knowledge, and do not produce accredited results. Thus, Muhammad Abduh (d. 1905 C.E.), invoking the rationalist Mu'tazilite school of the second Islamic century, exalted reason and science in imitation of the West, but failed to convert either the people or the *ulama* to the cause. When in practice he sought legal reforms, he fell back on collaboration with the ruler and his *siyasa*-based authority to legislate whatever combinations (*talfiq*) of Sunni views were most utilitarian, ignoring *usul* niceties. In contrast, the recent trend has been toward what is methodologically most pristine or most microcosmic (for example, abandoning *taqlid,* dispensing with school loyalty, following the view with strongest textual proof). It seems now that *fiqh* liberalization will succeed and endure only if it deals in the coin of the sole method that possesses widespread esteem, or, to change the metaphor, if it passes through the heart of the classical system. Many feel that the classical law has been too readily dismissed, and that it must now have its say.

The second major shortcoming of past reforms has been a lack of proponents capable of carrying out innovations. The *ulama,* once leaders in all spheres of society, nowadays fill social roles, and effect popular representation, that make it difficult for them either to claim unquestioning support from the people or to defend the *shari'a* before the power of the state. Feeling insecure, the *ulama* are all the more likely to cling conservatively to the standard doctrines and to the decaying institutions that once served them well. With their ability to innovate and their institutions both so weak, they may simply resort to supporting on *siyasa*-style grounds any regime that gives them prestige, and forego the far more difficult and controversial *ijtihad* enterprise the situation now demands of them. While this pattern of behavior may have helped preserve the *shari'a* through centuries of Western cultural onslaught, much more is now demanded. The enormity of the task the *ulama* face only increases with delay. Their inability to undertake it effectively has caused many Islamists to portray them as unresponsive to people's needs, as co-opted, as "government *ulama.*"

If they reject being co-opted, *ulama* seemingly have only two alternative courses of action. One, which also ducks the slow, hard work of *ijtihad,* is to go over to Islamism and seek to convert the politically alienated to it. Some taking this choice focus on fomenting group activism, even violence and terrorism, toward attaining the "Islamic state." Shaikh Umar Abd al-Rahman of the Egyptian Jama'at Islamiyya is an example. Others less radical simply work to convert nominal Muslims to fervent upholders of traditionalist Islamic piety, ethics and social mores, again to prepare the way to return to the "Islamic state" and "the rule of *shari'a.*"[24] Common to both approaches is the assumption that *shari'a*, being divinely revealed and researched for a millennium, is unproblematic and well known.

The *ulama's* second alternative is far less commonly practiced: to ally themselves with the "silent majority" and take up the *ijtihad* dictated by their needs. Such *ulama* have to convince the majority that they have answers that are both authentic and workable for novel, often Western, challenges. Accomplishing this, in turn, requires that they courageously exploit old methods of Islamic legitimation, gradually evolve new methods from old ones, and be responsive to experts of other fields and non-*ulama* Islamic scholars. They must learn to credit the lessons of practical experience and broad popular opinion as criteria by which to judge the success of their answers. Few *ulama* possess the education and outlook to take up all these difficult tasks at once. Doing so is rarely rewarding, since departing to any degree from stable and authoritative answers and methodologies, or from the stricter positions on any issue, too often exposes one to accusations of co-optation. While there are scholars who have ventured into this gap, they have not attained a critical mass. One can find promising demonstrations of this approach only outside politics, as in Islamic banking, discussed later.

The third major obstacle for legal reform has been the lack of a viable institutional setting for *ijtihad.* Such a setting cannot fall within the *siyasa* realm, since, as we have posited, genuine reforms must engage *ijtihad* not *siyasa,* given the latter's diminished legitimacy and flexible criteria; therefore, the setting must be at some distance from immediate state interests. Practicality counsels this in any event, since otherwise states will suppress talk of Islam for fear of costly disruptions or Islamist opportunism. This suggests that innovators should consider reaching a pact or truce with the existing regimes: like quietist Islamic movements, they would renounce the Islamist objective of replacing the current regime with an "Islamic state," but, unlike the quietists, they would obtain in return a defined zone of autonomy for Islamic legal and political experimentation. One might even argue that, for the present at least, this sort of truce would perform the function of securing individual and group autonomy that secularism, "civil society" and related concepts play in Western systems. Note, however, that the autonomy sought here, unlike some analogies in the West, is not for pursuit solely of private, individual, apolitical or civil-society objectives; rather, since the reforms involve *ijtihad,* they perforce will engage aspects of governance, such as legislation and adjudication.[25] Finally, such a truce—which we here arrive at on other grounds—is in keeping with the religious doctrine that counsels against rebellion, and exactly parallels the medieval constitutional pact between *ulama* and rulers, by which *ulama* granted rulers a concessive, de facto legitimacy in return for autonomy in private law and adjudication.

Overcoming these three shortcomings of reform efforts—all of which are the consequences of neglecting microcosmically rooted *fiqh* methods and institutions—seems a prerequisite for lasting liberalizing innovations and reforms in Islamic law.

GULF CASE STUDIES

Saudi Arabia

Of all the Gulf countries, Saudi Arabia is the one to which the framework just outlined is most easily applied. Following a rigorously textualist-legal *(salafi)* philosophy inspired by Ibn Taymiyya, its *ulama* articulate a strongly microcosmic vision of law, and, applying Hanbali *fiqh,* exercise a broad independent jurisdiction in all three branches of government. Again following Ibn Taymiyya, constitutional authority is shared between the ruling family and the *ulama* according to an explicit *siyasa / fiqh* distinction.

Almost alone in the Muslim world, Saudi Arabia possesses a legal system drawn on classical models. The system is, however, far from untouched by modernization. *Ulama* institutions have been greatly transformed, not always to the augmentation of their power, but their central position within the regime is still secure. Presently, the greatest threat to their authority comes, not from modernization or secularization, but from *ulama* more stringent than themselves.

The transformation of Saudi Arabia into a modern nation state has inevitably vastly augmented the king's powers. The manifold centralizing effects of modernization and vast state revenues give the king the means to influence events independent of either the tribes or the *ulama*. At the same time, the cultural, economic and legal spheres over which the king traditionally holds sway have greatly increased in importance, while the realms over which the *ulama* are the keepers are simply less vital to the daily life of most citizens. In such a context, the continued tension between the microcosmic and macrocosmic principles becomes critical. Islamic public law theory, the explicit source of the constitution, offers no formal or positive check on the mounting *siyasa* powers of the king. The restraints are the informal ones of *ulama* doctrines and institutions. Protections of individual interests, rights and freedoms come only from assertions of the microcosmic principle, of which the *ulama* are the keepers.

Two areas in which the *ulama* and the microcosmic principles they espouse have played particularly visible roles are the controversy over codification of civil laws, and the Basic Law of March 1, 1992, and the debates leading up to it.

Codification. In Saudi Arabia, a great part of applicable law—almost all civil, commercial, criminal, family, inheritance, land tenure and procedural law—is not codified, but taken directly from the *fiqh*, usually Hanbali. This is an extraordinary state of affairs, especially for a country that has in a short span of time adopted many modern institutions and spent hundreds of billions of dollars on development. The country has incurred many extra billions of dollars in additional development costs to compensate outsiders for uncertainties about and unfamiliarity with the legal system. Saudi businessmen regularly call for rationalization of its legal system. Given such pressures for change it may seem puzzling why Saudi Arabia has not adopted the sort of modern codes common to all its neighbors, including Iran and the GCC countries. The answer is straightforward: emphasis on *shari'a*, opposition to "man-made" law, and the influence of *ulama*, who feel that even the present balance is weighted far too much toward man-made law and non-religious courts. The most fundamental and persistent controversy within the Saudi legal system since the country's founding has been whether to codify the basic laws of the kingdom.

In most Islamic states other than Saudi Arabia, the legal system is bifurcated: one part is based on man-made, positive *(wad'i)* law; the other part on Islamic law. The first part usually exists in the form of comprehensive codes similar to those of European civil law systems, and the second in the form of Islamic law, usually codified as well. The positive legal system provides the basic or residual law, while the Islamic law is exceptional, supplementary and relatively narrow in scope. There is a similar bifurcation in the institutions that apply the law, for example, between positive law tribunals and religious law courts.

Saudi Arabia also has a dual legal system, but the relative roles of the two sides are reversed. The Islamic component of the legal system is fundamental and dominant. The positive law, on the other hand, is subordinate, constitutionally and in scope. Saudi positive law consists of decrees (*nizam*) issued by the king with the advice of his Council of Ministers (and now also Consultative Council) under *siyasa shar'iyya* authority. His constitutional power to legislate is limited to laws needed to supplement the *fiqh* in furtherance of public welfare, on condition that these laws offend no clear text or fundamental principle of *shari'a*. This power has been exercised only in relatively discrete areas, typically reflecting problems arising in modern times (for example, laws on nationality, customs, trademark, traffic laws and narcotics). The *nizam*s are small in scope compared to the positive law corpus of other countries. To accompany these *nizam*s, the king also created specialized tribunals. With respect to the other, the *fiqh*-based, side of the legal system, because *fiqh* is uncodified and because the Saudi *ulama, salafi* Hanbali in orientation, are committed to a microcosmic vision of *fiqh*, law is determined by the judge *(qadi)*. The judge is required to practice *ijtihad* to the best of his ability, though he is encouraged to consult with other *ulama*. The *qadi*s and *ulama* are the legislators (in the sense of law-finders) of the applicable *fiqh*.

Saudi adjudication exhibits both the advantages and disadvantages of microcosmic law-making. It devolves authority for a highly important aspect of governance—legislation—away from the ruler to a professional class, whose prestige depends a great deal on the respect of the people. Since *shari'a* is the fundamental law and holds over inconsistent positive law, every judge (and even every regulatory tribunal) is to some degree a constitutional court, capable of checking the authority of the state. Its disadvantages are that it risks unbridled judicial discretion, the proverbial Weberian "*qadi*-justice." It provides an unsystematic approach to legal problems, treating them atomistically and solving them ad hoc, with no overall plan or consistency. It lowers the system's defenses against irrational, provincial, ignorant or corrupt judges.

To control these disadvantages and to secure the stability of the system, Saudi *qadi*s have mitigated its microcosmic character in practice, though not in theory. They do not in fact determine the law in rigorous microcosmic fashion, each case tested against the revealed texts. They are rather predictable: most of the time they apply the Hanbali school, and when they deviate from it, they try to do so as a group. Their conformity is achieved by non-doctrinal means: a common education steeping all *ulama* in Hanbali rulings and methods of derivation; group loyalty and consultation; respect for senior *ulama*, whose *fatwa*s have almost legislative effect; and adherence to views announced by the courts of appeal, which, though formally not binding, "guide" the lower courts. These means have in turn their own disadvantages: they weld the *ulama* into a cohesive, introspective, conservative elite, wedded to the views of their most senior members and tending to identify legal development with the perpetuation of their own influence.

If they expect to respond sufficiently to the needs of modern interactions, Saudi laws and courts have only three alternatives. One is codification, which would mean ceding the full power of legislation to the king and his *siyasa* authority, thereby relinquishing a vital constitutional check on his authority. Judges protest that they would lose their independence and prestige. Though outsiders may view codification as a step toward rationality and the rule of law, it would represent a further tilt toward the macrocosmic principle, already too strong. We should not confuse such legislation with laws passed in a Western environment of separation of powers and the rule of law. So far this alternative has been blocked by the *ulama*.

The second alternative is to exploit the various present legislative methods now in force to deal more successfully with contemporary needs. The principle of judicial *ijtihad,* supported by the cohesiveness of the *ulama* system as shown in judges' voluntarily following higher scholars and courts, means that, if they wished, the *ulama* could effectively legislate, with either no or supplementary legislation by the king. Comparative law offers analogies suggestive of how this could be achieved, such as judge-made law in common-law systems, scholarly treatises in civil-law systems, or the American Law Institute's expert Restatements in American law. But the innately conservative *ulama* seem unwilling to take up the task. This is exemplified by their passivity on commercial law, a topic that in Saudi terms falls within their jurisdiction. Long neglecting the vigorous *ijtihad* needed to reflect the country's development, *ulama* finally agreed to shift jurisdiction to the Grievances Board, an administrative court based on old *shari'a* precedents. Even on this court commercial law remains the concern of individual judges with *shari'a* training, with results still far from satisfactory to businessmen.

The third legislative alternative is more hypothetical, but still instructive. The *ulama's* passivity might change if ordinary Saudis assumed for themselves the individualist microcosmic rights and responsibilities so strikingly advocated by Ibn Taymiyya and by *salafi* thought. If lay Saudis demanded that the *ulama* not only inform them of the *fiqh* rules being applied to them (now not even this is done), but also convince them that the rules are at once Islamically legitimate and legally and practically suitable, the *ulama* then would be forced to develop the law that is needed in many areas of life, such as commercial law, and to consult non-*ulama* experts in these areas. Outcomes could then be "legislated" through existing *ulama* institutions. The public's strong desire for an Islamic solution in finance and banking, discussed below, is encouraging just such an open collaboration among the public, lay experts and *ulama*. Were such a collaboration on new laws called for in Saudi Arabia, the government might even favor it and admit it to public fora, as long as it offered hope both of resolving the codification impasse and of relieving pressures for greater participation and greater Islamization in public life. No doubt the government would do so only if the debate remained responsible and pragmatic and avoided "politics." If in such circumstances the *ulama* refused to take up the challenge, they would be neglecting their role as representatives of the people's interests.

This discussion of Saudi Arabia illustrates several key points: first, the costs of leaving the microcosmic principle wholly in the control of *ulama* in their modern condition; second, the gains hypothetically achievable from invoking microcosmic approaches, particularly in offering a way around the worsening stalemate between traditional Islamic and modern Western legal forms; and third, the likelihood that, without a conscious effort led by Muslim intellectuals, the microcosmic angle will not be developed, falling victim to lack of imagination, incongruence with Western models, and the narrow class interests of both *ulama* and Westernized elites.

Basic Law. On March 1, 1992, King Fahd promulgated three documents that defined the structure and function of government for the first time in written form.[26] Their issuance followed agitation in the country during the buildup to the Gulf War, aroused by the humiliation of inviting in foreign troops to confront Iraq. Striking evidence of this agitation was the novel phenomenon of petitions to the king (leaked to the public) signed by prominent citizens and voicing complaints about the Saudi system of government. One, submitted by important businessmen and technocrats in 1990, demanded the creation of a consultative council, reform of the civil laws, and elimination of corruption and special privilege. Momentous in itself, it was overshadowed in spring 1991 by a second petition signed by some of the highest and most influential *ulama* among others, which demanded the following:

- establishment of a council for consultation *(shura)* to decide upon domestic and foreign affairs, the members of which shall be from those possessing various specializations and of attested probity and sincerity, with complete independence and without any pressure that would affect the actual responsibility of the council.
- review and drafting of all rules *(la'iha)* and laws *(nizam)*, whether political, economic, administrative or otherwise, in accordance with the rules *(hukm)* of the Islamic *shari'a*, and, accordingly, abrogation of anything in conflict with (those rules). This is to be accomplished through reliable and competent *shari'a* committees.

  . . .
- upholding justice in the distribution of public wealth among all classes and groups within society . . .

  . . .
- unifying the judicial institutions and endowing them with complete and actual independence . . .
- guaranteeing the rights of the individual and the society, and ending any restrictive influences on the will of the people and their rights, in order to fulfill human dignity according to recognized *shari'a* standards.[27]

This document is extraordinary in its mixture of the standard institutional goals of the *ulama*—fortifying the independence of the judiciary, purifying *siyasa* laws of conflicts with *shari'a,* enhancing *ulama* legislative powers—with broader social and political aspirations, both microcosmic and macrocosmic in content. The last section is particularly striking in its demand for freeing both the individual and society from "restrictive influences."

Other petitions appeared. One, about a year later, was submitted by opposition religious scholars and totalled 45 pages. The high *ulama* establishment, however, withdrew support for further petitioning and denounced those engaging in it, ending a period during which *ulama* and technocrats were partly aligned in their demands. Yet this alignment may have been one of the chief reasons for King Fahd's issuance of the March 1992 Basic

Law, fulfilling promises he and earlier kings had many times made but postponed.

The Basic Law makes many concessions to the *ulama*, who were reportedly pleased with its contents, and adopts many of their most characteristic ideas. Most importantly, it reflects the microcosmic ideal of law—the *shari'a* remains transcendent over any man-made legislation. Thus, the constitution of the country is said to be "the Book of God . . . and the Sunna" (Art. 1) which are to remain "sovereign over this law and all *nizams* of the state" (Art. 7). The judiciary is assured its independence and general jurisdiction, and is obliged to apply only "the rules of the Islamic *shari'a* as indicated by the [textual] proofs of the Book and the Sunna, and the *nizams* issued by the ruler that do not contradict the Book or the Sunna" (Arts. 46, 48). The king's authority, in contrast, is only that of *siyasa shar'iyya*: he "undertake[s] the governing [*siyasa*] of the nation in accordance with [the *shari'a*] . . ." (Art. 55); the state's legislative power is only to "attain welfare and avoid harm in the affairs of the state, in accordance with the general rules of the Islamic *shari'a*" (Art. 67). To none of these positions can the *ulama* raise any objection.

The document acknowledges the broader political rights the petitions had called for but gives them no concrete implementation. It reads: "The state shall protect human rights in accordance with the Islamic *shari'a*" (Art. 26). It guarantees the privacy of homes and of communication (Arts. 26, 40), freedom from arbitrary imprisonment (Art. 27), and certain social and economic rights. No mention is made of a number of other rights, however, such as rights against gender discrimination, of religious freedom and of association. The rights granted are not given any means of enforcement beyond the courts and laws as already constituted. Juristically the Basic Law is only an expression of the king's will and is subject to change. It institutes no new constitutional basis for the Saudi government.

The associated Consultative Council (*Majlis al-Shura*) Law created a council of sixty members all appointed by the king for a four-year term. The powers of the council include initiating draft legislation; "interpreting" *nizams*; reviewing all *nizams*, treaties, international agreements and development plans before their adoption; "requesting" the attendance of ministers; and "requesting" the provision of government information. Decisions of the council are to be submitted to the president of the Council of Ministers (for instance, the king), who refers them to the Council of Ministers. If both councils agree, then decisions become final "upon the king's consent." If they should disagree, then "the king has the right to decide as he deems fit." The Basic Law allows the king to dissolve and to reconstitute the council at will.

Is there any conflict here between the protection granted the *ulama*-dominated legal system and the rights given ordinary citizens? In one respect there is none: the Basic Law faithfully reflects the Islamic legal system as conservatively understood in the kingdom. For example, because classical *fiqh* contains no rules with positive, effective force on the matter of *shura,* theory is divided over whether a ruler is obliged to follow the opinion of a *shura* council or may do as he thinks best.

But from another perspective we can draw new lessons from this episode. First, the petitions submitted by the *ulama* are a strong indication of the way the *ulama's* microcosmic approach might align partly with the political reform program of a liberalizing, Westernizing merchant/technocratic group, and of the power such an alignment might wield. Opposition *ulama* and other Islamic activists are today the most outspoken critics of abuses of power in the kingdom. *Ulama,* courts and other decisionmakers may draw encouragement from the Basic Law to oppose offenses against rights on Islamic law grounds. But, cutting the other way, the Basic Law episode also shows us how a program shaped solely by *ulama* may prove inadequate to the task of protecting individual rights. *Ulama* aligned with the state in Saudi Arabia may not hold out for more than their traditional privileges. After all, *fiqh* content and history encourage the *ulama* to see the reinforcement of their own power as the best safeguard for individual rights, and to insist on little else.

Iran

Events in Iran since the revolution stand in strong contrast to the traditionally microcosmic approach of *fiqh*—even Shi'i *fiqh.* Shi'i public law doctrine is very different from that of Sunni law. Yet when viewed in terms of system and function, political thought and practice in past Shi'i states was not unlike that of Sunni states. In both systems *ulama* maintained a pessimistic, detached attitude toward actual rulers, whom they considered corrupt in degrees and whom they sought to guide toward the fulfillment of *shari'a.* In both systems the *ulama* specialized in microcosmic law and left macrocosmic concerns to the state. They never had, nor sought the opportunity to seize, the power to use the levers of the state directly to further their religious program. Imam Khomeini's doctrine of "leadership by the jurist" (*velayat-e faqih*) here represents stark innovation.[28] This doctrine approaches theocracy in eliminating the checks and balances provided by the separation of *fiqh* from *siyasa,* of those who wield religious legitimacy from those who wield power. Joining the authority to rule with religious authority tends to totalitarianism and saps the microcosmic impulse of religion. The authority of the texts, of which the *ulama* have always seen themselves as just a vehicle, becomes confused with the authority of the *ulama* themselves. Khomeini's innovation certainly does overcome the tendency of *ulama* in Saudi Arabia, with their traditionally microcosmic approach and weakened institutions, to overlook the macrocosmic needs of citizens, particularly in such matters as political participation, positive legal protections for rights, and economic justice.

It is in their degree of sympathy for macrocosmic means and ends that Iranian intellectuals and religious leaders of the revolutionary era most strikingly distinguished themselves.[29] Ali Shariati's writings lay emphasis on collectivities over individuals as the basis of Islamic legal rights and duties. The influence of a long-time opponent, Marxism, is evident. For example, in being described as religiously privileged *mustaz'afin,* "oppressed," the urban proletariat, the foot-soldiers of the revolution, gained a status in religious discussions inconceivable in classical law. As to law, contemporary Iranian statements on law continue to be distinguished most clearly from Sunni rhetoric by their macrocosmic emphasis. Khomeini, although he endorsed other perspectives on occasion, provided the most dramatic demonstrations of the newly macrocosmic character of Islamic law. They are crystallized in his 1988 *fatwa* mentioned above that the interests of the Islamic revolution supersede the five pillars of the faith.[30]

Was Iran's invocation of the *fiqh's* prestige for macrocosmic ends worth the costs? Most outsiders would say that the experiment has failed miserably in advancing the religious interests—microcosmic or macrocosmic— of Iranians. Many assert even that piety is waning in Iran. One way to assess the Iranian revolution Islamically would be to use the table provided on pages 268-69 (or a Shi'i version of it) to discover whether the religious elite in power tried to govern according to the ideal microcosmic paradigm of *fiqh* (the first column), or whether it seized on the *fiqh's* unstructured delegation of power to rulers (the third column) for its own benefit. Classically, the *ulama* delegated power to the ruler as part of a larger strategy to advance the *fiqh's* application in less than perfect conditions, under rulers considered unjust and incorrigible. To adopt such a position in an "Islamic Republic" under *ulama* control was to apply it outside that context. The record shows that the regime tortured and killed persons for their opinions on religion and religious law, even crushing great *ulama* for expressing views that were not only perfectly legitimate *ijtihad* but were strictly orthodox. Recently, Professor Abdolkarim Soroush was forced from the country for arguing philosophically for a sphere of secularism in Islam, for freedoms and democracy, and for the separation of the *ulama* from politics. Evidence accumulates of corruption among *ulama*, particularly in the immensely wealthy, unregulated *bonyads* (foundations). Under its constitution Iran has developed impressive political institutions including an elected parliament and an active press, both effective to a degree rare in the Middle East. But they may operate only within channels narrowly defined by the *ulama*, and power remains firmly in the control of the clergy, who, for example, have the right to approve the Islamic credentials of all candidates for parliament.

Whatever microcosmic and macrocosmic ends may justify the *ulama's* seizing power, the Iranian case suggests that they will garner for themselves the powers of both spheres. They do not check themselves in their exercise of worldly authority even in the interests of their traditional microcosmic goals. Not surprisingly, many Iranians, among them some *ulama*, call for the *ulama* to leave politics for good.

Trends in Iran since Khomeini's death show a weakening in macrocosmic class-driven politics and a turn toward more microcosmic patterns in economics and law. Ayatollah Khamenei has not been able to step into Khomeini's shoes, and *mullas* are able to talk more openly about abandoning politics. The regime has been unable to control in its favor the recent designation of the supreme scholar *(marja')* of the learned hierarchy of Twelver Shi'ism. In the end, perhaps Khomeini's totalitarian grasp of both secular and religious power will be seen as an aberration brought about by a charisma he alone possessed.

Contemporary Shi'ism in Iran is only one instance, though by far the most monumental and prolonged, of a contemporary tendency to understand *fiqh* macrocosmically, a trend found also in the ideologies of many Sunni Islamist movements. Some scholars argue that even before the Iranian revolution, Sunni Islamism innovated in its utopianist obsession with the goal of erecting the "Islamic state," and in reconstructing *fiqh* as a model for political and social revolution and transformation.[31] Many Islamist movements no doubt imagine that their state will be led by their religious leaders, *ulama* or not, and, dangerously enough, do not specify what "*shari'a*" (i.e., what *fiqh*) these leaders intend to apply. Nor do they comment on either the novelty or the risks of conjoining religious and temporal leadership. A new apparent case of political leadership by Sunni *ulama* is afforded by the insurgent Afghani Taliban movement, ruled by a "*shura* council" of *ulama*.

The Land Reform Controversy

An important series of legal disputes in Iran, for which ample studies do exist, concern clashes between Parliament and the Council of Guardians over social legislation, particularly land reform.[32] Land reform laws were drafted to allow the seizure for redistribution to peasants of lands abandoned by persons fleeing the revolution. The Council of Guardians, charged by the constitution to review the *fiqh* propriety of all legislation before its promulgation, several times rejected these laws after they were voted by Parliament, on the ground that they offended the *fiqh*'s protections of private property. The case offers a clear example of conflict between the class-based macrocosmic values of the revolution and the *fiqh*'s characteristically microcosmic moral concerns. In 1988 when these clashes had risen to the level of constitutional crisis, Khomeini sided with the parliament, and ordered the creation of a new board to break impasses of this sort, called the "Council for Discerning Utility," which subsequently was added to the constitution.[33]

The controversy is not entirely new: religious scholars have always permitted individuals as well as states to deviate from *fiqh* norms on grounds of extreme necessity. For example, land may be expropriated with compensation for public need, and in *siyasa* contexts, individual rights, however sacred, are often overridden, at times on religious grounds such as *jihad* but at times for pressing collective necessity. What is new here is that the *ulama* and the *fiqh* define and control both sides of the equation, and at times the action is advocated, not as an exceptional deviation, but as the everyday fulfillment of *fiqh*. Two versions of *fiqh* are in conflict, one that avails itself of the macrocosmic perspective of an Islamic state and another that does not. Presumably ruling *ulama* are developing a *fiqh* to guide the new council that will decide when individual rights ought to be overridden in order to redress class inequities.

Islamic Finance and Banking

All these examples leave us pessimistic about the likelihood of governance reform in the Gulf. When, however, we look outside politics (as our paradigm suggests we should), we find grounds for greater optimism. If development is succeeding there, distance from politics may be one important reason for that success. Development outside government may yield clues about how Islamic innovation might advance, even in areas of politics.

Islamic finance has lately developed rapidly, and shows signs of one day generating viable Islamic modes of investment and banking that are distinct from Western models. Admittedly, legal innovation in finance is relatively easy, because new financial practices can be adopted merely by private agreement, without state action. No doubt, governments have had to enact a few laws and regulations for the creation and regulation of Islamic banks, but these measures arouse little concern for their effects on political or economic stability.[34]

What drives innovation in Islamic finance is a popular, religiously motivated rejection of, or discomfort with, conventional practices due to the Quran's emphatic prohibition of *riba*, which, classically interpreted, includes interest on loans. Most patrons of Islamic banking are not radicals, but fall within the silent majority of believing Muslims. After the concept of the "Islamic bank" was invented (notably, not by *ulama*), the *ulama* have helped to find workable means to reconcile banking and financial transactions with the classical law. Their early *fatwa*s vacillated between the impractically strict and the overly permissive. Among the latter were *fatwa*s condoning Islamically improper practices ad hoc for reasons of "necessity," namely the survival of Islamic banks. Recently *ulama* opinions on Islamic banking have become stricter, more rooted in Islamic sources, and better researched and reasoned. Legal conceptions long ago declared "not contradictory to Islamic principles" when enacted in *siyasa* context as part of post-colonial law codes now arouse long, illuminating comparative-law debates when scholars try to ground them in *ijtihad*. This trend is driven by public opinion disillusioned by the banks' more expedient practices. The public also has become better informed about the theory of Islamic banking and no longer accepts permissive *fatwa*s without question. Customers inquire as to which scholar issued a particular *fatwa*, and which scholars serve on a bank's *shari'a* supervisory board charged with determining the permissibility of transactions.

In rejecting interest, Islamic banking rejected the opinions of many liberalizing, reforming scholars of the last century, many of them *ulama*, who declared bank interest permissible. Today various classical opinions, even inconvenient ones, are being followed, even by participants and scholars who in other contexts adopt more flexible opinions. It is as if Islamic banking has set itself the task of seeing whether the game can be won even playing by strict rules. The voice of traditionalist *ulama* is sought on banks' supervisory boards and in *fatwa* academies. Non-*ulama* generally advise, research and propose, but do not decide. Islamic banking has proven a boon for traditionalists, who for the first time in many years have gained well-paid positions in the private sector, opportunities to declare on practical problems outside the spheres of ritual and the family, and a respectful hearing among men of the world.

As Islamic finance continues to develop, scholars are finding it more difficult to make progress, as increasing sophistication creates demands for additional transactions that in the West are achieved by means contradicting Islamic law. Deprived of any easy solution, scholars are obliged to inquire into the underlying economic problem and into novel ways of solving it. In the process they must collaborate with experts outside their field, such as bankers, financiers, economists and lawyers, and must find solutions not only in legal rulings and transactions but through institutional change and creation. In this way the demand for particular microcosmic relationships generates new macrocosmic institutions. For example, insurance is highly suspect under *fiqh*, but, now that the idea has spread of providing coverage through a private institution dedicated to Muslim charitable and mutual aid (called a "solidarity company"), it is more widely accepted. The Islamic finance industry is also developing a number of new institutions (in addition to the Islamic banks and insurance companies themselves), including the *shari'a* control board as a structural part of banks; new accounting and auditing standards organizations; international boards and conferences of *ulama* to study and standardize *fatwas*; industry-wide trade organizations; and, soon, secondary financial markets. As these innovations emerge, Islamic financial contracts and institutions evolve away from their original Western models.

Another significant trend is Islamic finance's growing impact on governmental interests and policies. Pressure is building on governments to facilitate Islamic financial development or lose out on a growing economic sector. Competition among countries has set in, leading Bahrain, as it aspires to become a new Islamic financial center, to look over its shoulder at Malaysia. Governments have become customers for Islamic finance. Several nations, among them Pakistan, Sudan, Jordan and Malaysia, have financed development projects using Islamic techniques. Countries like Saudi Arabia, with strongly Islamic populations and low domestic private investment rates, are considering the possibility of using Islamic techniques to attract private investment for development projects, reducing deficits and foreign borrowing.

Can we draw analogies between these innovations and potential Islamic political development? People are even more dissatisfied Islamically with the political status quo than they are with banking or finance. But there is no "marketplace" for experimenting, for binding negotiation and compromise, in the development of Islamic political institutions. If the *ulama* were called upon to consider the manifold legal and political problems of Islamic governance in microcosmic contexts, we might begin to learn what, in practice and not just in theory, Islamic sources (texts, history and sociology) can be made to say about modern constitutional, political and legal institutions. Admittedly, governments are unlikely to permit speculation, much less experimentation, on issues central to their stability, such as the Islamicity of *velayat-e faqih* in Iran or of monarchy in Saudi Arabia. But in civil areas progress may be possible. In Iran pressure for economic liberalization seems to grow, as the government moves away from nationalization and class-conscious politics toward encouragement of private property and enterprise. In Gulf countries other than Iran the case for economic liberalization and privatization of government services is much easier, and Saudi Arabia has such projects on the table. Experimentation with Islamic governance in such contexts would ease transitions demanded in the political system, such as removing religious prerequisites to election in Iran; widening the electorate in Kuwait, particularly to women; or enhancing employment opportunities for women in Saudi Arabia.

Islamic banking in Pakistan, Iran and the Sudan contrasts with that elsewhere in that in these three countries the governments have decreed that all banking must be Islamic. Significantly, banking has succeeded in Islamic terms in neither Iran nor Pakistan (information on the Sudan is scanty). Practices condemned by Islamic law persist, often in the form of shallow pretenses of Islamic legality. In Pakistan, inventory financing is achieved using a fictitious double-sale: first the inventory is sold to the bank for cash, and then the customer immediately repurchases it on credit. Lending to government and abroad is exempted from Islamic rules. In Iran, while the Islamic contract of profit-sharing partnership is used to lend to businesses, the central bank fixes the amount of "profit" for all contracts in each sector in advance.

The Iranian banking industry is near collapse, but bankers maintain that it is not the Islamic banking practices that have caused the dire situation. They ascribe the problem rather to the nationalization of banks following the revolution and to the government's habit of using the banks to finance governmental deficits and to pursue agendas unrelated to banking.[35]

Islamic banking in Iran has failed because the state has subjected it to its macrocosmic agendas, particularly to bolster the state's legitimacy and to support certain economic goals. *Siyasa* prerogatives of the state defeat and obscure the distinct task of achieving Islamicity in each transaction. The sudden adoption of nationwide Islamic banking precluded an organized transition, and uniform state-mandated procedures stifle innovation and competition among banks to be "more Islamic." The pattern is characteristically Iranian: Islam is in the macrocosm.

Saudi Arabia falls at the other extreme from these nationally mandated systems. Unlike most Muslim countries, Saudi Arabia, with one exception, has refused to license Islamic banks (the exception, al-Rajhi Bank, was obliged not to mention its intentions to comply with Islamic law in its charter). Presumably the finance ministry blocks "Islamic" banking because designating one portion of the banking system "Islamic" would imply that all other banking practices are "non-Islamic," inspiring demands to abolish them, while the government believes that "Islamic" banking as now understood cannot meet the country's needs. Allowing extensive "Islamic" banking might feed a spirit of doctrinalism and religious over-bidding in other areas of Saudi life, seeking to make them also doctrinally and ideologically pristine. Yet Saudi Arabia remains one of the world's leading markets for Islamic finance. The central bank has permitted conventional banks to open non-interest branches and windows, the floating of mutual funds that undertake to comply with Islamic law, and the sale of off-shore Islamic investments. Two of the largest multinational Islamic banking conglomerates were founded and are still controlled by Saudis. Saudi Arabia hosts several of the world's most important institutions for research on Islamic banking.[36] Establishment *ulama* are strong advocates of Islamic banking, and reportedly members of the governmental Council of Senior *Ulama* serve on al-Rajhi's board of *shari'a* advisers. In sum, apart from its refusal to sanction a separate banking industry denominated as "Islamic," Saudi authorities seem tolerant of the phenomenon and inclined to allow private experimentation. They have not attempted to influence, alter or reduce *ulama* opposition to interest banking, and Saudi private individuals, scholars and institutions have been leaders in developing interest-free alternatives.

Prognosis for Gulf Governance

Many questions for further analysis and evaluation are suggested by the foregoing. Should there be greater recognition that historical and sociological research on past and present legal systems must inform present Islamic political, legal and constitutional debates? Should the compromises with Islamic principle common over the long history of Islamic rule (see table) cease to serve as norms, at least of explicitly Islamic states? To what extent might the methods and aspirations of the microcosmic domain of *fiqh*, hitherto the concern of *ulama* and *fiqh* theory, be aligned with calls for liberal democracy?

Probably the central issue is whether a microcosmic vision of *fiqh*, if urged now as fundamental to the Islamic legal enterprise, might gradually win broader autonomy for the people from both the ruler and the *ulama*. While supporting regimes in power, could such a vision diminish the overweening power (and overwhelming responsibilities) of the modern nation state, as new means for individual and communal religious realization emerge through privately generated norms and institutions?[37]

This possibility is a mere hypothesis. What chance is there that any groups in GCC countries will adopt it? (Iran is left to one side as wholly unfavorable to such an initiative.) To explore this, let us consider what the strategy would be in opposition to it, were regimes in power intent solely on retaining a maximum of power and confident that they could do so without concessions either to Islam or liberal-democratic forms. In that case these regimes would be best advised—given the religiosity of their populations—to present all state action as mere *siyasa*, even when exercising it in the sphere of legislation. They should represent the demands of Islamic law as met by the ruler's largely symbolic, external or formal recognition of them, overseen by establishment *ulama*. For example, the law's application could be presented as a matter merely of amending the few positive laws that conflict directly with unquestioned Islamic principles. *Shura* Councils would be advisable, since they show respect for the demands of religion, but could be set up without real power, since traditional doctrine about them is vague. Democracy, on the other hand, is easily claimed to be un-Islamic since it is rule of the people rather than God. Western allies will usually concede this, since they are ready in many cases to support the regimes in power as bulwarks against Islamism. If the society should succeed in following this trajectory for a long time, life will increasingly distance itself from the concerns of religion, and the power of the *ulama* will continue to diminish. In this way the population will gradually be secularized, but without acquiring the ideals of universal individual political participation and fulfillment that in the West undergird and justify secularism. Continued augmentation of state functions will render *siyasa* authority ever more comprehensive and invasive.

Probably, however, even with their extraordinary economic means none of these governments has the option of such a course, and will wish in any event to develop new forms of popular participation to strengthen a legitimacy no longer as easily replenished from customary sources. A highly relevant customary source of legitimacy is the "*majlis*," a sort of open house conducted regularly by those in power, with roots both tribal and Islamic. In theory, any citizen may, without hindrance or hesitation, use the *majlis* to convey directly to a man in power his or her opinion, advice, grievance or petition. While the *majlis* is still a vigorous institution, its use is becoming more difficult, as the population grows, the complexities of life, of problems and of governing increase, and as the numbers and variety of interest groups and lines of influence multiply. In this case, these countries could take two possible courses. One would be to adopt Western-style democratic institutions—Kuwait struggles toward this goal, aided by a post–Gulf War atmosphere, internal and external, insistent on democracy. Such a course may or may not in the end satisfy either the populace, the Islamists or the government. If it succeeds, it will be a historic turning point for Gulf and Islamic politics; if it does not, the democrats will once more be frustrated. Another alternative, the one suggested here, would be to generate, using *fiqh* problems as a vehicle, forms of participation in governance by individuals *qua* Muslims, and thereby devolving, privatizing, the immediate control of sectors of public life from the state to society as a whole.

In revolutionary Iran, of course, neither of these options was chosen. Instead, the religious leadership seized the authority of both *siyasa* and *fiqh* in its own hands, and shared power with the people in a limited way using institutions modeled on those of Western democracies. The critical contrast between Iran and other Gulf countries, and one that dictates their continued divergence, is between the social groups driving change in the two cases: in one an urban mass responding to a populist message, and in the other an emerging educated middle class demanding power-sharing and accountability. Until now only the latter group has had importance in Saudi Arabia and other GCC countries.[38]

These points all suggest that, compared to the rest of the Muslim world, the GCC countries possess traits most conducive to emergence of the patterns sketched here. None of them is likely to abandon aspirations to Islam in the political sphere, to adopt patently Western institutions, or to accept an Iranian-style totalizing solution. This combination of traits may just spell stalemate. Key determinants will be whether a middle class emerges with the motivation and power to demand concessions from the government. If the power of such a group proves insufficient, they may seek an alliance with the state's traditionalist supporters. If they approach the *ulama* and gain their support, this might usher in courses of action like those portrayed here.

Notes

1. This article has benefited from comments by my colleagues at the Harvard Law School summer workshop. I also thank David Westbrook for extensive comments and criticisms.

2. Useful recent publications include Olivier Roy, *The Failure of Political Islam*, trans. Carol Volk (Cambridge: Harvard University Press, 1994); Dale Eickelman and James Piscatori, *Muslim Politics* (Princeton, NJ: Princeton University Press, 1996).

3. Francis Fukuyama, in *The End of History and the Last Man* (New York: Free Press, 1992), p. 46 states that Islam "cannot challenge liberal democracy . . . on the level of ideas," and predicts the inevitable eclipse of Islamic ideologies. Compare this with Samuel P. Huntington, "The Clash of Civilizations?" *Foreign Affairs* 72, no. 3 (Summer 1993); "The West and the World," *Foreign Affairs* 75 (November-December 1996), p. 28.

4. It is often important for the outside commentator, as it is for many Muslims, to maintain the distinction between *shari'a* or the perfect divine law, and *fiqh* or the human effort (jurisprudence) to discern the former. Only the latter can admit of errors, flaws or incompleteness. I often use the term "classical law" to refer to the *fiqh* as Muslim scholars knew it at approximately the beginning of the eighteenth century. This article (except where indicated) confines itself to Sunni *fiqh*.

5. See Yvonne Yazbeck Haddad, "Islamists and the Challenge of Pluralism," *Center for Contemporary Arab Studies Occasional Papers* (Washington, DC: Georgetown University, 1995).

6. Olivier Roy, in *The Failure of Political Islam*, chapter 4, sees this as a common trait of Islamist groups.

7. While this article appears to propose to certain Muslims ideas for their politics, it does so indirectly and with apologies, acknowledging its lack of standing. Its goal is a paradigm for comparisons between Western and Islamic systems, with liberal democracy as an important case. Most Muslim

liberalizers have chosen to support existing regimes over Islamist oppositions, even ones contesting elections. Those committed more to Western liberalism than Islamic governance may like this article's hypothetical alternative even less, since it involves the embrace of certain classical legal tenets.

8. These discussions depart considerably from the terminology and frameworks used by *fiqh* works themselves. This is necessary to build a basis for comparisons. For example, *ijtihad* is called "legislation" and "law-making."

9. Bukhari, Muslim, Abu Dawud, Tirmidhi, Nasa'i, Ibn Maja.

10. See, e.g., Ibn Taymiyyah, *Majmu'at fatawa Shaykh al-Islam Ahmad Ibn Taymiyya*, A. al-'Asimi, ed.(Riyadh: Matabi al-Riyadh, 1961-67), 35, pp. 379, 374.

11. Bukhari, Muslim, Abu Dawud, Tirmidhi.

12. For a complete explanation of the microcosmic/macrocosmic distinction and related conceptions, see Frank E. Vogel, "Islamic Law and Legal System: Studies of Saudi Arabia," Ph.D. dissertation, Harvard University, 1993.

13. While intended for more general application, the framework draws on fiqh public law doctrine and practice in the period after the thirteenth century C.E.

14. Marshall G.S. Hodgson, *The Venture of Islam,* vol. 2, *The Expansion of Islam in the Middle Periods* (Chicago: University of Chicago Press, 1974), 350. Some of the ideas of this section were inspired by Hodgson's account of the "Middle Period."

15. Similarly, Muslim minorities, and even non-Muslim minorities, might move toward more equal civil status as microcosmic understandings of their stance and its treatment gain emphasis. On issues of women's status, a similar situation obtains, though as to these the examples in the text are less illustrative. Suggestive here is the Quran's emphasis on the innate equality, indeed identity as "insan," of man and woman before God.

16. The dangers of the most invasive doctrines are shown by the recent upsurge in state intolerance brought about by their literal application. There have been executions for apostasy in Sudan and Saudi Arabia; suits for divorcing apostates in Jordan and Egypt; actions against authors disrespectful of Islam in Bangladesh, Egypt and Iran (Rushdie); and trials and mob killings of Christians in Pakistan for alleged insults to the Prophet.

17. See Lino J. Lauro and Peter A. Samuelson, "Toward Pluralism in Sudan: A Traditionalist Approach," *Harvard International Law Journal* 37, no. 1 (Winter 1996), pp. 65-138.

18. Shaul Bakhash, "The Politics of Land, Law and Social Justice in Iran," *Middle East Journal* 43, no. 2 (Spring 1989), pp. 186-201, 198; Eickelman and Piscatori, 50.

19. See Ellis Goldberg, "Smashing Idols and the State: the Protestant Ethic and Egyptian Sunni Radicalism," *Comparative Studies in Society and History* 33, no. 1 (January 1991), pp. 3-35, n. 1, citing comparisons with sixteenth-century Calvinism.

20. But one should not confuse this with the individualism of liberal Western societies. What is likely is not each individual's judging Islam for himself or herself, still considered unacceptable. *Ulama* remain the bearers and protectors of the revelation and its message, though new Islamic intellectuals generate most new ideas and, for Sunnis, provide the forceful religious leadership. Abbasi Madani, accounting himself not of the *ulama*, reserved for *ulama* left unnamed "the last word" on the law a FIS government would apply, while calling for consultative dialogue between the people and the ulama to correct the latter's errors ("Pour une nouvelle légalité islamique" [interview with Slimane Zéghidour], *Politique internationale* 49 (Autumn 1990), pp. 177-92). See also M. Al-Hanaf, B. Botiveau and F. Fregosi, *L'Algérie par ses islamistes* (Paris: Editions Karthala, 1991), chapter 2. Even Islamist movements violently opposing establishment *ulama* have turned to *ulama* for their *fatwas*, for example, Shaikh Umar Abd al- Rahman in Egypt.

21. See Tariq Al-Bishri, "La Question juridique entre *shari'a* islamique et droit positif," in *Les Intellectuels et le pouvoir: Syrie, Égypte, Tunisie, Algérie* (Cairo: Centre d'études et de documentation économique, juridique et sociale, [1985]). In series, *Dossiers du Cedej* 3 (1985), pp. 182, 191ff.

22. Useful in this regard is the expanding literature on contemporary Arab civil society.

23. The exception is probably the Sudan, where secularly educated, Islamically informally taught Dr. Hasan al-Turabi has reportedly been able to give free rein to his theories. See his *Tajdid usul al-fiqh al-islami* (Khartoum: Dar al-Fikr, 1980); *Islam, Democracy, the State and the West*, Arthur L. Lowrie, ed. (Tampa, FL: World & Islam Studies Enterprise, 1993).

24. Roy distinguishes such movements from Islamism because of their gradualism, calling them "lumpen Islamism" and "neo-fundamentalism" (chapter 5).

25. It is in this sense that Islamic initiatives affect "civic" as well as "civil" society. See for a useful discussion Nazih N. M. Ayubi, *Over-stating the Arab state:*

Politics and Society in the Middle East (New York: I.B. Tauris, 1994), pp. 438-45. Described here is a path distinct from movements emphasizing a piety-and-personal-improvement (Meccan) phase before a political (Medinan) phase. It is distinct also from a "neo-fundamentalism" as portrayed by Roy that, while focusing on social transformation, evades legal innovation and seeks shariʿa enactment by the state (Roy, chapter 5).

26. With the exception of the Organic Instructions of the Kingdom of Hejaz, 1926.

27. Emphasis added. My translation of a widely circulated, but otherwise unauthenticated, petition by Saudi *ulama* and others submitted to King Fahd in early 1991.

28. Said Amir Arjomand, *The Turban for the Crown: The Islamic Revolution in Iran* (New York: Oxford University Press, 1988); compare Abdulaziz A. Sachedina, *The Just Ruler in Shiʿite Islam* (Oxford: Oxford University Press, 1988).

29. Indeed, this is a key factor in comparing Iranian scholars with each other. See Ali Rahnema and Farhad Nomani, *The Secular Miracle: Religion, Politics and Economic Policy in Iran* (London: Zed Books, 1993).

30. See note 18 on page 293.

31. Roy, chapter 3.

32. Chibli Mallat, *The Renewal of Islamic Law: Muhammad Baqer as-Sadr, Najaf and the Shiʿi International* (Cambridge: Cambridge University Press, 1993), pp. 79-107; Asghar Schirazi, *Islamic Development Policy: The Agrarian Question in Iran,* trans. P. J. Ziess-Lawrence (Boulder: Lynne Rienner, 1993), pp. 201-32.

33. Mallat, pp. 105-6.

34. At times governments favor or resist Islamic banking for political reasons, treating it as a symbol of openness to Islamist causes. Examples are Malaysia and Saudi Arabia. Also, in several instances—the Sudan—Islamic banks have bankrolled Islamist movements.

35. For recent information on Iranian banking, see Said Saffari, "Islamic Banking in Theory and Practice: the Experience of Iran," unpublished case study by the Islamic Investment Project, Harvard University, October 20, 1995, especially pp. 24, 58 and 113.

36. The Fiqh Academy of the Organization of the Islamic Conference is one, and exemplifies an important new institutionalization of "group *ijtihad*" with

promise for the future. Its attention so far has been focused on historically novel, politically neutral, *fiqh* issues.

37. This process may well have already begun, and existing experiments in Islamic governance—successful and not—need study for the rich empirical evidence they will offer. Why in particular the ongoing innovations of traditionalist Islamic systems are so neglected is unclear, unless it is a false and facile assumption that, if such systems' claims to traditional form are valid, they are irrelevant to modernity, and if their claims to traditional Islam are false, they are hypocritical or deluded.

38. The recent unrest of the Shi'i majority of Bahrain offers an exception. Is this a unique situation, or a trend?

CHAPTER 11

THE ISLAMIC MOVEMENT: THE CASE FOR DEMOCRATIC INCLUSION

Roy P. Mottahedeh and Mamoun Fandy

For two decades a revival of identity among the world's approximately one billion Muslims has brought to the fore the extremely varied and changing faces of the encounter between Islam and politics. Most people in the United States (and the West in general) see this revival as a springboard for the emergence of an Islamintern: a coordinated conspiracy of single-minded fanatics who are addicted to violence and sworn to the hatred of America and the oppression of women; in short, a present-day analogue to what the Communist-hunting Senator Joseph McCarthy called "A conspiracy so immense and an infamy so black." And, within the Islamic world, many autocratic regimes hostile to the Islamic revival know that, no matter how distasteful their policies might be, this is the button to press in order to get American support; hence America's covert support during a long period of the Iran-Iraq War for Saddam Hussein's Iraq, which had taken on the archetypal Islamic regime, Iran.

Yet the very example of Iran—as an important test case for many Muslims as well as Americans—shows how the Islamic revival, when it enters the centrifuge of real politics, becomes, like every ideal exalted or otherwise, hostage to the world and its conflicting forces. Muslims in Iran, Egypt, Turkey, and elsewhere have understood the relation of religion and politics in significantly different terms based on various longstanding and strongly-held local political and civic traditions. As a result the Islamic revivalist movements of different countries have been strikingly different.

The example of Iran, where such a movement's leaders have long been in power, offers a very useful point of comparison with the Islamic revival movements in other parts of the Middle East, which have not achieved power. To the degree that they hope to reach or succeed in finding a place in the political process, such aspiring movements are often obliged to pursue national political traditions and interests; in Iran, with an Islamic revivalist regime in charge, national political traditions and interests often seem to have completely overtaken "Islamic" ideology. Iran is not only an example of what other Islamic revivalist movements might turn into, it is also—and more importantly—an example of the many conflicting pressures on such a regime when and if it does come to power. For, after many years of fairly open debate, continuing disagreement within and between the ruling and religious elites in Iran makes it increasingly uncertain whose vision of revived Islam will prevail. Many Iranians must be reminded of a certain Persian proverb: When there is more than one midwife, the baby's head is sure to come out the wrong way. Not only for Iran but for all these movements, the adjective "Islamic" by itself explains very little indeed.

ISLAM IN IRAN

There is no better place than a conclave of the Iranian clergy to understand the undoubtable influence but neglected limitations of that group. When such a conclave meets in Qom, the Iranian city of shrines and religious colleges, to choose the Shi'i spiritual leader, a sort of "Pope," these meetings are steeped in traditions that are far, far older than the Islamic revival. The meetings resemble congressional caucuses; their purpose being, according to tradition, to declare who is "most learned," yet to avoid choosing a political incompetent. For decades the leading religious scholars of Qom (who are member of what is now called "the Association of Teachers") have gathered in the handsome library of the most prestigious religious college in Iran. Built by a nineteenth century shah as a sitting room for his visits to Qom, through its origins this library represents the tradition of arms-length respect that the government and the religiously learned (in Iran called *mullas*) have maintained toward each other in most periods and most places throughout the history of Islamic societies. The king would visit the shrine city to pay his respects to religion; but the *mullas* had to come to the king's own building to pay their respects to the king.

To understand what happened at these meetings, and the dramatic shift they signalled in the relations between the religious establishment and the state in "the Islamic Republic," one must go back to a meeting some years ago. After Ayatollah Khomeini's death in 1989, when the Association of Teachers met to choose a new supreme leader of the Shi'i, there were no more shahs in Iran. Further, the post-revolutionary constitution of Iran had given recognition of spiritual leadership new importance. According to this constitution, "the governance and leadership of the nation" should preferably be given to a single individual from among those very few *mullas* who were *marjas,* or Grand Ayatollahs, having the qualifications of "political and social perspicacity, courage, strength and the necessary administrative abilities."[1]

A small number of *mullas*—probably never more than two hundred at one time— have the authority to give a recognized opinion on disputed points of Islamic law; these men are qualified "doctors of the law" and usually enjoy the title *ayatollah.* Their authority has been received from similarly qualified teachers whose own authority can, according to Shi'i belief, be traced back in a continuous chain to the founder of Islam, the Prophet Muhammad (somewhat as apostolic succession is traced back to Jesus). But only a few of these "doctors of the law," seldom as many as eight at one time, get any acceptance as *marjas;* and normally only one, the "most learned," is "the supreme *marja.*" These *marjas* author the most popular manuals about the basic practice expected of an ordinary Islamic believer (who bears no guilt before God for error in disputed matters as long as he or she follows one of the *marjas* as a "source for imitation").

During the last years of Khomeini's life, the majority of Iranian Shi'i believed that he embodied all of these qualifications: he was a *marja* and the charismatic leader of the revolution. Few government officials or *mullas* dared to oppose him openly from the time the constitution was ratified in December 1979, until he died on June 3, 1989. Insofar as one can speak in Iran of religion and state (for these are Western terms, not always useful in non-Western contexts), Khomeini was the embodiment of both.

With Khomeini's death the basic constitutional problem was laid bare for everyone to see. In its opening statement the constitution states its sixth general principle to be: "The affairs of the country must be governed by reliance on public opinion, as determined by elections." Elsewhere, the constitution seems to disregard the elective process and gives great direct power to the spiritual "Guide" of the nation, including the power to appoint the highest officials in the armed forces, the head of the judiciary, and so forth.[2]

Constitutions are like caterpillars; they feed frenziedly on events and the hurried decisions of influential people until they emerge as utterly metamorphosed creatures unpredictable from their earlier shapes. The great English historian Thomas Babington Macaulay, in prophesying the shipwreck of the American Constitution, said it was "all sails and no anchor"; now it is the oldest written constitution still in use in the world. In the Iranian case, the framers of the constitution had a clear mandate to create a truly "Islamic government"; what is surprising is not that they created a constitution with ambiguities, but—given the immense uncertainty and disagreement as to what "Islamic government" might mean—that they came up with anything at all.

Islamic government is for many Muslims what the late-twentieth-century phrase "civil society" is for many liberals: a repository of collective hope and an aspiration that the fundamentally good values at the roots of their traditions will be reformed and strengthened. But the actual, agreed-upon content of Islamic government remains very limited and, more often than not, severely disputed. According to most Sunni Muslims, who constitute approximately 85 percent of the world's Muslims, true Islamic government existed only from 622 to 661, that is, in the latter part of the life of the Prophet Muhammad and under his four immediate successors. According to most Shi'i Muslims, who constitute about 15 percent of the Islamic community, such government existed only in the latter part of the life of the Prophet, from 622-632, and under the rule of Ali, his cousin and son-in-law, from 656 to 661. In both cases the life of the Prophet is the overwhelming source from which examples of Islamic government are derived.

Yet the Prophet's full "legislative" authority could not be inherited by anyone. Who, for example, should say how the many (and necessarily quite different) arrangements made by the Prophet for the collection of taxes (to be paid in some cases in textiles, in others in coin; in some cases per head, in others according to agricultural yield) should be generalized into a uniform and truly "Islamic" system of taxation? In this instance a general consensus was worked out, the details of which, however, remain disputed among Muslims up to the present. Khomeini, in his manifesto calling for Islamic government, claims that the medieval Islamic consensus view of taxation satisfies all the needs of modern government. Iran has yet to adopt tax laws, such as the pre-modern Islamic flat twenty percent tax on agricultural production, that reflect Khomeini's prescription. Such taxes would seem to most Iranians profoundly irrelevant to their situation.

In fact, it is far from clear that Islamic government requires a constitution; and some ayatollahs openly say as much. Saudi Arabia, which considers itself a truly Islamic government, has no constitution in the Western sense. (Although some consider the Saudi Basic Law a start toward a constitution.) Then why did Iran adopt a constitution? Because no government, Islamic or otherwise, without a constitution would be legitimate in the eyes of Iranians, who in 1906 had the first successful constitutional revolution in Asia. Iranians, in their own way, obsess about constitutions nearly as much as Americans. Islamic government in Iran, as elsewhere, had to be articulated in the political language known by its practitioners. In Iran this language is dramatically different from, for example, that of Saudi Arabia, with its traditions of monarchy and tribal consensus, or of Libya, with its anti-clerical and egalitarian traditions.

When, however, the "doctors of the law" met in Qom in December 1993 and December 1994 to choose the spiritual leader for Iran's Shi'i, they did not go to their customary meeting place of the former shah's sitting room turned library; they met in the house of one of the members. In 1979 the religious establishment had taken over the government; fourteen years later the religious establishment was energetically trying to avoid being controlled by elements of the very government that supposedly embodied its interests.

Why had events since 1979 defeated so many of the Iranians' early expectations about the nature of Islamic government? Before his death Khomeini had foreseen that no one could dominate the government as he had; shortly after his death a revision of the constitution, which said that the spiritual "Guide" of the nation need only be a "doctor of the law" and not necessarily a *marja*, was ratified. This revision allowed a fast round of musical chairs. Ali-Akbar Hashemi-Rafsanjani, an engaging and politically astute *mulla* of moderate learning, became the President, an office that now was given real power. Khamenei, holder of the formerly ceremonial presidency, received Khomeini's position as spiritual "Guide," although everyone knew that he would have to struggle to reclaim even a portion of those powers exercised by Khomeini.

If, for Iranians, Islamic government had its origins in the spiritual leadership of an overwhelmingly popular *marja*, then, with the appointment of Khamenei, not only individuals but also ideas had played musical chairs. Until Khomeini's death, Khamenei, a well-spoken and presentably grey- and white-bearded gentleman in his forties, had never been considered one of the "doctors of the law" (ayatollahs) qualified to give an independent opinion. Khomeini's son (not an ayatollah) and a certain ayatollah fortuitously present reported that Khomeini, on his death bed, had recognized Khamenei as an ayatollah. Khamenei, who had been a cooperative player with Rafsanjani, was quickly approved for the office of "Guide" by the relevant bodies, including the influential Association of Teachers. The brute fact was that politics, and the political needs of elected leaders like Rafsanjani, had made it impossible to keep the most learned religious leaders—who were almost invariably too independent in their political views—in the government.

It can be said of Khamenei, as it was said of Truman, that he was put forward by men who, speculating beyond the death of their leader, knew what they wanted but had absolutely no idea what they would get. Chosen as a reliable member of the circle of Rafsanjani, Khamenei felt inspired by his new office to be a genuine holy man. He undertook fasts and prayer vigils; he sometimes returned from these spiritual exercises inspired with opinions that were, in the view of President Rafsanjani's circle, positive embarrassments. He thundered against Salman Rushdie, the question of whom the Rafsanjani group hoped would recede into the background. He worried about lax standards for modesty in dress, and he urged greater government involvement in the economy at a time the government was trying quietly to restore a free market. To his critics, Khamenei seemed in eager pursuit of the larger role of "Guide" as it had been understood in the lifetime of Khomeini. To his supporters, he seemed to strike the populist note that was otherwise absent in the government after Khomeini's death.

On Thursday, December 9, 1993, Ayatollah Golpayegani, who the majority of Iranians recognized as their "Pope," died at the estimated age of ninety-six. When the Association of Teachers in Qom convened to choose his successor, Khamenei wanted to represent himself as the heir of Golpayegani. Not only the family of Golpayegani (who denied Khamenei an important role in the funeral) but also the leading members of the clergy were determined to prevent him from seizing that chance. In the clergy's view it was putting one aspect of religious tradition out of the reach of the nation's "official" religious "Guide."

In the end the Association of Teachers, by the vote of a slim majority, decided that "the office of *marja* is exclusively established in the Grand Ayatollah Hajj Shaikh Mohammad Ali Araki."[3] This terse statement was not unexpected. Araki, once fairly learned, once a moral example to the young clergymen of Qom, had by now largely turned himself over to the state of contemplation his ninety-nine years had earned him. He seemed to illustrate the wisdom of the Arabic proverb that says "Better a mute sage than a fool who speaks." One of the very few clergymen opposed to photographs of people, he was now too old and too diffusely focused to notice that he was being photographed. And, the choice of Araki coincided with the wishes of the circle around Rafsanjani.

A year later with Araki's death on November 24, 1994, the senior Shi'i clergy stepped back to a yet earlier period in their history. Araki had conveniently been unconscious for about two weeks before his death, during which time this century's most bizarre and bellicose ayatollah, Ahmad Jannati, declared that political shrewdness was the most important quality for the *marja*, an obvious reference to Khamenei and a complete reversal of 150 years of Shi'i tradition. Shortly after, a fairly prestigious nongovernmental group, the Association of Militant Clergymen of Tehran issued a list of six ayatollahs appropriate to be *marjas,* which did not include Khamenei's name. Finally, when Araki died, the Association of Teachers met and, on December 2, issued a list of the seven *marjas* acceptable for people to imitate, adding the name of Khamenei to the six proposed by the Militant Clergymen, but without indicating that any one of the seven was superior to any other. The text accompanying the list was almost as significant as the list itself: it said that freedom of choice of religious leaders had always been a positive aspect of Shi'i belief and that, in past times, lists of several names had been put forward—an obvious reference to what had happened after the death of Ayatollah Borujerdi in 1961. Plurality of leadership in 1961 had been regarded as abnormal; now it was being promoted as a positive step. Elements in the government including Ayatollah Yazdi declared a victory for Khamenei; but in fact it still seems overwhelmingly likely that Khamenei will *not* be the *marja* accepted in religious matters by most Iranians, and attempts to pretend that he will be will widen the gap between the upper clergy and the government. Khamenei had been included in the list so that there would not be an open confrontation with the government; but to avoid the government's embrace, the clergy had dissolved (at least temporarily) the "Papacy." The Shi'i clergy may as a result have become weaker, but as a group they were, and still are, certainly harder to grasp and manipulate.[4]

In 1979, in the person of Khomeini, the clergy gained control of the government. In the 1989 revision of the constitution, the government installed Khamenei, a cleric of only modest religious learning, but presumed to be cooperative with the clergy as the Islamic "Guide" of the nation. In December 1993 and again in December 1994, in the face of Khamenei's activism, the higher clergy attempted to hold the government at arm's length, first by selecting an aged candidate who would reign but not rule and then by selecting so many candidates that none could rule.

Now a nation of 60 million (the overwhelming majority of whom are Shi'i Muslims), Iran, eighteen years after its revolution, has the longest running experiment in non-monarchical Islamic government. But the example of Iran shows how unpredictable and influenced by cultural setting Islamic government can be, particularly when some element of popular sovereignty remains. Iranian culture, with over a 2,000-year history, is a wily and powerful creature. The Islamic tradition, with fifteen centuries of extremely varied history, has all the rich diversity that such length and breadth would imply. It should come as no surprise that the Iranian tradition and the Islamic tradition can find in each other's baggage clothes that comfortably suit.

ISLAM IN THE ARAB GULF STATES

Turkey and Egypt are the other two giants in the Middle East, each with a population of over 60 million. In both countries, *Islamists*—advocates of government by Islamic law—have shown the same openness of agendas and the same adaptability to the political cultures of their countries. These countries' experiences add to an understanding of the importance for Islamists of local contexts. For instance, in Egypt, the courts and syndicates (professional organizations) have been the locus of struggles between the Islamists and the government. In the more open system of Turkey, where the locus is quite naturally the parliament, the Islamist party has more often than not had to compromise both before the electorate and in the legislature in order to seek a role and, subsequently, maintain their participation in government.

Countries of the oil-rich Gulf region other than Iran are also battlegrounds between the Islamists and local governments. The relationship between these Islamic movements and their governments differs depending on the local government's willingness to include the Islamists in the political process. This relationship also depends on the discourse of each Islamic movement and its willingness to deal with the question of pluralism as a basis for political life. Some countries in the Arabian peninsula, such as Kuwait and Yemen, have opted for what Michael Hudson calls "limited accommodation"; others, such as Bahrain, so far have excluded Islamists completely from the political process. Saudi Arabia, Oman, Qatar, and the UAE stand somewhere in the middle.

Kuwait has been one of the most successful Gulf countries in accommodating and containing the Islamists. In the Kuwait parliament of 1981, the Islamists won 4 seats. Their leaders campaigned to change the second article in the Kuwaiti constitution to make Islamic Shari'a the main source of legislation in Kuwait. In the 1985 elections, the Islamists won 5 seats; 2 members of the previous parliament remained. This parliament lasted for only one year before the amir dissolved it, ending parliamentary life in Kuwait for the next six years.

In contrast, the elections of post-war Kuwait show an upsurge in the Islamists' representation in parliament. In the 1992 election, the Islamists won 16 seats (30 percent). Following this election, the Islamists joined the government and were appointed to 3 cabinet positions. The Islamists debated a range of issues and were accepted as legitimate players in Kuwaiti politics. In the 1996 elections they won 16 seats for the second time. This suggests that 16 seats is probably the maximum number that the Islamists can win.

Furthermore, the Kuwaiti Islamists are not a monolithic group. These 16 seats can be broken down into the following categories: 8 seats for the Islamic Constitutional Movement, 6 seats for the Salafis, and 2 seats for the National Islamic Alliance (a Shi'i group). It is also interesting to note that the distribution of seats among the various factions of the Islamic movement is to some degree similar to the distribution of seats among Kuwaiti tribes. For instance, the Awazem tribe won 7 seats; the Mutairi tribe won 6 seats; the Rashayda and the Ajman tribes won 3 seats each. It is this balance between the tribes and Islamic organizations that provides stability to the Kuwaiti polity.

In Yemen, the Islamists have been part of the most recent two parliaments. Parliamentary life and democratization started to take hold in Yemen after the union of North and South Yemen in 1990. In the 1990-93 parliament, the Islamists had about 47 members. This number increased dramatically in 1993 with the election of the new parliament. The dominant Islamic party, al-Islah, won 62 seats; in addition there were some 20 other members who sympathized with the Islamic agenda. The Islamic leadership seems committed to work within the democratic framework. The deputy leader of al-Islah, 'Abdul Wahhabe al-Anisi, said "We do not see any formula that serves the Islamic interest best except the democratic formula." Here, it is important to realize that Islamism alone could not effect a major change in Yemeni politics without its falling back on tribal connections. The strong showing of Abdulla Al-Ahmar and his Islah Islamic party could not have been achieved if it were not for Shaikh Ahmar's position as chief of the Hashid tribal federation.

In contrast, violence erupted in Bahrain in 1994 and continues until the present. The Islamic movement in Bahrain has expressed itself in different forms, including such militant actions as street riots and the occasional bombing of hotels. But the Islamists have also expressed their views in non-violent political forms. This included thousands of people attending the anti-government rallies of Shi'i clerics, especially the charismatic shaikhs Salman and al-Jamri. The power of these clerics became obvious when Sheikh Salman convinced twenty thousand Sunni and Shi'i activists to sign a petition urging the amir to reinstate parliamentary and constitutional rule in Bahrain.

Bahrain has a population of some 600,000. The majority of this population, over 70 percent, are Shi'i Muslims; the ruling class, however, is a minority Sunni group headed by the royal family of Al-Khalifa. However, it is misleading to portray the conflict in Bahrain as the result of tension between a dominant Sunni minority and a dominated Shi'i majority. Characterizing the power struggle in Bahrain in sectarian terms (Sunni versus Shi'i) is counterproductive. There are a host of political, economic, and constitutional issues driving this very powerful resistance to the ruling family. The opposition in Bahrain consists of four major groups. Two of them are Shi'i (the Bahrain Islamic Freedom Movement and The Islamic Front for the Liberation of Bahrain), and two are liberal groups with mixed Shi'i and Sunni membership. Three of these groups call for peaceful change of the status quo by petitioning the Emir of Bahrain to reactivate the constitution that was suspended in 1975. Since then Bahrain has been ruled by decree. This constitutional crisis of Bahrain started in 1974 when the emir wanted to enact laws to deal with workers' riots. When the parliament refused to go along with his desires, the amir dissolved the parliament. Neighboring states in the gulf, particularly Saudi Arabia, supported the amir's decision, since Saudi Arabia views any democratic institutions in the region as a threat to its own stability.

In addition to demanding a return to parliamentary representation in Bahrain, the opposition calls on the amir to improve the conditions of the Shi'i areas and to remove the foreign security forces from the country. Currently, Shi'i areas are the worst off in terms of economic development, and the unemployment rate among the Shi'i in general exceeds 20 percent. Human rights organizations, including Amnesty International, accuse the security forces of using torture to gain confessions from their political prisoners. Still, the Bahraini government recently asked the assistance of Saudi riot police to quell demonstrators.

Not only are Islamists and liberals trying to convince the amir to revive the parliament, some 300 Bahraini women recently petitioned the amir to release political prisoners, allow freedom of speech, improve economic conditions in the rural areas and in Shi'i communities, and restore parliamentary and constitutional life in the country. So far the amir hasn't listened to either domestic or international voices, including those of some U.S. congressmen and members of the British Parliament. Many in the region also appealed to the amir to take reasonable measures toward reconciliation with the opposition. These voices included a number of Kuwaiti parliamentarians and many human rights and non-governmental organizations. Thus, Bahrain not only excludes the Islamists, but almost all civic organizations. The politics of exclusion in Bahrain has led to destruction of public buildings and the loss of human lives.

Saudi Arabia is unique in its treatment of Islamists in terms of inclusion and exclusion. Saudis argue that the Islamists are already included in the political system; because Saudi Arabia is an Islamic state. There is some truth to this argument since the *ulama* have a say, at least formally, in approving certain policies or issuing fatwas to justify certain government actions. However, in spite of this, there are many opposition groups in Saudi Arabia who use Islam as a vehicle to express their dissatisfaction with the Al-Saud family and the way it runs the Kingdom.

In Saudi Arabia, political Islam takes different forms. Different groups represent various degrees of threat to the regime. In response, the Saudi government has dealt with them differently, in terms of inclusion and exclusion. There are five Saudi opposition groups: (1) religious preachers, like Safar al-Hawali and Salman al-Auda, who emerged during the Gulf crisis; (2) the Committee for the Defence of Legitimate Rights (CDLR); (3) the Movement for Islamic Reform (MIRA); (4) the Committee for Advice and Reform (CAR) led by Usama bin Laden; and (5) the Shi'i Reform Movement. The regime sees the CAR, under the leadership of Usama bin Ladin, as the most dangerous group; Mr. Bin Laden has made it clear that he supports those who carry out violent acts against the Saudi government. The government has also arrested Shaikh al-Auda and Shaikh al-Hawali and many of their followers.

With regard to the CDLR, the Saudi government has asked Britain to deport its leader, Mohammed Mas'ari from London and to dismantle his anti-Saudi media operation there. The king issued decrees to establish a Shura Council and a Basic Law as a response to Islamist petitions for reform. Thus, in a way, the regime is responsive to Islamists' criticism.

The only Shi'i organization that has challenged the Saudi regime is the Reform Movement led by Shaikh Hassan al-Saffar. After a long struggle against the government, the Shi'i managed to gain some concessions. In return for ceasing their activities they were allowed to return to the Kingdom. Since its inception in 1975, the Shi'i movement in Saudi Arabia has shown a great ability to cope with local, regional, and international changes.[5] Its first phase (1975-1980) was militant, showing little understanding of the regional or international implications of its activities. Ideologically, the main aim of the movement was to purify Islam from "Sufi practices and the selective usage of Islam to bolster a certain regime's legitimacy." In that stage, radical discourse dominated the movement's publications. The monthly, *al-Thawrah al-Islamiyya,* was the main voice of the movement. By 1979, political events, namely the installation of an Islamic government in Iran, the uprising of the Eastern Province, and the siege of the Grand Mosque, helped to further radicalize the movement. The leaders of the movement followed the Iranian line. Until 1985, the discourse was uncompromising. In an interview, one of the leaders stated that their position toward the royal family was one of "No negotiation with a regime that violates Islamic teachings." al-Saffar said,"We cannot negotiate with a regime that has no regard for the rule of law."

A notable shift occurred in Shi'i discourse in 1988, signalling an end to revolutionary rhetoric in favor of a broader agenda of democratization and human rights. Shi'i criticism began to focus on the human rights abuses of the Saudi regime and on the absence of a constitution or any national assembly. It called for broader participation by Saudis in running the affairs of their government, for limiting the absolute power of the king, and for curtailing police power to detain and arrest those who verbally criticized the regime.

In 1990, Shaikh al-Saffar published, *al-Ta'adudiya wal Hurriya fi al-Islam,* which seems to have greatly influenced both the Reform Movement's political dialogue and political agenda, raising the movement to a new and more sophisticated plane by addressing the Islamic basis of freedom and pluralism. This book paved the road for a transitional period that took the movement away from the rhetoric of revolution and the influence of Khomeinism to a more moderate discourse anchored in the theology of Abdolkarim Soroush. Since its appearance in 1990, Muslims in various

Arab countries have written a number of books on the subject of Islam and democracy.

This shift in the movement's orientation led to the emergence of the magazine *al-Jazeera al-Arabia* (1990-94). Unlike *al-Thawrah al-Islamiyya, al-Jazeera al-Arabia* appeared to be a very solid publication focused on reporting events in the kingdom and providing serious analysis. Its purpose was not to incite a revolution against the royal family; instead, it focused on human rights, tolerance, public administration, and government corruption. The magazine's credibility made many take the movement seriously, including the Saudi government.

In June 1992, Shaikh al-Saffar signaled a willingness to negotiate with the government, saying,"We do not refuse any initiative for a dialogue between us and the government as long as we are talking about issues." Two years after this interview, the government provided an initiative acceptable to the Shi'i opposition, and on October 24, 1994, many of the Shi'i opposition leaders returned to Saudi Arabia. They met with the king, Prince Sultan, Prince Salman, and Prince Muhammad bin Fahd, the governor of the Eastern Province. Government openness toward the Shi'i came at a time of momentous political changes. Locally, the royal family had come under strong criticism from Sunni religious groups concerning the use of Western soldiers in the holy land. Presumably, they hoped an accommodation with the Shi'i would free them to focus on the potentially more threatening Sunni opposition. Moreover, the Gulf War and the uprising of the Iraqi Shi'i against Saddam Hussein changed local perceptions of the Shi'i to some degree. Thus, the change in the Saudi government's attitude toward its Shi'i opposition was not merely a function of a change of al-Saffar's discourse alone, but the result of pressure on the Saudi government both internally and externally. Nevertheless, the conciliatory discourse of Al-Saffar contributed a great deal to this outcome.

In the Saudi case, both the concessions that the government made to the Shi'i and the enactment of the Shura Council and the Basic Laws came as responses to popular demands. They suggest that the government accepts a notion of limited accommodation of demands, though not of power sharing. The groups themselves, especially the Shi'i, show that they are political rather than religious organizations. The change over time in both their language and their responses to issues as well as shifts in their views vis-à-vis the government reveal a great deal about their political pragmatism. The pattern of moving from a radical point of view to a watered-down version of the same discourse to accommodate the government and improve negotiation positions parallels what is taking place in Iran, Egypt, Turkey, Jordan, and Kuwait.

The Kuwaiti, Yemeni, and Jordanian cases suggest that there is a ceiling for the number of seats that the Islamists can win. In Jordan, in fact, the Islamists lost some seats during the last election. If such a formula exists in three Arab countries, then it is possible that some degree of accommodation can take place in other countries threatened by the Islamists. However, it appears that countries with strong civil-society organizations are more capable of accommodating Islamists than those with weak civil societies. The unit of civil society in the Arab world that has proved most capable of resisting the state is the tribe. This is perhaps why tribal societies such as Yemen, Jordan, and Kuwait can afford to accommodate the Islamists without risking the stability of the political system. In the views of some secularists, in relatively non-tribal societies, such as Egypt and Algeria, the only force that can constrain the power of the Islamists is that of the military. In these cases we find either a bloody conflict, as in Algeria, or total exclusion of Islamists, as in Egypt.

THE DIVERSITY OF ISLAMIST MOVEMENTS

The largely mistaken idea that the Islamists are a coordinated movement lies behind much of the West's fear of them; that somewhere a black turbaned ayatollah meets with the elegantly-suited Prime Minister of Turkey, Necmettin Erbakan, and an Egyptian lawyer in his lumpy Cairo-made suit to synchronize watches for the next terrorist act their Western-hating minds have spawned. And how deeply satisfying this specter is to Western imaginations, for some curious reason more so than imagining a conspiracy of the remaining Communist leaders, some of whom have the worst human rights records in the world. Alas for the writers of colorful copy, the non-radical Islamists, in spite of occasional gestures of friendship to each other, are really no more a coordinated movement than are the animal protection movements and conservation societies of the world. Their attitudes toward inter-Muslim conflicts tell the story of their primary connection to local circumstances and their primary concern in protecting their local organizations. Attitudes toward Iran range from admiration to contempt; actual knowledge of Iran's post-revolutionary history is virtually non-existent.

The Islamists' range of attitudes toward Iran is well demonstrated by the way the Muslim Brothers have reacted to that country at various times. At the time of the Iranian Revolution in 1979 the Brothers were overwhelmingly enthusiastic about Khomeini's success. But in 1982 the Syrian regime, then a close ally of Iran, mercilessly suppressed the Muslim Brothers, in Syria, claiming that they intended armed rebellion. The Syrian Muslim Brothers felt the Iranian government had, by its official silence in the face of this suppression, let them down completely. By contrast, the Muslim Brothers of Sudan are ready to work with Iran because they admire Iran's independent and avowedly Islamic stance. The Egyptian Muslim Brothers fall somewhere in between. (Even though they are the oldest branch of the organization, they have only "fraternal" relations with branches in other nations.)

Most curious is the position of the Muslim Brothers of Jordan. Long protected and, since 1984, partly enfranchised by King Hussein, they have distanced themselves from their early support of Iran because they want to be seen as a loyal opposition to the King's government. (The King's government has fairly consistently maintained a distance from Iran.) Their relation is such that, when King Hussein agreed to meet Israeli Prime Minister Yitzhak Rabin on the White House lawn, the Muslim Brothers made a totally non-confrontational move by declaring a "Day of Mourning." King Hussein—whose political gifts never cease to amaze—had for months prepared the Jourdanians for his entry into the peace process by telling them that the country had to move in unison, or it would again fly apart. (Jordanians remain traumatized by the tensions between their citizens of Palestinian origin and those of a more ancient Jordanian origin, which erupted in a short but bloody civil war in 1970.) On the "Day of Mourning," out of loyalty to the king, few Islamists or Jordanians of any stripe chose to mourn in public, however much they may have mourned in private.

At the end of July 1994, the Jordanian Muslim Brothers chose a new man, predictably enough a lawyer, to replace their extremely aged leader. By his public pledge to continue opposition to the agreement only by legal and constitutional means, this new leader has assured Jordanians that the chosen arena for most Islamists in that country is the unusual building—a kind of marriage between a basketball arena and an oriental palace—in Amman in which the Parliament sits. Recently a member of Hamas who directed an Islamic foundation was asked which model he favored for Hamas's future political struggle: that of Algeria, Iran, or the Sudan. Without hesitation, he replied "Jordan"—by which he meant that Hamas, anxious that it might be excluded by the PLO, sought democratic inclusion in Palestinian politics. His may be a minority view in Hamas; but with the experience of democratic inclusion, it may well become the majority view.

The Gulf War of 1990-91 offered yet further scenes of Islamists reflagging themselves according to changing sentiment and local political interest. The Turkish Welfare Party was at first pro-Saddam, but after a September meeting with King Fahd, it assumed a position that hovered between neutrality and mild criticism of Saddam. The Muslim Brothers in Egypt were in some disarray; while most were contemptuous of Saddam's new claim to be a pan-Islamic leader, they were alarmed to see Western armies sorting out the problems between Islamic countries. The old guard among them knew that, in the past, financial support from sympathizers in the Gulf had been extremely important, and, thus, they did not want to support Saddam openly. The rank-and-file were outraged that the Americans were swaggering about yet another area—much of it sacred—of the Middle East and wanted Saddam to survive (which, to everyone's surprise, he did). Ultimately, the Muslim Brothers were less vocal about Egypt's involvement with the coalition against Iraq than had been expected, and the secular left, which was vocal, enjoyed a new popularity on Egyptian campuses.

The Iranians, as the Persian idiom has it, felt their hearts "chill" with relief to see Iraq, their opponent in an eight-year war, and the West—whom they knew, well before the Western public, had materially supported Iraq—go to war with each other. But it was the Iranian government's behavior in the aftermath of the Gulf War that spoke volumes on the limitations of Islamic internationalism: the Iranians may have allowed armed Iraqi refugees who were in Iran to cross back into Iraq when there was a massive uprising of their fellow Shi'i in southern Iraq, but the government understood the risks and kept well clear of significant direct involvement. Some Iraqi Shi'i still feel betrayed.

Why do large scale movements of Islamists lack (and sometimes even fail to seek) international Islamic coordination? Although the winds of religious revival blow strong among the one billion Muslims of the world, the majority of Muslims do not regard Islamic government as a priority. For the politically committed, there are other options besides the Islamist movements: liberal Islam is still very much alive, and anyone who has experienced an Egyptian Ramadan and seen the devotion with which secularist members of the liberal Wafdist party or leftists of the Nasserist party fast cannot doubt the sincerity of their faith. Yet an enormous number, probably the majority, of Muslims remain politically uncommitted. The pietists, those who emphasize inner religious development, are well represented by the largest Islamic movement in the world, the Tablighi Jamaat, which originated in South Asia and even has a following among the few million Muslims in North America. At yearly meetings, whether they are in Britain, Canada, or South Asia, the assembly of its adherents is second in size only to that of Muslims on the Pilgrimage. Yet the Tablighi Jamaat maintains that it is far more important to get Muslims to pray five times a day than, say, to oppose Hindus in the aftermath of their destruction of the Babri mosque at Ayodhya.

The Islamists know that, if they wish to capture the hearts and minds of the Muslim majority, they must offer that majority some of the practical things it wants and expects. And the deeper the Islamists become involved in mass politics, and in particular, in democratic politics, the more they articulate the desires and expectations of their fellow countrymen. The Hezbollah, the Shi'i organization in Lebanon, has the largest block in the Lebanese parliament; in its demand to have freedom to broadcast its own radio and television shows, it has become an ally both of the Leftists and the Christian right. (The religious leaders of the Lebanese Shi'i are now somewhat alienated from the leading Iranian clergyman because they were not invited to the election of Araki.) Erbakan tells his Turkish followers that his party, which has a fair amount of small merchant support, is the party of free enterprise and the private sector. The Muslim Brothers in Egypt are also free marketeers, although they continually point to their quite considerable social welfare projects as proof that Islam has strengthened their sense of social conscience. In Iran, where virtually all public discourse is Islamic, national politics have become stalled between the elected officials of a parliament that favors a free market and the statist programs of the economic radicals, who find support in social groups, such as militias, that owe their existence to the revolution. In any case, the economic radicalism that was an assumed part of the platform of Islamist groups eighteen years ago now seems to be the platform of fringe groups that consider the Muslim Brothers and their kind to be bourgeois sell-outs.

Mass movements also have to deal with long-term expectations about what is right and proper: like Iran, Turkey and the Arab states of the Gulf have ancient and artful cultures. In the eighteenth century the majority of Muslims around the world belonged to mystical brotherhoods, the Sufi orders, whose vivid ceremonials were designed to create mindfulness of God in the believers and were widely popular among the literate and illiterate alike. In no place were these orders more powerful than in Turkey, where the Ottoman sultan was proud to belong to a Sufi brotherhood. Small wonder that the original core of Erbakan's party was a group of adherents to Sufi brotherhoods. The Iranian Shi'i clergy has always frowned on Sufis, although they have been unable to suppress them. In Turkey a mass movement of Islamists cannot do without the Sufis; in Iran, Sufi support might be a liability. In Egypt, the power of the Sufis has decreased since the nineteenth-century, in part because nineteenth century Egyptian Muslim leaders saw Sufis as forces of backwardness. The Egyptian Muslim Brothers disapprove of Sufis, but at some political cost.

Yet it would be a mistake to think that the cultural world of Islamic countries is somehow rigid and that the West is—to use that indirect self-compliment used by Westerners in the past—faced with "the unchanging East." This ignorant fantasy has resurfaced in recent discussions of Islam's supposed incompatibility with democracy. The Prophet Samuel's anointing of Saul as king has not prevented Jews from becoming ardent democrats any more than the declaration of Jesus that his kingdom was not of this world has prevented Christians from supporting kings. The Quran is no more specific than the Bible—and, like it, is more explicit about the ethics than about the form of government.

The enfranchisement of women offers a compelling proof of the ability of Islamic political cultures to evolve. In general, women were granted the vote later in the Islamic Middle East than in the West, in part because of the resistance of religious conservatives. But the Islamist movements of Egypt, Turkey, and Iran now regard women as an absolutely fundamental element in their support and would never dream of disenfranchising women. (In Turkey, women are more effective as house to house canvassers for the Islamists than are men, to whom doors open only when adult male members of the family are at home.) The enfranchisement of women, however, has no built-in bias that favors Islamists; it is just an irreversible fact of politics. It is no accident that the three women who have recently been heads of state (none of them Islamists) in the Islamic world were elected in parliamentary democracies. Benazir Bhutto of Pakistan, Khaleda Zia of Bangladesh, and Tansu Ciller of Turkey led states with a combined population of more than two hundred-eighty million, far larger than the Arab world (which in the West is so often mistakenly assumed to be synonymous with the Islamic world). Advocates of Islamic government inside Pakistan also have had very limited success in national elections and only flourished under the patronage of dictatorship; and Hassan Turabi, the Islamist ideologue of the present regime in the Sudan, was never able to win a seat in parliament in the days when that country had real elections.

One aspect of the Islamic revival seems to have escaped most observers: it has introduced millions to organized politics. Formerly, relations between central governments and local communities took place through elites: landlords, great merchants, clergy and the like. Most of these elites have been swept away by reform and the redistribution of wealth or pushed to the side by modern communications that allow ordinary people to see and hear the state directly and to experience its interference in local affairs. Wherever religion has been the most basic element of self-identification, local organization has tended to take on a religious identity, whether in Christian Latin America or in the Islamic Middle East. Before the Islamic revival political parties in the Islamic Middle East were more often than not merely the followings of charismatic men. The new Islamist organizations have, in some cases, created genuine political parties, many of which will survive their leaders. They are, in this respect, in the vanguard of what the West calls "modernization."

THE CASE FOR DEMOCRATIC INCLUSION

Does this all mean that it would be in the world's interest and in particular in the interest of the world's Muslims, to favor inclusion of the Islamists in the political process? Two strong arguments have been raised against such inclusion. One says that the Islamists believe in democracy until their victory: that they believe in one man, one vote, one time only. Certainly, some of them probably do believe in this formula. This fear caused the Algerian government to halt the democratic process in Algeria in January 1992. But the results seem to indicate that one cost of stopping the Islamists at the ballot box may be to face them again as a mass movement, one that is wholly militant, without any stake in democracy, and without perceptible head or tail. It is no longer clear with whom Algerian authorities should talk if they wish to reach a compromise. In Egypt some secularist intellectuals argue for the inclusion of the Islamists because the Islamists have gained power through democratic means (and even relinquished power, in the Pharmacists' Syndicate, when voted out). They point to Jordan where the Muslim Brothers, after doing very well in the election of 1989, held positions such as Speaker of the House in Parliament. When a change in election laws and in public sentiment (the Islamist Ministers of Agriculture and Education were judged to have handled their portfolios poorly and to be righteous sloganeers who could not deliver) gave the Islamists fewer seats in the 1993 elections, the loyalty of the Muslim Brothers to the king, who supported their inclusion in politics, seemed, if anything, stronger.

Informed estimates give Egyptian Islamists about 30 percent of the electorate in free elections. Those who distrust the Islamists say they cannot allow Egypt to play Russian roulette: informed estimates may not be well enough informed. Cynics have suggested that even if the estimates are incorrect, one man, one vote, for one time may be better than one man, one vote at no time.

The second strong objection to the inclusion of the Islamists is that they refuse to compromise on several human rights issues because they believe these to be matters of Islamic law; the one common element in these movements is their demand that Islamic law be reintroduced. On this point both sides feel misunderstood and both sides are, in fact, genuinely misunderstood.

Americans, for example, are deeply shocked and horrified at the mistreatment of any person on the basis of religion; Iranian authorities seem to be deaf and blind to the reasons for this shock and horror. Consequently, some people in authority in Iran can only understand the several votes of the U.S. Congress condemning their persecution of the Iranian Baha'is as a cynical anti-Iranian plot without real support among Americans or any real basis in American political traditions. Iranians think that Americans see them only through the lens of the hostage crisis and their human rights record (some aspects of which are indeed deplorable) and refuse to recognize that there is some degree of popular sovereignty in Iran. Thoughtful Iranians admit that in Iran the subjects of debate are, in fact, restricted, but maintain that very real debate goes on. Likewise, candidacy for parliament is, unquestionably, highly restricted but elections are nevertheless largely honest and, consequently, vigorously contested.

The failure of some democratically-minded Islamists to understand that individual rights are a necessary complement to popular sovereignty may prove a fatal weakness in their programs. In terms of religion and/or ethnicity, most Islamic nations of the Middle East have enormous "minorities." To the degree that Islamist movements do not conceive of citizenship as full and equal for all, whether the citizens be Muslim, Christian, Baha'i, or atheist, or Palestinian, Berber, Armenian, Turkic, or Kurdish, such movements will not create successfully integrated societies and will eventually fail. There is some sign that in Iran, through the practical schooling of politics, an increasing number of religious Iranians—even an increasing number of Iranian clergy—are coming to realize this. Whether or not they will be able to articulate this realization in the form of a political movement is another matter.

The Islamic revolution in Iran has catapulted the shrine city of Qom into a different world in more ways than one. Laws enacted to move factories out of Teheran and a superhighway that connects Qom to Teheran have increased industry in the Qom area and, alongside it, the population has grown several fold to over a million. But the heart of the city belongs to the religious colleges, the number of whose students has also increased many-fold. The students follow the classic religious curriculum, but are fascinated by new books that discuss the possibility of a radical reconstruction of Islamic law. They too have been affected by political experience.

The victory of the genuine "doctors of the law" of getting their candidates appointed as the highest points of religious reference for the Iranian Shi'i often seems to have little meaning. It is significant that the battle over satellite dishes, extremely popular in Iran, has passed out of the hands of the ayatollahs with their conflicting rulings into the hands of Parliament. But in fact the "doctors of the law" knew that they could not create an effective hierarchy because in Shi'i Islam intellectual subordination of one of them to another is possible only to a limited extent. While tradition favors the appointment of a "most learned" ayatollah as a leader, no "doctor of the law" is supposed to follow anyone except himself: even the Shi'i "International" falls short of fantasies of an Islamintern.

Under the Rafsanjani administration, there is a three-way standoff in Iranian politics between a pragmatic administration, represented by the presidency, a socially and economically conservative parliament, and the radicals, who want more government intervention in everything. Khamenei, perhaps seeking his own constituency, has come to speak more and more for the radicals, while the ayatollahs are by and large economic conservatives. The struggles are now more economic and social than ideological. A large segment of the Iranian population, terrified about the state of their economy, does not know where to look. Politics, it seems, always has been, and always will be, politics, even in states with overtly religious agendas—whether they be former Papal States, the Holy Roman Empire, Buddhist Tibet, or contemporary Iran. After almost two decades of direct experience, many of the Iranian "doctors of the law"—consciously choosing not to follow in Khomeini's path—have become just as cautious about becoming too involved in politics as their nineteenth-century predecessors were. The pious shah who built the sitting room in Qom would probably understand.

Notes

1. See Mohsen Milani, "The Transformation of the Velayat-e Faqih Institution: From Khomeini to Khamanei," *The Muslim World* 82, nos. 3 and 4, (July-October 1992): 175-90 for a discussion of the clauses of the Iranian constitution relevant to leadership.

2. Ibid.

3. See Roy P. Mottahedeh, "Shi'ite Political Thought and the Destiny of the Iranian Revolution," in *Iran and the Gulf: A Search for Stability*, edited by Jamal S. Al-Suwaidi (Abu Dhabi, 1996), 76.

4. Ibid., 76-77, for a discussion of these matters as well as quotes from Jannati and other figures mentioned.

5. For a comprehensive study of the Shi'i Reform Movement and its aims, see Mamoun Fandy, "From Confrontation to Creative Resistance: The Shi'a Oppositional Discourse in Saudi Arabia," *Critique,* Fall 1996, pp. 1-27.

CHAPTER 12

PROSPECTS FOR CONFLICT AND COOPERATION: THE GULF TOWARD THE YEAR 2000

Anwar M. Gargash

For the past 30 years the Gulf region has been synonymous with political turmoil and conflict. Witness to two major wars and a host of minor skirmishes in the last decade alone, the importance of the Gulf states was reinforced by the mid-seventies rise in the price of oil, although this has also contributed significantly to the region's reputation for instability. The area, more than ever, is embroiled in a rivalry of great powers and today, to compound those problems, the Gulf faces new uncertainties because of the conflicting designs of regional powers.

These uncertainties notwithstanding, the petroleum age and the subsequent escalation of crude oil prices has had a momentous impact on the social structure of the region. Internal circumstances have experienced enormous change, propelled by the phenomenal pace of social and economic progress. Regional societies have been dramatically transformed, and the physical environment has been developed at unprecedented speed.

While these changes have taken place throughout the Gulf, they have been perhaps the most dramatic in Abu Dhabi, where, in 1961, the British Political Agent stated that life for the inhabitants of Abu Dhabi had not changed since the late eighteenth century.[1] Another observer noted that not a single yard of surfaced road existed in Abu Dhabi as late as 1965,[2] truly a remarkable statement when one considers that the United Arab

Emirates' capital is today one of the most modern cities of the developing world.

This paper will strive to encourage thoughtful contemplation about the future direction of Gulf politics, and to consider the course of significant issues that are destined to affect this future. Focusing on several key topics, the paper will address relations between the larger and smaller states, the security debate, border disputes and various issues connected with the internal politics of the region. Although this listing is by no means exhaustive, any identification of critical or relevant issues will surely include these.

Surprisingly little indigenous discussion takes place regarding the future of the area. No region-wide consensus or outlook is emerging, and no Gulf perspective is crystallizing regarding the future state of affairs. If the constant crises have not allowed the pause necessary to take a reflective look, or if the contentious and emotional nature of some of these issues causes us to overlook these critical questions, the result, in the long run, will prove disastrous. The fact that the area might face further serious tests in the near future emphasizes the need for greater and more incisive probing into the shape of the future.

One must note, at the outset, that each Gulf state is unique. Significant differences exist in their social, economic and political development, and the GCC states are not as monolithic as some tend to believe. Because of the dissimilarities, the perspectives of the Gulf states may differ sharply, and their perceptions are largely influenced by location, history, social composition and economic outlook. Despite these factors, it is also clear that many of the challenges facing these states are shared challenges, and certain issues are important to every one of them.

The role of this paper is to highlight and discuss some of these questions, and to consider, in as pragmatic a manner as possible, the issues that I have mentioned.

Compounding the problem, the Gulf region is party to many of the changes taking place in the world. The triumph of liberal democracy and the collapse of the totalitarian model with its centralized economy are global phenomena that have influenced the region. Similarly, the demise of bipolarity and the breakup of the Soviet Union have had important ramifications for the regional balance of power. The United States has emerged as the primary external power, and its influence does not suffer from any credible challenge.

There is a feeling, however, that the Gulf, as other parts of the Middle East, has been slower to respond to these changes than the rest of the world, a perception especially evident with respect to issues connected to internal reforms and political participation. While geostrategic concerns are diminishing in favor of economic priorities and large trading blocs are coming to the fore around the world, the outlook in the Gulf is different.

REGIONAL POWERS AND SMALL STATES

Geographic and demographic realities are difficult to ignore. Demographically, Iran and Iraq each have a population larger than the combined population of the six states that comprise the Gulf Cooperation Council. Saudi Arabia's area of 2,150,000 square kilometers dwarfs Bahrain, which has an area of 662 square kilometers, or Qatar, with an area of 11,000 square kilometers. Plainly, the Gulf is split between large regional states and smaller states, and affected by geographic and demographic facts that influence regional relations and produce mutual perceptions. Mistrust in regional relations, influenced by great variations in size, is one of the major impediments to the creation of a more congenial regional atmosphere, which in turn represents a formidable stumbling block when tackling sensitive issues such as territorial disputes.

Iran, Iraq and Saudi Arabia are in a league of their own. They are regional powers seeking to enforce their own dictum, and their conduct in the Gulf is one of relentless competition, infrequent accommodation and rare cooperation. The relationships within this triad have shaped Gulf politics for some time and will continue to do so in the coming decade. Furthermore, the ascent or decline in the fortunes of any of these powers has serious consequences for the others. Saudi Arabia, for example, was able to enhance its regional influence as a result of the Iran-Iraq War. Similarly, Iran was one of the main beneficiaries of Iraq's defeat in the Gulf War. The trouncing of Iraq's massive ground forces by the Coalition Partners tilted the geostrategic balance in the Gulf firmly in Tehran's favor, and secured, in the immediate term, its long and mountainous border.

Despite occasional reports of an Iranian-Iraqi rapprochement, the relationship of the Big Three will continue to be tense in the coming years. Attempts at accommodation are mostly tactical, and the search for greater influence represents the norm. This reading is based on three factors:

1. A recent history of confrontation and rivalry that includes the Iran-Iraq War, the Gulf War and various violent outbursts in the Hajj season. Efforts to reconcile Iran and Iraq in recent years have proved futile. The latest such attempt was prompted by a shared desire to

stand up to the United States, but early indications point out that this effort faces strong criticism in influential Iranian circles.[3]

2. The three states have conflicting aspirations concerning their respective Gulf roles. Each envisions itself as the primary Gulf power and seeks to consolidate its role, yet all three suffer from serious weaknesses. The lack of a substantial population base, limited access to Gulf waters, or ethnic and linguistic barriers are impediments to regional ambition. The post–Gulf War balance of power among the three regional powers does not encourage an imminent conflict, although some Gulf experts believe that the threat of hostility will increase significantly by the end of the decade.[4]

3. While the three states have different political systems, a more serious difference is that their state ideologies are self-righteous and diametrically opposed. Saudi Arabia is a conservative, status-quo regime and the cradle of the puritanical Hanbali school. Iran represents an anti–status quo revolutionary power seeking radical changes in the regional order while simultaneously laying claim to being the world's political center of Shiism. It is extremely difficult to envision the two regimes reconciled in the foreseeable future.

In addition to these three larger states, the Gulf is home to five smaller states of varying sizes. The larger powers, at times, do not accept that the smaller states are sovereign members of their region, and, in many cases, refuse to address issues important to their smaller neighbors. This was nowhere more evident than in Riyadh's insensitivity to Doha's complaints, or in Iran's refusal to accept that there is a legitimate UAE view on its occupied islands. Similarly, Iraq has been traditionally insensitive to Kuwaiti concerns, despite Kuwait's financial and logistical support during Iraq's war with Iran.

In dealing with their larger neighbors, the smaller states have sought different approaches. In Bahrain's case, its regional policy is to remain closely affiliated with Saudi Arabia. This historical connection was influenced by Iranian claims to the island, and consolidated in recent years by generous Saudi economic assistance. The recent Saudi-Qatari rift proves that even traditionally good relations in the area are not static and can deteriorate in a short period of time.

Alternatively, states such as Oman or pre-invasion Kuwait have searched for a neutral foreign policy, and have tried to keep their channels of communication open. It must be added, however, that the smaller Gulf states are less likely to choose republican Iran as a balancing power than monarchist Iran. A decade of revolutionary grandstanding has clearly prejudiced this decision.

The tension between the larger regional powers and the smaller states plays a significant role in the politics of the region. The lack of confidence inherent in the relationship is a complicating factor that contributes negatively to the various dimensions of inter-Gulf politics.

Smaller states simply do not trust their larger neighbors, and they fear their designs. Furthermore, they perceive their approach to many of the issues as self-centered and insensitive, some going so far as to characterize Saudi policy toward its Gulf neighbors as "imperial."[5] While Riyadh, to a certain extent, enjoys more links than the other two regional powers, its relationship with its neighbors is a mixture of love and hate.[6]

This lack of confidence has not been addressed frankly, and is in need of open, in-depth and honest debate. Such a discussion must involve decisionmakers and ruling elites, and must not be confined to well-meaning academics. Sadly, the prospects for such a debate's taking place are dim. The fact that these three powers have conflicting ambitions means that chances for mutual understanding are minimal, at best. As a consequence of these differences, a smaller state such as Qatar will continue to fear an ulterior Saudi agenda and the suspicions harbored by the United Arab Emirates concerning Iranian designs in the area will persist.

What, then, are the possibilities for the Gulf to break out of this cycle? By virtue of their size and power, the onus is, unequivocally, on the regional powers to initiate improvement in the regional environment. It is these states that must act as catalysts for harmonious inter-state relations and begin to erect political bridges in the area.

Specific actions may vary from ceasing irresponsible rhetoric on the part of Iran to greater flexibility on border issues in Riyadh's case. Furthermore, any actions must be implemented over an extended period of time to create credibility, and to demonstrate that there is indeed a new regional code of conduct. Sporadic improvements will only create temporary and, in many instances, tactical cooperation, which has, unfortunately, been the norm in the Gulf in the past.

THE SECURITY DILEMMA

The security of the Gulf states continues to be a concern of paramount importance in the coming decade. The war for the liberation of Kuwait and a turbulent past are heady reminders of the significance of this issue.

As one would expect, the security dilemma is an urgent and complicated matter, and an issue that divides the states of the region.

Thus far, perceptions of security differ sharply. The Gulf War demonstrated that regional threats are as serious, if not more so, than external threats, with the result being that the GCC states realize that an American presence is an essential element in any security formula. To these states, security of the region is intimately connected to Western power-projection capability.

Iran, on the other hand, considers such presence threatening and promotes a regional arrangement in which the Iranian role is preeminent. Indeed, the recent escalation of tensions between Iran and the United States casts a large negative shadow on the Gulf, and presents new complications in the region. The GCC member states are torn between backing their primary security partner and searching for better relations with Tehran.

Under the leadership of Saddam Hussein, Iraq continues to be a regional pariah state despite numerous attempts to break out of its isolation. In its current condition, as a result, it cannot significantly influence the security debate. With its authority challenged continuously at home, the power of the Baathist regime is not commensurate with Iraq's geostrategic importance. It is safe to say that Iraq is unlikely to passively accept a significant American role in the area in the immediate future. It is highly unlikely, as well, that a Saddam-led Iraq can play a role in any regional security arrangement.

In short, there are various conflicting approaches to the security dilemma, and it is extremely difficult to reconcile these diametrically opposed views. Not surprisingly, it is the Gulf Cooperation Council views on security that have radically "evolved" over the last decade. This evolution has been largely dictated by regional challenges and a realization by the GCC states that they are unable to confront these challenges on their own. Saudi Arabia, Kuwait and the United Arab Emirates have gone on record on numerous occasions against the presence of Western forces in the Gulf. With the carnage and devastation of the Iran-Iraq War and the escalation of the "tanker war," however, a fresh look was necessary. Old formulas can no longer be sacrosanct, and whatever doubts remained regarding Western assistance were quickly dispelled when Iraqi forces moved into Kuwait. Yet, despite earlier hopes, a unified GCC security plan of action did not emerge. Lingering mistrust kept cooperation to a minimum, and external security arrangements were concluded on a bilateral basis.

What did evolve was a general and shared perspective, however. Boosting the military capability of each state and ensuring a minimum level of cooperation between the GCC armed forces; fostering the security and diplomatic cooperation of key Arab states; and reliance on cooperation with the United States were the three components that formed an overall security outlook. While the last element—cooperation with the United States—is arguably the security linchpin, it is at once the most sensitive and problematic issue on more than one plane. It not only complicates regional relations, as was mentioned earlier, but also creates an association the GCC states must learn to carefully manage; it has the potential to influence the internal politics of participating states.

It goes without saying that maintaining balance within all of these factors is difficult, as Gause notes in Saudi Arabia's case: "Over-reliance on any one element could entail serious problems."[7] The instability of the whole picture led another commentator to state, prior to Iraq's invasion of Kuwait, that "The events of the last few years have thrust the West and the Southern Gulf states together. The forces involved, however, are unstable. They can either forge a lasting partnership or end in creating new divisions."[8]

For the GCC states, the acceptance of a regional security arrangement that includes Iran or Iraq is not realistic at the present time. Tehran and Baghdad are seen by various states as the main peril to security. It has been noted by another observer that any regional security organization that includes these regional powers "contains the dilemma of appointing the foxes to help guard the chicken coop."[9] Revolutionary rhetoric, aggressive policies and the sheer size of Iran and Iraq continue to augment these fears.

Deterrence literature refers to risk-averse and risk-acceptant decisionmakers. The member states of the Gulf Cooperation Council realize that their larger neighbors are clearly of the second type. While this does not mean that relations in this sphere between the GCC states and Iran have to be antagonistic, it does mean that an improved political environment is a precondition to any kind of security cooperation.

It is a truism that the GCC states, on the other hand, are not completely comfortable with the Western connection, and relations with the West are widely condemned in Arab nationalist and Islamic fundamentalist circles. This dichotomy constitutes a very real political liability. In addition, these states realize that the West has its own agenda and self-interest, and, as a result, fear greater Western interference in their internal politics. An example of this is Western pressure for internal reforms and greater political participation. Overall, there has not been a great amount of pressure in this respect, but the situation can change rapidly.

Iran's perception of the security of the region is diametrically opposed to that of its neighbors. The Islamic Republic is strongly opposed to any Western presence in the Gulf, insisting instead that security is the sole responsibility of the littoral states. This is a position that ultimately favors a strong Iranian role since Tehran is the largest regional power.

The gap between this position and the GCC states' reliance on the United States is clearly substantial and, on appearance, unbridgeable. In a recent statement, released after a meeting with the Omani minister of commerce and industry, President Rafsanjani called for the GCC states to stand against Western presence in the Gulf.[10] From a GCC perspective, the Iranian president's suggestion is unrealistic, since this same presence constitutes the underpinning of the GCC's security strategy. Iran, in reinforcing its position, does not favor extra-regional Arab involvement in Gulf security. Tehran is especially sensitive to the possibility of Egypt's playing an active role, a position that has been articulated in numerous Iranian criticisms and vitriolic attacks on the "Damascus Declaration." The propaganda war between Cairo and Tehran in the aftermath of the liberation of Kuwait made this abundantly clear.

Accusations aside, the American role will be especially evident in the security debate. The West in general and the United States, in particular, have vital interests in the area, and it would be naive to assume that these parties will not influence events in the future; external powers will continue to play an important role in regional politics.

To emphasize its point, Iran has made efforts to blame its economic woes on Washington, with President Rafsanjani at one time going so far as to accuse the United States and Israel of conspiring to hasten the collapse of the Iranian rial.[11] One must recognize, however, that there are basic policy differences between American concerns and regional concerns. The United States has a superpower outlook and a more comprehensive policy agenda, with the result that its views are not always shared by its traditional allies in the region.

To illustrate this point, while the Russian sale of nuclear reactors to Tehran is extremely alarming to Washington,[12] it is not a critical issue to some of the GCC states, a divergence that is also apparent on the issue of nuclear proliferation in the Middle East.

There is clearly a necessity for a frank debate on the security needs of the area, but any such debate, to be meaningful, must take into account the diversity of views and interests in the region. All must accept the fact that, since security is a core concern of any state, reaching an understanding will entail a gradual and protracted process. States must be patient and respect the security requirements of their neighbors. Such forbearance is especially necessary in the initial stages when a lack of confidence will be the norm.

The experience of the Association of South East Asian Nations (ASEAN) is relevant. Mistrust and border disputes characterize the relationships of these states, and to address them they have sponsored the ASEAN Regional Forum (ARF),[13] a gathering at which specific issues related to member security is discussed. Such a discussion would be especially helpful in promoting greater understanding between neighbors in the Gulf, as legitimate needs for weapons purchases and military exercises could be explained in a forum of this kind. What might seem like a provocative act to a certain state could be debated and discussed in the presence of all of the regional actors, and many ensuing crises could be aborted. Such a forum, moreover, would serve to cultivate better understanding among the military institutions in the region, and would, with the passage of time, accumulate enough credibility to tackle more complex affairs of state. An improvement in this arena would ultimately be connected to an improvement of political conditions between the states of the region.

The Territorial Disputes

Border disputes are an integral part of inter-Gulf politics, as well as of the oil age. Historically, borders have been an alien concept to an area accustomed to large nomadic migrations, with each principality having a fluctuating sphere of influence rather than fixed borders as a result. Areas of influence changed rapidly due to political and military considerations; although a stable core was more permanent, the power of a given shaikh would suffer as a result of his military defeats and the continuing allegiance of the tribes in his area. The example of Kuwait is illuminating. Following several defeats of Shaikh Mubarak and his son Salim's forces, Kuwait's sphere of influence was drastically reduced in the 1920s.[14]

Territorial disputes have traditionally had their roots in tribal competition and dynastic rivalry, particularly in the case of neighboring states. Economic considerations and the control of oil inflamed the issue. These disputes continue to play a disruptive role in the politics of the region. Interestingly, issues such as the Hawar dispute between Qatar and Bahrain and the Iraq-Kuwait border issue are as much a part of present-day politics as they were a feature of the politics of the 1930s.

Modern nationalism has been instrumental in complicating boundary issues in the Gulf. The region is home to two highly charged nationalisms—Arab and Persian—that still have not learned to co-exist. Border claims are usually advanced to increase a state's importance, and emotions fostered by rampant nationalism remain a serious obstacle to the rational solution of these disputes. The late shah of Iran's about-face on Bahrain, for example, was not favored in Iranian nationalist circles, and this ultimately influenced the shah's hard line on the islands dispute with the United Arab Emirates. Similarly, the strength of these sentiments are unmistakable in popular Iraqi convictions toward Kuwait.

One must stress, however, that boundaries are primarily political issues that are largely affected by prevailing political conditions between states and, at times, by regional and international considerations. The latest dispute between Qatar and Saudi Arabia underlines this point. What has traditionally been a brotherly relationship between a regional power and its smaller neighbor has steadily deteriorated, with the undesirable outcome being that incomplete border arrangements have assumed center stage and contributed negatively to the bilateral relationship. It is obvious that confronting and addressing the boundary issue in an effective manner is essential to the return of normal relations.

Solving territorial disputes is not an impossible task, and examples in the area prove this point. The obvious approach is to resolve these conflicts through bilateral negotiations with the assistance of a third party. It is imperative, however, that the political situation is ripe and that relations are generally cordial. Depending on the nature of the issue, negotiations can be detailed and protracted. A circumstance that causes both parties to be willing to reach an agreement—and in the process to compromise—is essential for these discussions to succeed.

Solidifying a temporary arrangement and building on its initial success is another route. The Uqair Conference of 1922, which addressed the Saudi-Kuwaiti border dispute, is one such example. Uqair created a 2,000-square-mile neutral zone to the south of Kuwait, stipulated a joint administration and prescribed an equal distribution of any oil income in the zone. This arrangement had been in place for a long time when, in 1965, the neutral zone was divided equally and the oil income evenly distributed, regardless of the location of each oil field. In this case, developing the earlier agreement was only possible because it had been in place for an extended period of time, and confidence had been established in the process.

A more recent success involves the border between Oman and Yemen. With the help of the Kuwaitis, the two states moved slowly from open hostility to a mutually agreed border demarcation. The protracted negotiations between Oman and South Yemen commenced in 1982, yet the concluding ceremonies were held a full thirteen years later. The agreement gives Yemen more territory and ends a contentious and bitter chapter in the history of two neighboring states.[15] It must be emphasized that this agreement was possible largely because of internal political changes in Aden that moved it away from previous dogmatic politics and because of regional changes that favored greater cooperation in inter-state relations.

A further course involves some form of regional arbitration, in which regard the GCC mechanism has failed miserably. Arab Gulf academics have been critical of the organization, pointing out that it has not dealt successfully with the border disputes of its members—witness the fact that the Bahrain-Qatar dispute over Hawar has, at more than one juncture, threatened the unity of the Gulf Cooperation Council. There is no question that this conflict has weakened the organization by damaging both its credibility and its ability to speak in a single voice.

As an alternative, the GCC has had to accept a peripheral role in this vital area, and stand as a hapless observer while the issue was debated by the International Court of Justice (ICJ), once described as the "neutral to end all neutrals;"[16] resorting to adjudication at the ICJ should be another acceptable norm in the area when bilateral negotiations fail. Border issues can explode at any time and must be dealt with actively and effectively. International arbitration offers a face-saving solution, while at the same time providing an established "system" created specifically to deal with such contentious issues.

Correspondingly, the Gulf presents examples of border agreements signed but ultimately not respected. Two clear examples emerge, one involving the 1975 Algiers agreement between Saddam Hussein and the late shah of Iran and the other, Iran's repeated transgression of the 1971 Memorandum of Understanding over Abu Musa. These breaches inject a further note of caution, especially in cases involving a large state and a smaller neighbor.

By the same token, a party's lingering feeling that an earlier agreement was unjust and signed under pressure can also contribute to continued tension. Feelings in the United Arab Emirates concerning the 1974 agreement with Riyadh fall within such a category. The fact that one of the major oil fields in the area—the Shaibah or Zarara field, one of the largest in the region with a potential production of 500,000 barrels of light, low-sulphur crude per day—was discovered in territory conceded by the UAE only exacerbates the situation.[17]

Improvement in political conditions is essential to solve many of the border issues effectively and to guarantee that all parties abide by the agreements. Negotiations should coincide with improvement of the political climate since, in many cases, stalled border disputes are a major obstacle to better political relations. Certain criteria are essential, including an agreement not to resort to violence and the primacy of peaceful means in dealing with these issues. Under no circumstances should occupation of territory by force be accepted, nor should force be allowed to form a basis for claims to any territory.

THE INTERNAL DIMENSION

The Gulf states are part of a wider world and are affected by various trends and developments in this world. With the collapse of the communist model, a democratic wave has swept the world with far-reaching consequences in areas as far removed as Latin America and Southeast Asia. One wonders about the effect of these changes on the governments of the Gulf region and how they will respond to these challenges.

The atmosphere that surrounded the Gulf War raised expectations in the GCC states to an exaggerated level. Large segments of the population thought the crisis constituted a watershed that would lead to a period of political openness and dynamism. Indeed, the crisis period witnessed an unprecedented "liberal" environment with various critical public lectures and open debate. On the one hand, governments realized that, at such times, the margin of free speech should be expanded, and "reasonable" opinions about some opening of the political system should be tolerated. On the other hand, government institutions are preoccupied at times of crisis and unable to exercise the same degree of control. In Saudia Arabia, for example, there were calls for greater political participation in the immediate aftermath of the Gulf War. Several petitions were circulated, exposing a great desire for reform. This was a feeling that encompassed a wide array of political opinion, from the views of professional "liberals" to those of conservative Islamists. This period was aptly termed by Ghazi Al-Gosaibi the "storms after the storm".[18]

All the same, a few years later the record remains confused. Drastic variation persists from state to state. Recent developments in several Gulf states—including Bahrain, Iran, Iraq and Saudi Arabia—have served to emphasize the need for internal reform, the urgency of which, in some states, is due to the changing economic landscape. A clear dichotomy between rich and poor Gulf states is in the process of crystallization, developments that will ultimately lead to greater pressures for reform.

It must be noted that in some states there is no significant call for reform from the population. Yet, regimes must be careful since what appears as a calm situation in the absence of a free press and other open forums might be a misleading indicator. A case in point is Prince Faisal's decision to lift press censorship in 1960 as part of his internal struggle with King Saud. No sooner had this been done than calls for constitutional reform and the formation of an elected council with broad legislative powers were among the first demands appearing in the newspapers.[19]

In cases such as the foregoing, the elites must have the foresight to bring about such changes, since a political situation can change radically in a frighteningly short period of time.

An example of such action is Sultan Qabus's decision to introduce limited elections and give the Shura Council relatively greater authority. This was followed by the election of women to the council. Significantly, there was neither internal nor external pressure on the sultan at the time, and his decision was based solely on his assessments of future developments in Oman.

The picture, however, is not monolithic. Some states, such as Kuwait, have more than thirty years' experience with parliamentary politics, and the experiment, while at times tenuous, seems to be working. Achievements in the Kuwaiti system have included frank and open debates as well as checks and balances, particularly with respect to the monitoring of state spending. The invasion of the state and reminders of a government in exile have consolidated Kuwait's democratic choice, and it would be extremely difficult for the government of Kuwait to attempt to reverse the tide now. Many point out, however, that the experiment suffers from exaggerated personal squabbles and drastic polarization that a small society can ill afford. In the past, Kuwaiti academics expressed the view that their experiment offered a viable model for other GCC states. While this sentiment still surfaces on occasion,[20] it is not heard nearly as often as in the past. It is obvious that the recent crisis has taken its toll, and post-war Kuwait is more inward-looking and less sure of its future course.

The Kuwaiti example is by no means the only model for the other GCC states. The historical conditions influencing Kuwait's choice and the conducive regional environment of the 1960s have changed dramatically.

If the Kuwaiti model is too ambitious or liberal, however, there are many alternative reform "packages" that could be implemented.

An internal reform package suitable to each state's stage of development can be put forward. Any such plan must emphasize the rule of law, financial accountability and greater freedom of speech and expression, the minimum requirements for a credible reform policy.

By contrast, many observers think that the Saudi reform package is too cautious. The introduction of a "Basic Law" and a sixty-member Shura Council are conservative steps in a fast-moving region. This represents the minimum present in all of the GCC states. The conservative nature of these reforms leads a sympathetic observer to note, "clearly basing everything on Islam and on tradition, the new law then went on to codify much that had been vague before, even if it had been generally applied in practice."[21]

At present, it is apparent that the traditional channels of participation are inadequate. The tribal *majlis* and its successor are ill-suited to handle the demands of a modern and diverse political system. Kings, sultans, and amirs are less accessible, and, without such access, the system cannot perform adequately. The sheer workload and trappings of statehood have made the mythical simplicity of the traditional *majlis* a relic of the pre-oil Gulf. Many of the modern issues confronting the area's polity are too technical or specialized, and the traditional *majlis*—where anyone present can air an opinion—is no longer an appropriate forum. Not surprisingly, the conservative Gulf states are caught in a transitional phase, and they find themselves in a rather uncomfortable situation. Their old channels of participation are inadequate, and their new channels are largely ceremonial and ineffective.

A cautionary note must be added at this point. The assumption that political reforms and change will bring a more rational and liberal form of government is not an accurate supposition. If changes should take place in the traditional dynastic systems it will not necessarily lead to an open-minded, liberal and Western-oriented alternative.

On the contrary, change is more likely to bring a better-organized authoritarian system disguised in military, Arab nationalist or fundamentalist garb, a gloomy prospect influenced by the prevailing fundamentalist and Arab nationalist opposition in the region. These groups, no matter how far one stretches the imagination, can never be described as "democratic." The rare experience of Arab and Islamic regimes where an open "liberal" system has been adopted is another indication that caution is warranted.

In the case of Iran, the constitution has been part of the country's modern history, but, with the exception of short periods of time, it has not functioned adequately. Since the birth of the Islamic Republic in 1979, Iran has created institutions that have enjoyed varying degrees of effectiveness; the *majlis* and other institutions cater to a single political trend in Iran's polity. It has not been able to accommodate the multitude of ideas and opinions present in Iranian society. These institutions are first and foremost the institutions of the clergy-based regime. As a consequence, the challenge facing the regime is to try to open up the political system in an orderly and peaceful fashion. The modern history of Iran, with its sharp twists and turns, is a poignant reminder that this, in fact, is an urgent matter that must be taken seriously.

The Gulf states have experienced a radical transformation over the last forty years. From rudimentary organizations with little impact on social and economic matters, they have flourished and undergone a remarkable change. Assisted by great oil wealth and a self-defined role as an all-encompassing, benevolent entity, the state played a major role in the social, economic and political realm, becoming the locomotive that led the progress and development of society. The scope of its activity was expanded, necessitating the employment of a majority of the population. The "cradle-to-the-grave" concept included free health care and education, and the regulation of economic activity. The population felt that this was compensation for the hardship of the past, and it was accepted that this was the most effective way to redistribute the oil wealth. The citizens depended on the state and realized that their well-being was intimately connected to its capabilities and programs.

The process, on the other hand, had its negative aspects as well, and was largely responsible for extinguishing the fires of personal enterprise and initiative. In many cases, a population that was entrepreneurial in spirit and actively involved in commerce was turned by the rentier state into under-achieving bureaucrats.

Significant changes, moreover, were not confined to the role of the state, and included a radical transformation of the region's social structure. Gulf society developed beyond recognition, casting away the simplicity of the past. Furthermore, economic development created occupational diversity and social mobility; new jobs were created and the average income rose substantially. The nucleus of a professional middle class was the logical outcome of ambitious education plans.

In its initial phases, the state was able to accommodate the increasing demand and to guarantee generous social services and employment. Yet, with changing economic conditions and growing populations, it was becoming clear that the welfare state was experiencing serious difficulties. The high expectations of a population long accustomed to services provided by the state without cost could no longer be guaranteed.

These changes naturally have political ramifications that Gulf governments cannot ignore. There is a clear connection between economic reforms and political reforms. As a state surrenders some of its economic and regulatory powers it becomes weaker, yet the success of its program depends on this surrender. Suddenly the Gulf states had to deal with previously unheard-of problems, such as unemployment and budget deficits. Concern over unemployment in Bahrain, for example, led the Ministry of the Interior to order foreign labor to rectify their documentation. The minimum monthly salary of an expatriate worker seeking to bring his family to the island was raised from 250 to 400 dinars.[22] Meanwhile, facing annual deficits of almost $800 million, the sultan of Oman has pledged to balance the budget by the year 2000, a goal that will have to be achieved through stringent fiscal policies and a reduction in state spending.[23]

Short-term concerns, however, are largely responsible for economic reforms in the Gulf. These include budget deficits and perceptions by the governments of future difficulties. Having said that, international pressure is not a major factor, while inflationary fears are an important determinant in Iran and Iraq. As a result of the area's economic difficulties, governments are forced to accelerate the pace of privatization. A large part of the economic sector in many Gulf states is currently targeted, although various regional Arab organizations complain of the slow process of privatization.[24]

The GCC states, in particular, are eager to undergo this process. Saudi Arabia, for example, has recently announced plans to privatize Saudia, its heavily subsidized national airline. In addition, it plans to actively involve the private sector in new industrial projects in Jubail and Yanbu worth an estimated four billion riyals.[25] Similarly, Abu Dhabi's General Industry Corporation has announced plans to privatize various plants and factories with a book value of $200 million.[26] In Kuwait, government shares in sixty companies valued at $2.7 billion are being sold successfully and in record time.[27]

Governments, as well, are urging the private sector to play a more active role in the economies of the region, a call heard all over the Gulf. It was most recently echoed by Sultan Qabus in an address to the Omani populace.[28]

The fact that the urgency of these economic reforms is largely due to political considerations does not give them the necessary credibility. For economic restructuring to be effective, it needs time and consistency. An observer offers the following remarks: "In Iraq the reforms instituted by Saddam Hussein's regime, such as the privatization of certain industries and agricultural lands—while impressive on paper—were, for the most part, politically calculated to reward a few individuals and improve a deteriorating foreign exchange situation."[29] Similarly, the Rafsanjani reforms in Iran have had to be compromised at various junctures, leading to a loss of credibility.

A frequently heard criticism is that reforms in the area perpetuate the influence of an already-entrenched private sector and do not necessarily enhance competitiveness.[30] Wealth is not expanded, as a result, and a few business oligarchies are the ultimate beneficiaries.

Time is needed to ensure the success of these measures. Gulf society will have to endure a period of austerity new to this area since the beginning of the oil age. It will be difficult for the population, especially the poorer sectors, to accept that previous distributive policies are no longer possible. This pill will be harder to swallow with the open nature of bureaucratic and financial corruption in some states. Since these structural changes will hurt the less-fortunate sectors, it is important to sustain these policies in order for them to work. This can be done by creating safety nets with programs targeted to help these groups.[31]

The economic dimension, following several decades of plenty, is presenting itself as a serious challenge. The state that is best able to restructure and adjust will be in an advantageous position, but the presence—side-by-side—of successful and failed economies in the region can go either way; it could create tension and hostility or it could promote healthy competition. Additionally, the tough fiscal policies adopted by the governments of the area could lead to internal disturbances, especially in states such as Iran and Iraq. Unstable internal political conditions can promote demagogic leadership and an escapist foreign policy. In the final analysis, stability in the region is a necessary ingredient for improving economic prospects in the area. Political turmoil and military adventurism are costly, and the Gulf will be hard pressed to afford them.

THE NEED FOR COOPERATION

The protracted issues addressed above present a formidable obstacle to stability in the region. Consolidating the search for areas of cooperation will ultimately help ease the tension associated with many of these matters. It is natural that differences over serious issues such as boundary disputes, oil policies and internal reforms, are substantial. Furthermore, differences are exaggerated by tendencies of new states to protect their sovereignty, as well as by an ethnocentric type of nationalism.

Bilateral cooperation is the most common type and one that is not unknown to the Gulf, Kuwait's assistance to various Gulf states being one example. Other examples include the arrangements governing the free movement of people and goods between the United Arab Emirates and Oman. Functional cooperation in shared oil fields is commonplace, as in the case of Iran and the UAE, Qatar and the UAE, and Saudi Arabia and Kuwait. While bilateral cooperation creates trust and goodwill, there is urgent need for a collective effort. The creation of institutions to foster cooperation is essential for this endeavor to succeed, and the establishment of effective procedures and mechanisms is an important part of this effort. The southern Gulf states—in the shape of the Gulf Cooperation Council— have been able to form an institutional framework to promote cooperation between the members. The record so far is spotty, and the results of more than a decade of effort are humble indeed. The entire experiment is in dire need of an overhaul, and urgent political and administrative reforms have been encouraged by many quarters in the Gulf.

The basic failures of the Gulf Cooperation Council can be grouped under three major subheadings:

1. The failure to tackle the border disputes within the GCC;
2. The failure to provide an effective security umbrella for its members;
3. The failure to become a grass-roots organization through relevant social and economic reforms.

While some of these criticisms are valid, others—especially those connected with the security of the member states—are unquestionably overstating the potential and capabilities of the organization. These limitations notwithstanding, the GCC has to be relevant to the people to succeed. A certain amount of popular input and support is required, and many feel that a GCC-wide parliament is the solution. A skeptic would wonder about the benefit of such a parliament if it mirrors the existing national assemblies and Shura Councils.

Cooperation need not exclude Iran and Iraq; without them regional cooperation is meaningless. In the early 70s, many projects and institutions were established with Iranian and Iraqi participation. Significantly, many of these projects were undertaken following the Algiers Agreement of 1975 and prior to the Iranian revolution.

Cooperation, above all, requires an environment of trust. There were several periods during which such an atmosphere seemed tenable. One lost opportunity was the prevailing environment in mid-1991, following the Gulf War.

The GCC states were clearly appreciative of Iran's responsible role during the crisis in Kuwait, and various high-level visits were exchanged which led to high expectations of a long-term Iran-GCC rapprochement. The mood of the period was captured by the statement issued following the meeting of Iran's foreign minister with his GCC counterparts in September 1991: "The guidelines spelled out are very appropriate, and will constitute a useful framework for regional relations; it spoke of the sovereignty of the parties; the inviolability of their international boundaries; the peaceful settlement of disputes; non-resort to force in their relations; the non-interference in the domestic affairs of others; and the encouragement of dialogue and mutual understanding.[32]

The necessity for constructive ideas such as these has led various Gulf Arab academics to speak of the need for a comprehensive "code of ethics" that will regulate relations between the various littoral states.[33] Nonetheless, skeptics would point to the realities of politics in the area, and to support their view they need only point to Saddam's "National Charter," which served to camouflage his expansionist designs.

The issue again is how to create confidence in state-to-state dealings in the Gulf. Only by succeeding in this effort will we be able to break out of this vicious cycle.

Concluding Remarks

In the coming decade the Gulf region will continue to be an important and sensitive area. Industrial powers and states seeking to play an important role on the world stage will continue to show interest in the region. International and regional interests will ensure that competition for greater influence will endure.

While the remarks articulated in this presentation are, more or less, a continuation of older trends in the Gulf, the situation is changing markedly. The old days of wealthy states seeking prestige and glory are over, at least for some. The Gulf states have to live with new fiscal constraints, amid the uncertainties of a radically different international scene.

Many of the old issues and problems persist, however. Questions concerning borders and security remain at the heart of regional relations, as they always have.

Internally, the current democratic wave is certainly not the final ideological chapter or the end of history. More likely, it is but another swing of the pendulum. Yet, as in the case of all great changes, it will leave an unmistakable mark, and any future swings will take careful note of this. In the midst of these historical trends, the Gulf states cannot isolate themselves or their societies. They must develop and open up their systems with a mixture of political and economic reforms. While there is a connection between the two, in the final analysis the Gulf regimes are expected to address both areas.

It is difficult to imagine how the Gulf states can deal meaningfully with an Iraq governed by Saddam Hussein. Perhaps some new emergency in the region will lead to such a scenario, or perhaps it will be due to the calculations connected to the balance of power in the area. Any such dealing, however, will be of a tactical nature, and a long-term contribution by Iraq to the politics of the region will have to wait for an internal change in Baghdad.

Tehran's role is rather more complicated. Iran is arguably the most important state in the region, and it does not suffer from the Baathist regime's lack of legitimacy. Furthermore, it enjoys good working relations with many of its neighbors. Contradicting those relations, Iran has never been successful in reaching out to its neighbors and dispersing their fears. The chaotic nature of its internal politics will ensure that this gap will not be bridged. What is clear is that there is an obvious and urgent need to build Arab-Iranian bridges. These need not be solely political, but can be economic as well. Ultimately, greater cooperation in the economic realm will lead to greater results in other fields.

Finally, future prospects concerning conflict and cooperation in the region are intimately tied to breaking the cycle of mistrust among the regional participants. The larger states in the Gulf must initiate this process; only then can one hope for consistent and steady progress in the quest for stability.

Notes

1. J. E. H. Boustead, *The Wind of Morning* (London: 1972), p. 228.

2. K. G. Fenelon, *The United Arab Emirates: A Brief Economic Survey.* 2nd edition (London: 1976), p. 18.

3. *Al-Sharq Al-Awsat,* May 31, 1995.

4. David E. Long, "Prospects of Armed Conflict in the Gulf in the 1990s: The Impact of the Gulf War," *Middle East Policy,* no. 1 (1993), p. 124.

5. David E. Long, "Saudi Arabia and Its Neighbors: Preoccupied Paternalism," in H. Richard Sindlar and J.E. Peterson, eds., *Crosscurrents in the Gulf* (New York: 1988), p. 181.

6. Ibid.

7. G. Gause, "Saudi Arabia: Desert Storm and After," in R. Freedman, ed., *The Middle East after Iraq's Invasion of Kuwait* (Gainesville: University Press of Florida, 1993), p. 210.

8. Anthony Cordesman, *The Gulf and the West: Strategic Relations and Military Realities* (Boulder: Westview Press, 1988), p. 456.

9. Graham E. Fuller, *The Center of the Universe: The Geopolitics of Iran* (Boulder: Westview Press, 1991), p. 101.

10. *Al-Hayat.* May 31, 1995.

11. *Al-Hayat.* May 10, 1995.

12. *Al-Hayat.* May 10, 1995.

13. "China Looks Abroad," *The Economist,* April 29, 1995, p.17.

14. Ahmad Mustafa Abu Hakima, *The Modern History of Kuwait: 1750-1965* (London: Luzac and Company, 1983), p. 123.

15. *Al-Sharq Al-Awsat,* June 7, 1995.

16. "The GCC Border Disputes Seminar," Gulf Centre for Strategic Studies (London: 1992), p. 21.

17. *Middle East Economic Survey (MEES),* March 27, 1995.

18. Al-Gosaibi, *The Gulf Crisis: An Attempt to Understand* (London: 1993), p. 142.

19. "A Saudi Revolution," *The Economist,* April 30, 1960.

20. Mohammad al-Rumaihi, "Kuwait: Oasis of Liberalism?" *Middle East Quarterly* 1 (September 1994), p. 35.

21. John Bulloch, *Reforms of the Saudi Arabian Constitution* (London: Gulf Centre for Strategic Studies, 1992), p. 2.

22. *Al-Sharq Al-Awsat,* June 7, 1995.

23. *Al-Hayat,* June 23, 1995.

24. "Gulf Push Toward Privatization," *The Middle East,* June 1995, p. 30.

25. Ibid.

26. Ibid.

27. *Al-Sharq Al-Awsat,* June 7, 1995.

28. *Al-Bayan,* June 3, 1995.

29. Henri Barkey, "Economic Reform and Democracy: Can the Middle East Compete?" *Journal of Democracy* 6, no. 2 (April 1995), p. 116.

30. Ibid.

31. Carol Graham, "The Politics of Safety Nets" *Journal of Democracy* 6, no. 2 (April 1995), pp. 142-43.

32. G. Gause, "Saudi Arabia: Desert Storm and After," in R. Freedman, ed., *The Middle East after Iraq's Invasion of Kuwait* (Gainesville: University Press of Florida, 1993), p. 215.

33. See comment by Abdul Rida Assiri in *Al-Khaleej,* June 17, 1992.

CONTRIBUTORS

Gary G. Sick is the Executive Director of Gulf/2000. Dr. Sick served on the U.S. National Security Council staff under Presidents Ford, Carter and Reagan, where he was the principal White House aide for Persian Gulf affairs from 1976-81. He is the author of two books on U.S.-Iranian relations and many other articles and publications on Middle East issues. Dr. Sick is a captain (ret.) in the U.S. Navy, with service in the Persian Gulf, North Africa, and the Mediterranean. He was the deputy director for International Affairs at the Ford Foundation from 1982 to 1987. Dr. Sick holds a Ph.D. in political science from Columbia University, where he is Senior Research Scholar and Adjunct Professor of International Affairs. He is a member of the board of Human Rights Watch in New York and chairman of the advisory committee of Human Rights Watch/Middle East.

Lawrence G. Potter is Deputy Director of the Gulf/2000 Project and Adjunct Assistant Professor of International Affairs at Columbia University. A graduate of Tufts College, he received an M.A. in Middle Eastern Studies from the School of Oriental and African Studies, University of London, and a Ph.D. in History from Columbia University. He taught in Iran for four years before the revolution. From 1984 to 1992 he was Senior Editor at the Foreign Policy Association, a national, nonpartisan organization devoted to world affairs education for the general public. He has written a number of articles on Iranian history and U.S. policy toward the Middle

East, and recently completed a monograph on the Persian Gulf for the Foreign Policy Association's *Headline Series* (forthcoming, 1997).

Anthony H. Cordesman is a Senior Fellow at the Center for Strategic and International Studies in Washington, D.C., an Adjunct Professor of National Security Studies at Georgetown University, and a military analyst for ABC News. He recently was a Fellow at the Woodrow Wilson International Center for Scholars at the Smithsonian and was National Security Assistant to Senator John McCain. He has previously served in senior positions for the Office of the Secretary of Defense, the State Department, the Department of Energy, and the Defense Advanced Research Projects Agency. He has also served in numerous overseas posts. Professor Cordesman has written and lectured extensively on the Gulf and the Middle East, the United States and Soviet military balance, U.S. forces and defense budgets, and the lessons of war. His recent books include *The Gulf War* (Westview, 1995) and *Iran and Iraq: The Threat from the Northern Gulf* (Westview, 1994).

Munira Ahmed Fakhro is an Assistant Professor at the University of Bahrain. She earned an M.A. from the School of Social Work and Social Research at Bryn Mawr College and a D.S.W. in social welfare from the Columbia University School of Social Work. She has previously worked as the Head of the Welfare Section of Bahrain's Ministry of Labor and Social Affairs. Professor Fakhro is a member of various local and regional societies and organizations and has published many articles on women and family as well as two books, entitled *Women at Work in the Gulf: The Case of Bahrain* (London: Kegan Paul International, 1990) and (in Arabic) *Civil Society and the Democratization process in Bahrain* (Ibn Khaldun Center, 1995). Her current research interest is civil society and democracy in the Gulf.

Anwar Mohamed Gargash is an independent scholar who specializes in the Gulf. He was formerly an Assistant Professor of Political Science at the United Arab Emirates University. Dr. Gargash received his B.A. and M.A. from The George Washington University and his Ph.D. from King's College, Cambridge.

F. Gregory Gause III is Associate Professor of Political Science at the University of Vermont and has taught at Columbia University. He received his

Ph.D. from Harvard University in 1987. During 1992-1993 he was a Fellow for Arab and Islamic Studies at the Council on Foreign Relations in New York. He has published two books, *Oil Monarchies: Domestic and Security Challenges in the Arab Gulf States* (Council on Foreign Relations Press, 1994) and *Saudi-Yemeni Relations: Domestic Structures and Foreign Influence* (Columbia University Press, 1990) as well as a number of scholarly articles, including "The Gulf Conundrum: Economic Change, Population Growth, and Political Stability in the GCC States" (*The Washington Quarterly*, Winter 1997) and "The Illogic of Dual Containment" (*Foreign Affairs*, March/April 1994).

Richard K. Herrmann is the Associate Director of the Mershon Center and Professor of Political Science at The Ohio State University. He holds a Ph.D. and an M.P.I.A. from the University of Pittsburgh. Dr. Herrmann served on the Secretary of State's Policy Planning Staff at the U.S. Department of State from 1989-1990. He has written extensively on the United States and Soviet foreign policy and the politics of the Middle East. He is the author of *Perceptions and Behavior in Soviet Foreign Policy* (1985) and has contributed articles to a number of journals, including *International Security, World Politics, American Journal of Political Science, Political Science Quarterly, International Organization,* and *Political Psychology.* **R. William Ayres** is a Visiting Instructor in Political Science at St. Mary's College of Maryland and a Ph.D. candidate in Political Science at The Ohio State University. His research interests include regional conflicts and conflict resolution, especially in the Middle East.

Roy P. Mottahedeh was born in New York City and educated at Harvard University, where he received his Ph.D. He has taught at Princeton University. An internationally recognized scholar, he is currently Gurney Professor of History and Chairman of the Committee on Islamic Studies at Harvard. Dr. Mottahedeh has received numerous academic awards, including a Guggenheim and a MacArthur Prize Fellowship. He is the author of *The Mantle of the Prophet: Religion and Politics in Iran* (New York: Pantheon Books, 1985) and *Loyalty and Leadership in an Early Islamic Society* (Princeton University Press 1980), as well as numerous scholarly articles, including "The Clash of Civilizations: An Islamicist's Critique," in *Harvard Middle Eastern and Islamic Review* 2 (1995). **Mamoun Fandy** is Research Professor of Politics at Georgetown University's Center for Contemporary Arab Studies, specializing in Egyptian and Gulf politics. He holds a Ph.D. from Southern Illinois University, Carbondale. His articles on Middle Eastern politics have appeared in *The Middle East Journal, Middle East Policy, The New York Times, Los Angeles Times,* and more regularly in *The Christian Science Monitor.* His book, *Saudi Arabia and the Politics of Dissent,* is forthcoming from St. Martin's Press.

Karim Pakravan is a Vice President at the First National Bank of Chicago. As a Senior Economist and Credit Manager, he has regional responsibilities that include Western Europe, the Middle East, North Africa, and Venezuela. Dr. Pakravan holds a B.A. in economics from the University of Geneva in Switzerland, an M.S. in econometrics from the London School of Economics, and a Ph.D. in economics from the University of Chicago. He has held teaching and research positions at a number of academic institutions including the Free University of Iran, the University of Chicago, the Hoover Institution, and the University of Santa Clara. Dr. Pakravan is the author of several publications on oil, energy, and the Middle East, including *Oil Supply Disruptions in the 1980s: An Economic Analysis* (Hoover Institute Press, 1984).

Richard N. Schofield is Deputy Director of the Geopolitics and International Boundaries Research Centre at the School of Oriental and African Studies, University of London, and an Associate Fellow of the Middle East Programme at the Royal Institute of International Affairs. He is the author of *The Evolution of the Shatt al-Arab Boundary Dispute* (Menas Press, 1986), *Kuwait and Iraq: Historical Claims and Territorial Disputes* (Royal Institute of International Affairs, 1991; 2nd ed. 1993), and *Unfinished Business: Iran, the UAE, Abu Musa and the Tunbs* (Royal Institute of International Affairs, 1997 forthcoming). He is the editor of *Arabian Boundary Disputes* (Archive Editions, 1992) and *Territorial Foundations of the Gulf States* (St. Martin's Press, 1994), and edits the tri-annual journal *Geopolitics and International Boundaries* (Frank Cass, 1996-).

Paul J. Stevens is BP Professor of Petroleum Policy and Economics at the Centre for Petroleum and Mineral Law and Policy at the University of Dundee in Scotland. Professor Stevens was educated as an economist and as a specialist on the Middle East at Cambridge University and the School of Oriental and African Studies, University of London, where he received his Ph.D. in 1974. He has taught economics at the American University of Beirut and the University of Surrey and was a founding member of the Surrey Energy Economics Centre and the Third World Energy Policy Studies Group. Professor Stevens has worked as an oil consultant in Beirut and continues to advise governments and companies on economic issues. He has published widely in the areas of energy economics and development economics.

Frank E. Vogel is Assistant Professor of Law and Director of the Islamic Legal Studies Program at Harvard Law School. Prior to assuming his present post, Professor Vogel spent five years in Riyadh, Saudi Arabia, researching the Islamic legal system and practicing law. He has taught courses on the Islamic legal system, Islamic contract and commercial law, human rights and Islam, and the comparative law of the Arab Middle East at Harvard. Professor Vogel received his A.B. in 1972 from Harvard College, J.D. magna cum laude in 1975 from Washington College of Law, American University, and Ph.D. in law and Middle Eastern studies from Harvard University in 1993.

INDEX

Abd al-Rahman, Shaikh Umar, 273, 293n20

Abdallah, Diana, 81n16, 81n17, 82n27

Abduh, Muhammad, 272

Abu Dhabi, 102, 106-7, 129, 133, 135, 151, 155, 235, 319

Abu Dhabi National Oil Company, 106

Abu Hakima, Ahmad Mustafa, 339n14

Abu Musa Island, 131, 133, 135, 136, 142-53, 155-8, 205, 237, 240

Abu Safa oil field, 184

Adelman, M. A., 110n28, 110n32

Afghanistan, 249
war in, 36, 195

Aghassi, Haji Mirza, 144

Alavi Foundation, 117

Albright, David, 228n42

Algeria, 76, 96, 222, 234, 251, 310, 311, 315

Algiers Accord (1975), 131, 137, 237, 329, 337

Allen, Robin, 28n4, 29n18, 30n30

Amirahmadi, Hooshang, 247n48

Amnesty International, 306

Amuzegar, J., 126

Ancel, Jacques, 132, 137, 138, 158, 160n11

al-Anisi, 'Abdul Wahhab, 305

Arab Gulf. *See* Persian Gulf

Arab-Israeli peace process, Clinton administration's investment in, 39

Arabian American Oil Company, 120

Arafat, Yasir, 47, 52, 243

Araki, Grand Ayatollah Hajj Shaikh Mohammad Ali, 302-3, 313

Argentina, 233

Arjomand, Said Amir, 294n28

Armenia, 195

Arms Control and Regional Security talks, 234-5, 243

Arnett, Eric, 246n34

Askari, H., 126

Assad, Hafez, 52

Assiri, Abdul Rida, 340n33

Association of South East Asian Nations, 42, 327

Atomic Energy Organization, 212

al-Auda, Salman, 307

ayatollah, 299

Ayatollahi, Mohammed Sadegh, 213

Ayres, R. William, 6, 343

Ayubi, Nazih N. M., 293n25

Azar, Edward, 80n1

Azerbaijan, 195, 197

Azmeh, Youssef, 82n19

Azzam, Henry, 28n9, 29n11

Bab al Mandab, Strait of, 88

Bahrain
border disputes, 87, 127-8, 130, 137, 141-2, 146, 148, 154, 157-8, 327-30
economic difficulties in, 78

Saudi Arabian Basic Industries Corporation, 71, 123
Saudi Arabian Monetary Authority, 68, 121-22
Saudi Aramco, 101
Saudia (airline) 123
Schirazi, Asghar, 294n32
Schofield, Clive H., 161n27
Schofield, Richard, 7, 109n12, 159n1, 159n3, 159n6, 159n10, 160n12, 160n14, 160n15, 160n18, 160n20, 160n25, 161n26, 161n27, 162n31, 162n35, 162n28, 162n42, 162n43, 162n45,162 n47, 162n48, 162n49, 162n51, 165n68, 165n70, 237, 245n21, 245n24
Sciolino, Elaine, 57n23
Seymour, I, 110n32
Shah of Iran, 2, 12, 15, 213
Shaibah oil field, 101-2, 133, 329
Shamlan, Ahmad, 188n17, 188n18
Shariati, Ali, 282
Sharjah, 107, 131, 133
Shatt al-Arab, 131, 136-40, 237
Sheikoleslam, Hussein, 239
Shihi, M., 110n32
Shi'i Muslims, 2, 36, 50, 52, 66, 78, 80n6, 168, 169, 170, 173, 175, 176, 179, 180-2, 183, 187, 194, 219, 262, 281, 282-3, 298-9, 306, 307, 308-9, 312-3, 322; Arab, 46
Shobokhsi, 120
Shuey, Robert, 226n29, 228n45
Shura councils, 175, 180, 185, 250, 252, 284, 289, 308, 309, 331-2
Sick, Gary, 3, 6, 10n4, 244n1, 341
Sindlar, H. Richard, 339n5, 339n6
Singapore, 103
Sirri islands, 206
Sirri oil fields, 101
Soroush, Abdolkarim, 283, 308
South Africa, 103
South African Strategic Field Fund, 103
South Korea, 76
Soviet Union, 2, 15, 241
  collapse of, 32, 33, 35, 104, 320
  see also former Soviet Union

Spector, Leonard, 227n37, 228n43, 228n48
Stauffer, T., 110n32
Stavins, R. N., 110n20
Stein, Janice Gross, 246n30
Stein, Peter, 244n8
Stevens, Paul, 7, 109n2. 109n3, 109n5, 109n6, 109n10, 110n15, 110n16, 110n17, 111n37, 112n47, 344
Sudan, the, 195, 219, 222, 249, 252, 286, 287, 311, 314
Suez Canal, 88, 168
Sultan, Nader, 99, 239
Sultan, Prince, 309
Sunna, Prophet's, 254-5, 259, 263
Sunni Muslims, 36, 50, 52, 78, 169, 170, 175, 176, 182, 262, 272, 281, 282-3, 306
Supreme Petroleum Council, 100
Al-Suwaidi, Jamal S., 318n2
Swindells, Steven, 81n14, 82n29
Switzerland, 210
Syria, 47, 52, 135, 208, 234, 238, 311

Tablighi, Jamaat, 312-13
Taimurtash, Abd al-Hussein, 146
Taiwan, 76
Tajikistan, 48; war in, 34
Taylor, John W. R., 223n10
Tehran Stock Exchange, 122
Al-Thani, Amir Hamad bin Khalifa, 69
Timmerman, Kenneth R., 226n34
Toye, Patricia, 163n40
Treaty of Islamic Friendship and Brotherhood, 1934 (Treaty of Taif), 127, 130
Tripp, Charles, 160n17, 239, 246n30
Truman, Harry S., 302
Tunb islands, 131, 136, 142-58, 205, 237
Tunisia, 234, 235, 251
al-Turabi, Hasan, 293n23, 314
Turkey, 22, 36, 42, 52, 53, 93, 108, 195, 221, 297, 304, 310, 313-14
Turkmenistan, 42

Ulamatova, Sazhi, 54n2
Umm al-Maradim, 129
Umm Al Nar, 106